MW00328193

THE HUMAN BEING

The Human Being

A THEOLOGICAL ANTHROPOLOGY

Hans Schwarz

William B. Eerdmans Publishing Company
Grand Rapids, Michigan / Cambridge, U.K.

© 2013 Hans Schwarz

All rights reserved

Published 2013 by

Wm. B. Eerdmans Publishing Co.

2140 Oak Industrial Drive N.E., Grand Rapids, Michigan 49505 /

P.O. Box 163, Cambridge CB3 9PU U.K.

Printed in the United States of America

19 18 17 16 15   7 6 5 4 3 2

Library of Congress Cataloging-in-Publication Data

Schwarz, Hans, 1939-

   The human being: a theological anthropology / Hans Schwarz.

       pages   cm

   Includes bibliographical references and index.

   ISBN 978-0-8028-7088-9 (pbk.: alk. paper)

   1. Theological anthropology — Christianity.   I. Title.

BT701.3.S35   2013

233 — dc23

                               2013029737

www.eerdmans.com

Contents

CONTENTS

Preface

Anthropology is a vast terrain even if narrowed down to Christian anthropology. I have in front of me three anthropologies. One rather recent publication is the massive two-volume work by David Kelsey, *Eccentric Existence: A Theological Anthropology* (Westminster John Knox, 2009). It is written in the ecclesial context for the believer who wants to know what being a human being entails. It may also be beneficial for people outside the theological circle who want to know what Christians think a human being is all about. Central are the incarnation and resurrection of Jesus Christ, human sin, and redemption. It is strange that in his extensive bibliography Kelsey does not even mention Wolfhart Pannenberg's *Anthropology*. Genetics is given at the most four pages, concluding with Charles Hodge. This is very different from the anthropology by Philip Hefner, *The Human Factor: Evolution, Culture, and Religion* (Fortress, 1993). It reflects Hefner's long interaction with scientists and so we read about nature and nurture, altruism and love, and freedom and determinism. It seems to be written for those who today want to know whether one can still say human beings are created in God's image and what that means. Finally, there is Pannenberg's *Anthropology in Theological Perspective* (Westminster, 1985). He writes first about the human being in nature, and then inquires about the uniqueness of humans, their openness to the world, and their being created in the image of God. There follows the social being where identity and sin are important issues. Finally, Pannenberg touches on culture and the social institutions and the place of humans in the world. Here I see the attempt to connect knowledge about the faith with knowledge about the world to show that both belong together in elucidating who we are. To sum it up, a theological anthropology can be written in many different ways.

This anthropology was written with a threefold emphasis: the biblical testimony, the historical unfolding by its major voices through the centuries, and the present affirmation of this tradition in view of rival options and of the factual evidence the various sciences have unearthed. It starts with our place in the world, ponders our freedom, and concludes with the premise that we are a community of men and women in this world and in the world beyond.

Some of the issues presented here I have treated more extensively in earlier works but have updated everything as much as possible. Of course, much more could have been said, but I trust that the general thrust has become clear.

At this point I want to thank first of all my longtime secretary Hildegard Ferme, who typed the manuscript with her usual speed and accuracy; Dr. Terry Dohm, who undertook the arduous task of improving my style; Dr. Bong Bae Kim, who helped with compiling the indices; and my colleague Dr. Rüdiger Schmitt, a geneticist, who read through the science section to correct any inaccuracies. Nevertheless, all remaining mistakes must be attributed to me. But, as our son once said when he was a little boy, "Nobody's perfect!" We are still on this side of heaven.

HANS SCHWARZ

Abbreviations

ACW   *Ancient Christian Writers.* Ed. Johannes Quasten and Joseph C. Plumpe. Westminster, MD: Newman Press, 1946-.

ANF   *Ante-Nicene Fathers.* Ed. Alexander Roberts and James Donaldson. 10 vols. Grand Rapids: Eerdmans, reprint of the 1884-86 edition. Reprint, Fortress, 2000.

CD   *Church Dogmatics,* by Karl Barth. Ed. Geoffrey W. Bromiley and Thomas F. Torrance. Trans. Geoffrey W. Bromiley. Edinburgh: T&T Clark, 1936-62.

FC   *The Fathers of the Church.* Ed. R. J. Deferrari. Washington, DC: Catholic University Press, 1947-.

HDT   *Handbuch der Dogmen- und Theologiegeschichte.* Ed. C. Andresen. Göttingen, 1983-.

LW   *Luther's Works, American Edition.* Vols. 1-30, ed. Jaroslav Pelikan. St. Louis: Concordia, 1955-67. Vols. 31-55, ed. Helmut T. Lehmann. Philadelphia: Fortress, 1955-67.

NPNF   *Nicene and Post-Nicene Fathers of the Christian Church.* Ed. Philip Schaff. Grand Rapids: Eerdmans, 1983, reprint edition.

ST   *Systematic Theology,* by Paul Tillich. 3 vols. Chicago: University of Chicago Press, 1951-63.

TDNT   *Theological Dictionary of the New Testament.* Ed. Gerhard Kittel and Gerhard Friedrich. Trans. Geoffrey W. Bromiley. 10 vols. Grand Rapids: Eerdmans, 1964-76.

TDOT   *Theological Dictionary of the Old Testament.* Ed. G. Johannes Botterweck, Helmut Ringgren, and Heinz-Josef Fabry. Trans. John T. Willis et al. Grand Rapids: Eerdmans, 1977-.

TRE   *Theologische Realenzyklopädie.* Ed. Gerhard Krause and
         Gerhard Müller. 36 vols. Berlin and New York: Walter de
         Gruyter, 1977-2007.

WA   *D. Martin Luthers Werke: Kritische Gesamtausgabe.* Vols. 1-.
         Weimar: Hermann Böhlau, 1983-.

Introduction

If I were one of the other primates, I could not write this book. Only humans can entrust their thoughts to written documents. Whether other living beings can muse about the world or themselves, we do not know for sure. Only human beings develop something like a philosophy by which they ponder existential issues, such as the difference between being and non-being, the existence of a living soul, and the beginning and the end of the world.

While every living being, from an earthworm to a gorilla, is special, human beings are unique. Many birds and mammals can make tools, a craft once thought to be restricted to humans. But only human beings have developed a culture that embraces every expression of life. Though insects, such as ants, can live in extreme regions, humans alone have developed strategies by which they can comfortably live on every continent. But humans are not very specialized. Their five senses are only average. Yet even though these specializations are present in other living species but missing in humans, like smell for dogs and sight for birds of prey, the shortfall is overcome in humans since it is counterbalanced by the ability of humans to run, jump, swim, dive, see, and hear like no other species if all these faculties are considered together.

There is still another uniqueness of the human being. Although there is an insect called a *praying mantis,* its name is only derived metaphorically from its stature since it looks as though it is praying. Yet from their very beginning, humans seem to have an awareness of something higher than themselves with which they try to relate. Human destiny, as it comes into focus in the cult of the dead, has been of vital concern to humans since their beginning. Humans reflect on themselves, their origin and final destiny, the world around them and its origin. With these preliminary human characteristics in mind, in Part I we want to elucidate first the special place that human beings occupy in this world. We will do this from the perspective of the biblical documents and also from the view of the natural sciences, focusing especially on the life sciences. In our secular age we dare not omit some reflections from the secular side and its projection of the human future.

In Part II we address the issue of human freedom. In the Christian tradition it has always been emphasized that humans are not as free as they want to be, or as free as they might feel. But from the time of the Enlightenment human optimism has abounded. Many learned disciplines intended to show that neither sin nor evil is an insuperable obstacle on the way to human fulfillment. Yet more recently various sciences from psychoanalysis to brain research have told us that human freedom is rather limited if it exists at all. It seems that humans, though strong in their approach to the outside world, actually have feet of clay.

With this caveat we move to Part III, investigating human beings as a community of men and women. Is there an actual difference between men and women and, if so, how are both related to each other? Finally, we will ask: What is the specific place of humans in this world and what destiny might they expect? This is indeed a full agenda. It may at times be treated only cursorily, though I hope not superficially. It is, however, important that we cover the landscape as extensively as possible to map out what it means to be human.

I. A Special Place in the World

In the last century it became more and more evident that human beings occupy a special place in this world. Through their unprecedented population growth they are crowding out more and more living species. If they continue to consume nonrenewable natural resources at such prevailing rates, they will also in the long run crowd themselves out, or at the least make the present standard of living in "developed" countries a thing of the past. When we look at the biblical account, we also find there an ambivalent assessment of human existence.

1. The Biblical Perspective

In Psalm 8:4 the psalmist raises the all-important question "What are human beings that you are mindful of them, mortals that you care for them?" With the creation narrative in Genesis 1 we could answer that the reason God cares for humans is that God created them. Whereas the God relationship is expressed there, this does not tell us anything about the constitution of humans.

1. The Old Testament View

There are three or perhaps even four Hebrew terms that describe a human being: *nefesh, basar, ruah,* and perhaps *leb.* These terms point to the essentials of a human being and are translated roughly as soul, flesh, spirit, and heart.

a. Humans as Living Beings

The term **nefesh** occurs at least 750 times in the Old Testament and is translated 680 times as "psyche" in the Septuagint, the Greek version of the Old Testament.[1] Yet each of these renderings remains wanting. We notice this at once when we read in Genesis 2:7, "The Lord God formed man from the dust of the ground, and breathed into his nostrils the breath of life; and the man became a living being." The original Hebrew *nefesh hayah,* trans-

---

1. According to Horst Seebass, *"nefesh,"* in *TDOT,* 9:503.

5

lated as "living being," certainly does not mean a living soul or a living psyche. A human being does not have a *nefesh* (soul or psyche), but is one and lives as one. As we see in 1 Kings 17:17ff., when the breath leaves the child (v. 17) and only returns after the prophet Elijah uses mouth-to-mouth resuscitation, the *nefesh* is what makes a person a living being. Since a human being breathes, *nefesh* is also the breath and it can be strong (Exod. 15:10) or laborious (Isa. 42:14). As soon as the breath stops, life ends. This means the *nefesh* has no existence outside the body, but is always tied to a bodily existence. Therefore *nefesh* can simply be equated with "life."[2] The throat, the visible organ for breathing, can also be called the *nefesh* (Ps. 69:2[1]). But the Old Testament is not very discerning, anatomically speaking. Therefore the throat can also be said to experience hunger (Deut. 23:25[24]), thirst (Prov. 25:25), and appetite (Mic. 7:1). As the agent of life, *nefesh* can also be identified with the blood (Deut. 12:23). Since *nefesh* is so closely tied to life, it can also denote the power to live. When Rachel's *nefesh* departed, she died (Gen. 35:18). At the same time, *nefesh* can also mean one's own self. For example, Isaac said to Jacob that he should bring some of the wild game so that "I [my *nefesh*] may bless you" (Gen. 27:25).

When we read the command "You shall love the Lord your God with all your heart [*leb*], and with all your soul [*nefesh*], and with all your might" (Deut. 6:5), we notice not just a close relation of *leb* and *nefesh,* but also a summons to the innermost core of a human being. The same goes for Psalm 103:1, where the psalmist says, "Bless the Lord, O my soul [*nefesh*], and all that is within me, bless his holy name." The whole human existence is denoted by *nefesh.* It comes as no surprise that even human feelings and passions, such as hatred (2 Sam. 5:8), longing (Ps. 42:2), and affection toward other people (Gen. 34:3, 8), are expressed with this term.

"*Basar* can sometimes denote the whole man as well as *nefesh.*"[3] So we read in Deuteronomy 12:23, "For the blood is the life [*nefesh*]," connecting *leb* (blood) and *nefesh.* In Leviticus 17:11 we then read, "For the life [*nefesh*] of the flesh [*basar*] is in the blood [*leb*]," whereby the blood as spreading through the whole human being contains the life of the body. Yet *nefesh* is not an indestructible core of personal existence that could stand in contrast to the body and exist independently of the body. Therefore the translation of *nefesh* with "soul" is misleading. "Though much is said about *nefesh* as the life, any cult of

---

2. Seebass, "*nefesh,*" in *TDOT,* 9:512.

3. Edmond Jacob, "*psychē.* B. The Anthropology of the Old Testament," in *TDNT,* 9:622.

life or death is lacking, and with it also every speculation about the fate of the 'soul' beyond the borders of death."[4] The psalmist, however, prays to God: "For you do not give me [my *nefesh*] up to Sheol, or let your faithful ones see their Pit" (Ps. 16:10). Human life is under the protective care of God and no other powers have any claim on it. When the "I" becomes synonymous with *nefesh,* it shows that humans do not have a *nefesh* but as living beings they are a *nefesh.* So *nefesh* can denote an individual person (Lev. 22:3) or even in the plural a whole group of people (Gen. 9:5).

b. Humans as Bodily Beings

When we consider the term "flesh" *(basar),* we notice that it is exclusively used for living beings. "Whereas *nefesh* is applied to God in at least three percent of its occurrences in the Old Testament, there is not a single instance in the case of *basar.*"[5] *Basar* stands for living beings and their bodily existence. As Hans Walter Wolff (1911-93) has shown, out of the 273 occurrences of *basar* in the Old Testament, 104 are references to animals. The term largely connects humans with animals. With reference to the latter, *basar* can simply mean the flesh or meat of animals, such as the roasted meat that is eaten (Isa. 44:16) or the flesh of animals that are still alive (Job 41:23). When one reads in Leviticus of animal offerings, reference is made quite often to the flesh of animals (Lev. 4:11). Yet in the same book one can also read of the curse that falls on Israel on account of its disobedience to God. Then "you shall eat the flesh of your sons, and you shall eat the flesh of your daughters" (Lev. 26:29). Human flesh can also be contrasted to bones, as can be seen in the creation story. In creating Eve God took one of Adam's ribs "and closed up its place with flesh" (Gen. 2:21).

Basar not only denotes the distinction between flesh and bones, but it is also used "euphemistically" of the sexual organs, as is seen in the injunction on cultic uncleanness: "When any man has a discharge from his member [*basar*], his discharge makes him ceremonially unclean" (Lev. 15:2).[6] Similarly, we hear "when a woman has a discharge of blood, that is a regular discharge from her body [*basar*], she shall be in her impurity for seven days"

---

4. Hans Walter Wolff, *Anthropology of the Old Testament,* trans. Margaret Kohl (Philadelphia: Fortress, 1974), 20.

5. Wolff, *Anthropology,* 26, including the following.

6. N. P. Bratsiotis, *"basar,"* in *TDOT,* 2:319.

(Lev. 15:19). While the New Testament can distinguish between skin and flesh, often *basar* simply means the whole body, including the skin. The Israelites are admonished, for instance, not to make any gashes in their flesh (Lev. 19:28), a custom that is still observed today by some tribes who inflict on themselves such gashes or wounds as ornamentation. "*Basar* is probably the most comprehensive, most important, and most frequently used anthropological term for the external, fleshly aspect" of human nature.[7]

Nefesh basar (a bodily living being) can also represent a person, as we read in Psalm 119:120: "My flesh [*basar*] trembles for fear of you, and I am afraid of your judgments." Besides being used for an individual, *basar* can also denote a human togetherness, for instance, when the first man said concerning the first woman, "This at last is bone of my bones and flesh of my flesh" (Gen. 2:23). Moreover, it can be used for a certain relationship, as is expressed by the brothers of Joseph when they say about him, "He is our brother, our own flesh" (Gen. 37:27). When Yahweh promises Israel that he "will remove from your body the heart of stone and give you a heart of flesh" (Ezek. 36:26), we notice that, like *nefesh,* flesh denotes here something living. Yet in the same vein it is also something that is limited in duration, as can be seen in Job 34:14f.: if Yahweh "should take back his spirit to himself, and gather to himself his breath, all flesh would perish together, and all mortals return to dust." The fact that the flesh is alive is not to be taken for granted, but ultimately rests on God's *ruah,* on God's spirit. One need not even be afraid of such a mighty king as Sennacherib of Assyria, as Hezekiah of Judah states, "With him is an arm of flesh; but with us is the Lord our God, to help us and to fight our battles" (2 Chron. 32:8). Human flesh is always limited in its duration and power, and life is not an innate human faculty. Therefore we hear God in Ezekiel's vision of the valley of dry bones saying, "I will cause breath to enter you, and you shall live. I will lay sinews on you, and will cause flesh to come upon you, and cover you with skin, and put breath in you, and you shall live" (Ezek. 37:5f.). This breath (*ruah*) that comes from God and makes the difference between life and death is not just *nefesh* as in Genesis 2:7, but is more fittingly translated "spirit."

---

7. Bratsiotis, *"basar,"* in *TDOT,* 2:325.

c. Humans as Theomorphic

Ruah can be used in two ways. First, almost one-third of its usage in the Old Testament denotes a natural power, namely, the wind.[8] Second, it is used almost equally often to signify the *ruah* of God and to a somewhat lesser extent of humans, animals, and idols. When *ruah* is compared with *nefesh, nefesh* is only rarely used with reference to God, but *basar* is never found in this context. We agree with Hans Walter Wolff who calls *ruah* "a theo-anthropological term."[9]

Ruah is used to denote the wind as a natural power. For instance, we hear that "the trees of the forest shake before the wind" (Isa. 7:2). In the story of the crossing of the Red Sea, we hear that "the Lord drove the sea back by a strong east wind all night, and turned the sea into dry land" (Exod. 14:21). When the wind is called a "natural" power in this context, it should be noted that the wind is God's tool to rescue the Israelites. The modern bifurcation between the natural and the supernatural spheres is unknown to the Old Testament. The wind is a mighty power that is at the disposal of Yahweh, as we read in Ezekiel 13:13: "Therefore thus says the Lord God: In my wrath I will make a stormy wind break out, and in my anger there shall be a deluge of rain, and hailstones in my wrath to destroy it."

In its theo-anthropological meaning, however, *ruah* is first of all the human breath, so to speak the human wind that endows a human being with life. Again, this breath is nothing natural to be taken for granted as we read in Isaiah 42:5: "Thus says God, the Lord, who created the heavens and stretched them out, who spread out the earth and who comes from it, who gives breath to the people upon it and spirit [*ruah*] to those who walk in it." This is the difference between God's creatures and the idols made by human beings. Whether they are made of stone or wood, whether they are gold- or silver-plated, "there is no breath [*ruah*] in [them] at all" (Hab. 2:19). Only Yahweh alone can endow things with *ruah*. On the one hand, this *ruah* is the spirit or breath of life that belongs to humans because "when their breath departs, they return to the earth" (Ps. 146:4). But it is also God's life-giving breath, or Spirit, as we see in Job 34:14f.: "If he should take back his Spirit to himself, and gather to himself his breath, all flesh would perish together, and all mortals return to dust." The Israelites knew that as long as someone breathes, this breath, spirit, or wind is inhaled and exhaled and

---

8. For the exact statistics, see Wolff, *Anthropology,* 32.
9. Wolff, *Anthropology,* 32.

there is life in that person. In this way they can talk about *ruah* in a very mundane way. We read, for instance, in Job 19:17: "My breath is repulsive to my wife; I am loathsome to my own family." Here *ruah* is equated with bad breath.

Yet the Israelites knew that this spirit of life is nothing natural, as being derived from nature. It is God's creative power and makes the difference between life and death. We read in Genesis 6:3: "The Lord said, 'My Spirit shall not abide in mortals forever, for they are flesh.'" In the last analysis *ruah* is God's life-giving Spirit that determines how long a person will live. If this Spirit is given in abundance, humans enjoy exceptional qualities. Therefore the Egyptian Pharaoh looked for a person "in whom is the Spirit of God" (Gen. 41:38), so that this person would have sufficient wisdom to take appropriate measures to avoid the threatening famine. Like the *ruah* Yahweh endows a person with artistic abilities (Exod. 31:3). This would mean that both life itself and the faculties that go with it, such as strength, wisdom, and creativity, are not innate in humans, but are ultimately gifts of God.

The Spirit can also be an almost independent agent given by God to certain people, which can then be distributed to others, as we see, for instance, in the case of Moses in Numbers 11:17. There God first put his Spirit on Moses, and then took some of that Spirit and put it on the seventy elders, so that they could help Moses in governing the people. Since *ruah* is primarily this life-providing element, it can also characterize certain emotional states. For instance, when the queen of Sheba noticed Solomon's wisdom, his palace, the food on his table, the attire of his servants, and all the other splendor with which Solomon surrounded himself, "there was no more spirit in her" (1 Kings 10:5). This means she was simply dumbfounded. God can even stir up the *ruah* of the people (Ezra 1:5) so that they do certain things. There is only a small step from emotions to will and intentions, which can also be subsumed under the term *ruah*. Yet there is still a very different quality in a person, closely connected to life but distinguished from all these more natural qualities. It is somehow connected to human reason, the heart (*leb*) of a person.

d. Human Reason

Hans Walter Wolff writes: "The most important word in the vocabulary of Old Testament anthropology is generally translated 'heart.' . . . [It] is the commonest of all anthropological terms."[10] Heart (***leb***) is almost exclusively used to denote something in humans. It is found more than 800 times in the Old Testament. It is misleading to equate it with today's understanding of heart. The Israelites did not think about a human being the way we do since they did not have our contemporary knowledge of the function of our bodily organs. For instance, it is stated about rich Nabal: "his heart died within him; he became like a stone. About ten days later, the Lord struck Nabal, and he died" (1 Sam. 25:37f.). If the heart becomes like a stone and no longer moves, the person would be considered dead. But then we learn that Nabal lived for another ten days before he actually died. We might therefore assume that when he became like a stone he was just paralyzed and continued to live for another ten days until his heart gave out. Similarly, we hear regarding David's son Absalom that Joab "took three spears in his hand, and thrust them into the heart of Absalom, while he was still alive in the oak. And ten young men, Joab's armor-bearers, surrounded Absalom and struck him and killed him" (2 Sam. 18:14f.). When Absalom was caught with his hair in the branches of an oak tree hanging there defenselessly, David's commander Joab took three spears and thrust them into the heart of Absalom. If three spears are thrust into the heart of anyone, one can be reasonably sure that the person is dead. But then we hear that the armor-bearers of Joab struck Absalom again and killed him. Evidently, what is called "heart" here cannot have been Absalom's heart, but must have been his chest or simply his upper body. The Israelites, however, were not totally ignorant of human anatomy, as we can see in Jeremiah when the prophet talks about the walls of his heart (Jer. 4:19). When he mentions the pain that his heart causes because it "is beating wildly," it is assumed that the pain is felt more in the chest than actually in the walls of the heart. As in the analogy about Absalom, perhaps Jeremiah also means the chest in which his wildly beating heart is located.

Since the heart is not accessible as long as a person lives, "heart" can also denote that which is inaccessible. For instance, Moses stood at the foot of the Holy Mountain "while the mountain was blazing up to the very heavens." Actually in Hebrew it reads "to the heart of the heavens" (Deut. 4:11). The inaccessible is also that which is secret. Therefore the heart can be the location of human secrets (Ps. 44:21). With this reference we are already moving beyond the anatomical to the spiritual and emotional realm. Besides the already mentioned feelings of anguish and pain, *leb* also denotes

10. Wolff, *Anthropology,* 40.

human temper. We read the admonition "Do not let your heart envy sinners, but always continue in the fear of the Lord" (Prov. 23:17). There are also positive emotions associated with the heart; for instance, there are "wine to gladden the human heart, oil to make the face shine, and bread to strengthen the human heart" (Ps. 104:15). The heart is the location of gladness caused by wine, and of strength brought about by bread. Moreover the heart is also the seat of human desires when we hear that God has given the king "his heart's desire" (Ps. 21:2).

When we still pray today with the psalmist, "Create in me a clean heart, O God, and put a new and right spirit within me" (Ps. 51:10), we might ask that evil desires be banished from us. Yet the clean "heart" can point to another part of the human anatomy, namely, to that which is today circumscribed by our head or even more precisely by our deliberative faculty. There should be no unclean thoughts or evil deliberations in our mind. This is exactly the overwhelming designation of *leb* in the Old Testament, namely, as the seat of our intellectual and rational human motions. After enumerating how short human life is, the psalmist requests that God "teach us to count our days that we may gain a wise heart" (Ps. 90:12). And Solomon asks God to "Give your servant therefore an understanding mind to govern your people, able to discern between good and evil" (1 Kings 3:9). An "understanding mind" is actually represented in Hebrew as a "hearing heart." This shows that wisdom and knowledge were understood to be located in the heart. Similarly, we read in Proverbs 18:15, "An intelligent mind [actually in Hebrew 'an insightful heart'] acquires knowledge, and the ear of the wise seeks knowledge." The heart can give knowledge and insight to a person. If one is wanting of a heart, this means not as we assume today that one has a heart of stone and cannot be moved by someone else, but that one is simply unreasonable or even stupid. When Abraham, for instance, heard about God's promise of an heir, he "fell on his face and laughed, and said to himself [in Hebrew: 'said in his heart'], 'Can a child be born to a man who is a hundred years old?'" (Gen. 17:17). Today we would not use the term "heart" in this situation but rather "mind."

When God promises the Israelites, "I will give them a new heart, and put a new spirit within them; I will remove the heart of stone from their flesh and give them a heart of flesh, so that they may follow my statutes and keep my ordinances and obey them" (Ezek. 11:19f.), the heart of stone is one that does not listen to God's commands and makes the Israelites unwilling to follow God's orders. The new heart, the heart of flesh, however, is an insightful heart that moves them to obey God's will. Heart is here the seat of discernment between good and evil, but also that which makes human beings act in accordance with God's will or against that will. This presupposes the faculty of discernment and deliberation.

Leb is a very comprehensive anthropological term embracing bodily functions as well as emotional, intellectual, and intentional modes. It "functions in all dimensions of human existence and is used as a term for all the aspects of a person."[11] Nevertheless, the Bible primarily views the heart as the center of the consciously living person.[12] But the heart extends beyond the human sphere to God's own self. For instance, God says in 1 Samuel 2:35, "I will raise up for myself a faithful priest, who shall do according to what is in my heart and in my mind." Here "heart" and "mind" are used synonymously, expressing God's will and intentions. When Job asks God, "What are human beings, that you make so much of them, that you set your mind [*leb*] on them?" (Job 7:17), God's attention is mentioned with the term "heart." This shows that "heart" can also be used to indicate that God is not an immovable, eternally decreeing being. God considers the state of humans and interacts with their doing both positively and negatively.

While the Old Testament terminology describing the human makeup only partly coincides with our modern knowledge, which reflects our vastly increased anatomical insights, three things become clear:

1. A human being is in many ways not different from other living beings. It is intimately connected to the whole realm of living beings.
2. Life in its various forms and expressions is neither self-sustained nor self-originating. In whatever form it shows itself life is ultimately a gift of God. It is not to be taken for granted and is definitely finite.
3. A human being is not just a living being, but also a reasonable being with the power of considerable deliberation, intention, and willfulness. In that latter category there is a similarity to God's own self who is characterized by similar faculties.

2. The New Testament View

When we look at the New Testament, we encounter a terminology that is much more akin to our modern-day thinking. The New Testament is writ-

11. Heinz-Josef Fabry, *"leb,"* in *TDOT,* 7:412.
12. See Wolff, *Anthropology,* 55.

ten in Greek, and Greek conceptuality has very much influenced our way of thinking about a human being. There is, of course, continuity between the Old and the New Testament views. For instance, Luke reports that at Pentecost "all of them were filled with the Holy Spirit and began to speak in other languages, as the Spirit gave them ability" (Acts 2:4). This means that God's Spirit gave them the ability to exercise the extraordinary faculty to speak in other languages. As Swiss New Testament scholar Eduard Schweizer (1913-2006) states: "*Pneuma* [spirit] is used in Mk. and Mt. in the thoroughly Old Testament sense of God's power to perform special acts."[13]

a. Bipartite and Tripartite Anthropology

In contrast to the Old Testament, a human being in the New Testament is seen in either a twofold or threefold anatomical way, or spiritually in a twofold perspective. One distinguishes between body and spirit, as evidenced when Jesus admonishes his listeners: "Do not fear those who kill the body but cannot kill the soul; rather fear him who can destroy both soul and body in hell" (Matt. 10:28). Here the distinction is made between body and soul as the two components of the human being. On the other hand, we see in Romans 8:10 that when the body dies, there is also a "redemption of our bodies" (Rom. 8:23). Against the Platonic idea that there is a disembodied soul while the body slowly decays, Paul affirms that "this mortal body puts on immortality" (1 Cor. 15:54). This does not mean that somehow the atoms or molecules of the body will be reassembled, but that a soul will never be naked, that it will always be enclosed by a body.

Sōma (body) is the most comprehensive term with which Paul denotes a human being. "For Paul there is no human identity apart from bodily existence, and so he also thinks of the resurrection reality and the postmortal existence in bodily terms."[14] To some extent *sōma* is analogous to the Hebrew *basar.* One does not have a *sōma* but is *sōma.* Any dualism between body and soul is excluded. Since the body is created, it is perishable and weak. It can be tempted and indeed does succumb to temptation. Paul can even talk about "the body of sin" (Rom. 6:6). The body perishes and will be

---

13. Eduard Schweizer, *"pneuma,"* in *TDNT,* 6:397.
14. Udo Schnelle, *Theology of the New Testament,* trans. M. Eugene Boring (Grand Rapids: Baker, 2009), 284.

redeemed through the creation of an imperishable body. When Paul writes, for instance, "For the wife does not have authority over her own body . . . likewise the husband does not have authority over his own body" (1 Cor. 7:4), then the body is not something that only externally belongs to a human being. It is an inseparable part of his or her makeup. Therefore Paul admonishes his readers: "Do not let sin exercise dominion in your mortal bodies" (Rom. 6:12).

While for Paul *soma* is the main anthropological term, *psychē,* or soul, is used by him relatively seldom. Rudolf Bultmann (1884-1976) writes: "Just as Paul does not know the Greek-Hellenistic concept of the immortality of the soul (released from the body), neither does he use *psychē* [soul] to designate the seat or the power of the mental life which animates man's matter, as had become the custom among the Greeks. Rather *psychē* means primarily the Old Testament *nefesh* (rendered *psychē* in the Septuagint) — 'vitality' or 'life' itself."[15]

Often the term *psychē* is not rendered with the English word "soul," but with "life," as, for example, in Romans 16:4, where Paul greets those "who risked their necks for my life [*psychē*]." German New Testament scholar Hans Conzelmann (1915-89) even claimed: "The soul belongs to man's earthly existence. It does not exist without physical life. It is not, say, freed from death, then to live in untrammeled purity. Death is its end."[16] This is an overstatement. Admittedly, *psychē* is clearly placed on the side of *sarx* (flesh) by Paul when he contrasts, for instance, the *psychikos* human being with the *pneumatikos* human being (1 Cor. 2:14f.).[17] But this does not mean that there is a void after death. Any existence after death, just as our existence here and now, is dependent on God and will be an embodied existence. Like the often interchangeable use between *nefesh* and *ruah, psychē* can also be used like *pneuma,* though the human spirit must be distinguished from the divine Spirit (Rom. 8:16). Paul wants people to be holy "in body and spirit" (1 Cor. 7:34). Here spirit *(pneuma)* could also stand for soul *(psychē).*

Paul also distinguishes spirit and soul when he wishes for the Christians

15. Rudolf Bultmann, *Theology of the New Testament,* trans. Kendrik Grobel (New York: Charles Scribner's, 1970), 1:203f.

16. Hans Conzelmann, *Theology of the New Testament,* trans. John Bowden (New York: Harper & Row, 1969), 179.

17. See Werner Georg Kümmel, *Man in the New Testament,* trans. John J. Vincent (Philadelphia: Westminster, 1963), 43, where he also refers to the "promiscuous use" of various terms by Paul to describe the "inner human being."

in Thessalonica that their "spirit and soul and body be kept sound and blameless" (1 Thess. 5:23). Here a threefold distinction is made in the human anatomy between body, soul, and spirit. It is interesting that this tripartite anthropology is not of body, soul, and reason, but of body, soul, and spirit.

Reason *(nous)* is not a special organ that endows a human being with reasonableness, but it is the knowledge and understanding that also involves certain intentionality. It is analogous to the Old Testament *leb,* which is usually rendered in the Greek Septuagint as *nous.* Although the term *nous* occurs twenty-one times in the Pauline corpus, it is used only three other times in the rest of the entire New Testament. This shows that it is not a favorite New Testament term to talk about a human being. In Luke it occurs in the sense of "mind" when the resurrected One, in addressing his disciples, "opened their minds to understand the scriptures" (Luke 24:45). Here it denotes the faculty to understand and acknowledge something. It is also used in a similar way in the book of Revelation (Rev. 13:18; 17:9).

Paul's use of *nous* becomes at once clear when he says about sinful humanity: "God gave them up to a debased mind [*nous*] and to things that should not be done" (Rom. 1:28). Then he challenges the Ephesians "to be renewed in the spirit of your minds" (Eph. 4:23). *Nous* is not the freely deciding and deliberating human reason, or the objective human mind. Paul puts it very bluntly: "I see in my members another law at war with the law of my mind, making me a captive of sin that dwells in my members" (Rom. 7:23). As God's creatures humans should be focused on their creator. Yet they contradict this orientation by doing what their mind (*nous*) tells them, resulting in a life of sinful alienation. There is the discrepancy between intention and action. Human beings cannot do what they want to do, but only what they do not want to do. Paul phrases it this way in his famous assessment in Romans 7: "I do not understand my own actions. For I do not do what I want, but I do the very thing I hate. . . . I can will what is right, but I cannot do it. For I do not do the good I want, but the evil I do not want is what I do" (Rom. 7:15, 18f.). Human *nous,* or reason, is in its actual tendency directed toward the good, but in fact it is moving toward evil. The human *nous* does not have the double possibility of an "understanding will with the alternative of being for God or against Him."[18] Human *nous* is not the freely deciding rationality that humanity often claims to possess.

18. This is what Bultmann optimistically claims in *Theology of the New Testament,* 1:213.

b. Flesh or Spirit?

As Martin Luther (1483-1546) pointed out against Erasmus of Rotterdam (1466-1536) in his treatise *The Bondage of the Will,* no person lives on an island. We are always influenced by the context in which we live. Paul could even say that we are enslaved to sin. Therefore he puts human existence in an either-or position: we live either according to the flesh *(kata sarka)* or according to the Spirit *(kata pneuma).* Moreover, he contends that human beings have already missed their actual being because their intentionality is wrong, even evil. While all people have the faculty to know about God, "they did not honor him as God or give thanks to him, but they became futile in their thinking, and their senseless minds were darkened" (Rom. 1:21). Since sin and death as ruling powers entered this world through the first human being, all people are sinners. This wrong intentionality of humans is usually identified by Paul as living according to the flesh *(sarx),* which means the material corporality of a human being.

While *sarx* in the sense of all flesh (Rom. 3:20: trans. "human being") can also mean everyone, it usually denotes the corporality of an individual human being in his or her humanness, meaning his or her weakness and transitoriness. In this way *sarx* is contrasted to God and his *pneuma* (Spirit). "In the flesh" (Gal. 2:20) can mean the actual or natural life without implying an ethical or theological judgment, and it can also stand for a life lived contrary to the way it ought to be lived, in opposition to God's Spirit or to faith (Rom. 7:5). The same is even more true of "according to the flesh" *(kata sarka)* when, for instance, Abraham is claimed as "our ancestor according to the flesh" (Rom. 4:1). But then *kata sarka* is used in a theological way when Paul talks about walking "according to the flesh" or "according to the Spirit" (Rom. 8:4). He explains: "For those who live according to the flesh set their minds on the things of the flesh, but those who live according to the Spirit set their minds on the things of the Spirit." Flesh and Spirit are the parameters within which a person can live.

Since all people live their lives in the flesh, meaning in their natural bodily and finite existence, the decisive question for Paul is whether one can then live freely, either setting one's mind on the fleshly and therefore sinful norm, or on the spiritual and therefore sinless norm. Especially in his Letter to the Romans Paul endeavors to show that regardless of how free they feel, humans are enslaved to sin and they willingly, though not always intentionally, follow a path that leads them away from God and his commandments. As Rudolf Bultmann pointed out, flesh and sin are *"powers to which man has fallen victim,* and against which he is powerless. The personification of these powers expresses the fact that man has lost to them the capacity to be the subject of his own actions."[19] In the aforementioned chapter 7 of Romans Paul explains: "I am of the flesh, sold into slavery under sin.... I see in my members another law at war with the law of my mind, making me captive to the law of sin that dwells in my members" (Rom. 7:14, 23). Humans become objects of sin, their own ego dies, and sinfulness rules supreme. It is not surprising that the end result is death because at the judgment sinners can only expect to be rejected by God.[20] This alienation from God is so pervasive that even nature is implicated in this process and also "has been groaning in labor pains until now" (Rom. 8:22). In late apocalyptic thinking the appearance of the Messiah is often thought of as being preceded by "apocalyptic labor pains" through which all earthly problems are intensified. Whether Paul is thinking of that remains uncertain.[21]

There is no doubt for Paul that redemption is not confined to humans alone. Yet how is such redemption accomplished? Of course, underlying God's redemptive act in Jesus Christ are his sacrificial death and his glorious resurrection. Through God's identification with humanity on the cross and the display of new life in Christ's resurrection there is the possibility for humans, too, to die to one's self and to be raised to new life as Paul had shown in Romans 6. Yet how is the transition accomplished from living "according to the flesh" to a life lived "according to the Spirit"? In his discussion with the Christians in Galatia Paul may give us a clue. He questions their approach, saying, "Are you so foolish? Having started with the Spirit, are you now ending with the flesh? Did you experience so much for nothing? — if it really was for nothing. Well then, does God supply you with the Spirit and work miracles among you by your doing the works of the law, or by your believing what you heard?" (Gal. 3:3-5). Then referring to Abraham and his faith and quoting Habakkuk 2:4b Paul writes: "The one who is righteous will live by faith" (Gal. 3:11). Paul scolds the Galatians by saying they had begun their new life in the Spirit, but then attempted to complete it in the flesh, meaning by their own human power and intentionality. He asks them if they did not realize that it was God who worked "miracles"

---

19. Bultmann, *Theology of the New Testament,* 1:245.

20. Schnelle, *Theology of the New Testament,* 319, rightly cautions here: "It would be a total misunderstanding to subsume Paul's anthropology under a pessimistic view of humanity; *his view of human beings is not merely pessimistic, but realistic."*

21. So Joseph A. Fitzmyer, *Romans,* The Anchor Bible (New York: Doubleday, 1993), 33:509, in his comments on Romans 8:22.

among them by their believing the gospel which they had heard. As the life according to the flesh is lived under the domain of sin, the new life according to the Spirit is lived under the domain of faith that is enabled by God. Paul summons the Christians in Galatia to lead their lives trusting not the flesh but in the Spirit as the formative power of their new existence.

c. Two Kinds of Existence

There are also other antinomies involved in the old and new existence, such as living by the law or living by the gospel, or glorying in one's own works or glorying in Christ Jesus. Paul sums up his advice: "If you sow to your own flesh, you will reap corruption from the flesh; but if you sow to the Spirit, you will reap eternal life from the Spirit" (Gal. 6:8).

It would be wrong to assume that Paul is alone in juxtaposing two kinds of existence. This either-or existence reverberates throughout the New Testament. For example, according to John, Jesus told his audience: "You are from below, I am from above; you are of this world, I am not of this world" (John 8:23). Here "from below" and "from above," "of this world" and "not of this world" are juxtaposed, not only to indicate from where people are, but also to indicate where they will go and where they cannot go. Yet this is not a cosmological dualism, but *"a dualism of decision"* by which Jesus summons the people to do God's will.[22] In the Gospel of John we notice that there are two kinds of people, those who are "from God" and hear God's word, and those who are "not from God" and do not hear God's word (John 8:47). Of course, the world is in darkness and those who do evil hate the light "and do not come to the light" that shines into this world (John 3:20). But again, escaping from darkness is not a human possibility. As Jesus tells his audience: "For God so loved the world that he gave his only Son, so that everyone who believes in him may not perish but may have eternal life. Indeed, God did not send the Son into the world to condemn the world, but in order that the world might be saved through him" (John 3:16f.). In his graciousness God sent his Son to redeem the world. Through him the question is directed to those who are in darkness whether they want to stay there or want to accept God's grace.

In the Synoptic Gospels we encounter a similar situation when the people are summoned to change their ways. According to Mark, we read that Je-

22. See Bultmann, *Theology of the New Testament,* 2:21.

sus began his ministry saying, "The time is fulfilled, and the kingdom of God has come near; repent, and believe in the good news" (Mark 1:15). Living in accordance with God's will and living with the perspective of becoming a part of God's kingdom is only possible by responding to God's initiative and not through one's own efforts. This means that a human being, at least insofar as the issue of salvation is concerned, has no free will to decide for the good or for the bad. One can only turn to God on God's own invitation.

While in spiritual matters humans are not as free as they often think, the freedom to choose is in other respects also not totally unfettered. Swiss philosopher Jean-Jacques Rousseau (1712-78) already showed in the eighteenth century in his novel *Émile* that human beings are heavily influenced in their decisions by their social context. As Rousseau says, "Education comes to us from nature, from man, or from things."[23] Of course, Rousseau presupposed that all humans are equal and good in their behavior. Only their social conditions corrupt them. Yet again, no human being is an island. We all live in a certain context that influences our thinking and therefore our decisions. Moreover, biology has also told us that genetic makeup can severely influence our decisions and limit their range. Therefore we should be even more cautious than Martin Luther, who conceded human freedom at least in secular matters. The biblical writers, however, did not make that kind of distinction between the spiritual and the secular. They saw an intimate relation between the created and the creator. For instance, with the Old Testament description of a person they emphasized, as we have seen, that all our actions presuppose God as the giver of life. God alone allows for human actions. In order to elucidate the place of humanity in this world, we must now turn our attention to what it means that humanity was created by God.

3. God's Special Creature

While there are two creation accounts right at the beginning of the Bible, the priestly account in Genesis 1:1–2:4a and the Yahwistic account in Genesis 2:4b-25, only the latter one gives a detailed account of the creation of the first human beings. In the priestly account we are only told that God made human beings, but we are not told how. Moreover, immediately after the

23. Jean-Jacques Rousseau, *Émile,* trans. Barbara Foxley (New York: E. P. Dutton, 1943), 6.

first human beings (Adam and Eve) were created, God enters into a dialogue with them. Although there are other references to God having created human beings (see Ps. 139:13f.; Job 10:8-12), prime attention has always been given to the creation narratives at the beginning of the Bible.

One might think that God's creative activity culminates in the creation of humanity. Yet at the end of the priestly creation narrative there is no mention of humanity but of God, who instituted the Sabbath day as a day of rest. Humanity is mentioned right before that day. Although four verses are devoted to humanity and its creation, there is not even a special day reserved for the creation of humanity. On the sixth day "living creatures of every kind: cattle and creeping things and wild animals of the earth of every kind" were brought forth from the earth (Gen. 1:24) and then God also created humanity. Not even a special kind of food is reserved for them. They are supposed to eat "every plant yielding seed" and the animals "every green plant." Both animals and humans are depicted as vegetarians. Death and the killing of other living beings for food is "not in accord with the will of the creator at the beginning although it is necessary in the present world."[24] — Like the fish of the seas and the birds of the air, humans are blessed and given the command to be fruitful and multiply. This shows the intimate connection between animals and humans. Indeed, when we remember how humans lived at the time when the priestly account was put down in ink, most likely in the sixth or fifth century B.C. after the Babylonian exile, such a statement is not surprising. People lived together with the animals, sharing with them shelter and quite often also food. But this is not that different from the way many people treat their pets today. Only in farming communities, at least in the West, have humans and animals very distinct and separate quarters. Also, their food is quite different.

In Genesis 1:27 we read three times that God created humanity as if to emphasize that humans are definitely God's creatures, no more and no less. In other creation accounts humans have a very different status. According to Hesiod, for instance, "the beginnings of things were the same for gods as for mortals."[25] Humanity is born from the earth, just as the earliest gods were born from Gaia, the earth goddess. Historian of religion Mircea Eliade (1907-86) mentions that in ancient Sumer there existed at least four narra-

24. So Claus Westermann, *Genesis 1–11: A Commentary,* trans. John J. Scullion (Minneapolis: Augsburg, 1984), 164, in his comments on Genesis 1:29f.

25. Hesiod, *Works and Days* (108), trans. Richmond Lattimore (Ann Arbor: University of Michigan Press, 1959), 31.

tives that explained the origin of humanity.[26] In one myth, for instance, we are told that the first human beings sprouted from the ground like plants. In another version humans were fashioned from clay by certain divine artisans. One modeled a heart for the first human being, and the other gave it life. In a third text the goddess Arura was the creator of human beings, and finally in the fourth version humanity was formed from the blood of two gods who were immolated for that purpose. This last version then, according to Eliade, gave rise to the famous Babylonian cosmogonic poem *Enuma Elish.* The latter myth is especially interesting because there it states that the god Ea created humans from the blood of Kingu and "imposed the service of the gods upon them."[27] By contrast we read in Genesis 1:26ff.: "Then God said, 'Let us make humankind in our image, according to our likeness; and let them have dominion over the fish of the sea, and over the birds of the air, and over the cattle, and over all the wild animals of the earth, and over every creeping thing that creeps on the earth.'" We hear nothing here of humans being servants to the gods. On the contrary, the purpose of humanity focuses on activities within the world, that is, to have dominion over animals. "The creation of human beings introduces the possibility of a hierarchical order which is characteristic of 'being in the world.' The goal of the creation of humans is detached from the life of the gods and directed to the life of this world."[28] Now we can see the reason for the creation of humanity. Humans have their own task here on earth and are not created as domestic servants of the gods.

Nevertheless, it is asserted that humanity was created in God's image. When the Hebrew language uses two different words to denote this, *demut* and *tselem,* therewith not two different kinds of images are implied, but the two words are to be understood as being synonymous.[29] Yet the later Latin tradition distinguished between *imago* and *similitudo* and asserted that the *imago* image was lost through the fall, while the *similitudo* image remained. Since only man and woman were created in God's image it is not surprising that humanity has an elevated position over against other creatures. The be-

---

26. See Mircea Eliade, *A History of Religious Ideas,* vol. 1, *From the Stone Age to the Eleusinian Mysteries,* trans. Willard R. Trask (Chicago: University of Chicago Press, 1978), 59, for the following.

27. *Enuma Elish,* tablet 6, line 36, in Alexander Heidel, *The Babylonian Genesis: The Story of Creation* (Chicago: University of Chicago Press, 1942), 37.

28. Westermann, *Genesis 1–11,* 159.

29. Horst Dietrich Preuss, *"damah,"* in *TDOT,* 3:259, states "that very little distinction can be made between the two words."

ing that was created "in the image of God" is distinguished from all other creatures made by God. We should not speculate, however, which parts or functions of humanity correspond especially well to being created in God's image. Such differentiating speculations are foreign to this text. We are simply reminded that the whole person is created in God's image.

A view of the cultural-historical context can be enlightening.[30] In Mesopotamia and in Egypt images of the gods were often used in religious cultic life. The significance of an image did not lie in the fact that it would describe or actually depict the godhead, though this may not have been completely off the mark. Decisive is that the image was the place at which the godhead was present and made manifest. The presence of the god and the blessing of his or her presence were mediated through the image. In Egypt the Pharaoh was even regarded as the earthly manifestation of the godhead and he functioned analogously to the image of the god that was kept in the temple. In Mesopotamia the king was only considered for a short period as the representative of the godhead. In Israel, according to Genesis 1, the image of God was not confined to the king but was extended to humans in general. Therefore being created in the image of God means "that the human being rules over the rest of creation as king, governor, and God's representative on earth."[31]

According to Genesis 1:26ff., being created in the image of God does not imply a special ontological quality, but is an assertion about the function of humanity. That is to say that humanity has been created and is called forth to rule over the rest of creation. This is also expressed in Psalm 8, where the psalmist writes: "What are human beings that you are mindful of them, mortals that you care for them? Yet you have made them a little lower than God, and crowned them with glory and honor. You have given them dominion over the works of your hands; you have put all things under their feet" (Ps. 8:4ff.). Being created in the image of God is not intended to deify or idolize humanity; it is also no license to exploit creation and to subjugate it to one's desires. Being created in God's image means rather to act in God's place, as his administrator and representative.

This understanding is reinforced in the New Testament where the Pauline corpus is the main — almost exclusive — source. To be created in God's image means to be ethically shaped in conformity with God and to act in a

---

30. For the following, see Edward M. Curtis, "Image of God (OT)," in *The Anchor Bible Dictionary,* 3:390f.

31. Jacob Jervell, "Bild Gottes I," in *TRE,* 6:492.

manner for which God serves as the prototype. Such conduct can be derived from God's ways as they are transparent in Jesus of Nazareth (see Phil. 2:5; Rom. 15:5).

As humans we are supposed to represent God and to model our conduct according to God. This also illustrates the limits of human freedom. It is not a freedom to do whatever we want to do; rather it is the freedom to live according to God's intentions. We should remember that every creative act of God was described as "very good." As God's representatives we should maintain and preserve this "very good." We should direct and channel everything that stands against God's creation, which is destroyed, corrupted, and in bondage to decay, in the direction of this "very good." If we did that we would truly be creatures, but also co-creators because we would exercise our responsibility for creation so that it does not run counter to its original intention or is used contrary to it. We are God's representatives and we derive our self-understanding from our task of representing God.

Burdening creation, however, through mindless procreation and pushing it beyond its carrying capacity (Gen. 1:28 says that we should merely fill the earth not overpopulate it!), and exploiting its natural resources so that subsequent generations are surrounded by garbage dumps, have nothing to do with representation but with egotism. Our experience of God as a loving and caring God should give us pointers to how we as God's representatives should be experienced by others. The concept of being created in the image of God not only suggests authority but also includes humility. Decisive action would be paired with caring, and loyalty in service to others with dignity.

Contrary to God's original intention and in an emancipating way we could also use our own selves to define our existence. Then we would be the sole measure of all things and everything would have to serve us. As individual human beings we would not only be confronted with nature, but with all other human beings as well. Our postmodern experience as solitary, isolated, and individual human beings shows ever more clearly the precariousness of our existence if we no longer understand ourselves as being created in God's image. We abandon our responsibility of caring for and cultivating God's creation. Instead, we regard it as our property while simultaneously ignoring its comprehensive context. By trying to gain the world for ourselves, we are about to lose it and ourselves in the process. If finite human beings became the measure of everything, they would end up absolutizing themselves and would see themselves as infinite.

Putting humanity in charge of all other living beings has often been understood as a license to subjugate everything on earth for our own advantage and to use it according to our own ideas. American historian of medieval history Lynn White Jr. (1907-87) called Christianity the most anthropocentric religion the world has ever seen because nature's sole purpose for existence is to serve us.[32] In a similar manner German critical essayist Carl Amery (1922-2005) wrote of the merciless consequences of Christianity.[33] Already in the nineteenth century philosopher Ludwig Feuerbach (1804-72) asserted: "Separation from the world, from matter, from the life of the species, is therefore the essential aim of Christianity."[34] However, environmental ethicist Paul Santmire, in an insightful study, showed that the theological tradition of the West is neither ecologically bankrupt, as many assert, nor does it just suggest simplistic solutions for averting our ecological crisis. Santmire contends that the Christian faith contains starting points "for a rich theology of nature."[35] At the same time Santmire also admits that in Western theology humanity always has to rise far beyond nature to enter into communion with God.[36] The subsequent rift between humanity and nature can, of course, become problematic for both. Therefore Jürgen Moltmann (b. 1926) calls for a "naturalization of the human being."[37] This is not a call to a romantic "return to nature." But "men and women should find a new understanding of themselves, and a new interpretation of their work in the framework of nature." Humans are neither of divine stuff nor are they left by themselves on earth. They are also not simply God's helpers. God has entrusted to them a certain task here on earth through which they should define themselves. This object-focused definition of people is often pronounced today when certain persons are defined by the task they perform in and for society.

When we now look at the Yahwist creation narrative, which begins in Genesis 2:4b, then strictly speaking it presents only an account of the creation of humanity. The actual creation of the world is presupposed and the

---

32. Lynn White Jr., "The Historical Roots of Our Ecologic Crisis," first published in *Science* 155 (March 10, 1967): 1203-7, and since then often reprinted.

33. Carl Amery, *Das Ende der Vorsehung: Die gnadenlosen Folgen des Christentums* (Reinbek bei Hamburg: Rowohlt, 1972).

34. Ludwig Feuerbach, *The Essence of Christianity,* trans. George Eliot, intro. Karl Barth, foreword H. Richard Niebuhr (New York: Harper & Row, 1957), 161.

35. So H. Paul Santmire, *The Travail of Nature: The Ambiguous Ecological Promise of Christian Theology* (Philadelphia: Fortress, 1985), 8.

36. See Santmire, *Travail of Nature,* 188.

37. See Jürgen Moltmann, *God in Creation: A New Theology of Creation and the Spirit of God,* trans. Margaret Kohl (Minneapolis: Fortress, 1993), 49f., for this and the following quotation.

sole reminder of such a creation is seen in the fact that God has not yet caused it to rain on the earth. Only the immediate environment of humanity is described, and it is a matter of fact that God has created everything and that he also gives rain that allows life to thrive. In contrast to the priestly account in which humanity is placed at the end of the creative process, here everything is created around humanity so that it can feel at home in God's creation. The Hebrew word that is used to denote the human being, *adam,* is a collective word, actually meaning "humankind." Only later does it become a proper name for Adam as the first human being.

The Yahwist creation narrative shows that the creation of humanity is exclusively the work of God. We read: "Then the Lord God formed man from the dust of the ground, and breathed into his nostrils the breath of life; and the man became a living being" (Gen. 2:7). German Old Testament scholar Gerhard von Rad (1901-71) called this verse "a locus classicus [a classical assertion] of Old Testament anthropology."[38] There is nothing divine in humanity since it is closely associated with matter. Though we might expect the creation narrative to make a distinction between body and soul, such a distinction is foreign to Old Testament understanding. Contrary to Hellenism, there is no human soul as a life-causing agent that enters the body from the outside and enlivens that body. Humanity is perceived as a unity. A human *(adam)* is taken from earth *(adamah).* Therefore we read toward the end of the story of the fall, "you are dust, and to dust you shall return" (Gen. 3:19). Humans go back to nature from which they were taken. But as we also saw in the priestly account the earth does not simply yield humans. The priestly writer reports that the earth brought forth living creatures of every kind (but no humans). There is no natural necessity for humans to emerge. God himself gives his breath to a human and so there emerges a living human being. Human life is a gift of God and it is not to be taken for granted. We receive our human existence by participating in God's life-giving Spirit. When many people question today whether humanity has a chance of surviving the environmental crisis, this reference to the gift character of human life takes on renewed significance. Humanity has no right of its own to survive. Life and the future that is necessary for life to unfold are God's gifts.

The creator of all of humanity is at the same time the creator of each individual human being (see Isa. 17:7). The psalmist writes of this creator: "For it was you who formed my inward parts; you knit me together in my

---

38. Gerhard von Rad, *Genesis: A Commentary,* trans. John H. Marks (Philadelphia: Westminster, 1961), in his exegesis of Genesis 2:7.

mother's womb. I praise you, for I am fearfully and wonderfully made. Wonderful are your works" (Ps. 139:13f.). Similarly, we read in Job:

> Your hands fashioned and made me; and now you turn and destroy me. Remember that you fashioned me like clay; and you will turn me to dust again? Did you not pour me out like milk and curdle me like cheese? And you clothed me with skin and flesh, and knit me together with bones and sinews. You have granted me life and steadfast love, and your care has preserved my spirit. (Job 10:8-12)

Though the writer of the book of Job describes the procreative process, that the semen is injected into the female organism and a solid embryonic body is formed ("Did you not pour me out like milk and curdle me like cheese?"), this whole process is, at the same time, understood as a work solely wrought by God. It is beyond the imagination of the Old Testament writers that nature should do its part and then God would do the rest, or that the natural processes would involve some kind of automatism.

Martin Luther captured well the biblical understanding of the dependency of human life on God when he said that God "could give children without using men and women. But He does not want to do this. Instead, He joins man and woman so that it appears to be the work of man and woman, and yet He does it under the cover of such masks."[39] Each human being is totally God's work regardless of his or her earthly progenitors. The question of whether life evolved "naturally" (unaided) from inanimate matter, though scientifically significant, is theologically secondary. Both inanimate nature and all living creatures are God's creation. Whenever and wherever human life appears it is a gift of God.

After this brief survey of additional assertions concerning creation we must once more return to the Yahwist creation narrative. Humanity's creaturely position is not only indicated by the Yahwist when he mentions that humans are taken from dust and created through the life-giving Spirit of God. Their reddish-brown skin reminded the Israelites of the reddish-brown dust of the earth. Moreover, animals are seen in close relationship to humans. Like humans they are created from dust and they are even introduced as possible helpers for humans (Gen. 2:18f.). Finally, the first human being was supposed to name the animals. The animals receive the designation that the first human attributes to them.[40] The naming of the animals is

---

39. Martin Luther in his exegesis of Psalm 147:13, in *LW,* 14:114.
40. For the following, see Westermann, *Genesis 1–11,* 228, in his exegesis of Genesis 2:19.

no magic act through which a human might obtain power over the animals; rather, with these names this human puts them into a place in his world. They are part of his world and belong to him. Since today more and more species of animals are destined to become extinct, the human world becomes impoverished. Animals belong to humans and are part of the richness of the human world.

When we turn to the creation of the woman, we notice that God's creative activity does not tolerate any spectators. Adam falls into a deep sleep when Eve, the mother of all living beings, is created. We are only allowed to view God's creation retrospectively. "The creation of woman from the rib of the man should not be understood as a description of an actual event accessible to us."[41] Through the creative event itself, the mutuality of man and woman is explained. The woman is from the same "material" as the man, from human stuff. Man *(ish)* notices this immediately and calls her "woman" *(ishah)* similar to the old English meaning of "woman" (female human).

In the beginning of the narrative we read that God created "a helper as his partner." This was often interpreted to mean that the woman was to help the man in agriculture. Feminist theology has rightly corrected this exegesis, which demeans the woman as the handmaiden of the man. As the Yahwist creation narrative shows, such a devaluing of the woman is not intended, but there is expressed a personal correspondence between man and woman. With the creation of the woman the creative process of humanity is concluded. Therefore one could even regard the woman as the pinnacle of God's creation. Yet the woman does not stand alone. Only now can there be "the personal community of man and woman in the broadest sense — bodily and spiritual community, mutual help and understanding, joy and contentment in each other."[42] When we read in the concluding sentence that a man leaves his father and mother and clings to his wife this is to show again the strong relationship between man and woman, which is sustained through the love between them and against which even the bond with the parental home cannot supervene.

In the priestly account, too, we read: "So God created humankind in his image, in the image of God he created them; male and female he created them" (Gen. 1:27). There is no indication of some primal archetypal androgynous being since sexual differentiation is something given with creation. From the very beginning human beings are present in one of these

---

41. Westermann, *Genesis 1–11*, 230, in his exegesis of Genesis 2:21f.
42. So to the point Westermann, *Genesis 1–11*, 232, in his exegesis of Genesis 2:23.

two forms. Therefore they coexist, for better or for worse, in mutual inter-dependence. "Every theoretical and institutional separation of man and woman, every deliberate detachment of male from female, can endanger the very existence of humanity as determined by creation."[43]

While the two creation stories are quite different with regard to their often picturesque details, they are in fundamental agreement in their basic estimation of humanity. Humans are seen as creatures, placed in immediate vicinity of animals, but created in distinction to the animal world, and in a basic twofold appearance of men and women. The paradisiacal environment in which they were put did not imply an idle existence. In contrast to the more agricultural environment of Genesis 2, in which humanity was charged to till the garden and to keep it, is the priestly account in which humanity was given dominion over all living beings. Humanity is not in the world for itself. "From the beginning, the human creature is called, given a vocation, and expected to share in God's work."[44]

43. Westermann, *Genesis 1–11*, 160, in his exegesis of Genesis 1:27.
44. Walter Brueggemann, *Genesis* (Atlanta: John Knox, 1982), 46, in his interpretation of Genesis 2:4b–3:24.

2. *The Biological Perspective*

When we view from a biological perspective the special place of humans in the world, we notice especially two things that have often aroused much curiosity and controversy: human origin and the difference between humans and animals. Are the biblical creation narratives just stories when compared to the facts of the natural sciences? And, if the theory of evolution is correct, can there be anything special about humans, or are they so closely related to the animals that they are just another species of the primates? To address these vexing questions we must first take a careful look at human origins from a biological perspective and then compare the human constitution and the human potential with that of other living species.

1. Human Origin

Especially in the latter part of the nineteenth century progress was felt everywhere. It was the era of the great industrial revolution, especially in Great Britain but also in the emerging United States. This was the gilded age of John D. Rockefeller (1839-1937), Andrew Carnegie (1835-1919), and J. P. Morgan (1837-1913), but it was also the age of Charles Dickens (1812-70) and his social criticism and of Henry George (1839-97) with his proposal of a single tax to curb excessive land speculation. And Charles Darwin's evolutionary theory fit right into this progressive mood.

a. The Evolutionary Theory of Charles Darwin

Having published the *Origin of Species* in 1859, Charles Darwin (1809-82) concluded his project in 1871 with *The Descent of Man*. In the introduction of the latter book Darwin says: "The sole object of this work is to consider, firstly, whether man, like every other species, is descended from some pre-existing form; secondly, the manner of his development; and thirdly, the value of the differences between the so-called races of man."[1] Concerning the bodily structure of humans Darwin states: "It is notorious that man is constructed on the same general type or model as other mammals. All the bones in his skeleton can be compared with corresponding bones in a monkey, bat, or seal. So it is with his muscles, nerves, blood-vessels and internal viscera. The brain, the most important of all the organs, follows the same law."[2] From this common structure, Darwin then concludes that there must be a coherence or, as he calls it, a "community of descent."[3] While Darwin admits in his general conclusion that "many of the views which have been advanced are highly speculative, and some no doubt will prove erroneous," he holds "that man is descended from some less-highly organized form."[4] One of these highly speculative claims that have been proven wrong is his statement that "man is descended from a hairy quadruped, furnished with a tail and pointed ears, probably arboreal in his habits, and an inhabitant of the Old World."[5]

Darwin still allowed for a human having an immortal soul, though he found it impossible to determine "at what precise period in the development of the individual, from the first trace of a minute germinal vesicle to the child either before or after birth, man becomes an immortal being."[6] Then he asked why it seems more irreligious to explain the origin of humans as a distinct species by the descent from some lower form, through the laws of variation and natural selection, than to explain the birth of the individual through the laws of ordinary reproduction. "The birth of both of the species and of the individual are equally parts of that grand sequence of events, which our minds refuse to accept as the result of blind chance. The

---

1. Charles Darwin, *The Descent of Man and Selection in Relation to Sex*, intro. John Tyler Bonner and Robert M. May (Princeton, NJ: Princeton University Press, 1981 [1871]), 1:2f.

2. Darwin, *The Descent of Man,* 1:10.

3. Darwin, *The Descent of Man,* 1:32.

4. Darwin, *The Descent of Man,* 2:385.

5. Darwin, *The Descent of Man,* 2:389.

6. Darwin, *The Descent of Man,* 2:395.

understanding revolts at such a conclusion, whether or not we are able to believe that every slight variation of structure, — the union of each pair in marriage, — the dissemination of each seed, — and other such events, have all been ordained for some special purpose."[7]

Darwin points here to a dilemma that he himself had experienced: On the one hand, he seemed to have shown exactly how everything occurred in a natural manner. Yet on the other hand, it was impossible for him to believe that this was all the result of "blind chance."[8] This dilemma, he admits, is independent of whether we accept a teleological (divine) direction. As we remember, Martin Luther resolved that dilemma elegantly when he claimed that God rarely operates in a direct way in creation. He rather works in, with, and under the natural cause-and-effect sequence so that it seems that everything occurs naturally, while ultimately it is God's own doing. In 1859 Darwin's publication of *The Origin of Species* caused quite a controversy, though he had hardly mentioned the origin of humanity, except with his remark that "light will be thrown on the origin of man and his history." Once *The Descent of Man* appeared in 1871, the dust of the storm over the *Origin* had already settled.[9] Though the publication of *The Descent of Man* aroused a lot of attention and the book sold well, people more or less accepted it as just another book by Charles Darwin. The earlier controversy was not renewed with the same vigor. Indeed, if there is continuity from one living species to another, humanity can hardly be exempt.

b. The Present-Day Picture

Austrian biologist Franz Wuketits (b. 1955) claims that most biologists are still of the opinion "that in principle Darwin was right, but that his view of evolution needs decisive expansions."[10] Wuketits himself is very adamant

---

7. Darwin, *The Descent of Man,* 2:396.

8. Charles Darwin wrote to J. D. Hooker in 1870: "I cannot look at the universe as the result of blind chance, yet I can see no evidence of beneficent design, or indeed of design of any kind, in the details." As reprinted in *The Autobiography of Charles Darwin, 1809-1882,* ed. Nora Barlow (New York: W. W. Norton, 1969 [1958]), 162.

9. Charles Darwin, *The Origin of Species,* A variorum text, ed. Marse Peckham (Philadelphia: University of Pennsylvania Press, 1959), 757.

10. See Franz M. Wuketits, *Evolutionstheorien: Historische Voraussetzungen, Positionen, Kritik* (Darmstadt: Wissenschaftliche Buchgesellschaft, 1988), 171, for this and the following quote.

that evolution as a natural process is the starting point of biology. "Any refuge in a metaphysical frame of reference or even into creationism would be a relapse into a long overcome way of thinking." Whether the theory of evolution excludes any metaphysical perspective, meaning a reference to that agency that brought everything physical into being, is questionable. Nevertheless, we agree with Wuketits when he claims that "evolution is the key to the understanding of everything living."[11] Of course, Darwin's claim that humans are only modified apes can no longer be maintained. Yet that humanity emerged within a larger evolutionary process is the overwhelming consensus of most biologists. Of course, details will always remain in flux as long as new data are unearthed.

The following picture seems relatively uncontested. As far as we can tell the predecessors of humanity emerged when a large part of the African and Asian rainforests disappeared and savannahs emerged. Some of the predecessors of the anthropoid apes such as the *Kenyapithecus* adjusted to living at the seams of the savannahs, roughly 14 million years ago in eastern Africa. From these primates the hominids then emerged approximately 5 million years ago. In 2001 in the central African country of Chad the skull of a hominid was found that was judged to have lived approximately 7 million years ago. This *Sahelanthropus tchadensis* is of the size of a chimpanzee and has human features with regard to face and teeth. Yet the volume of the skull is only 350 cubic centimeters, which is less than that of present-day chimpanzees. So this creature seems to be related to both chimpanzees and humans. Other finds of these hominids occurred in eastern Africa and date back 5 million years. So far several hundred bones of these precursors of humanity, called *Australopithecines,* have been found. When we come closer to our own time, approximately 3 million years ago, we also find them in southern Africa.

In 1995 near Lake Turkana in Kenya, Meave Leakey found the remains of hominids a little more than 5 million years old. She called this find *Australopithecus anamensis.* Meave Leakey (b. 1942) is the daughter-in-law of the Kenyan paleoanthropologist and naturalist Louis Seymore Leakey (1903-72), who with his wife Mary Leakey (1913-96) in the late 1950s excavated in the Olduvai Gorge in Tanzania, East Africa, and there found remains of some *Australopithecines* who may have used simple tools. These "roughly trimmed pebbles and lumps of rocks . . . were later recognized as the oldest stone tools."[12] This means that the *Australopithecus* was the first

11. Wuketits, *Evolutionstheorien*, 173.

12. Patricia J. Ash and David J. Robinson, *The Emergence of Humans: An Exploration of*

toolmaker. Only forty-five kilometers south of the Olduvai Gorge at Laetoli, Mary Leakey found preserved in volcanic ash hominoid footprints of two individuals showing that they advanced in an upright position. As there were no knuckle impressions, it showed that these hominids walked upright habitually, and their feet had an arch typical of modern humans. Soft rain had cemented the ash layer without destroying the prints.[13]

Today one distinguishes between six different lines of *Australopithecines* who all lived in eastern or southern Africa. At least it is only there that their remains have been found. It appears that while three lines of *Australopithecines* that exhibited rather bulky body structure eventually died out approximately 1 million years ago, another two lines, the *Australopithecus afarensis* and the *Australopithecus africanus,* had a more delicate structure. They seem to be the predecessors of modern humanity. As far as we know, the *Australopithecus afarensis* lived approximately 4 million years ago and developed a million years later into the *Australopithecus africanus.* In 1974, 40 percent of a skeleton of an *Australopithecus afarensis* was found in Hadar, Ethiopia. The age of that skeleton was dated to 3.2 million years. It was classified as a female and later called "Lucy."[14] Since then further remains have been found and it appears that the female beings were considerably smaller than the males. The first *Australopithecus africanus* was discovered in 1924 and was the remains of a small child three to four years of age.

From these finds one could conclude that already 3 million years ago the Australopithecines moved around on two legs as efficiently as we do today. While the more bulky ones ate, among other things, hard nuts and seeds, the more delicate ones took to softer food. The grown-up *Australopithecines* had only one-third of the brain size of today's humans. From the more graceful species of the *Australopithecus* there evolved the first humans approximately 2.5 million years ago. Of course, they were much smaller than humans today, but again, the big difference was the brain size. To elucidate this more modern species, we refer again to Louis and Mary Leakey and their teams who excavated between 1960 and 1970 in eastern Africa between Lake Turkana, formerly Lake Rudolf, and the

the Evolutionary Time Line (Oxford: Wiley-Blackwell, 2010), 143; and see Theodosius Dobzhansky, *Mankind Evolving: The Evolution of the Human Species* (New Haven, CT: Yale University Press, 1962), 175, for this and the following.

13. See Mary Bowman-Kruhm, *The Leakeys: A Biography* (Amherst, NY: Prometheus, 2010), 113ff.

14. See Donald Johanson and James Shreeve, *Lucy's Child: The Discovery of a Human Ancestor* (New York: William Morrow, 1989), esp. 82-89.

Olduvai Gorge in Tanzania and discovered the *Homo rudolfensis* and the *Homo habilis.* The *Homo rudolfensis* lived between 2.4 and 1.9 million years ago, while the *Homo habilis* lived between 1.9 and 1.6 million years ago. Perhaps they are even the same species and, what is important, they now have a much larger brain than the *Australopithecines,* namely, between 500 and 730 cubic centimeters. The *Homo habilis* also has a smaller mouth and smaller teeth, which again shows that it consumed softer food than its predecessors. Approximately 1.9 million years ago the *Homo erectus* emerged and is found not only in Africa, but also in Asia and in southern Europe. These "people" settled in the tropics and subtropics, where natural food was plentiful and the climate was relatively warm. It has been generally assumed that there was an African genesis of the human family from where the other parts of the globe were settled. "But new evidence shows that the species occupied a West Asian site called Dmanisi [in present-day Georgia] from 1.85 million to 1.77 million years ago, at the same time or slightly before the earliest evidence of this human-like species in Africa."[15] For the next 1.3 million years the *Homo erectus,* meaning the upright human being, hardly changed. In 1984 Richard Leakey (b. 1944), the husband of Meave Leakey, found near Lake Turkana a nearly complete skeleton of a *Homo erectus,* a boy judged to be twelve years old at the time of his death who had lived 1.6 million years ago.

Another interesting find was made by Pierre Teilhard de Chardin (1881-1955), a French Jesuit and paleontologist who, together with others, found in Zhoukoudian, near Beijing, between 1923 and 1927 the *Sinanthropus pekinensis,* the so-called Peking Man (currently called *Homo erectus pekinensis*), who is dated to approximately 500,000 years ago. The excavators found in a cave the remains of approximately forty individuals and the ashes of an artificially set fire. In digging further, they also found burned animal bones, pieces of charcoal, and layers of yellow and red burned clay.[16] While the foreheads were relatively flat and the bones below the eyebrows rather pronounced, the teeth were relatively close to the ones humans have today. This indicates that these "people" ate softer food,

15. Bruce Bower, "Homo May Have Originated in Asia," *Science News* 180 (July 2, 2011): 8. This shows that the actual origin of humans and their eventual spreading over the globe may always be shrouded in a certain degree of uncertainty.

16. See for details Paul Overhage, *Menschenformen im Eiszeitalter: Umwelten — Gestalten — Entwicklungen* (Frankfurt am Main: Josef Knecht, 1969), 191. See also Camilo J. Cela-Conde and Francisco J. Ayala, *Human Evolution: Trails from the Past* (Oxford: Oxford University Press, 2007), 202f., who, however, do not mention Teilhard.

which means more meat and cooked food.[17] The brain size of the adult averages around 1,000 cubic centimeters, which is already two-thirds of what we find in present-day *Homo sapiens*.

In 1997 in Ethiopia near the village of Herto, bones of several individuals were found. The men had a cranial capacity of 1,450 cubic centimeters, which is even more than that which modern humans have. The finds were dated to around 160,000 years ago and these remains seem to stem from direct ancestors of modern humanity *(Homo sapiens sapiens)*. One estimate is that 100,000 years ago this species migrated to present-day Palestine, then to Southeast Asia, Australia, and Europe, and finally 20,000 to 15,000 years ago to the Americas. All humans who exist today are descendants of these "African emigrants." In Europe, these humans lived for a while side by side with the *Neanderthals*. The first *Neanderthals* also came from Africa and appeared in Europe as early as 350,000 years ago. Their cranial size was larger than that of modern humans, and they were robustly built. They used tools made of bones, antlers, and wood, and of course, also of stone. While it is evident that they are not a subspecies of the *Homo sapiens* of present-day humanity they share a common ancestor. The *Neanderthals* seem to have emerged as a species of humanity and were on the same developmental level as the *Homo sapiens*. Through DNA analysis Swedish biologist Svante Pääbo (b. 1955), one of the directors of the Max-Planck Institute of Evolutionary Anthropology in Leipzig, Germany, has shown that they intermingled and also intermarried with the *Homo sapiens* who came out of Africa since 1 to 4 percent of the Neanderthal genes are present in the genomes of present-day non-African individuals.

When 40,000 years ago the *Homo sapiens* migrated from Africa to Europe, they started the so-called Cro-Magnon culture, named after a cave near Cro-Magnon in southwestern France where in 1868 the first fossils of the *Homo sapiens* were discovered. These Cro-Magnon people were taller and more slender than the Neanderthals; they had a high forehead and a pronounced chin. Yet they had much in common with the Neanderthals, including a large brain and a long childhood, and both ate meat and used fire. They lived in caves, but also constructed primitive huts, and were excellent hunters and makers of stone tools. Of course, they also used human language. After approximately 10,000 years when a glacial period made living in Europe more difficult, the Neanderthals died out about 30,000 years

17. See Hong Shang and Erik Trinkhaus, *The Early Modern Humans from Tianyuan Cave, China* (College Station: Texas A. & M. University Press, 2010), 202.

ago. Due to their robust stature they needed up to three times as much food as the Cro-Magnon people, which was a decided disadvantage in a time of food shortage. Only the Cro-Magnon people survived since they were more flexible at adapting themselves to the more difficult living conditions.

In 2008 Russian archaeologists who had been working in the Denisova Cave in the Altai Mountains in Siberia found a fragment of a finger of a young human female who lived about 40,000 years ago.[18] This cave had also been inhabited by Neanderthals and modern humans. Two years later a group of international scientists announced that "the stratigraphy of the cave where the bone was found suggests that the Denisova hominin lived close in time and space with Neanderthals as well as with modern humans."[19] They also claimed that analysis of the mitochondrial DNA (mtDNA) of the finger bone — the initial find — showed it to be genetically distinct from the mtDNAs of Neanderthals and modern humans. Since then more fragments have been found from what has been named the Denisovans. Subsequent study of the nuclear genome suggested that this group shares a common origin with Neanderthals. "Genetic data of unprecedented completeness have been pulled from the fossil remains of a young Stone Age woman. The DNA helps illuminate the relationships among her group — ancient Siberians known as Denisovans — Neanderthals, and humans."[20] One assumes that the Denisovans ranged from Siberia to Southeast Asia and lived among and mated with the ancestors of some present-day modern humans. Up to 6 percent of the DNA of Melanesians and Australian Aborigines derived from Denisovans. This means that modern humans may have mated with at least two groups of ancient humans: Neanderthals and Denisovans.

Many of these findings that were unearthed during the last century were accidental and their interpretation is still somewhat debated. But some conclusions are quite certain:

1. First of all and most important for some people, modern humanity did not descend from apes or monkeys. Of course, there is a close relationship especially with the great apes. We can see this by just visiting a zoo. This has also been shown more conclusively through genetic research.

18. Ker Than, *National Geographic News* (December 22, 2010).

19. Johannes Krause et al., "The Complete Mitochondrial DNA Genome of an Unknown Hominin from Southern Siberia," *Nature* 464 (April 8, 2010): 894.

20. Bruce Bower, "DNA Unveils Enigmatic Denisovans: Extinct Neanderthal Relatives Serve Up a Complete Genetic Playbook," *Science News* 182 (September 22, 2012): 5.

We share 95 to 98.8 percent of our genes with the anthropoid apes, such as gorillas and chimpanzees, so we can rightly say that we have a common ancestry. Yet we also share some genes with all other living species. This means that there is a fundamental unity and coherence among all living beings.

2. There is no straight line from pre-human forms of life to modern humanity. As the fate of the Neanderthals shows, some branches simply died out. They could not compete with a changing environment or with other groups of humans. We still see this in more recent human history when one civilization dies out and another originates and thrives.

3. From all we know today, there seem to be several waves of humans that came out of Africa.[21] An earlier wave of archaic *Homo erectus* spread as far as China, as the *Homo erectus pekinensis* indicates. But then this wave was overtaken and replaced by at least one other wave of *Homo sapiens* who settled the whole globe and replaced earlier humans. There is, however, also a multiregional model that says that in the *Homo sapiens* there is also some genetic admixture from more archaic humans.

How do we know that there were several waves? Here we must turn to DNA analysis. The human mitochondrial DNA is a circular, double-string DNA molecule. This mtDNA is only passed from the mother to her descendants. Furthermore the mtDNA mutates at a relatively constant rate, so that one can say fairly well how close in temporal proximity two tribes are related to each other if the predecessors of these tribes have separated. One can, for example, determine that the original population of the Americas is most closely related to the original population of Eurasia, meaning they have a common predecessor. Geneticists from the universities of Uppsala in Sweden and Leipzig in Germany compared the complete mtDNA of fifty-three people of different tribal groups. The result was a relatively stable genealogical tree with relatively great precision. Therefore mtDNA analysis and comparison of DNA sequences plus the fossil findings show that present humanity has its origin in Africa.[22]

---

21. So Cela-Conde and Ayala, *Human Evolution*, 217.
22. For details, see Cela-Conde and Ayala, *Human Evolution*, 304-9.

c. Biological and Theological Evaluations

What are the consequences when the biological perspective that we have just elucidated is confronted with the theological one that we presented earlier? Is the belief still tenable that God created human beings? Two possible options have emerged over and over again. One option resulted in a clear denial that God could have created human beings while the other option still affirmed the traditional Christian faith.

French molecular biologist and 1965 Nobel laureate **Jacques Monod** (1910-76) caused quite an uproar with his 1970 book *Chance and Necessity: An Essay on the Natural Philosophy of Modern Biology,* which was translated into English the following year. As the title of the book indicates, he saw two factors operative in the evolutionary process: (1) chance, by which certain changes or mutations occur in a living species, and (2) the necessity that if this change strengthens a living being in contrast to others who had not undergone this mutation or if such mutation even provides new possibilities, then this being will be more successful in propagating itself.[23] We remember the advantage that the Cro-Magnon had over the Neanderthal who was finally crowded out. Although a mutation is always a "chance occurrence," the necessity is that those who are fitter for survival will eventually prevail. This way there is usually an upward movement traceable in evolution.

Monod included religion in his evolutionary framework when he claimed: "The invention of myths and religions, the construction of vast philosophical systems — they are the price this social animal has had to pay in order to survive without having to yield to pure automatism."[24] This means that in order to develop a culture humans had to invent myths, religions, and philosophical systems. Since we have discovered that the metaphysical and philosophical systems in which humanity believed were its own creations, "man knows at last that he is alone in the universe's unfeeling immensity, out of which he emerged only by chance. His destiny is nowhere spelled out, nor is his duty. The kingdom above or the darkness below: it is for him to choose."[25] All religious and metaphysical interpretations of humanity, its origin, and its destiny are wishful thinking for Monod. We have to accept things "the way they are." While Jacques

23. See Jacques Monod, *Chance and Necessity: An Essay on the Natural Philosophy of Modern Biology,* trans. A. Wainhouse (New York: Alfred A. Knopf, 1971), 118f.

24. Monod, *Chance and Necessity,* 167.

25. Monod, *Chance and Necessity,* 180.

Monod was not a crusader for his "strictly scientific exposition" of the origin of humanity, the same cannot be said for present-day avowed atheists such as Richard Dawkins (b. 1941) and Peter Atkins (b. 1940).

Richard Dawkins, Professor of Public Understanding of Science at Oxford University from 1995 to his retirement in 2008, has especially crusaded against a God notion, opting for a strictly naturalistic understanding of evolution. He states: "The one thing that makes evolution such a neat theory is that it explains how organized complexity can arise out of primeval simplicity."[26] Then he concludes that "the theory of evolution by cumulative natural selection is the only theory we know of that is in principle *capable* of explaining the existence of organized complexity." Since such progress from simple to more complex forms of life, including the descent from pre-human life forms to humanity itself, can be explained without needing a God who is involved in this process, God is reduced to "a hypothetically lazy God who tries to get away with as little as possible in order to make a universe containing life."[27] Even if we allow for a designer who guided the whole evolutionary process up to the emergence of modern humanity, according to Dawkins, such a "supernatural Designer" would "explain precisely nothing, for it leaves unexplained the origin of the Designer."[28] For Dawkins a natural explanation or any kind of explanation cannot stop at a certain point but must be all-embracing. It must explain everything.

If we leave the realm of the finite and claim universality, as Dawkins does, then we abandon the realm of empirical observation. This is exactly what Dawkins and others who claim that evolution does not allow for God's creative involvement tend to forget. An evolutionary biologist talking about the evolutionary evolvement of humanity rightly pursues a methodological naturalism by which any reference to God is excluded. But Dawkins and his followers have turned this methodological naturalism into naturalism by principle. Since any reference to God is excluded in this methodological naturalism, their conclusion is that God cannot be involved in the evolutionary process. In pursuing this line of argument they become ideological and leave the security of scientific argumentation.

The other extreme position is occupied by creationists who hold a literalistic interpretation of the creation accounts in Genesis 1 and 2. The young

26. See Richard Dawkins, *The Blind Watchmaker: Why the Evidence of Evolution Reveals a Universe without Design* (New York: W. W. Norton, 1986), 316-17, for this and the following quote.

27. Richard Dawkins, *The God Delusion* (Boston: Houghton Mifflin, 2006), 118.

28. Dawkins, *The Blind Watchmaker*, 141.

earth **creationists**, for example, claim that our earth was created within the last 10,000 to 6,000 years. Though for scientifically informed people this may sound strange, a 2007 Gallup poll showed that as many as 66 percent of the people in the United States believe that God created human beings largely in their present form at one point in time within the last 10,000 years. In 1961 Henry Morris (1918-2006) and John C. Whitcomb (b. 1943) published *The Genesis Flood,* which provided the scientific undergirding for young earth creationism. Its authors claimed that "the Flood may have occurred as much as three to five thousand years before Abraham."[29] This would then lead to the creation of humans within the last 10,000 years. Henry Morris then founded in 1972 the Institute for Creation Research in Dallas, Texas.[30] Soon after, Morris and his followers attempted to have the teaching of creationism accepted in public schools along with the teaching of evolution. Through the great flood theory they argued that most of the geological strata were laid down in the space of a relatively short time and therefore they claimed that the case for evolution had become invalid. In May 2007 at the cost of 27 million U.S. dollars financed by donations, a creation museum was opened in Petersburg, Kentucky, near the Greater Cincinnati International Airport, attempting to convince its visitors of a young earth history theory that claims to discredit the theory of evolution. While the attempt to convince state legislatures in the United States to have creation science taught alongside evolutionary science has failed, the notion that evolution is all wrong and the creation of humanity is a fairly recent event is still very much alive, both in society at large and among advocates of young earth creationism.

These so-called experts and scholars of creation science are not interested in scholarly interchange outside their own group. As historian of religion Arthur McCalla says, they "do not submit their work to peer review journals, they do not seek funding from the National Science Foundation or other standard granting bodies, and they do not participate in collaborative research with non-Fundamentalist scientists."[31] As their endeavors with the public school curricula show, they are not really interested in a dia-

29. John C. Whitcomb and Henry M. Morris, *The Genesis Flood: The Biblical Record and Its Scientific Implications,* foreword John C. McCampbell (Philadelphia: Presbyterian and Reformed Publishing Co., 1961), 489.

30. See Ronald L. Numbers, *The Creationists: From Scientific Creationism to Intelligent Design,* expanded ed. (Cambridge, MA: Harvard University Press, 2006), 312ff., a very informative and well-researched book.

31. Arthur McCalla, *The Creationist Debate: The Encounter between the Bible and the Historical Mind* (New York: T&T Clark International, 2006), 179.

logue with the established sciences by which the evolutionary theory is taught, but want to establish their own science. Yet truth cannot be divided. One has to start with the science that exists and then dialogue with its advocates to see to what extent their foundations and conclusions are wanting. While it is the intent of creationists to free the people and especially the schools from teaching the "godless theory of evolution," in so doing they turn creation, and especially the creation of humanity, into another scientific theory. Thereby the existential claim that God is the creator of all life, including all human beings, is reduced to a scientific claim. If such a claim, however, could be reduced to a scientific claim, it would have no immediate existential appeal.

Another approach, though not fundamentally different, is offered by the so-called **intelligent design** movement. This movement is institutionally connected with the Center for the Renewal of Science and Culture at the Discovery Institute in Seattle, Washington. It first appeared under its present name in 2002.[32] Unlike creationism, it does not start with a literalistic interpretation of Genesis 1 and 2. Its starting point is therefore not the Bible, but nature itself where it seeks to ascertain whether evolution is a wholly undirected process or whether it is a product of chance, natural law, intelligent design, or some combination thereof. The scientists involved with the center attempt to prove that the "apparent design" in nature is genuine design, meaning the product of an intelligent cause, and not simply the product of an undirected process such as natural selection acting on random variations. In claiming that it can indeed prove such genuine design, it does not identify this intelligent cause detected through science as something or someone supernatural. In other words, its proponents do not say that behind the intelligent design, which they claim to prove, stands God. Like creationists, however, they attempt through legal acts to include their "intelligent design science" in public school curricula in the United States. Additionally, as creationists have done, the intelligent design movement has a worldwide network through which its ideas and goals are disseminated.

The founder of the intelligent design movement is Phillip E. Johnson (b. 1940), a retired law professor from the University of California, Berkeley, and author of the 1991 book *Darwin on Trial*.[33] He is also co-founder

---

32. According to McCalla, *The Creationist Debate,* 190. For more information, see Numbers, *The Creationists,* 381f.

33. Phillip E. Johnson, *Darwin on Trial* (Washington, DC: Regnery Publishing Co., 1991).

and program adviser for the Discovery Institute's Center for the Renewal of Science and Culture. He argues against an atheistic theory of evolution and for theistic realism. Another vigorous proponent of the intelligent design argument is the mathematician and philosopher William A. Dembski (b. 1960), currently research professor in philosophy at Southwestern Baptist Theological Seminary in Fort Worth, Texas. He also functions as senior fellow at the Discovery Institute's Center for Science and Culture. He argues that many things in nature are so complex that there can be no adequate materialistic explanation for them (molecular machines inside a cell, for example). "The only causal power we know that is able to produce systems like this is intelligence."[34] In arguing for some kind of intelligence or intelligent design, Dembski does not want to prove the truth of Christianity, including the Christian God as the creator, but he wants to discard the leading ideology, namely, "the scientific and Darwinian materialism" that leads so many people to reject this Christian God.[35] The issue that makes the intelligent design movement so suspicious is its indirect "scientific" support for the truthfulness of the Christian faith. While the Christian faith certainly rests on certain historical facts, for example, the birth and death of Jesus, and the claim by reliable people that he was resurrected, the conclusions drawn from these "facts" involve an existential commitment. Yet with the intelligent design argument the conclusions from historical facts can allegedly be scientifically proven. If that is the case there is then no existential commitment, meaning there is no need for faith. Whoever does not accept their conclusions is considered to be simply dumb but is not necessarily an unbeliever.

The underlying issue of the intelligent design argument, whether there is teleology in nature, meaning is there directionality that leads up to humans or not, is a much more acceptable proposition. For instance, John D. Barrow (b. 1952), professor of theoretical physics and applied mathematics at the University of Cambridge, and Frank J. Tipler (b. 1947), professor of mathematics at Tulane University in New Orleans, wrote *The Anthropic Cosmological Principle* in which they wanted to introduce a new teleology on a scientific basis. They refer here to a thesis of Australian theoretical physicist Brandon Carter (b. 1942), who presently conducts research at the Meudon campus of the Laboratoire Univers et Théories, which is part of

34. William A. Dembski, "Opening Statement," in *Intelligent Design: William A. Dembski & Michael Ruse in Dialogue,* ed. Robert B. Stuart (Minneapolis: Fortress, 2007), 19.

35. Dembski, "Opening Statement," 22.

the French National Centre for Scientific Research. Carter first introduced in 1974 the so-called **anthropic principle**. He claimed "that what we can expect to observe must be restricted by conditions necessary for our presence as observers. (Although our situation is not necessarily *central*, it is inevitably privileged to some extent.)"[36]

Tipler and Barrow start with the statement that there are a number of very unlikely — and coincidental — accidents that are totally independent of one another. These accidents seem to be necessary if an observer, whose basic building material is carbon compounds, is to emerge in our universe.[37] This leads them to establish three different anthropic principles.

First, there is the weak anthropic principle, which states: *"The observed values of all physical and cosmological quantities are not equally probable, but they take on values restricted by the requirement that there exist sites where carbon-based life can evolve and by the requirement that the Universe be old enough for it to have already done so"* (16).

The strong anthropic principle then goes one step further and claims: *"The Universe must have those properties which allow life to develop within it at some stage in its history"* (21).

Lastly, they formulate the final anthropic principle, which states: *"Intelligent information-processing must come into existence in the Universe, and, once it comes into existence, it will never die out"* (23). Tipler expanded on this principle in his 1994 book *The Physics of Immortality*.[38]

The weak anthropic principle is basically a circular argument saying that if the conditions are right, then life as we know it today can and does evolve. The claim of the strong anthropic principle, however, is only a claim: namely, that there must be certain conditions in our universe that are required in order for life to develop. The final anthropic principle, however, is even more tenuous. Who are we to say that once sentient beings have come into existence they will never die out? Tipler and Barrow simply wonder about the coincidences necessary that would have made possible the emergence of life and ultimately of humanity. Yet the conclusions they draw from these coincidences are beyond scientific proof, namely, that life

36. Brandon Carter, "Large Number Coincidences and the Anthropic Principle in Cosmology," in *Confrontation of Cosmological Theories with Observational Data*, ed. M. S. Longair (Dordrecht: D. Reidel, 1974), 291.

37. See John D. Barrow and Frank J. Tipler, *The Anthropic Cosmological Principle*, 2nd ed. (Oxford: Clarendon, 1988), 5, where they follow Carter's lead. The following page numbers in the text are from this book.

38. Frank J. Tipler, *The Physics of Immortality* (New York: Doubleday).

must evolve in the universe and that once sentient life, meaning human life, has evolved it cannot die out. Nevertheless, Barrow and Tipler are not alone in their musings.

Paul Davies (b. 1946), a British theoretical physicist and cosmologist, is presently professor at Arizona State University. In line with the anthropic principle, he toys with the idea that "the apparent 'fine-tuning' of the laws of nature necessary if conscious life is to evolve in the universe then carries the clear implication that God has designed the universe so as to permit such life and consciousness to emerge. It would mean that our own existence in the universe formed a central part of God's plan."[39] He also points to the fact that the design argument, abandoned by Charles Darwin, "has been resurrected in recent years by a number of scientists. In its new form the argument is directed not to the material objects of the universe as such, but to the underlying laws, where it is immune from Darwinian attack."[40] This means that this design argument, which is different from the intelligent design, talks about the basic structure of the universe as having been fine-tuned to enormous precision before the evolutionary process could even get started. Of course, Davies knows that the acceptance of such a "designer universe" cannot result from a strictly scientific proof. He therefore concludes with the confession: "I cannot believe that our existence in the universe is a mere quirk of fate, an accident of history, an incidental blip in the great cosmic drama. . . . We are truly meant to be here."[41] This confession sounds similar to that of Charles Darwin, who discovered certain laws by which humanity evolved and felt that this could not have occurred without God being involved. We note here scientific restraint, focusing on the empirical, and not shutting oneself off from that which is beyond and above empirical proof.

2. Human Constitution

After giving considerable attention to the origin of humanity, we must now ask what is so peculiar about humans. We have observed that there has never been a necessity for humanity to evolve the way it did. We are either

---

39. Paul Davies, *The Mind of God: The Scientific Basis for a Rational World* (New York: Simon & Schuster, Touchstone Book, 1993), 213.

40. Davies, *The Mind of God*, 203.

41. Davies, *The Mind of God*, 232.

the result of pure chance, as scientists such as Richard Dawkins tell us; or we are the result of a guiding power from without, as the proponents of the intelligent design movement claim; or perhaps we are even a mixture of both, as Paul Davies suggests.

As mentioned above, it is scientifically totally unfounded to claim in traditional popularized Darwinian fashion that humanity descended from monkeys as they are today or from some kind of primordial apes. There is, however, no doubt that chimpanzees and gorillas are closely related to us. As Genesis 1 intimates and biological science has confirmed, all the other living beings are related to us, too, whether oxen or crocodiles, peach trees or violets. We might even say that present-day primates branched off from the tree of life that then ascended to modern-day humanity. This would mean that there is something unique about humanity, even with regard to its biological nature. We will now try to find out what is unique about humanity both by comparing it with other living beings and by reflecting on its own potential.

a. Distinction between Humans and Animals

Charles Darwin postulated that most of humanity's behavioral and ethical patterns can be explained as having gradually evolved from the animal stage. In comparing different animals with each other and finally with humans, we get the impression that innate reactions that are due to rigidly fixed instinct patterns become gradually less determined. In higher stages of life psychic faculties, intelligent thinking, and consequent actions seem to replace more and more the fixed and predictable reactions of less advanced forms of life. Does this mean that we can only talk about transitions from one form of life to another, or did something truly unique emerge with the human species?

It is often claimed that humans have a unique possibility to enlarge and transform their environment according to their needs and desires.[42] Yet a progressive world-openness and the liberation from the restrictive dependence on the environment are characteristic of all vertebrates. Due to their physical development they can breathe through lungs, their extremities

---

42. For the following, see Otto H. Schindewolf, "Phylogenie und Anthropologie aus paläontologischer Sicht," in *Neue Anthropologie,* ed. Hans-Georg Gadamer and Paul Vogler (Munich: DTV, 1972), 1:279ff.

carry their body, some of them can even fly, their eggs have a protective cover or they bear young ones alive, and their blood temperature is no longer dependent on environmental temperature. Active transformation of the environment, however, as we detect in the often complicated structure of bird nests, is not a new acquisition of the vertebrate stage. When we look at the artistic structure of termite hills, we must admit that this faculty is already present in non-vertebrates. Yet there we are safe in speaking of the predominance or exclusiveness of instinctive behavior that regulates the transformation of the environment. When we reach the level of the anthropoid apes, we notice goal-directed experiments, planned shaping of tools, the beginning of reasoning and a deliberating intelligence. Even a language of gestures can be observed, which may be classified as a lower form of human language and which enables the handing on of tradition.

We have seen that the earliest traces of humanity are often associated with bone and stone fragments that leave open the question whether they were intentionally formed by human hands, were accidental human productions, or were simply produced by nature. It is difficult to determine whether primeval humanity used available artifacts as tools or deliberately produced tools that could be reused several times. Thus the exact location of the demarcation line between human and pre-human beings is imperceptible. Yet there is an immense difference between the first ambiguous human artifacts and the precisely hewn stone axes of the Neo-Paleolithic era. And there is also a huge difference between the domination of the environment expressed by the occasional use of fire and the human self-expression demonstrated in the beautiful cave paintings of Altamira, Spain, which were produced nearly 20,000 years ago. And yet there is a vast difference between these simple paintings from 20,000 years ago and the development and use of tools demonstrated in modern cancer research and in space exploration.

It was only in the Neolithic Revolution, which commenced around 12,000 years ago, that humans became autonomous beings who learned to dominate the earth and transform it through agriculture, animal husbandry, and the building of houses, roads, villages, and cities. When we talk about a transitional phase between human-like beings and humanity itself, we do not want to convey the impression that there is a clear-cut line when modern humanity began to exist. We simply want to suggest that somewhere within this phase, human beings as we now know them were born.

It is noteworthy that the physical structure of humans has by far not changed as drastically as their achievements. But why is it that their achievements have accelerated at such an amazing pace? Take, for example, the development of tradition, which is often regarded as something distinctly human.[43] Tradition enables a rapid evolution of ways of conduct and of achievements. But again, it is not something specifically human. German zoologist Adolf Remane (1898-1976), for instance, tells of titmice in England that learned to open milk bottles left on the doorstep by the milkman. This custom of opening milk bottles and stealing some of the milk had apparently spread by tradition from a specific location where it was first initiated. In one part of the country only bottles with silver tops were opened; in other areas only ones with golden tops were opened.

Another example is a group of chimpanzees in the forests of the west coast of Africa that use hammerstones to crack open nuts, something that the chimpanzees in the Gombe National Park in Tanzania do not do. However, the latter group uses sticks to extract termites from their mounds, something the other group does not do.[44] This shows that tradition works very exactly. By the use of tradition new customs can be spread over a territory in a matter of weeks, whereas by strictly mutational change the spread of the same practice would take many generations. Tradition can "remember" items for many generations and it can enable intellectually less gifted members to participate in the discoveries of more intelligent ones.

There is no doubt that mammals especially can truly act intelligently. They can solve a problem through direct use of properties as a means to achieve a goal, not just on a trial-and-error basis. Intelligent thinking has become the foundation for technological accomplishments. Again, however, humans distinguish themselves only gradually and not qualitatively from the same faculties that animals enjoy. Even recognition is not something through which we distinguish ourselves from other living beings. The Greek poet Homer (eighth century B.C.), for instance, mentioned in his *Odyssey* that the dog recognized his lord Odysseus when he returned to his home after many years of being away.[45] We know that after many years mammals and birds can also recognize their friends and enemies and their former homes. Again, with regard to the ability to recognize items and beings of the past, humans and animals differ only slightly.

---

43. For the following, see Adolf Remane, "Die Bedeutung der Evolutionslehre für die allgemeine Anthropologie," in *Neue Anthropologie,* ed. Gadamer and Vogler, 1:320ff. See also Cela-Conde and Ayala, *Human Evolution,* 325, who cite more recent literature.

44. Michael Alan Park, *Biological Anthropology,* 6th ed. (Boston: McGraw Hill, 2010), 145 and 173.

45. Homer, *Odyssey,* trans. S. H. Butcher and A. Lang, in *The Complete Works of Homer: The Iliad and the Odyssey* (New York: Modern Library, n.d.), 268f. (book 17).

The story is sometimes different when we investigate the power to re-member. One of the classical examples is the one in which lettuce is placed in a box and the box is closed in front of a monkey. Through a hidden mechanism the lettuce is removed and is replaced with a banana. When the box is opened again the monkey acts surprised, a sign that it remembered that the box should have contained something else. But the span of remembrance for monkeys and apes is relatively short, approximately one to two days at the most. Like small children, animals live almost exclusively in the present.

Human memory, however, spans almost a whole lifetime, from about the third year of life onward to the present. This immense difference between hu-mans and animals allows for the development of an abstract conceptual lan-guage that is peculiar only to humans. Of course, the elaborate language of bees is a well-known fact, as is the language of animals through which they warn their peers or beg for food. But this language is directed exclusively to the present or to the most immediate past. Even the interesting experiments with the bonobo Kanzi, who could communicate with humans by language and gestures, do not change these results. For instance, they were able to com-municate the difference between "eating peaches" and going "to the location in the forest where there usually are peaches."[46] But all communication re-mained in the present. It is exactly this amazing power to remember that opens for humans the realm of thought that provides the basis for culture.

One further characteristic of existence that needs illumination is be-havior. We notice, for instance, that the social behavior of ants, termites, and bees is highly structured. There is a clear division of labor and each community leaves the impression of harmonious social coexistence. When we watch monkeys, many social traits are observed that remind us of human behavior. While there is a definite social structure according to rank, rank is not automatically conferred but gained through demonstrations of physical strength and intelligence, or, as in baboons, through age and wisdom. The groupings are loose and can be joined to larger groups or split into smaller ones. Often the family is not even a social unit; there can be promiscuity and the females stay together except for copulation. This is, for instance, different from the social behavior of storks for which instinctive reactions ensure durable pair relationships.[47]

46. Pär Segerdahl, William Fields, and Sue Savage-Rumbaugh, *Kanzi's Primal Lan-guage: The Cultural Initiation of Primates into Language* (New York: Palgrave Macmillan, 2005), 81.

47. Konrad Lorenz, *On Aggression,* trans. M. K. Wilson (New York: Harcourt, Brace & World, 1966), 151ff.

Anthropoid apes which, except for humans, enjoy the longest childhood and youth among primates also exhibit the highest degree of individualization.[48] They often live in small groups of changing membership. Adult members often leave their own group to join another. The more highly evolved the living beings are, the more freedom there is for them to choose their own group. When we reach the human level, this tendency is furthered. However, we notice one additional phenomenon. While conspecifics among higher primates are usually spared from persecution, it is different with humanity. The broken bones and opened skulls of the *Sinanthropus* (Peking Man) and of some branches of the Neanderthals seem to indicate cannibalistic behavior.[49] Early humanity not only killed and ate animals; it also killed and ate members of its own kind. Humans are the first, and so far the only, living beings that developed war to persecute and kill members of their own species. This phenomenon is missing in the animal realm and seems to be a byproduct of our increased individualization.[50]

b. Inborn Forms of Human Behavior

So far we have been able to show only the difficulty of differentiating between humans and animals. Yet there are some significant differences that become apparent, first in the physical constitution and then in the behavior of the two.

Physical Constitution

The first characteristic difference is visible at birth and during infancy and adolescence. Though the form of the human growth curve is apparently a

---

48. John H. Relethford, *The Human Species: An Introduction to Biological Anthropology* (Boston: McGraw Hill, 2003), 225, states: "Primates show an amazing amount of variation in the ways in which their societies are structured."

49. See Paul Jordan, *Neanderthal: Neanderthal Man and the Story of Human Origins* (Phoenix Mill: Sutton, 1999), 106f. and 167.

50. Irenäus Eibl-Eibesfeldt, *Der vorprogrammierte Mensch: Das Ererbte als bestimmender Faktor im menschlichen Verhalten* (Munich: DTV, 1976), 100, points out that the findings of the first weapons by paleoanthropologists go hand in hand with the findings of violently damaged human skulls. Thus increasing individualization may not be the sole factor that contributed to this destructive human behavior; an additional factor may be the invention of weapons, which humanity still today has not learned to handle peacefully.

distinctive characteristic, at birth a human baby is much more helpless than the babies of its anthropoid relatives, the gorillas and the chimpanzees. Unlike the body proportions of a newborn anthropoid ape, those of a human baby are very different from that of an adult. This is mainly due to the larger brain size at birth. While the brain of most anthropoid apes weighs 130 to 200 grams, for human babies the weight is around 366 grams. Human babies also have larger body weight than the babies of anthropoid apes. While during the first year a human baby grows much more rapidly than does an anthropoid ape baby, its body development slows down considerably toward the end of the first year. This retardation of body development continues for humans throughout their youth. For instance, an elephant is full grown at age fifteen and a chimpanzee at age ten or eleven. But for humans it takes nineteen to twenty-one years, or even twenty-four years as recent measurements suggest, until he or she is fully grown. But between childhood and adulthood there comes with adolescence a new phase "not presaged among the non-human primates, not even the large-bodied apes."[51] This phase begins with the pubertal growth spurt, which starts for girls at age ten and ends usually with age eighteen; for boys it starts at age twelve and ends at age twenty-one. The initial helplessness of a human baby requires close attention of at least one parent, while the slow development necessitates longer dependence on adults than in all other cases of living beings.

Within the last 100 years, however, a dramatic acceleration, termed "secular acceleration," has occurred in the development of human beings. The age of sexual maturity has been lowered by two years and is now close to that of chimpanzees (ten to eleven years for chimpanzees compared to thirteen years for humans). The medium adult body length, too, has increased by 3 inches in the United States and in European countries, and human babies gain 3 to 4 pounds more body weight during their first year. The exact reason for this amazing acceleration is still unknown. Perhaps better food, more exposure to light through recreational activities, and more sensory stimulation in our technological world may be some of the factors that have led to some of the problems caused by an accelerated body growth coupled with the usual pace in mental and emotional maturation.

When we compare the human development of brain capacity with that of animals, we notice that in the development of a human baby its brain in-

51. Douglas E. Crews and Barry Bogin, "Growth, Development, Senescence, and Aging: A Life History Perspective," in *A Companion to Biological Anthropology,* ed. Clark Spencer Larsen (Oxford: Wiley-Blackwell, 2010), 135.

creases tremendously. While the brain of a newborn human "averages 366 grams, and in chimpanzees it averages 136 grams . . . the human brain grows more rapidly than the brains of apes, so that, at 18 months of age, human brains weigh more than 1,000 grams and chimpanzee brains average about 300 grams."[52] In comparison, the brain of adult humans is three times the size of anthropoid apes in relation to their body size, while at birth the difference is only about 20 percent. It would be wrong, however, to assume that parts of our brain find no equivalent in the anthropoid apes. Again, the difference is more quantitative than qualitative. The increase in volume of the human brain shows a progressive exponential evolution of brain capacity.

With the appearance of Cro-Magnon man, however, the adult human brain reached its maximum size and form. Until then the evolutionary increase in brain size was not uniform. The cranial volume of adult Neanderthals was even somewhat larger than that of the adult Cro-Magnon. Recent CT-based measurements of a Neanderthal baby's skull suggest that in contrast to present-day babies a phase of brain development after birth — decisive for differentiation in the neocortex — did not take place. Yet in human evolution it was mostly the neocortex that grew, while the paleocortex regressed. The optical system in particular evolved and so did the associative parts of the brain, while the smell areas regressed. When we look at the sensory and motor parts of the brain we notice a relatively large representation of the facial area, especially lips, tongue, and jaws, and of the arms and particularly the hands, each of the fingers, and also of the feet and toes. This emphasis of the brain is physically represented in the development of language and in upright posture.

"Compared to other large-bodied hominids (living apes and their direct ancestors) hominins (living humans and their ancestors) are habitually bipedal."[53] Though anthropoid apes can walk a few steps without using their hands, only humans have achieved truly upright posture. A newborn human has almost a straight spine and its pelvis is still fairly slanted. But soon the spine gains its typical S-like form and the pelvis is lowered. Through upright posture and by walking and standing on two legs, we gain the free use of our hands and arms. We can use tools or weapons with them while we walk, and our vision is much more able to comprehend our environment. We need no longer sit up like a rabbit to survey our environment, or stop feeding like a deer to pay attention to dangerous sounds or smells.

---

52. Crews and Bogin, "Growth, Development, Senescence, and Aging," 127.
53. Crews and Bogin, "Growth, Development, Senescence, and Aging," 136.

Since our hands are freed, we can also change our environment in ways that large-bodied apes cannot. When we consider slipped or crushed discs, prolapsed bowels, varicose veins, and circulatory diseases, we realize that we did not receive our upright posture as a mere boon. It has to be guarded carefully against many misuses.

We will now consider human language as our last point of comparison between humans and animals. The peculiarity of human language expresses itself rather obviously in the wide range of the human voice. When we talk we can span two octaves, and in singing we can cover even three and a half octaves. This is a much larger range than that of anthropoid apes, where it extends, for instance, only one octave in gibbons. Usually animal language, especially among anthropoid apes, is not detached from gestures so that we could call it a mixture of voice and gesture language. Human language, however, has its peculiarity in its wide range of communication. We can convey feelings, situations, objects, and most abstract and remote concepts, such as the cultures of extinct peoples. We can also use "a finite number of sounds and create an infinite number of words, sentences, and ideas from these sounds."[54]

A further advance in communication is the phenomenon of writing. The first evidences of writing are the symbolic code-signs scratched on bones at Paleolithic sites, the picture script in the cave paintings of the Neolithic age, and the pictographs of prehistoric Inuit and American Indians. The visual images induce associations with scenes of everyday life. At a more formalized stage come the stylized pictures of China and Egypt. There one must remember many images and combinations of them to express oneself. Finally, one comes to a total auditory stage at which a word is characterized by a certain sequence of consonants and then also of vowels. This allows for the strongest differentiation and for a continued creation of new words without burdening the memory with a huge amount of symbolic characteristics.

The development of language goes hand in hand with the development of a conceptual and symbolic world and allows for the development of a spiritual life. We could list many other characteristics of humans, such as the special form of the uterus, a life expectancy longer than that of other mammals, the non-specialization of hands, eyes, teeth, and ears, and the like. But we only wanted to survey the most important characteristics that, at the same time, are the main contributors to the human element.

54. Relethford, *The Human Species,* 290f.

Social Behavior

When we concern ourselves more with the distinctive social behavior of humans, we must first ask whether there is anything normative about their behavior which they have "by nature." The search for the "natural" is complicated by the fact that it is very difficult to exclude all of our traditions and cultural conditioning. However, the experiments of **Irenäus Eibl-Eibesfeldt** (b. 1928), a student of the Austrian behaviorist Konrad Lorenz (1903-89) and others, yielded very surprising results.[55] He experimented with babies born deaf and blind who are difficult to educate and, due to their impairments, have no means for imitation. Yet he noticed that such babies cry when they hurt themselves, they laugh when they are tickled, and they smile when they are patted. They of course never saw or heard those expressions from other people. When they are angry, they frown like normal children, stamp their feet, and sometimes even bite. This is true also for heavily brain-damaged children who could never have learned this simply by touching people. Like other children, the deaf and blind are afraid of strangers whom they recognize through their sense of smell, and they show signs of guilt and remorse when they have done wrong and they expect signs of forgiveness.

We can also observe that small children search for personal contact with a person to whom they can relate. If this desire is refused, there occur developmental disturbances.[56] Usually this contact is established naturally since there is an instinctive bond between the mother and the infant during the first half year after birth. Afterward this bond is continued in a kind of voluntary partnership.

Since humans are social beings, the question has often been raised as to whether many of the specifically human characteristics are inborn or are the result of social conditions. More specifically, the question has recently been posed as to whether the distinctive male and female modes of human behavior are the result of social conditioning. Observing preliterate societies,

---

55. See for this paragraph Irenäus Eibl-Eibesfeldt, "Stammesgeschichtliche Anpassungen im Verhalten des Menschen," in *Neue Anthropologie,* ed. Gadamer and Vogler, 2:13-18; and his *Ethology: The Biology of Behavior,* trans. E. Klinghammer (New York: Holt, Rinehart and Winston, 1970), 403-8, where he reports on pertinent studies conducted by other scientists.

56. See for the following Irenäus Eibl-Eibesfeldt, "Stammesgeschichtliche Anpassungen," in *Neue Anthropologie,* ed. Gadamer and Vogler, 2:13 and 50f.; see also *Ethology,* 442.

American anthropologist Margaret Mead (1901-78), for instance, suggested long ago: "If those temperamental attitudes which we have traditionally regarded as feminine — such as passivity, responsiveness, and a willingness to cherish children — can so easily be set up as the masculine pattern in one tribe, and in another be outlawed for the majority of women as well as for the majority of men, we no longer have any basis for regarding such aspects of behavior as sex-linked."[57] British-American anthropologist Ashley Montagu (1905-99) finally declared: "The notable thing about human behavior is that it is learned. It is nonsense to talk about the genetic determinance of human behavior." Of course, we should be aware that such a categorical statement can easily be refuted. We might think here, for instance, of the impact of certain hormones on the male/female behavior in humans, which enhances or diminishes sex-specific behavior. American anthropologist Michael Alan Park is correct when he states: "Certainly we come into this world with some behavioral responses built in. Facial expressions such as smiling, the newborn's instinct to nurse, the bond between a mother and her offspring, the drive to walk uprightly, and learn languages — those are all recognized as universal in our species and are preprogrammed in our biology."[58]

"Sex differences, like other heritable traits, are determined by the interaction of genetic-hormonal and environmental factors."[59] But these differences do not automatically dictate or totally preordain the course of postnatal dimorphism of behavioral differentiation. Thus it is as wrong to say that males and females develop different patterns of preferred behavior only because they are treated differently, as it is wrong to claim that they are treated differently only because they demonstrate different behavior patterns right from the beginning. On the contrary, sex-specific behavior patterns are partly given as a biologically conditioned potential and partly developed through cultural conditioning. There are biologically determined characteristics that contribute to subtle differences of potential between the sexes. In most societies these differences are implicitly recognized in the

---

57. For the quotations in this paragraph, see Margaret Mead, *From the South Seas: Studies of Adolescence and Sex in Primitive Societies,* part 3, *Sex and Temperament in Three Primitive Societies* (New York: William Morrow, 1939), 279f., and Ashley Montagu, ed., in his intro. to *Man and Aggression,* 2nd ed. (New York: Oxford University Press, 1973), xvii.

58. Park, *Biological Anthropology,* 158.

59. Charlotte M. Otten, "Genetic Effects on Male and Female Development and on the Sex Ratio," in *Male-Female Differences: A Bio-Cultural Perspective,* ed. Roberta L. Hall et al. (New York: Praeger, 1985), 155.

process of sex socialization. Thus the sex-differentiated behavior indicates that certain models of behavior are more easily learned by one sex or the other. Though there is a sizeable degree of overlap, "females tend to outperform males slightly but significantly on tests of verbal ability" and have greater fine motor skills — as needed, for instance, by neurosurgeons — while males test better on the average "for perception and manipulation of spatial relationships."[60]

The majority of ethnographic reports indicate that "males are more interactable, egoistic, spatially more explorative, rougher, less prosocial, and more peer-oriented, whereas females are typically more compliant, prosocial, less spatially explorative, less rough, and more involved in interaction with adults than are boys."[61] One might still want to argue that these typically gender-oriented differentiations are expected by society and therefore are the result of cultural conditioning. Yet in observing Kalahari Bushmen, American anthropologist Patricia Draper noted that these sex differences in the cultural behavior of children are not necessarily expected or intensified under certain cultural conditions. Other observations have also shown that when new items were introduced into the traditional Bushmen culture, such as pictures of airplanes and automobiles, there resulted among the children specifically sex-related preferences of interests that had no precedence in their own culture. Under conditions of a culture change to a sedentary economy, however, certain elements of male- and female-differentiated behavior are indeed explicitly enhanced by society in the process of increasing sex differentiation.

Some of these sex-related modes of behavior, however, are not exclusively human characteristics. Irenäus Eibl-Eibesfeldt, for instance, reminds us that male characteristics, such as "a desire for higher rank and increased aggressiveness, are characteristics we share with other primates."[62] Since humans are also culturally conditioned beings, one must ask whether this common biologically engendered heritage should be culturally reinforced. For example, it would be an oversimplification to discard certain Pauline assertions on male (church) leadership (see 1 Cor. 7:4; 14:34) with the argument that they are culturally outdated. Yet the recognition that we encoun-

---

60. Dean Falk, *Braindance: New Discoveries about Human Origins and Brain Evolution,* rev. and exp. ed. (Gainesville: University of Florida Press, 2004), 111, in the relevant chapter on "Boy Brain, Girl Brain" (103-25).

61. Patricia Draper, "Cultural Pressure on Sex Differences," *American Ethnologist* 2 (1975): 603.

62. Eibl-Eibesfeldt, *Ethology,* 453.

ter in these statements of Paul inborn norms does not automatically sanction them either. Naturally these norms are open to change through societal pressures as are any other "instincts." The question that must be left open at this point is whether and in which direction such change should be sought. Reference to nature alone will not suffice to answer this question.

There are also many biologically engendered human characteristics that are basic to both sexes. For instance, there is a distinctive inclination among adults to establish durable pair relationships. This does not necessitate monogamy, however, since polygamous arrangements can also be durable. Since sexual activity is no longer restricted to special mating seasons, as in most animals, it can be used in pair relationships for mutual gratification and consequent deepening of these relationships. Also, a rank relationship with the rule of some and the submissive and obedient behavior of others is biologically given, as Sigmund Freud (1856-1939) asserted.[63] It has been shown in experiments that this behavior of natural obedience to authority can be exploited among humans and can lead to disastrous results, including the ruthless killing of fellow human beings. Fidelity of husbands, faithfulness of friends, courage in situations of extreme exigency, and even compassion and helpfulness are founded in our biological constitution and did not originate through cultural input.

Of course, biologically given norms of conduct need not be just a blessing or something that can be easily adapted to today's situations.[64] The human appendix shows us very drastically how painful biologically inherited relics can become. Today's anonymous mass civilization is very destructive of lasting relationships and it impairs our "natural" feelings of compassion and helpfulness. More and more people find it easy to cheat the anonymous Internal Revenue Service or to steal from a supermarket, an unknown and

63. Sigmund Freud, *"Warum Krieg?"* letter to Albert Einstein (September 1932), in *Gesammelte Werke: Chronologisch geordnet,* vol. 16, *Werke aus den Jahren 1932-1939* (London: Imago, 1950), 24, where he says: "It is part of the inborn inequality of mankind which cannot be eliminated that distinguishes mankind in leaders and dependents." For the following, see Eibl-Eibesfeldt, *Ethology,* 446ff.

64. Wolfgang Wickler, in his interesting book *The Sexual Code: The Social Behavior of Animals and Men,* intro. Konrad Lorenz, illus. Hermann Kacher (Garden City, NY: Doubleday, 1972), 281, rightly says: "Man is different from animals. His behavior is that of a thinking being, so it cannot be assessed in terms of biology alone; but neither can it be assessed without biology." See also Konrad Lorenz, "Psychology and Phylogeny" (1954), in *Studies in Animal and Human Behavior,* vol. 2, trans. R. Martin (Cambridge, MA: Harvard University Press, 1971), 194, who points out the difficulty of adapting innate norms to today's problems and emphasizes "the gradually developing inadequacy of species-specific *killing inhibitions.*" For this particular problem, see his book *On Aggression.*

often unknowable business conglomerate. But the same persons who find cheating or stealing so easy would have never dared to commit these crimes against their own family members or in a local country store. Yet it is not just society that is to blame if "natural" norms cease to work. We are the ones who tend to reduce our innate norms by allowing the dominance of our intellect over our instinctive behavior. For instance, we tell ourselves and others that our opponents are not human beings, but sub-human beings. Thus in order to eradicate any natural affection for their enemies during World War II the American propaganda depicted the friendly Japanese people as ape-like, ugly Japs and the Germans as marauding Huns.

Beyond the strictly biological level there are other important formative sources of human behavior. The first to be mentioned is the phenomenon of imprinting.[65] We mentioned that, once the instinctive bond between a newborn and its mother is waning, the newborn establishes a relationship with a caring person, usually the mother. This relationship with a caring person is established between the third and the eighteenth month and is constitutive for the infant's normal development. "Human infants require intense physical and emotional interaction with their primary caregivers. Children who do not receive this interaction fail to develop the part of the brain that is involved in emotional connectedness, trust, and the ability to love. When deprivation is extreme, such infants simply die."[66]

The impressions received during a child's fourth to seventh year predetermine which general features will be attractive for the child in its future love relationships on the adult level. Any erotic attraction at this early stage, which especially Sigmund Freud emphasized with his concept of an Oedipus complex, is the exception rather than the rule. From the second year on, discovery, curiosity, play, and imitation are characteristic for toddlers. These very different actions enable young children to discover their environment, to develop all abilities that they need to learn, and to assume the conduct of adults. In other words, curiosity, discovery, play, and imitation prepare a child to become an operative member of the human community. In this context learning can be enhanced through spatial and temporal continuity; through rewards and punishment; and through the readiness to discover, play, and imitate. Learning usually modifies instinctive, that is, in-

---

65. See for the following paragraph, Bernhard Hassenstein, "Das spezifisch Menschliche nach den Resultaten der Verhaltensforschung," in *Neue Anthropologie,* ed. Gadamer and Vogler, 2:64ff.; and Eibl-Eibesfeldt, *Ethology,* 232-37.

66. So the psychologist Carrie A. Miles, *The Redemption of Love: Rescuing Marriage and Sexuality from the Economics of a Fallen World* (Grand Rapids: Brazos, 2006), 172f.

born action, but it does not result in a reduction of inborn reflexes. For instance, if someone moves his or hand toward me as if to slap me, I will undoubtedly blink, even if I know that he or she will not actually slap me.

While willpower plays an important role in modifying human behavior, there are two important items that influence it:[67] (1) the respective condition of life, and (2) the milieu to which a human being was subjected during her or his childhood. For example, if food resources are scarce, people will attempt to satisfy their biological needs in spite of their intentions not to steal. Consequently, burglaries will increase. If a person is frequently subjected to hunger as an infant, there may be a tendency when he or she becomes an adult to satisfy oral needs through excessive eating, drinking, or smoking.

Yet none of these influences or tendencies is slavishly binding. If we arrive at a conclusion after having considered several options, we can attempt to enforce our will in opposition to the biologically or behaviorally conditioned patterns of conduct. However, the stronger these patterns are, the less chances our will has to enforce its choice. This means we are not always free to do exactly what we want or will. Our actions are not as free as our reflections. Occasionally they are swayed by biological determination. Only human beings whose biological needs are satisfied and who understand the impact their environment has on them can act in true freedom. In order to further this kind of humanness, we do not want to advocate a return to the animal stage. But we must recognize and fulfill our basic human biological need for food and shelter and we must understand the pressure our environment places on us. Once this has been accomplished, true freedom, and not biological and environmental necessities, will become the driving force in the history of humanity. The beginning of this we have witnessed through so-called cultural evolution.

Cultural Evolution

A unique development occurred with humanity in cultural evolution in which we can discern four significant steps:[68]

---

67. See Byron A. Campbell and James R. Misanin, "Basic Drives," in *Annual Review of Psychology*, vol. 20 (Palo Alto, CA: Annual Reviews, 1969), 77, who rightly claim that the so-called basic drives, such as hunger, thirst, sex, and maternal behavior, are themselves controlled by "a complex of interactions among environmental stimuli, hormonal states, physiological imbalance, previous experience, etc."

68. The following reflections are largely based on Rüdiger Schmitt, "Phänomen Mensch," unpublished paper (2009).

1. The first use of stone artifacts and of fire (2 million years ago)
2. The development of human language (100,000 years ago)
3. The Neolithic Revolution (12,000 years ago)
4. The scientific technological revolution (500 years ago)

Primates can use stone artifacts and even birds have been observed using available objects as tools to obtain desired results. Yet only with humans do we notice the use of fire and also the intentional shaping of stone artifacts. But from our perspective, this seems to have been a long, drawn-out process lasting more than a millennium. From thereon, however, human evolution continuously accelerated. The development of human language and the already mentioned Neolithic Revolution had thus far the most significant impact on the development of present-day humanity. We are not wrong to assume that approximately 50,000 years ago the sudden development of new technologies in production of artifacts and in art and also hints of burial rites and religion may have resulted from this newly acquired differentiated language ability of modern humanity.

Again, this advancement may be genetically conditioned. The gene *FoxP2* has decisive significance for articulation in speech. In humans, mutations of *FoxP2* cause severe speech and language disorders. Only two amino-acid substitutions distinguish the human *FoxP2* proteins from that found in chimpanzees, gorillas, and orangutans. These primates also lack the facial and linguistic expressions typical of humans. Yet both Neanderthals and Cro-Magnons had these human *FoxP2* proteins, as far as we can tell, and therefore may have been able to communicate with each other.

The Neolithic Revolution indicated another important shift. After nearly 2 million years as nomadic hunter-gatherers, our forbears settled down approximately 12,000 years ago in areas such as the Fertile Crescent, that is, present-day Iran and Iraq, but also as far away as Melanesia. This meant a more agrarian-based life with the domestication of various plants and animal species. In the Fertile Crescent emmer and barley were cultivated and animals such as sheep, goats, pigs, and cattle were domesticated. Since food could now be obtained in a more calculated way by planting crops and raising animals, this allowed for a higher density of population in the same area. Therefore villages and towns such as Jericho were founded where the first attempts were made to cultivate crops and domesticate animals. The first traces of a settlement in Jericho date back at least 12,000 years. We notice a tension between the farmer and the hunter-gatherer reflected in the Genesis story of Cain and

Abel. Though one was no longer alone, life in general was not safe in these settlements since in Jericho the first city wall was already built in ca. 8,000 B.C.. While human life as a hunter and gatherer had lasted for nearly two millennia, within 4,000 years the new agrarian culture had spread from Turkey westward throughout Europe.

Yet did the farmers push westward, or was it the new idea of living that advanced? A comparative study shows that 80 percent of European men have the Y-chromosome of the Cro-Magnon who approximately 40,000 years ago migrated to Europe, while barely 20 percent are descendants of Neolithic farmers and later immigrants. For Europe at least this means the Neolithic Revolution was a cultural event and not caused by a change in the genetic makeup in contrast to the evolution of language. Through cultural mediation, of course, also facilitated by language, one can spread information very quickly within the same generation and need not wait for the emergence of the same trait in the next generation. The same is true for the next big change, the scientific technological revolution, which began approximately 500 years ago.

This scientific technological revolution is often connected with Nicholas Copernicus (1473-1543), who put the sun in the center of our solar system and thereby threatened the human self-understanding that had assumed that the planet we inhabit is at the center of the universe. Copernicus, however, was more interested in developing a system that would reinstate the classical Greek concept of harmony instead of breaking ground for a new worldview.[69] The actually important representatives of modernity were Johannes Kepler (1571-1630), who discovered the laws of planetary motion named after him; Galileo Galilei (1564-1642), who came into conflict with the Inquisition by advocating the Copernican heliocentric worldview; and René Descartes (1595-1650), who introduced radical doubt into philosophy. This revolution has since then increased at an ever more rapid pace. Scientific discoveries and their subsequent technological applications resulted in the industrial revolution of the nineteenth century and then in the various oil-based revolutions of the twentieth century. While initially every new advancement was greeted with enthusiasm, we are discovering ever more painfully that the spirits we unleashed provide a mixed blessing, often short-lived prosperity on the one side but destructive tendencies on the other. Especially in recent years, we have become more and more skeptical with regard to our own progress.

69. See Hans Schwarz, *Creation* (Grand Rapids: Eerdmans, 2002), 3f.

3. Human Potential

Ever since Charles Darwin explained the phenomenon of humanity within an evolutionary framework, it has been claimed that if humans have evolved so far, they could also evolve to new and unprecedented heights. That a change in humanity is taking place cannot be denied, for instance, when we consider that during the last 150 years each new generation has become taller than the preceding generation. We could also cite many other examples of change, such as increasing baldness and increasing recession of the so-called wisdom teeth. Yet these phenomena do not necessarily point in the direction of human betterment. If we want to assess the human potential for creative evolution, three areas should receive prime attention: neurological and genetic aspects, behavioral aspects, and socio-philosophical aspects.

a. Neurological and Genetic Aspects

When we look at the human brain size, we notice that since the Neanderthals the adult brain has not significantly enlarged.[70] We could conclude from this observation that the human brain is no longer evolving. But this would overstate the case. As German neurologist Hugo Spatz (1888-1969) points out, a child attains a nearly full-grown brain size between the age of seven and ten.[71] This is exactly the time when in terms of learning and achievement most processes actually start. This means there is a difference between the development of cerebral potential and that of cerebral efficiency. We might be safe in assuming that it took roughly 2 million years until the human brain evolved to its present cerebral potential.[72] This period may have concluded with the emergence of the Neanderthals. The

70. See Harry J. Jerison, *Evolution of the Brain and Intelligence* (New York: Academic, 1973), esp. 401 and 424, who also provides extensive statistical material.

71. See for the following Hugo Spatz, "Gedanken über die Zukunft des Menschenhirns und die Idee vom Übermenschen," in *Der Übermensch: Eine Diskussion,* ed. Ernst Benz (Stuttgart: Rhein-Verlag, 1961), 342f. See also Alan Bilsborough, "Some Aspects of the Evolution of the Human Brain," in *The Biology of Brains: Proceedings of a Symposium Held at the Royal Geographical Society London on September 28 and 29, 1972,* ed. W. B. Broughton (New York: John Wiley, 1974), 211, who suggests that "structural and organizational changes have perhaps been of greater importance in the evolution of the human brain than mere increase in size."

72. Bryan Kolb and Ian Q. Whishaw, *Fundamentals of Human Neuropsychology,* 5th ed. (New York: Worth, 2003), 44.

emergence of the Cro-Magnons then started a period of evolution of cerebral efficiency that takes us from prehistoric time to our present history and even beyond. This period in which the tempo of change has continuously quickened led to our cultural and technological evolution.

Spatz raises the question whether the evolution of the cerebral potential of the brain has already ended or whether there are certain parts of the brain that are still in a stage of development.[73] Mainly through comparison with closely related animals Spatz arrives at the conclusion that the outer parts of the human brain seem to be the youngest. Brain parts that are still impressible in the human skull are in a process of expansion and have not yet completed their evolutionary development. Spatz finds this true especially for the basal neocortex of the human brain. Its progressive development could lead to a future evolution of the human brain in terms of both cerebral efficiency and potential. Yet such speculative reflections do not take into account that though "the brain comprises less than 2% of the body, it uses 25% of the body's oxygen and 70% of its glucose. As a result it generates a great deal of heat and is at risk of overheating under conditions of exercise or heat stress."[74] This places a limit on how big the brain can be.

Of course, Spatz cannot avoid the burning question of whether an increase in cerebral efficiency alone or an increase in both efficiency and potential would lead to rather dangerous results.[75] He knows that some people fear that a further development of the human brain may lead to the extinction of humanity. Yet are such anxieties justified? It is not without significance that Charles Darwin claimed: "A moral being is one who is capable of comparing his past and future actions and motives, — of approving some and disapproving of others; and the fact that man is the one being who with certainty can be thus designated makes the greatest of all distinctions between him and the lower animals."[76] Increased cerebral efficiency could therewith lead to an increase in moral deliberations. When we look at the evident cannibalism of earlier human forms or the pride with which Babylonian kings boasted of cutting off so many prisoners' hands and tongues,

73. See for the following Spatz, "Gedanken über die Zukunft," 344.

74. Kolb and Whishaw, *Fundamentals of Human Neuropsychology*, 41.

75. See Spatz, "Gedanken über die Zukunft," 371f. Spatz, however, refers here to Julian Huxley, *Evolution in Action* (New York: Harper & Row, Perennial Library, 1966), 124-29, who is convinced of the progress of human "psycho-social evolution," as it expresses itself, for instance, in the discovery of the primacy of the human personality in which society is seen as existing for the individual and not vice versa.

76. Darwin, *The Descent of Man*, 2:391f.

or when we remember the frequent human sacrifices in the religious cults of the Aztecs, then we notice that these deliberations have gone a long way. But we should not pat ourselves on the back and be content with what we have gained. Modern technological evolution has given us tools for good and for bad that were undreamed of barely 100 years ago. In many instances the results of technological evolution are used to torture political prisoners scientifically and to "pacify" enemies chemically. Yet the atrocities of modern wars and the torture applied to prisoners are no longer a matter of national pride. These deeds are systematically concealed since we know that they ought not to be done. Even if the Universal Declaration of Human Rights adopted in 1948 by the members of the United Nations is too often not adhered to, it has been signed and therefore one can appeal to it. The increase in cerebral efficiency may indeed be an ambivalent blessing.

Instead of waiting for a possible evolution of humanity, others suggest that we should take evolution into our own hands. The discovery and basic understanding of the function of the genetic code seem to have especially opened up new vistas. Pierre Teilhard de Chardin, for instance, claims: "With the discovery of the genes it appears that we shall soon be able to control the mechanism of organic heredity ... we may well one day be capable of producing ... a new wave of organisms, an artificially provoked neo-life."[77] Through the Human Genome Project completed in 2003 "the base sequence for all 20,000-25,000 human genes was known."[78] This allowed the establishment of a definite relationship between a given genetic constitution and certain diseases. Through premarital genetic screening, one can determine in advance whether one of the partners is afflicted with the deleterious dominant trait or whether both partners are carriers of a recessive deleterious genetic constitution. While by far the 3 billion chemical base pairs that make up the human DNA have not been analyzed according to their impact on the human constitution, it is now already feasible to eliminate certain genetically caused diseases, such as Tay-Sachs disease or cystic fibrosis. By taking genetic counseling seriously typhoid or smallpox can be eradicated. Even the proclivity to certain diseases can be determined through genetic analysis.

A very controversial issue is the pre-implantation genetic diagnosis

---

77. Pierre Teilhard de Chardin, *The Phenomenon of Man,* trans. B. Wall, intro. Sir Julian Huxley (New York: Harper, 1959), 249f.

78. See David E. Newton, *DANN Technology: A Reference Handbook* (Santa Barbara: ABC CLIO, 2010), 35, and for the following.

(PGD), which is possible since the deciphering of the genetic code. PGD is a form of genetic diagnosis performed prior to implantation. This implies that a woman's egg cells should be fertilized *in vitro* and the embryos, possibly at blastocyst stage comprising 100 to 200 cells, be kept in culture until the diagnosis is established; they can then be implanted. PGD is available for a large number of genetically caused disorders. Increasingly, PGD is also used for sex selection for non-medical reasons. This raises several ethical issues since the blastocysts that are not implanted are discarded. The process involves those embryos in which a potential disease has been detected as well as the other "healthy" blastocysts that are not implanted. Moreover, as the issue of sex selection shows, there is the idea of a designer baby looming in the background that has room neither for diseases nor for the unwanted boy or girl.

Some geneticists go even further. They do not want to confine themselves to detecting and eliminating defective or undesirable constitutions but seek to change them. One possibility would be to change the reproductive cells through a kind of genetic surgery. Due to the immense number of male sperm cells this seems impossible with men, but women ovulate only 500 to 1,000 eggs during their reproductive period. It may be feasible that one could repair at least some genetic abnormalities in this relatively small number of cells and afterward replant the cells into the ovaries and let them develop naturally.[79] Apart from the technical difficulties that would arise with these experiments, two big problems emerge. First, the human genetic system is immensely complicated, consisting not only of the 20,000 to 25,000 genes in the human DNA, but also of the 3 billion base pairs that make up the human DNA. As already mentioned, however, important advances have been made in identifying and locating certain genes and the base pairs that make them up. But we still have to clarify the exact way in which a certain trait (or disease) is genetically expressed. Moreover, frequently several traits are interrelated and most traits are regulated by more than one gene. This means that some of these ideas border on wishful thinking. We are still far away from being able to make precise repairs.

We are much more on the safe side with genetic screening of adults. Through some tests, a medical diagnosis is made and a physician can be directed toward appropriate treatment. In other cases, genetic screening al-

---

79. Leroy Augenstein, "Shall We Play God?" in *Changing Man: The Threat and the Promise,* ed. Kyle Haselden and Philip Hefner (Garden City, NY: Doubleday, 1968), 97, toys with this idea.

lows families to avoid having children with devastating diseases or identifies people at high risk for conditions that may be preventable, such as colon cancer or breast cancer. These tests, however, give only a probability for developing a certain disorder. Even if one has noticed the disease-associated mutation, it may never develop into a disease since there are also other factors involved in the actual outbreak of the disease.

Much more radical types of genetic surgery have been advocated that change the whole phenomenal appearance of humanity. American geneticist and biologist **Joshua Lederberg** (1925-2008) coined the term "euphenics" for this endeavor.[80] Through prenatal or early postnatal intervention, for instance, the size of the human brain could be regulated. Another possibility that has been highly publicized is the so-called cloning process or the nonsexual reproduction of body cells, especially for therapeutic cloning. The resulting genetic material in therapeutic cloning is identical with one's own and thus one would no longer need to rely on organ donors, and the problem of rejecting transplanted organs through the immunization process would be eliminated. Even if a whole human being or some of its "spare parts" would be successfully cloned — for the first successfully cloned animal, the sheep Dolly, it took 277 egg cells — the risk of early aging and of age-related illnesses would be quite high. But it is now possible to grow human tissue in cell cultures, especially human epidermal tissue grown from epithelial cell lines for the purpose of transplantation.[81] Nevertheless these tissue cultures have a limited lifespan and only go through a limited number of cell cycles. While this type of replacement seems to point in a very promising direction, we are still far away from providing even the simplest spare parts through clonic reproduction.

Another possibility of genetic euphenics lies in the interference with human reproduction. Already in the 1950s cell nuclei of frog eggs were replaced by other nuclei on which the eggs were parthenogenetically fertilized, that is, without the aid of a male sperm. Similarly, one could transfer a nucleus from a donor cell to an egg from which its nucleus had been removed. If the egg then begins to divide normally, it could be transferred into the uterus of the surro-

80. G. Pontecorvo, "Prospects for Genetic Analysis in Man," in *The Control of Human Heredity and Evolution,* ed. Tracy M. Sonneborn (New York: Macmillan, 1965), 83; see also Joshua Lederberg, "Biological Future of Man," in *Man and His Future,* A Ciba Foundation Volume, ed. Gordon Wolstenholme (London: J. & A. Churchill, 1967), 269f.

81. See Sophie Paquet-Fifield et al., "A Transfer Model for Human Epidermal Skin Regeneration," in *Epidermal Cells: Methods and Protocols,* 2nd ed., ed. Kursad Turksen (New York: Humana, 2010), 369f.

gate mother; the resulting children would be clones of their genetic parent and also similar to each other as identical twins. Neglecting the influence of the environment, their pattern of conduct would be predictable to a higher degree than is possible with normally procreated children because they would now be subject to the genetic influence of only one parent. Due to their similar genetic constitution the children could learn from the mistakes of their parents. However, in deciding whether it is right to produce such a human being artificially Lederberg rightly admits that *"we simply do not know enough about the question at either a technical or ethical level (and these are intertwined) to dogmatize about whether or not it should ever be done."*[82] The same Joshua Lederberg who had earlier advocated changing the appearance of humanity when this was only a future possibility now rightly cautions against it once we have come closer to making it an actual possibility. Moreover this reproductive cloning has not yielded what one actually hoped for since the cell itself contains a small portion of mitochondrial DNA that might produce clones that are not strictly identical.

A far more promising possibility for the future was discovered in so-called stem cell research. There are two types of stem cells, embryonic stem cells and adult stem cells. Adult stem cells are found in adult tissues, especially in the umbilical cord blood and in bone marrow. Bone marrow stem cells have been used for many years to successfully treat leukemia and other bone- and blood-related cancers through bone marrow transplants. They are usually multipotent and able to develop into various types of cells (yet only into those of a closely related family of cells). There they can act as a repair system, replenishing specialized cells. Yet unlike embryonic stem cells they do not reduplicate indefinitely and are therefore restricted to a few therapeutic applications. Embryonic stem cells are usually harvested from a fertilized egg cell once it has developed into a blastocyst containing approximately 100 to 200 cells. They are pluripotent, that is, they can develop into many different kinds of cells, and are relatively easy to harvest, but through that harvest the potential human being is destroyed. Because of that and the risk that they might initiate cancerous growth, there are still no approved treatments or clinical trials using embryonic stem cells. Therefore the potential promises connected with them are mitigated by legal restrictions.

---

82. So Joshua Lederberg, "Genetic Engineering and the Amelioration of Genetic Defect" (1970), in *Human Genetics: Readings on the Implications of Genetic Engineering,* ed. Thomas R. Mertens (New York: John Wiley, 1975), 94, with regards to the so-called clone-a-man process.

Though technically more difficult, work with adult stem cells seems to open more possibilities for treatment, such as Alzheimer's disease, Huntington's disease, and even multiple sclerosis.[83]

Similarly, breeding of humans with three or four sets of chromosomes seems to be a very remote possibility. Where such triploid or tetraploid sets of single chromosomes have occurred, they have always had deleterious effects. Hermann J. Muller's prediction seems to be justified that "for a long time yet to come (in terms of the temporal scale of human history thus far), man at his present best is unlikely to be excelled, according to any of man's own accepted value systems, by pure artifacts."[84]

But **Hermann J. Muller** (1890-1967), 1946 Nobel prize winner for physiology and medicine and professor of zoology at Indiana University, also wanted to influence the genetic constitution of humanity.[85] For more than fifty years he advocated artificial insemination as a first step toward controlling our own future development. Artificial insemination has the economic advantage of being relatively inexpensive and the technical advantage of being easy to administer. Of course, such a prospect of artificial insemination does not actually enlarge the human potential. As we learned from Gregor Mendel (1822-84) and the laws of heredity that he discovered, we would be thrown back to the potential of our own genetic pool and even the most careful mating process would only result in new combinations of already latent possibilities.

b. Behavioral Aspects

When we look at the behavioral basis for the human potential, we must mention neuroscience, which gives us unprecedented ways to understand

83. See Samuel S. W. Tay, "Mesenchymal Stem Cells: Culture, Characterization, and Therapeutic Applications in Neurodegenerative Disease," in *Stem Cell Technologies: Basics and Applications,* ed. Kaushik D. Deb (New York: McGraw-Hill, 2010), 417, who writes: "Stem cells have been well-recognized as the potential resource for restorative approaches for degenerative diseases and traumatic injuries."

84. Hermann J. Muller, "Genetic Progress by Voluntarily Conducted Germinal Choice," in *Man and His Future,* ed. Wolstenholme, 255.

85. Hermann J. Muller, "Human Evolution by Voluntary Choice of Germ Plasm" (1961), in *Human Genetics,* ed. Mertens, esp. 130-38, as a sample of the numerous articles Muller devoted to this topic. It is interesting that John Cartwright, *Evolution and Human Behavior: Darwinian Perspectives on Human Nature* (London: Macmillan, 2000), 322-24, in his discussion of eugenics does not mention Muller.

the human mind and to predict, influence, and even control it. It is especially the control of human behavior that must be mentioned. It is, for instance, commonly known that male hormones influence masculinity and aggressiveness while administration of female hormones increases the motherly instinct. But there is a new group of drugs that has little to do with gender but with lifestyle. These "lifestyle drugs" have a worldwide market of tens of billions of dollars.[86] These are drugs to satisfy non-health-related goals, such as oral contraceptives and male erectile functioning, to treat baldness and obesity, to mitigate the nicotine withdrawal symptom, or to enhance athletic performance as we see especially with cyclists and weight-lifters. Then there are drugs increasingly used for pharmacologic enhancement, including memory, executive function, mood, appetite, and sleep. In many retirement homes the residents are sedated to make it easier for their caretakers. Similarly, more and more school children are taking Ritalin since their behavior "is viewed as abnormal."[87] If we do not like the way our body functions or our mental behavior, we resort increasingly to drugs to obtain the desired state. There is also a group of psychoactive drugs, usually illegally used, which cause transient psychotic states. These include psilocybin, mescaline, and LSD-25 (lysergic acid diethylamide), to name just a few. Though some of these mind drugs were used in ancient times for religious rites (Sibylic oracle, Peyote cult),[88] we have only recently learned to what an amazing extent human behavior is not fixed and static, but open to modification.

The plasticity of human behavior is also emphasized by behavioral psychologists such as **B. F. Skinner** (1904-90). Fascinated by the work of Russian physiologist Ivan Pavlov (1849-1936) on conditioned reflexes and the ideas of the first explicit behaviorist John B. Watson (1878-1958), Skinner concluded that "stimulation arising inside the body plays an important part in behavior."[89] Skinner attempts to understand human behavior largely in terms of physiological responses to the environment. Of course, he is well aware that environment cannot explain everything. Behavior is not endlessly malleable, primarily because of the restrictions set by one's innate endowment or one's genetic constitution. Yet Skinner encourages us "to ex-

86. Rod Flower, "Lifestyle Drugs: Pharmacology and Social Agenda," in *Neuroethics: An Introduction,* ed. Martha J. Farah (Cambridge, MA: MIT Press, 2010), 19.

87. Lawrence H. Ditter, "The Run on Ritalin: Attention Deficit Disorder and Stimulant Treatment in the 1990s," in *Neuroethics,* ed. Farah, 43.

88. See Weston La Barre, *The Peyote Cult,* enl. ed. (New York: Schocken, 1969).

89. B. F. Skinner, *About Behaviorism* (New York: Alfred A. Knopf, 1974), 219.

amine the reasons for one's own behavior as carefully as possible because they are essential to good self-management."[90] Skinner even goes on to say that

> this is no time, then, to abandon notions of progress, improvement, or, indeed, human perfectibility. The simple fact is that man is able, and now as never before, to lift himself by his own bootstraps. In achieving control of the world of which he is part, he may learn at last to control himself.[91]

If we are to interpret this statement as an appeal for a new heroism, we are far from what Skinner intended.

In his book *Beyond Freedom and Dignity* (1971), Skinner states that the abolition of autonomous humanity "has long been overdue."[92] Scientific analysis of behavior tells us that autonomous humanity does not exist. We are controlled by the world around us and in large part by other people. Yet we are not the victims because our environment is almost wholly of our own making. Skinner considers the evolution of culture as a "gigantic exercise in self-control . . . through which the individual controls himself by manipulating the world in which he lives."[93] Thus "the controlling *self* must be distinguished from the controlled self, even when they are both inside the same skin." Such a distinction, however, limits the role of self-expression since we are always also reactors to circumstances.[94] This outside stimulus can be expressed by brutal force or by simply trying to get others to change their minds.

Since Skinner maintains that some kind of external control of human behavior is inevitable, the question is whether this control in effective cultural design should be left to accidents, to tyrants, or to ourselves.[95] Skinner is realistic enough to know that the danger of a misuse of power looms greater than ever. Yet Skinner sees an effective defense against tyranny in two steps: (1) the fullest exposure of controlling techniques, and (2) restriction of the use of physical force. In understanding the techniques we able to realize when guid-

---

90. Skinner, *About Behaviorism,* 171.

91. B. F. Skinner, "Freedom and the Control of Men" (1955/1956), in *Cumulative Record: A Selection of Papers,* 3rd ed. (New York: Appleton-Century-Crofts, 1972), 4.

92. B. F. Skinner, *Beyond Freedom and Dignity* (New York: Alfred A. Knopf, 1971), 200.

93. See Skinner, *Beyond Freedom and Dignity,* 206, for this and the following quotation.

94. For the following, see Skinner, "Freedom and the Control of Men," 7ff.

95. For the following, see Skinner, "Freedom and the Control of Men," 10f.

ance becomes brainwashing and when by eliminating physical forces we prevent the stronger from pushing the weaker around. As he outlined in his utopian novel *Walden Two,* Skinner is convinced that humans should be deliberately conditioned to certain behavior instead of leaving the behavioral results to mere chance.[96] "Automatic goodness" is for him a desirable state of affairs.[97] Skinner is aware that such egalitarianism of the good does away with heroic deeds. But in the long run, Skinner is convinced that these will no longer be necessary. Gradually we will no longer need to submit to punishing environments or engage in exhausting labor. We will move more and more toward making food, shelter, clothing, and labor-saving devices more readily available. Skinner concludes that "we may mourn the passing of heroes but not the conditions which make for heroism."[98]

We could ask Skinner why he wants to reinforce a particular kind of goodness in the conditioning process. But he would easily justify his position by pointing to some of the values that evolved in the history of humanity.[99] Yet the decisive question has to come with the distinction between the controller and the controlled. If we are always both victim and victor, how can we be so optimistic in our attempt to bring about paradisiacal conditions? Contrary to Skinner's assumption we are discovering that the non-human-made environment (e.g., natural resources) seems in the long run to pose bigger problems for human progression toward "the better" than the human-made environment does. Therefore our situation of being controlled and of living in a finite environment poses more restrictions than Skinner could have envisaged. The human potential expressed in the polarity of controller and controlled is in reality too analogous to the Christian understanding of *simul justus et peccator* (justified and sinner at the same time) to allow for self-redemption.

Austrian Nobel prize winner and director of the Max Planck Institute for Behavioral Psychology **Konrad Lorenz** seems to provide a more realistic appraisal of the human potential. Since Lorenz experimented with animals for nearly his entire life, we are not surprised that he attempts to assess

---

96. B. F. Skinner, *Walden Two* (New York: Macmillan, 1948).

97. Skinner, "Freedom and the Control of Men," 14.

98. Skinner, "Freedom and the Control of Men," 16.

99. See Skinner, *Beyond Freedom and Dignity,* 125f., for further discussion on what constitutes the good. For some of the discussion on Skinner, especially with regard to his "abolition of freedom," see *Beyond the Punitive Society: Operant Conditioning; Social and Political Aspects,* ed. Harvey Wheeler (San Francisco: W. H. Freeman, 1973), which also contains a very helpful reply by Skinner to his critics.

human potential in strict analogy to the animal world. He disagrees with German anthropologist Arnold Gehlen (1904-76) that humans are defective beings.[100] While humans lack explicit specialization in one specific field, Lorenz finds that their non-specialized approach to the environment serves as an adaptive advantage. Even in physical respects their versatility to be able to jump, climb, swim, and dive distinguishes them from most animals. Like many higher animals this non-specialization is coupled with curiosity and leads them to become cosmopolitan. But in animals the exploratory and creative discourse with the environment ceases once adulthood is reached. As the proverb says, "You cannot teach an old dog new tricks."

With humans, however, the openness to the world is a characteristic feature that accompanies them until senility sets in. This fundamental and significant characteristic of humans — their continuous, creative, and active discourse with the environment — can therefore be classified as a phenomenon of neoteny, of being mature while still growing up.[101] Humans always retain some of their "immature characteristics" in adulthood; they are always becoming and never definitely set in their ways. This allows for the peculiarly human freedom of action uninhibited by rigidly structured norms for action and reaction. Humans can dialogically interact with their environment and become reasonable beings.

Yet Lorenz notices an immense dichotomy between our success in mastering our environment and the failure to control our own affairs. Lorenz, however, does not maintain that social problems are simply more difficult to master than environmental ones. Rather, he finds the clue to this evident dichotomy in the way conduct is shaped in animal populations.[102] For instance, even among the highest animals their conspecific ways of conduct, that is, their behavior toward members of their own species, are much more determined by inborn components than by rational achievements. Their interaction with the extra-specific environment, however, is governed more by reason and less by innate patterns.

However, we no longer live by our natural ways so that inborn components could decisively inform our behavior. Both with regard to our kin and with regard to those creatures and things not of our kin we have created our

---

100. For the following, see Konrad Lorenz, "Ganzheit und Teil in der tierischen und menschlichen Gemeinschaft" (1950), in *Mensch und Tier: Streifzüge durch die Verhaltensforschung* (Munich: Piper, 1973), 242f.

101. So among others, see Bryan Kolb and Ian Q. Whishaw, *Fundamentals of Human Neuropsychology,* 5th ed. (New York: Worth, 2003), 41f.

102. See for the following Lorenz, "Ganzheit und Teil," 251f.

own environment. Experimenting in a dialogical and questioning manner with our environment, we increasingly dominate our surroundings. We also developed a language through which transindividual knowledge could be handed on to future generations and a culture could be founded. These developmental steps introduced such rapid and profound changes in our living conditions that the adaptability of the inborn components of our behavior to these new situations was overextended. Lorenz arrives at the conclusion that "man is not so evil from his youth, he is just *not quite good enough* for the demands of life in modern society."[103] What would happen, Lorenz asks, if animals were given different tools, for instance, if a chimpanzee would be given a hammer or a pigeon the beak of a hawk? The results would certainly be devastating because the natural equilibrium between the opportunity to kill and the instinctive inhibition to kill would be disturbed. Lorenz claims that this is the situation in which we find ourselves.

The first stone axe in his hand gave man the possibility to kill his brother so quickly and surprisingly that the victim had no chance to activate inhibitions in the aggressor through cries or a submissive posture.[104] With modern weaponry we are so removed from the consequences of our actions and from the victims themselves that our natural inhibitions to endanger or kill conspecifics are well "protected" against activation. For instance, a person who would be too inhibited to become aggressive enough to spank his child would find it easy to push the button to launch a ballistic missile. In recent wars many gentle and caring fathers flying high above the

---

103. So Lorenz, *Das sogenannte Böse: Zur Naturgeschichte der Aggression,* 33rd ed. (Vienna: G. Borotha Schoeler, 1973), 333. The earlier English translation, *On Aggression,* 251, has this quote somewhat misleadingly modified to: "The imagination of man's heart is not really evil from his youth up, as we read in Genesis." Niko Tinbergen, a longtime friend of Lorenz, arrives at similar conclusions. See Tinbergen's essay "The Search for Animal Roots of Human Behavior" (1964), in *The Animal in Its World: Explorations of an Ethologist, 1932-1972,* vol. 2, foreword Peter Medawar (Cambridge, MA: Harvard University Press, 1973), 171ff.

104. See for the following Lorenz, *On Aggression,* 241f. Edward O. Wilson, *Sociobiology: The New Synthesis* (Cambridge, MA: Harvard University Press, 1975), 246f., however, objects here saying: "The evidence of murder and cannibalism in mammals and other vertebrates has now accumulated to the point that we must completely reverse the conclusion advanced by Konrad Lorenz in his book *On Aggression.* Murder is far more common and hence 'normal' in many vertebrate species than in man." Of course, the question must be asked here what Wilson understands by murder. If he does not mean reflective killing, but an intentional and willful act, then humanity may indeed be the more dangerous species. No other living beings have ever staged systematic genocides, such as the Nazis against the Jews, or as did other "cultured" nations by "relocating" native populations.

clouds mercilessly killed innocent women and children in air raids. But it is not just the rapid development of modern weaponry that produced such a precarious situation.

We are also not "good enough" for the demands of our increasingly anonymous world community that insist we relate to any unknown person as we would relate to a personal friend.[105] Lorenz claims that through natural inclination we would obey those of the Ten Commandments that refer to our conduct toward fellow human beings without having to develop responsible morals, provided that the fellow human beings are well-known friends or associates. Yet overburdened with social obligations of all kinds, crowded in small city apartments with the constant stress of modern life, interhuman relationships are becoming more and more shallow and so aggressive behavior erupts.[106] The demands on us are mounting. We should restrain our aggressive drives and our instinctive feelings and with responsible self-examination check the implications of our behavior for the future.

Lorenz realizes that our task of attaining responsible behavior is getting more and more difficult. But in his influential book *On Aggression,* he does not end on a negative note.[107] He calls first for increasing research into the causes of our own behavior. Then he suggests that we look for responsible substitute objects in order to redirect the original form of our aggressive drives that no longer are allowed an outlet in modern society. Third, he points out that with the help of psychoanalytic research, ways could be found to sublimate these drives.[108] But he is not optimistic enough to assume that aggression can be eliminated through moral legislation or by removing triggering causes. Lorenz also rejects the idea of genetic manipulation to eradicate aggression because aggression is tied in with many positive features, such as love, enthusiasm, energetic drive, and the like. Insight into

---

105. For the following, see Lorenz, "Ganzheit und Teil," 254f.; and *On Aggression,* 251ff. See also Tinbergen, "Functional Ethology and the Human Sciences" (1972), in *The Animal in Its World,* 2:220f., where he mentions the problems of human disadaptation and readaptation in our urbanized, crowded, and anonymous living conditions.

106. See Konrad Lorenz in his provocative book *Civilized Man's Eight Deadly Sins,* trans. M. K. Wilson (New York: Harcourt Brace Jovanovich, 1974), 12ff.

107. For the following two paragraphs, see Lorenz in his concluding chapter in *On Aggression,* 275-99, which has the characteristic title "Avowal of Optimism."

108. The question is whether there are such aggressive drives that need periodic release. Brad J. Bushman and L. Rowell Huesmann, "Aggression," in *Handbook of Social Psychology,* 5th ed., ed. Susan T. Fiske et al., vol. 2 (Hoboken, NJ: John Wiley, 2010), 839, claim that "Freud undoubtedly influenced Lorenz" and "little empirical evidence has ever been found" to support this theory.

the causes of one's own behavior, however, is for Lorenz the first step in mastering conflicts in cases in which a categorical imperative alone would not suffice.

The most promising aspect for the future, however, is seen in the redirection of our aggressive drives. As a good way of redirection Lorenz advocates sports because in sports aggression and fairness are paired. He is quick to caution, however, that sports are not always beneficial in fostering understanding between nations. The best way to overcome national aggression would be for individuals from different nations to meet and get to know each other. Lorenz also advocates enthusiasm as a way to release aggressive energy. Here the arts and sciences deserve a boost as collective properties of the whole human family. Even humor is suggested as a means of showing a brotherly spirit. Trusting in human reason and in the power of selection, Lorenz concludes that this, "in the not too distant future, will endow our descendants with the faculty of fulfilling the greatest and most beautiful commandment of true humanity."[109]

One may wonder, however, whether Lorenz's optimism is justified. Undoubtedly, in today's anonymous mass society and with the increasingly perceived powerlessness of large segments of many societies oppressive drives build up in societies and between societies. But this has little to do with inborn aggressive drives that need periodic satisfaction. Aggression is not an isolated phenomenon, but has been detected with certainty only as a support for other biological functions, such as the procuring of food or attainment and defense of one's rank. As Eibl-Eibesfeldt asserts, there are "some universal innate human dispositions, such as man's aggressive emotionality and the preparedness for group defense, dominance striving, territoriality, and disposition to react to agonal signals from strangers."[110] Yet having played through the different possibilities we can freely decide what to do, regardless of how causally determined our genetic disposition functions. As we learn from the animal kingdom and as Lorenz has shown, physically strong species, such as lions or bisons, usually do not kill their own kind.[111] On the contrary, strong animals living in societal groupings usually use submissive postures and have inhibitions against killing conspecifics if they belong to their own group. With humans, however, "aggres-

---

109. *On Aggression,* 299; our quotation is from the German original, *Das sogenannte Böse,* 368.

110. Irenäus Eibl-Eibesfeldt, *Human Ethology* (New York: Aldine de Gruyter, 1989), 421.

111. This is different, for instance, with a male lion killing the offspring of a lion mother with whom he wants to have offspring of his own. He eliminates these to further his own kind.

sion is the consequence of situational factors interacting with predisposing factors."[112] If weapons are readily available or if there is poor self-control, aggression can more easily erupt. This means it is up to us to bring these various factors under control to live together peacefully.

If this analysis proves to be correct, it makes it difficult to channel peacefully the aggressive drives set free and/or engendered by the lifestyle of our modern industrial society. Lorenz may have sensed some of this dilemma when in a later book on *Civilized Man's Eight Deadly Sins* (1972) he concedes that "there is no lack of obstacles to be overcome if humanity is not to perish. . . . When we consider all that has happened and is happening in the world today, it is difficult to argue with those who believe that we are living in the days of anti-Christ."[113] Perhaps Lorenz's present position may be assessed correctly when we say that by comparing humans with the animal world he perceives humanity's Promethean potential but at the same time is afraid that it may be misused in a self-destructive way.

Eibl-Eibesfeldt asserts that human aggressive behavior "is indeed pre-programmed," but can be increased or restrained through education.[114] "Even in peaceful cultures children develop, for instance, a certain kind of behavior of rejecting foreigners and of aggression . . . even if they have not had any bad experiences with them."[115] Similarly, "whenever people enter a new developmental stage by becoming part of a new community, they tend to explore the limits of their freedom to act."[116] In this aggressive social exploration a child, for instance, asks what is and what is not permissible. Aggression, therefore, cannot be termed as something altogether undesirable. Yet when the innate aggressive dispositions are enhanced and those that restrict aggression are suppressed, as happens, for instance, in war when the opponent is supposed to be annihilated, then this kind of aggression is a product of cultural evolution and needs to be evaluated as such. This means that humanity has to shoulder its responsibility for such activity and determine whether it wants to continue this trend.

---

112. So Bushman and Huesmann, "Aggression," in *Handbook of Social Psychology,* ed. Fiske et al., 2:844.

113. Lorenz, *Civilized Man's Eight Deadly Sins,* 42 and 59.

114. So Irenäus Eibl-Eibesfeldt, *Der vorprogrammierte Mensch: Das Ererbte als bestimmender Faktor im menschlichen Verhalten* (Munich: DTV, 1976), 116, and see 102.

115. Irenäus Eibl-Eibesfeldt, *Menschenforschung auf neuen Wegen: Die naturwissenschaftliche Betrachtung kultureller Verhaltensweisen* (Munich: Fritz Molden, 1976), 14.

116. Irenäus Eibl-Eibesfeldt, *Der Mensch — das riskierte Wesen: Zur Naturgeschichte menschlicher Unvernunft* (Munich: Piper, 1988), 212.

Few books have created such a heated debate as E. O. Wilson's *Sociobiology: The New Synthesis* (1975). Sociobiology is "the systematic study of the biological basis of all social behavior."[117] American biologist **Edward O. Wilson** (b. 1929) was charged by some of his critics with attempting to enable us "to understand all of human behavior and even to solve the ancient philosophical questions of how we ought to live."[118] He was also accused of advocating the status quo because he allegedly claimed that "what exists is adaptive, what is adaptive is good, therefore what exists is good."[119] Others claimed that they have yet to meet or hear of a sociobiologist "who believed that because a human behavior has evolved, it is necessarily desirable."[120] It is therefore a mistake to confuse "what is" with "what ought to be."

While in *Sociobiology* Wilson paid explicit attention to humanity only in the final chapter, his book *On Human Nature* (1978) is exclusively devoted to an investigation of human behavior. At the beginning of this latter book he points out that there are innate censors and motivators in the human brain "that deeply and unconsciously affect our ethical premises; from these roots, morality evolved as instinct."[121] This means that there are inborn forms of behavior that ensure our survival, something that traditional theology called "orders of preservation."

Wilson is not convinced that human genes specify certain traits. They rather prescribe the capacity to develop a certain array of traits. In some cases the array of traits is limited and one can hardly alter the outcome, whereas in other cases the array is so vast that the outcome can easily be influenced. This means that human behavior is specified to varying degrees. While Wilson agrees with the materialist basis for human behavior as advanced by the representatives of behaviorism, he cautions that their basic assumptions for control of behavior are too simplistic. Human behavior can be specified theoretically because genetic constraints and the restricted number of environments in which human beings can live "limit the array of possible outcomes substantially."[122] Yet even short-term predictions of de-

---

117. Michael J. Reiss, "Human Sociobiology," *Zygon* 19 (1984): 117.

118. So Peter Singer, "Ethics and Sociobiology," *Zygon* 19 (1984): 141.

119. So Elizabeth Allen et al., "Against 'Sociobiology,'" in *The Sociobiology Debate: Readings on Ethical and Scientific Issues,* ed. Arthur L. Caplan (New York: Harper & Row, 1978), 261.

120. Reiss, "Human Sociobiology," 137.

121. Edward O. Wilson, *On Human Nature* (Cambridge, MA: Harvard University Press, 1978), 5.

122. Wilson, *On Human Nature,* 73.

tailed behavior of an individual human being might be beyond the capacity of any conceivable intelligence. There are too many variables to consider and minute degrees of imprecision might easily be magnified and might alter the prediction considerably.

Wilson is convinced that human social evolution is obviously more cultural than genetic. He even claims that "conscious altruism is a transcendental quality that distinguishes human beings from animals."[123] While animals act in an altruistic way so that the survival of their species is ensured, they are generally not conscious of what they are doing since they are driven by certain biological mechanisms. Humans, however, can choose their moral principles through knowledge and reason remote from biology. Like Lorenz, Wilson would claim that our instinctive drives no longer necessitate but only suggest a certain behavior. But the question then arises: "Can the cultural evolution of higher ethical values gain a direction and momentum of its own and completely replace genetic evolution?"[124] Wilson responds to this question in the negative. "The genes hold culture on a leash. The leash is very long, but inevitably values will be constrained in accordance with their effects on the human gene pool." Even if our behavior is driven and guided by deep emotional responses, ultimately this behavior is a technique "by which human genetic material has been and will be kept intact."

Wilson concludes, therefore, that "morality has no other demonstrable ultimate function" than to assure our survival. While we have no choice but to concede that any other practical function of morality cannot be demonstrated, we should remember that not every species has so far survived. Though in every species there is certainly an intention to assure its own survival, such survival is not guaranteed by the evolutionary process itself or by the genetic constitution guiding and directing the process of life. Though Wilson concludes his book *On Human Nature* with a chapter on hope, he rightly speaks there of "the mythology of scientific materialism."[125] Any guarantee for survival cannot be given by the finite material base that gave rise to life. In that respect there is as much an intertwining of the finitude of life with the finitude of matter as there is of behavior with its genetic base.

For Konrad Lorenz and his followers morality was natural. Sociobiology,

---

123. Wilson, *On Human Nature,* 150.

124. See Wilson, *On Human Nature,* 167, for this and the following quotes. In a more recent but highly controversial book, *The Social Conquest of Earth* (New York: W. W. Norton, 2012), Wilson now claims that group selection and not the "selfish gene" has been the driving force of human evolution.

125. Wilson, *On Human Nature,* 209.

however, cautioned against such optimism and showed that altruism among members of the same species is the result of the fact that the actual carriers of biological evolution are not individuals, whether species or single members, but the genes that cooperate in order to survive.[126] This means that which looks externally altruistic is genetically egotistic. Natural selection, therefore, does not primarily further the maximizing of personal fitness, but rather the fitness of the whole, which is measured in terms of individual success in reproduction plus the reproduction of genetic relatives in which those are preferred that are closer to oneself. German anthropologist Christian Vogel (1933-94) phrases this kind of natural morality in these words: "Help your relatives according to their corresponding genetic relationship to you but when in doubt help them less than yourself and your own reproduction!"[127]

In contrast to Lorenz's assertion, behavioral geneticists disclaim that there is natural morality. Though natural dispositions may be contained in our moral behavior, they do not constitute part of the moral quality of our actions. The reason for this hesitancy in talking about moral qualities arises from the realization that as a scientist one describes what is and does not prescribe what ought to be. Furthermore, genetic influence is embedded in the complexity of interactions among genes, physiology, and environment. "It is probabilistic, not deterministic; it puts no constraints on what could be," notes American psychologist Robert Plomin (b. 1948).[128] Yet to discover genetic interaction is important because the more one knows about a trait genetically as well as environmentally, the more likely rational intervention and prevention strategies with regard to undesirable consequences can be devised.

Behavioral genetics is not, however, totally void of moral implications. It is still concerned with survival. In contrast to Darwin, who considered the survival of individuals or of groups, behavioral geneticists have realized that individuals certainly do not survive and groups quite often do not survive either. Only genetic units last long enough to evolve for the purpose of survival. These units have evolved to survive by helping their copies reproduce wherever those copies may live. This means, on the human level, we are "selfish individualists to the extent that our behavior maximizes the survival by reproduction of those copies of our genes residing in our own bod-

---

126. See for the following Christian Vogel, "Gibt es eine natürliche Moral? Oder: Wie widernatürlich ist unsere Ethik?" in *Die Herausforderung der Evolutionsbiologie,* ed. Heinrich Meier (Munich: R. Piper, 1988), 205f.

127. Vogel, "Gibt es eine natürliche Moral?" 207.

128. Robert Plomin, *Development, Genetics and Psychology* (Hillsdale, NJ: Lawrence Erlbaum Associates, 1984), 21.

ies; and we are group altruists to the extent that this behavior maximizes the survival by reproduction of copies of our genes residing in the bodies of others."[129] We may conclude, therefore, that behavioral genetics has not moved away from the issues of selfishness and altruism. It has become more differentiating and now also investigates the genetic base that leads to selfishness or to altruism. But behavioral genetics still focuses on the issue of survival. As we look now at the philosophico-religious side, we will see that the assessment of the human constitution is generally not much more optimistic.

129. Richard D. Alexander, "Evolution, Culture and Human Behavior: Some General Considerations," in *Natural Selection and Social Behavior,* ed. R. Alexander and Donald Trinkle (New York: Chiron Press, 1981), 511.

3. The Philosophico-Religious Perspective

With the various scenarios that are presented with regard to global warming, overpopulation, and the diminishing of natural resources, our present situation seems to be serious, perhaps more serious than any human situation before. Through the millennia one civilization after another rose to power and eventually was replaced by another. But today we talk about a global civilization in which no nation is isolated from the rest of the global community. And yet the existence of this global community is threatened by a possible ecological holocaust. In looking at the evolutionary stream of life and its material base, we have no reason for hope except that possible doom looms farther in the distance. There have always been some thinkers who wanted to break through the strictures that nature seems to impose on us. Their options, however, have not been very promising.

It would be shortsighted, however, to say that we now have scientific proof that the *eschaton* is imminent. Teilhard de Chardin rightly warned us against the attempt to equate any global or sidereal disaster with the coming of the *eschaton*. Such a disaster would only affect part of the world but not the total world and it would lead only to destruction but not to fulfillment as a new beginning. All we can gather from what we have seen so far is that this world in and of itself does not contain any long-range hope or the promise of an entirely new beginning. At most, we can have variations of what we already had, and in the end death still looms. When we now consider the options provided by philosophical inquiry, then secular existentialism at least seems to affirm this scientific analysis. Moreover, "existentialism is the only philosophical movement of the past hundred years to have captured the popular imagination, and its popularity has endured."[1]

1. The Option of Secular Existentialism

For Søren Kierkegaard (1813-55), the founder of existentialism, life was a venture sustained by trust in a gracious God. Secular existentialism, however, has emancipated itself from the all-embracing assurance of God's grace and starts with the assumption that ultimate questions are beyond our grasp. Existence does not find its fulfillment in the *eschaton,* but is basically defined as "being there" and "being in the world."

a. Life Bounded by Death

Martin Heidegger (1889-1976), one of the pioneers of modern secular existentialist thought, conceives of life as being in the world; it is a being-there and a being-toward-death. Temporality and death are constitutive factors of being-there. Since in our being-there we face death as the end of life, this final end of our possibilities causes anxiety as a basic phenomenon of life. Yet it would be foolish to flee from our being-toward-death or to cover up this characteristic feature of our being-there. In so doing we would be living an inauthentic existence and, turning anxiety into fear, we would attempt to hide from ourselves. Heidegger instead opts for resoluteness and an authentic existence. He claims that we must recognize anxiety "as a basic state-of-mind" and as "Dasein's [being-there's] essential state of Being-in-the-world."[2] Similarly, "*authentic* Being-toward-death can *not evade* its ownmost non-relational possibility, or *cover up* this possibility by thus fleeing from it, or *give a new explanation* for it to accord with the common sense of the 'they.'"[3] Since death is being-there's innermost possibility, "being toward this possibility discloses to Dasein [being-there] its *ownmost* potentiality-for-Being, in which its very Being is the issue."[4]

1. So rightly James Woelfel, *The Existentialist Legacy and Other Essays on Philosophy and Religion* (Lanham, MD: University Press of America, 2006), 1.
2. Martin Heidegger, *Being and Time,* trans. J. Macquarrie and E. Robinson (London: SCM, 1962), 234.
3. Heidegger, *Being and Time,* 304f.
4. Heidegger, *Being and Time,* 307.

Heidegger describes existence as occurring strictly within this world. While he could substantiate his claim by a phenomenological survey that all being-there ultimately faces death, his secular premise notwithstanding, he goes beyond the verifiable and calls for authentic existence as the optimum and goal of human existence. Yet this goal can really no longer be grounded in the being-there, and therefore Heidegger leaves the impression that his appeal is arbitrary.[5] There is no possible justifiable transition from "is" to "ought," from the way things are to the way things ought to be, unless we go beyond the phenomenologically given.

Ernest Becker (1925-74), in his award-winning book, *The Denial of Death,* emphasizes with convincing clarity "that the fear of death is a universal."[6] Largely following the psychology of Sigmund Freud and combining it with the existential portrayal of humanity provided by Kierkegaard, Becker points out that "we are hopelessly absorbed with ourselves."[7] We hope and believe that the things we create in society are of lasting worth and meaning, "that they outlive or outshine death and decay."[8] Thus the urge to heroism is natural. But there is no escape from death. We are "doomed to live in an overwhelmingly tragic and demonic world."[9] We can drown our senses, but as soon as we awake we realize anew that we do not understand the purpose of creation and therefore the direction of life's expansion. "We only feel life straining in ourselves and see it thrashing others about as they devour each other."[10]

According to Becker, fear of death is a fundamental human motif and the repression of death anxiety can make human beings more dangerous in the way they relate to their worldviews and use those against one another. Although Ernest Becker won the 1974 Pulitzer Prize for general nonfiction for *The Denial of Death,* generally his work was dismissed at that time by academics because they thought that it was just another wild speculation "based on psychological constructs of dubious validity derived from psychoanalysis."[11]

---

5. Herman Philipse, *Heidegger's Philosophy of Being: A Critical Interpretation* (Princeton, NJ: Princeton University Press, 1998), 27, notices "a persistent contradiction or tension in *Sein und Zeit:* Heidegger on the one hand stresses that we cannot free ourselves from the One or Everyman, and on the other hand claims that we have to liberate ourselves from it in order to become authentic."

6. Ernest Becker, *The Denial of Death* (New York: Free Press, 1973), ix.

7. Becker, *The Denial of Death,* xi and quote on 2.

8. See Becker, *The Denial of Death,* 5.

9. Becker, *The Denial of Death,* 281.

10. Becker, *The Denial of Death,* 284.

11. See for the following, including the quote, Sheldon Solomon, Jeff Greenberg, and

But some social psychologists thought differently and reasoned that the ideas contained in that book were profound and could have powerful implications for understanding and affecting human behavior. Sheldon Solomon, Jeff Greenberg, and Tom Pyszczynski then developed the terror management theory and "acquired a large body of experimental evidence in support of Becker's central claim that concerns about mortality play a pervasive role in human affairs." Empirical research indeed validated Becker's claims. Yet Becker did not want to stay with the empirical.

As he noted in *The Denial of Death,* a sober examination of the motivational underpinnings of human behavior leads beyond psychology and directly to religion — to find the "courage to face the anxiety of meaninglessness."[12] Solomon, Greenberg, and Pyszczynski realized that psychological equanimity "requires a meaningful conception of reality and no such conception can ever be unambiguously confirmed, [since] all such meanings are sustained by faith and are hence fundamentally religious."[13] But the road to the religious was quite difficult for Becker.

Initially, like Heidegger, Becker was not content with our yearning to overcome death through heroic deeds. In his last book, posthumously published, he argued that our "natural and inevitable urge[s] to deny mortality and achieve a heroic self-image are the root causes of human evil."[14] He was not as optimistic as Heidegger, however, that we can introduce a system by which we could live without causing pain and sorrow for each other. Still he refused to give up in despair. He closed his book, hoping for "that minute measure of reason to balance destruction."[15] Such hope is certainly not grounded in empirical data. But since the whole religious realm was explained by Becker as a device to escape the reality of "death and the dread of it,"[16] he could no longer resort to metaphysical powers. Neither was he willing to give up living and hoping. This hope without faith, against overwhelming odds, is the trademark of modern secular existentialism.

Yet Becker's life story has one more twist to it. After finishing *The Denial of Death* and before receiving the Pulitzer Prize, Becker was diagnosed with terminal cancer. He faced his own death true to his own books with a Stoic form of

---

Tom Pyszczynski, "Tales from the Crypt: On the Role of Death in Life," *Zygon* 33 (1998): 10. It is noteworthy that the main feature of this issue of *Zygon* is on the work of Ernest Becker.

12. Becker, *The Denial of Death,* 279.

13. Solomon, Greenberg, and Pyszczynski, "Tales from the Crypt," 39.

14. Ernest Becker, *Escape from Evil* (New York: Free Press, 1975), xvii.

15. Becker, *Escape from Evil,* 170.

16. Becker, *The Denial of Death,* 12.

heroism yet, as he added, with "the qualification that I believe in God."[17] He had been an atheist for many years, but it was not the prospect of dying that made him more religious. Long before that, at the birth of his first child, it dawned on him that new life was created, so to speak, out of nothingness. According to Becker, this must have something to do with God. Confronting death, he read one or two psalms each morning and one of them (Psalm 131) made him ask: "What can man do when he has seen his own pitiful smallness, his inability to do and to understand, except 'hope'?"[18] Becker discovered here not only the finitude of life, but also his own creatureliness and thereby realized that all he could do was to cast himself on the mercy of his creator.[19]

Again, the discovery of his own creatureliness did not result from facing terminal illness. Before that, in a letter of September 20, 1965, he wrote to Harvey Bates: "At least I have been fortunate to learn that we do not achieve anything; that anything is achieved, [is achieved] by grace. This is an immense discovery to me that is slowly transforming my whole world." But then he added:

> Your view of Christianity as a self-discipline which grows out of thanksgiving for what is already given, and not for what is to come, is perhaps the highest one could achieve. . . . It is gratitude for being born to serve. Evidently, the genuine Hebrew religiousness — and Buber's — is very similar: the belief that when man has done all he could, then God would do the rest, he would act.[20]

Creatureliness did not mean for Becker simply to be relegated to inactivity, but being grateful for having been born to serve. He also realized that any service a human being could do remains within the limits of creatureliness. God, indeed, would have to do the rest. Having emphasized the dark side of life and realizing that "there is evil in the world,"[21] Becker had basically three options: to resign oneself to fate, a stance that he considered inadequate for a human being; to resort to heroic measures, that is, so to speak, to "save the world," something that he was convinced would only contribute to misery; or finally, to serve and hope even in the face of overwhelming

---

17. As quoted by Sam Keen, "A Conversation with Ernest Becker," *Psychology Today* (April 1974): 78.

18. As quoted by Harvey Bates, "Letters from Ernest," *Christian Century* 94 (1977): 218.

19. For the following, see Sally A. Kenel, "A Heroic Vision," *Zygon* 33 (1998): 64ff., who emphasizes that Becker's anthropology is marked by "the religious symbol of creatureliness."

20. As quoted by Bates, "Letters from Ernest," 219.

21. As quoted by Keen, "A Conversation with Ernest Becker," 74.

odds. This truly existential note fortified by a religious conviction that was not worn on his sleeve allowed him to courageously face his own finitude.

b. Humanity Thrown upon Itself

When we come to **Jean-Paul Sartre** (1905-80), the French existentialist who radicalized Heidegger's philosophy, we are candidly confronted with a humanity that has lost its metaphysical reference point. Humanity is conceived of as an agent basically free of its destiny. Since there is no longer anything or anyone given, but only manifestations of our own — how we look at the world and human relations and how we shape them — we are radically free.[22] In contrast to Heidegger, Sartre can no longer understand human freedom as beneficial. Humanity is "condemned to freedom."[23] We have no God, no truth, and no values, in the traditional sense of these terms. This individualized and non-directed world encounters us as a basically antagonistic world. Others are encountered as evil, even as "hell," desiring to infringe on our freedom.[24]

Sartre claims that *existence* precedes *essence* and that our essence is "what has been," or in short, our past. But there is no common essence according to which we can act.[25] Rather, each of us makes his or her essence as we live our lives. This individualistic stance excludes history as a communal category, and Sartre answers the question whether history is essential to us with a flat-out "No."[26] Thus we must transcend the non-conscious level of *being-in-itself* and rise to the conscious level of *being-for-itself*. At this level we express lack of being, desire for being, and relation to being. Yet in opting for being-for-itself we bring nothingness into the world since we now stand out from being and can judge other being by knowing what it is not. Sartre emphasizes that we must be-for-ourselves if we want to escape from "bad faith."[27] This bad faith arises if we oscillate between relying on the past

22. See Jonathan Webber, *The Existentialism of Jean-Paul Sartre* (New York: Routledge, 2009), especially the beginning of his chapter on "Radical Freedom" (59f.).

23. Jean-Paul Sartre, *Being and Nothingness: An Essay on Phenomenological Ontology*, trans. and intro. H. E. Barnes (New York: Philosophical Library, 1956), 485. Sartre's claim of support from Heidegger seems to be unwarranted at this point.

24. Jean-Paul Sartre, *No Exit*, in *"No Exit" and Three Other Plays*, trans. L. Abel (New York: Knopf, 1949), 47.

25. Sartre, *Being and Nothingness*, 555-56.

26. Jean-Paul Sartre, *Critique of Dialectic Reason*, vol. 2, *The Intelligibility of History*, ed. Arlette Elkain-Sartre, trans. Quinlin Hoare (London: Verso, 1991), 450.

27. Sartre, *Being and Nothingness*, 70.

and projecting ourselves toward the future or, what is equally bad, if we attempt to synthesize both. It is our destiny to venture toward the future without relying on the past or on any pre-established norms.

It is a grim picture that Sartre offers us. We exist toward the future, solely relying on ourselves and in continuous conflict with others who, in a similar way, want to exist for themselves. British journalist Philip Mairet (1886-1975) rightly characterizes this stance as "pitiless atheism."[28] But what should our motivation be for existing in this kind of solipsistic activism? One would find neither comfort nor assurance in such a world and would rather opt for traditional values rather than relying solely on oneself.

Sartre's compatriot **Albert Camus** (1913-60) attempted to move beyond an arbitrary existentialist position to a moralist one.[29] In his novel, *The Myth of Sisyphus* (1942), he describes the situation in which he found himself after having discovered that none of the speculative systems of the past can provide positive guidance for human life or guarantee the validity of our values.[30] Unlike Sartre, he at least poses the question of whether it makes sense to go on living once the meaninglessness of human life has been fully recognized. Camus maintains that suicide cannot be regarded as an adequate response to the experience of absurdity that results from our discovery that we must live without the value-supporting "standards" and ideas of the past. Cutting through the tension-provoking polarity between being human and the world by committing suicide would only be an admission of our incapacity. Camus argues that we have too much self-pride to seek this easy way out. Only by living in the face of our own absurdity can we achieve our full stature.

Camus realizes that our revolt against metaphysically guaranteed directives for conduct does not really improve the human predicament. Like Sartre, he portrays in his literary works the persisting injustice and cruelty committed by one human being against another. In his philosophical essay, *The Rebel* (1951), he concludes that it is precisely the revolt against metaphysics, against human conditions as such, that has led to twentieth-century totalitarianism.[31] Camus

28. Jean-Paul Sartre, *Existentialism and Humanism,* trans. and intro. Philip Mairet (London: Methuen, 1948), 15, in the intro. by Mairet.

29. For a good assessment of Camus over against Jean-Paul Sartre's position and Camus's sober limitation to concrete experience, see Germaine Brée, *Camus,* rev. ed. (New Brunswick, NJ: Rutgers University Press, 1972), esp. 210-11.

30. Albert Camus, *The Myth of Sisyphus and Other Essays,* trans. J. O'Brien (New York: Vintage, 1991).

31. Albert Camus, *The Rebel: An Essay on Man in Revolt,* foreword Sir Herbert Read, trans. A. Bower (New York: Knopf, 1961). Yet already at the conclusion of this book Camus

now rejects the metaphysical revolt and opts instead for an ethical revolt. He recognizes that the metaphysical revolt, while attempting to impose on humanity a new world order, has resulted in the nightmare of an unrestrained power struggle. Yet Camus still calls for nihilism as a cathartic device. While he now knows that it does not provide a principle for action, he is still convinced that it will clear the ground for new construction by disposing of any kind of mystification by which we might try to rid ourselves of our radical contingency and confer on ourselves a cosmic status. But how can this "new ground" be filled with positive content once it is cleared? Even an essentially non-metaphysical and strongly moralistic humanism must derive its directives from somewhere; otherwise it would fall prey to what Camus rightly calls a "metaphysical" revolution.

In his last major work, *The Fall* (1956), Camus seems to imply that directives for ordering our lives cannot come from ourselves.[32] In this utterly pessimistic work Camus abandons political and social revolt. Evil is no longer understood as originating from the unjust social institutions in which we are doomed to exist; evil stems from the human heart. Then where does the incentive for life and living come from? In his short story "The Growing Stone" (1957), Camus seems to give an answer to this all-decisive question.[33] When the French engineer D'Arrast substitutes for the exhausted mulatto ship cook and picks up the stone to fulfill the cook's vow, he does not carry that stone to the cathedral, the place where the cook had vowed he would deposit it. Instead, D'Arrast carries the stone back to the little hut in which the man lives. In other words, Camus indicates that help for us can only come from human solidarity in taking on ourselves each other's burdens. But for Camus such solidarity must serve a human purpose and not a metaphysical one.

We wonder, however, whether this alternative that Camus poses could not, and even should not, be bridged by suggesting that one can serve the metaphysical purpose in fulfilling a human need. If we are strictly confined to ourselves and the world around us, how could we ever experience "a fresh beginning of life" that D'Arrast so vividly senses? Admitting human depravity, secular existentialists opt for a heroic stand in the midst of an antagonis-

---

mentions that "rebellion cannot exist without a strange form of love" (304), without, however, elaborating any further on the meaning of love. David A. Sprintzen in his preface to *Sartre and Camus: A Historic Confrontation* (Amherst, NY: Humanity Books, 2004), 14, points out that "Camus was appalled by the totalitarian direction of revolutionary movements."

32. Albert Camus, *The Fall,* trans. J. O'Brien (New York: Knopf, 1961).

33. Albert Camus, "The Growing Stone," in *Exile and the Kingdom,* trans. J. O'Brien (New York: Vintage, 1965), 159-213.

tic world. But they are unable to explain what would give us the continuing courage to wage a losing battle, nor are they in a better position to elucidate how there could be a fresh beginning. The root problem is that secular existentialists claim that humans "freely invent all values," which then remain "postulates of subjectivity" but cannot lay an ultimate claim on us nor provide for hope.[34] In other words, secular existentialism provides us with an accurate assessment of the human situation, but it is unable to lead us to a new future or even provide hope for the future unless it reintegrates its secular stance into a religious sphere.

2. Utopia from the Left

The term "utopia" dates back to Sir Thomas More (1478-1535), who in 1515-16 wrote his two books on the subject describing a pagan and communist city-state in which institutions and policies were entirely governed by reason. The order and dignity of such a state stood in stark contrast to the unreasonable polity of Christian Europe divided by self-interest and greed for power and riches. Though this utopia, a composite from the Greek words *ou* and *topos,* meaning "no place" or "nowhere," was meant by More as a satire, utopia in a positive sense is a dimension of human yearning, often associated with wishful dreams, or theologically, with the dimension of the future *eschaton.* **Karl Marx** (1818-83) and **Friedrich Engels** (1818-95) especially advocated their socialist realm of freedom as a concrete utopia.

a. A New World through Revolution

Karl Marx stated his goal very precisely when he wrote: "The philosophers have only *interpreted* the world in various ways; the point is to *change* it."[35] Marx and Engels, the founders of the Marxist movement, were influenced by a variety of sources. Progressive industrialization and popularized Darwinism gave them their optimistic outlook; labor conditions in the early years of the industrial revolution showed them the plight of the working class; biblical criticism, especially of the Tübingen school, removed for

34. Woelfel, *The Existentialist Legacy,* 16.
35. Karl Marx, "Theses on Feuerbach" (1845), in Karl Marx and Friedrich Engels, *On Religion* (Amsterdam: Fredonia Books, 2002 [1955]), 72, in thesis xi.

them most of the supernaturalness of the Bible; and Bruno Bauer (1809-82), a left-wing Hegelian and onetime close friend of Marx, gave them the idea that as a world religion Christianity was the product of the Greco-Roman world.[36] Especially for Karl Marx two further influences need to be mentioned. Both of his parents were of Jewish descent, though they had converted to Protestantism. While he may not have had much of a religious upbringing, his vision of a new and perfect society had implicit religious overtones.[37] We must also note the influence of Ludwig Feuerbach and his book *The Essence of Christianity,* in which Feuerbach re-established materialism as the prime concept. Engels tells us that Marx "enthusiastically welcomed this new concept."[38] It is built on the idea that nature exists independently of all philosophy, and is the foundation for the claim that human beings are products of nature. The suggestion is that nothing exists outside nature and humanity, and that "higher beings" are creations of religious fantasy and are simply fantastical reflections of our own being.

The idea that Christianity, or religion as Marx and Engels usually call it, is the product of its environment was decisive for their thinking. But Marx felt that Feuerbach had only accomplished half of the task. It is not sufficient to label religion as the projection of our unfulfilled desires on the screen of the beyond; it is necessary to recognize that this projection is a "social product" that belongs to a particular form of society, modern capitalism. If capitalism falls, religion will also disappear as will many other products of the bourgeoisie, such as the division of labor and the structures of the state.

Though the founders of Marxism admitted that early Christianity had notable points of resemblance with the modern working-class movement, being originally a movement of oppressed people, they faulted Christianity for refusing to accomplish social transformation in this world. Instead, Christians hoped for salvation from their plight in heaven, in eternal life after death, in the impending "millennium."[39] Thus Marx concluded con-

---

36. See Friedrich Engels, "On the History of Early Christianity," in *On Religion,* 324.

37. For details of his religious background and his own early views of God, see Walther Bienert, *Der überholte Marx: Seine Religionskritik und Weltanschauung kritisch untersucht* (Stuttgart: Evangelisches Verlagswerk, 1974), 15-17.

38. See for the following, including the quote from Friedrich Engels, "Ludwig Feuerbach und der Ausgang der klassischen deutschen Philosophie" (I), in *Texte zur materialistischen Geschichtsauffassung von Ludwig Feuerbach, Karl Marx, Friedrich Engels,* ed. with an intro. Helmut Reichelt (Frankfurt am Main: Ullstein, 1975), 549.

39. Friedrich Engels, "On the History of Early Christianity" (1894/1895), in *On Religion,* 317.

temptuously: "The social principles of Christianity preach cowardice, self-contempt, abasement, submission, dejection."[40] Since the proletariat needs courage, self-esteem, pride, and a sense of independence to attain its goal, it must do away with religion. "The criticism of religion ends with the teaching that *man is the highest essence for man,* hence with the *categoric imperative to overthrow all relations* in which man is a debased, enslaved, abandoned, despicable essence."[41]

Since the religious world is but the reflection of the real world, Marx demanded that we abandon the search "for a superman in the fantastic reality of heaven" where we can find nothing but the reflection of ourselves.[42] Marx therefore claimed that "the abolition of religion as the *illusory* happiness of the people is required for their *real* happiness."[43] As soon as religion as the general theory of this world is abolished — a theory that provides the justification for the exploitation of the working class and the consolation of a better future — we will abandon the fantastic heavenly reality and face our reality on earth.

When we remember the overwhelming otherworldliness of the so-called negro spirituals, in which the slaves usually dared to claim for themselves only a better beyond and not a better earth, we can understand Marx's claim that "religion is the sigh of the oppressed creature." But we cannot agree with his conclusion that religion "is the *opium* of the people." Religion has certainly been used for this purpose, but since the Judeo-Christian faith is by its very nature a forward-looking and world-transforming faith, this could have never been its main intention. There is undoubtedly also some truth in the claim that religion is a tool of the capitalists to exploit the working class and to sanctify this exploitation with the comfort of a better hereafter. But it is a gross oversimplification to assert that religion is simply an interpretation of present conditions. Religion is just as decisively an anticipation of the "beyond" in earthly form. Engels may have sensed some of this when he conceded that "in the popular risings of the Christian West . . . a new . . . economic order . . . arises and the world progresses," while in the context of other religions, even when the uprisings "are victorious, they al-

---

40. Karl Marx, "The Communism of the Paper *Rheinischer Beobachter,*" in *On Religion,* 84.

41. Karl Marx, "Contribution to the Critique of Hegel's Philosophy of Right," in *On Religion,* 50.

42. Marx, "Contribution to the Critique of Hegel's Philosophy of Right," 41.

43. See Marx, "Contribution to the Critique of Hegel's Philosophy of Right," 42, for this and the following two quotes.

low the old economic conditions to persist untouched. So the old situation remains unchanged and the collision recurs periodically."[44] But both Engels and Marx were influenced by Feuerbach so much that they could not have had any confidence in the function of religion.

Karl Marx opted for "a total revolution" in the antagonism between the proletariat and the bourgeoisie.[45] Once the working class is emancipated, "we shall have an association in which the free development of each is the condition for the free development of all."[46] It is not without significance that the word "free" appears twice in the above sentence. Instead of enslavement and force Marx envisions "the true realm of freedom" when socialized people as "associated producers regulate their interchange with nature rationally, bring it under their common control, instead of being ruled by it as by some blind power."[47] While the "savage" must wrestle with nature to satisfy his wants and to be able to live, modern socialized humanity is "beyond the sphere of material production in the strict meaning of the term." Humanity has passed the point "where labor under the compulsion of necessity and of external utility is required." Then the realm of freedom emerges. This new economic structure of society and the new cultural development thereby determined are eloquently praised by Marx:

> In a higher phase of communist society, after the enslaving subordination of individuals under division of labor, and therewith also the antithesis between mental and physical labor, has vanished, after labor has become not merely a means to live but has become itself the primary necessity of life, after the productive forces have also increased with the all-round development of the individual, and all the springs of the cooperative wealth flow more abundantly — only then can the narrow horizon of bourgeois right be fully left behind and society inscribe on its banners: From each according to his ability, to each according to his needs.[48]

44. Friedrich Engels, "On the History of Early Christianity," in *On Religion*, 317f., in a footnote.

45. Karl Marx, *The Poverty of Philosophy* (1847), in *Karl Marx: The Essential Writings*, ed. with an intro. Frederic L. Bender (New York: Harper Torchbook, 1972), 239. There is a 2nd ed. (Boulder: Westview Press, 1986). But this has in part different selections even from the same book and the original titles are difficult to find.

46. Karl Marx and Friedrich Engels, *The Manifesto of the Communist Party* (1848), in *Karl Marx*, 263.

47. For this and the following quotes, see Karl Marx, *Capital* (vol. 3), in *Karl Marx*, 429f.

48. Karl Marx, "Critique of the Gotha Program" (1875), in *Karl Marx*, 281.

What does it mean that "labor has become not merely a means to live, but has become itself the primary necessity of life"? If necessity still rules supreme, where then is the realm of freedom? Of course, if matter is the basis of life, we can only get from matter what we put into it. Though we are now agents of our own fate, fate indeed it is, because as soon as our energies cease just for one moment, whatever we have built will collapse.

To establish here and now the ideal world once envisioned in the beyond, reason is able, according to Marx, to control the material processes of life. Nature is subjected to humanity to serve humanity's needs and desires. Here nineteenth-century unbridled optimism that humanity is able to bend nature according to its desires provides the wider context for Marx's ideas. The question is not even whether nature will yield what Marx envisions for humanity, but whether humanity can really exercise that reasonable supremacy. Already Marx's notion (that in a fully developed socialism we need no institutions and no legal order since everyone cooperates freely) has been contradicted by the communist surveillance state. Furthermore, the division of labor and the overcoming of the distinction between mental and physical labor is a pipe dream, as Mao's permanent revolution indicated when university professors were sent into the fields to farm and peasants were supposed to teach.

While Marx developed a vision of paradisiacal dimensions, he forgot two essentials: when Feuerbach called religion a projection, he claimed that humanity projected on the screen of the beyond that which it could not attain in the here and now. Humanity then accorded divine attributes to that kind of deification. Yet it was exactly that ideal vision that Marx projected back on earth. Therefore he overestimated humanity and — as the Marxist revolution showed — his utopian vision ended in a catastrophe of apocalyptic dimensions. Furthermore, by disclaiming any concept of the "beyond," Marx never allowed the possibility that humanity could relax since there was no one who could provide for humanity except humanity itself. This means his vision of a realm of freedom turned into a realm of new enslavement.[49]

b. Concrete Utopia

Neo-Marxist philosopher **Ernst Bloch** (1885-1977) was born in Germany to Jewish parents and betrays an optimism about the future as Marx does. Our

---

49. For a good critique of Marx's vision, see Bienert, *Der überholte Marx*, 261-70.

journey moves irresistibly ahead toward "that secret symbol toward which our dark, seeking, difficult earth has moved since the beginning of time."[50] In his monumental work, *Das Prinzip Hoffnung (The Principle of Hope)*, written in exile from Nazi Germany in the United States, Bloch shows that the principle of hope is a universal characteristic of humanity. From the first cry of a helpless baby who wants to draw attention to its desires, to the tired old person who is waiting for eternal bliss, human existence is characterized by hope and a movement to the future. Bloch is convinced that Marxism will realize this future because its motivation and goal is nothing "but the promotion of humanity."[51] In its own way Marxism aims for the human goals of the revolutionary bourgeoisie and strives for the immanent realization of religious transcendence.

Bloch even calls Marxism the "quartermaster of the future" because it overcomes the antithesis of soberness and enthusiasm by letting both cooperate toward "exact anticipation" and "concrete utopia."[52] Unlike most abstract social utopia, the Marxist striving toward a better world is not compelled to forget the world at hand, but to transform it in a dialectical and economic way. Marxism is not mere futurism; it "takes the *fairytale* seriously" and "takes the *dream of a Golden age* practically."[53] Like Marx, Bloch contends that the comforting aspect of the Marxist worldview lies not in contemplation but in guidelines for action.

For Bloch humanizing humanity is a calculable and reachable goal, and the "unfinished world can be brought to its end."[54] Thus Bloch advocates a militant optimism and, unlike Kant, does not need a purgatory to assure the perfection of humanity. His confidence is not based on past experiences since the essential is that which is not yet but that which strives for self-realization in the core of being and expects its own genesis. Since real, objective hope provides its own foundation for Bloch, he seems to resort here to an Aristotelian first "unmoved mover" to endow the future with a direction and a hidden goal that is the same for all of humanity. It is insignificant for Bloch whether one calls this goal eternal happiness, freedom, the golden age, a land of milk and honey, or union with Christ in the resurrection. All

50. Ernst Bloch, *Thomas Müntzer als Theologe der Revolution* (Frankfurt am Main: Suhrkamp, 1969), 229.

51. Ernst Bloch, *The Principle of Hope*, 3 vols., trans. Neville Plaice et al. (Cambridge, MA: MIT Press, 1986), 3:1358.

52. Bloch, *The Principle of Hope*, 3:1368.

53. Bloch, *The Principle of Hope*, 3:1370.

54. Bloch, *The Principle of Hope*, 3:1373.

of these symbols and pictures illuminate hope and lead it to the ultimate goal that no one has yet reached and that will be our actual "homeland." *"True genesis is not at the beginning but at the end."*[55]

Bloch goes beyond the primitive projection hypothesis of Feuerbach and claims that this projection (i.e., the future), is certainly our god.[56] God is the utopian hypostasis of unknown humanity. When identity between our true humanness and our present condition is reached, we will occupy the place of God and religion will cease to exist. Consequently, Bloch has no reason to be hostile toward religion because it enlightens hope and gives hope its direction. But the metaphysical dimension of religion collapses into the physical since the future of the resurrected Christ and the future of God are the future of the hidden humanity and the hidden world. Bloch thus offers a meta-religion, *"transcending without any heavenly transcendence"* and conceiving the metaphysical as our ultimate goal in the physical.[57] Eschatology under these presuppositions becomes fictional, and we end up with a new earthly kingdom without God.[58]

Bloch is certainly right and realistic when he points to the discrepancy between our actual existence and our selfhood, between the individual and the society, and between humanity and nature, which must be overcome if we want to attain the ultimate identity we are striving for. But even if we concede to Bloch that achieving this identity is an attainable goal, we are still faced with the ultimate discrepancy between being and nothingness. Jürgen Moltmann captures this deficiency when he states:

> All utopias of the kingdom of God or of man, all hopeful pictures of the happy life, all revolutions of the future, remain hanging in the air and bear within them the germ of boredom and decay — and for that reason also adopt a militant and extortionate attitude to life — as long as there is no certainty in face of death and no hope which carries love beyond death.[59]

It is one of the bizarre tragedies of history that Karl Marx and Ernst Bloch have emerged as the leading messianic prophets in modern history of truly

---

55. Bloch, *The Principle of Hope,* 3:1375.

56. See Jürgen Moltmann, "Hope and Confidence: A Conversation with Ernst Bloch," *Dialog* 7 (1968): 43.

57. See Bloch, *The Principle of Hope,* 3:1288, in his discussion of Feuerbach.

58. See the striking title of Alfred Jäger's investigation into Bloch's eschatology: *Reich ohne Gott: Zur Eschatologie Ernst Blochs* (Zürich: EVZ-Verlag, 1969).

59. Moltmann, "Hope and Confidence," 49.

Old Testament stature and yet by denouncing the God-inspired hope that made such messianic figures possible have denied their own origin and proclaimed a new world of their own desires.[60]

c. The Right to Be Lazy

At least parenthetically we must mention here **Paul Lafargue** (1842-1911), who married Karl Marx's daughter Laura. He was a close friend of Friedrich Engels, who financially supported both him and Marx.[61] Lafargue's grandfather on his mother's side was a Jew of French nationality who had lived in Haiti, and also on his mother's side there was some French blood. To family and friends Marx initially called Lafargue "the 'gorilla,' the 'negrillo,' and the 'nigger.'"[62] Only later, after Lafargue had married Laura, did Marx call him the "African." Engels was less racially discriminatory against him. Lafargue had studied medicine, but never exercised his profession since, like Marx, he became a professional revolutionary, being the co-founder of the Spanish Socialist Party and one of the leaders of the French workers' movement.[63]

In 1883, the year in which Karl Marx died, Lafargue published a small pamphlet with the title *The Right to Be Lazy*, a refutation of the "right to work" demanded in 1848 in the *Communist Manifesto*. Initially this pamphlet was considered as satire, but Lafargue wanted to refute with it the hyper-Puritanical work ethos of the new communist movement. In *The Right to Be Lazy* he advocated the old mythical dream of a socialist paradise that could be established through the help of the new technological age and would contribute to the liberation of humanity. Lafargue first pointed to the plight of the working class during the industrial revolution. Women and children, attempting to compete with manufacturing machines,

60. Pierre Bauretz, *Witnesses to the Future: Philosophy and Messianism,* trans. Michael B. Smith (Baltimore: Johns Hopkins University Press, 2010), 462, rightly mentions the "messianic imprint" in Bloch's works.

61. For the following, including details of Lafargue's life, see Ernst Benz, *Das Recht auf Faulheit oder Die friedliche Beendigung des Klassenkampes* (Stuttgart: Ernst Klett, 1972), 13-17.

62. According to Leslie Derfler, *Paul Lafargue and the Founding of French Marxism, 1842-1882* (Cambridge, MA: Harvard University Press, 1991), 46.

63. It is interesting that Marx wanted by all means that Lafargue finish his medical studies and practice medicine instead of joining the revolutionary workers' movement. See Irving Fetscher, "Paul Lafargue," in *Paul Lafargue: Essays zur Geschichte, Kultur und Politik,* ed. Fritz Keller (Berlin: Karl Dietz, 2002), 7.

worked up to sixteen hours a day, whereas even slaves and prisoners in the West Indies worked only ten hours a day or less. While the working class had been confined to an ascetic lifestyle, the bourgeoisie had the duty of overconsumption. The produced goods were exported all over the world, yet there was still an industrial surplus. The proletariat continued the trend of being obsessed with work and "hoisted the banner, 'He who will not work Neither shall he Eat.' Lyons in 1831 rose up for bullet or work [the uprising of the silk weavers]. The federated laborers of March 1871 called their uprising 'The Revolution of Work.'"[64]

Lafargue suggested that on account of overproduction and the limited raw materials one should simply distribute work more equally "and force every workingman to content himself with five or six hours per day throughout the year instead of getting indigestion from twelve hours during six months" and then being laid off for another six months without remuneration.[65] Fewer hours of work per day, he claimed, would not slacken productivity, but perhaps even increase it. Lafargue used the United States as an example where they employed modern machinery in agriculture and as a result the workers could sit down in leisure and enjoy a pipe instead of straining their backs as French farmers did. Once the technological means are even more perfected, the working class would also have to increase its consumption of what it produces. While the proletariat wanted to be employed by the capitalists for ten hours a day in mines and factories, Lafargue claimed: "To strengthen human production it is necessary to reduce the hours of labor and multiply the pay days and the feast days."[66]

Lafargue was convinced that through modern industrial production there would be less and less need to work and therefore the lost paradise could be regained through social revolution. Yet Marxist theory, being developed in Great Britain, was much more infected by a Puritanical spirit. Work was essential for Marx, as we can see in both the *Communist Manifesto* and the *Capital*. In later communism, work heroes were highly decorated and the young Lenin who delivered a eulogy at the graveside of Lafargue became the spiritual head of that form of communism that perfected the right to work, abolished Sunday as a day of rest, introduced the gliding work week, and, through massive pressure of the party apparatus,

64. Paul Lafargue, *The Right to Be Lazy and Other Studies,* trans. Charles H. Kerr (Chicago: Charles H. Kerr, 1917), 38f.

65. Lafargue, *The Right to Be Lazy,* 44.

66. Lafargue, *The Right to Be Lazy,* 46.

made workers "voluntarily" exceed the stated production goals.[67] It is no surprise, therefore, that Ernst Bloch in his three-volume *Principle of Hope* does not even mention Lafargue and that in the official communist literature he has become a nonperson.

Lafargue himself seemed to have gradually realized that the social revolution could not regain paradise lost. Therefore he and his wife committed suicide on November 25, 1911, in their home in Paris. As church historian Ernst Benz (1907-78) wrote: "He wanted to bring the kingdom of heaven down to earth and realize it here through social revolution. Once it became clear that the programming of a perfect life on earth was unrealizable, he programmed his death and thereby forcibly pushed open the gate to another world which he thought he could negate."[68] The failure of modern utopia results from a wrong understanding of human possibilities. It erroneously assumed that humanity can be developed in any direction needed and once developed it will remain that way. Against this fallacy American theologian and social critic Reinhold Niebuhr (1892-1971) cautioned: "The utopian illusions and sentimental aberrations of modern liberal culture are really all derived from the basic error of negating the fact of original sin."[69]

3. The Impact of Religiosity

Most of the secular varieties of hope use the Judeo-Christian tradition as a negative foil against which they construct their own hope-filled futures. Yet Immanuel Kant (1724-1804) had claimed in his famous essay *What Is Enlightenment?* that human reason should seek its own way without resorting to external guidance. This demand has become especially true in contemporary religiosity.

For many centuries people relied on a priestly caste from which they expected guidance in religious matters. This situation changed drastically in the Christian West through the Reformation movement. The notion of the priesthood of all believers did away with a special priestly caste. Now the territorial princes and kings assumed ultimate responsibility for religious uniformity with the notion that there was supposedly only one religion in a

---

67. For details, see Benz, *Das Recht auf Faulheit,* 115.

68. Benz, *Das Recht auf Faulheit,* 119.

69. Reinhold Niebuhr, *The Nature and Destiny of Man,* vol. 1, *Human Nature* (New York: Charles Scribner's 1964 [1941]), 273 n. 4.

given territory. This changed in Europe in the late eighteenth century with the French Revolution when throne and altar were separated. When the New World with the nascent United States claimed its independence from Europe, a gradual disestablishment of religion took place and an unprecedented religious diversity emerged. The numerous Christian denominations were still quite homogeneous with regard to their own membership. Yet in recent years in both the United States and Europe, but also in other parts of the world, there are a growing number of people who no longer pledge allegiance to their traditional denominations and churches but assert their own religious independence. They borrow from traditional Christianity, from Asian religions, and from esoteric movements, creating their own "patchwork religion." For instance, in the larger German cities such as Frankfurt am Main only one-third of the population belongs to the mainline churches (Protestant and Roman Catholic), while another one-third has no Christian affiliation and the rest of the population has created a religion of their own liking without any church affiliation.

Adherents of this "patchwork religion" are usually not without guidance. They often rely on the authority of human leaders in a way in which most Christians refuse to pledge allegiance to their religious superiors. At the same time this new religiosity is highly individualized since one no longer carries an official church membership. Since individuals see themselves in charge of their own religion, this "patchwork religion" is characterized by an "up-beat" feeling. "A spontaneous consensus has sprung up around the evolutionary image of human potentiality."[70] The individual human being forges his or her own religion, freely borrowing from here or there and continuously looking for new insights and better solutions.[71] This vagabond guru religiosity is especially noticeable in that which is generally called the New Age movement and its varieties of eschatology.

---

70. So very perceptively Theodore Roszak, *Unfinished Animal: The Aquarian Frontier and the Evolution of Consciousness* (New York: Harper & Row, 1975), 4.

71. While this self-styled religion "is capable of enhancing the quality of lives of those participating," as Paul Heelas, *The New Age Movement: The Celebration of the Self and the Sacralization of Modernity* (Cambridge, MA: Blackwell, 1996), 213, perceptively notes, he also admits that this movement "does not score well when it comes down to *well-informed* practices."

a. A Homespun Religion

There are many roots and antecedents to this new religious movement, for instance, the Hippies, the flower children, the anti-Vietnam movement, the new left, and all that which American social critic Theodore Roszak (b. 1933) called the counterculture. It claims many significant figures as its forbears, such as Hildegard von Bingen (1098-1179), Pierre Teilhard de Chardin, and even Werner Heisenberg (1901-76). It is often referred to as the New Age movement. Dutch historian of religion Wouter J. Hanegraaff (b. 1961) distinguished three movements: New Age in a restricted sense, New Age in a general sense, and New Age in an improper sense.[72] Participants in the first movement wanted to help create a new age. The aim of the second was to create new ways of living for which Marilyn Ferguson may serve as the prime example. The third "wave" is made up of a variety of "alternative" movements and tendencies usually vaguely connected with the term "spiritual."

The New Age movement should not be confused with new religious movements such as scientology or ISKCON (International Society for Krishna Consciousness). Although it contains many diverse elements represented through its teachings and leaders, there are a remarkable consistency and organic unity in the New Age movement. This is largely due to the social and cultural milieu out of which it arose. British author Michael York (b. 1939) perceptively states:

> The New Age movements that emerged chiefly in the second half of the twentieth century constitute together an expression of the personalization of religion that has characterized modern Western spirituality in the wake of an increasing decline of institutional religious influence on social concerns, the increase of secularization as a non-religious option and the growing search for individual solace in the face of cultural uncertainties and bureaucratic hegemonies.[73]

In the wake of the weakening of traditional religious ties, people who face the uncertainties of modernity are looking for spiritual guidance in nontraditional places. We want to mention just two prominent representatives of this movement, Fritjof Capra and Marilyn Ferguson.

72. Wouter J. Hanegraaff, "The New Age Movement and the Esoteric Tradition," in *Gnosis and Hermeticism from Antiquity to Modern Times,* ed. Roelof van den Broek and Wouter J. Hanegraaff (Albany: State University of New York Press, 1998), 362f.

73. Michael York, *Historical Dictionary of New Age Movements* (Lanham, MD: Scarecrow, 2004), 1.

Fritjof Capra (b. 1939) writes: "In the seventies, the change in paradigms in California was especially propagated by humanistic psychology, the so-called Human Potential Movement and the Movement of Integral Health. Additionally there were different spiritual movements and a general strong interest in esoterics and the so-called extra-sensory or paranormal phenomena. The followers of these trends called themselves at that time the New Age Movement."[74] It is not without significance that this movement started in California, the state in the United States that enjoyed in the latter part of the twentieth century huge migrations, both from Asian countries and also from the eastern United States, and therefore was less settled in its ways. Only much later did this movement spill over to Europe as the religious hold on the general population by the established churches began to wane. In 1975 Capra claimed that with his first book, *The Tao of Physics,* he himself was at the center of the New Age movement.[75] Yet he did not use the term "New Age" after 1980, except to denote those who stayed with the spiritual mentality of the 1970s and did not participate in the widening of the social and political consciousness. This does not mean that Capra is no longer at the center of things.

In his 1996 book, *The Web of Life,* he calls for a new paradigm, deep ecology, and attempts to demonstrate the complexity and interrelatedness of the universal ecosystem that gave rise to life. "The success of the whole community depends on the success of its individual members, while the success of each member depends on the success of the community as a whole."[76] This ecological web needs to be understood and utilized for life to thrive and survive.

Most revealing is his book *Uncommon Wisdom* (1987), an autobiography in which Capra shows how, as a physicist, he was part of the Hippie movement of the late 1960s and how deeply he also was influenced by Hindu spirituality.[77] But then his 1975 bestseller, *The Tao of Physics,* appeared. There he attempted to overcome the old mechanistic worldview that he thought was expressed in Newton's universe in which there were discrete fundamental properties that remained as fixed data. "In the new world-view, the universe is seen as a dynamic web of interrelated events. None of the properties of any part of this web is fundamental; they all fol-

74. Fritjof Capra, "Die neue Sicht der Dinge," in *New Age: Kritische Anfragen an eine verlockende Bewegung,* ed. Horst Bürkle (Düsseldorf: Patmos, 1988), 15.

75. Capra, "Die neue Sicht der Dinge," 16.

76. Fritjof Capra, *The Web of Life* (New York: Doubleday Anchor Books, 1996), 298.

77. See Fritjof Capra, *Uncommon Wisdom: Conversations with Remarkable People* (New York: Simon and Schuster, 1988), 4 and 27-31.

low from the properties of the other parts, and the overall consistency of their mutual interrelations determines the structure of the entire web."[78] Already here he emphasized the universal web of life and attempted to provide a holistic and interdependent worldview. Capra sees a close affinity to Eastern mysticism in which the laws are embedded in nature, but are not decreed by a divine lawgiver.[79] Therefore, as evidenced in the title of his book, *The Tao of Physics,* Capra sees in science and mysticism two mutually complementary manifestations of the human spirit, the rational and the intuitive. The extreme specialization of rational comprehension is complemented by an extreme sharpening of intuitive awareness.

Capra's emphasis on a new paradigm, on a turning point, and on immediately threatening catastrophes reminds us of an apocalyptic view of the end-time.[80] Over against this a new age is dawning. In his book *The Turning Point* (1982) Capra points to a crisis in perception since we live in a poisoned environment and other ecological catastrophes, in an arising flood of violence and crime, in an energy crisis, in a crisis of health care, and so forth.[81] Therefore we need a new paradigm, a new view of reality, and a fundamental change in perception and values. With reference to systems theory, the theory of evolution, and anthropology, Capra sketches out a system that concentrates on a dynamic of self-transcendence that allows us to understand biological, societal, cultural, and cosmic evolution as stemming from the same model of systems dynamics even if the different kinds of evolution presuppose very different mechanisms.[82] The emergence of the spirit is seen in close connection to the properties of self-organizing systems and it is an essential property of living systems, but it is not something that stands over against the material.[83] Capra sees in Teilhard de Chardin a mystic who comes closest to this new idea of systems biology since for him, too, evolution ascends

---

78. Fritjof Capra, *The Tao of Physics: An Exploration of the Parallels Between Modern Physics and Eastern Mysticism,* 2nd rev. ed. (New York: Bantam, 1988), 276.

79. See Capra, *The Tao of Physics,* 279.

80. See Christoph Bochinger in his comprehensive study *"New Age" und moderne Religion: Religionswissenschaftliche Analysen* (Gütersloh: Chr. Kaiser/Gütersloher Verlagshaus, 1994), 453, who points out the analogy to apocalypticism.

81. See Fritjof Capra, *The Turning Point: Science, Society, and the Rising Culture* (New York: Simon and Schuster, 1982), 15, where he lists various threatening phenomena and calls for a radically new way of perception and action.

82. See Capra, *The Turning Point,* 265.

83. See Capra, *The Turning Point,* 285f.

to increasing complexity and thereby to an increase in consciousness and human spirituality.[84]

Over against a surface ecology, Capra calls for a deeper ecology that understands the transcending human spirit:

> as the mode of consciousness in which the individual feels connected to the cosmos as a whole, it becomes clear that ecological awareness is truly spiritual. Indeed, the idea of the individual being linked to the cosmos is expressed in the Latin root of the word religion, *religare* ("to bind strongly"), as well as in the Sanskrit *yoga,* which means union.[85]

By obtaining this new understanding that we are connected to the whole universe and that the human spirit is not just the center but the pinnacle of an evolutionary movement, we are ascending to new heights and are leaving the trivia of the old world behind us.

Capra has moved from physics to religion, and from research in physics to writing bestsellers. Now earning his living mainly from the lecture circuit and teaching at his Center for Ecoliteracy in Berkeley, California, he calls for a change of paradigms to save humanity from self-destruction and from destroying the world in which we live. Capra is not the only voice. There are many other interpreters who have secular qualifications but mediate religious content to an audience that no longer seems to listen to professional theologians and church dignitaries. It prefers those who come from a very different field and still find religion significant. "The best qualification for the credibility of a 'religious mediator' in the free religious scene is, therefore, his or her descent from a sector . . . that is as remote from 'religion' as possible: If a physicist deals with 'religion,' then there 'must something be to it.'"[86]

Another important interpreter is **Marilyn Ferguson** (b. 1938) for whose book *The Aquarian Conspiracy* (1980) Capra wrote the preface. In a 1973 book on *The Brain Revolution* one could already see that Ferguson was not entranced with technological possibilities such as cloning, organ transplants, and guaranteeing probable IQs. Instead, she followed the lead of William James (1842-1910), Carl Jung (1875-1961), and Teilhard de Chardin that there is a good chance of "emerging from relative unconsciousness into the fuller

84. See Capra, *The Turning Point,* 303f.

85. Capra, *The Turning Point,* 412.

86. So very correctly with significant details Bochinger, *"New Age" und moderne Religion,* 511.

awareness."[87] This could also result in psychic self-healing whether through meditation, autogenic training, or relaxation-visualization techniques. Instead of engineering larger human brains we should use what we already have since the brain can take us wherever we might want to go.

> The human brain, that "perfect instrument," that "fabulous electronic dance," can be our open sesame to an infinitely richer life than we have believed possible. The fluent, liberating, creative, healing attributes of the altered states can be incorporated into consciousness. We are just beginning to realize that we can truly open the doors of perception and creep out of the cavern.[88]

Ferguson is opting for human self-development, not in terms of using super-technology but by self-evolving to new heights, new experience, and new wholeness. This was masterfully expressed in her "cult book," *The Aquarian Conspiracy*.[89]

In the preface Capra lauds Ferguson for being a leading figure in establishing networks among individuals and groups.[90] Ferguson claims that though she is ignorant in astrology, she has been enthralled by the symbolic content of a pervasive dream in our culture, the thought that after a dark and violent "era of the pisces," an era of love and light is appearing, as is described in the well-known song from the musical *Hair*, which speaks of "harmony and understanding" and "the mind's true liberation" in the age of Aquarius.[91] The "age of the pisces," which is connected with the names of René Descartes and Isaac Newton (1642-1727), is the time of the big dualisms that ultimately led to all the crises of the present.

Inescapably the new age is dawning and has the trademark of a new consciousness through which the rescue of our world is made possible.[92] It

87. Marilyn Ferguson, *The Brain Revolution: The Frontiers of Mind Research* (New York: Taplinger, 1973), 337.

88. Ferguson, *The Brain Revolution,* 344.

89. On the back cover of Marilyn Ferguson, *The Aquarian Conspiracy,* with a new afterword and an updated resource list, foreword John Naisbitt (Los Angeles: J. Tarcher, 1987), the book description states: "*The Aquarian Conspiracy,* which *USA Today* called the handbook of the New Age."

90. See Fritjof Capra, "Preface," in Marilyn Ferguson, *The Aquarian Conspiracy* (Los Angeles: J. Tarcher, 1980), 14.

91. See Ferguson, *The Aquarian Conspiracy* (1987), 19, where she also refers to the theme song of the Aquarian Age.

92. For a good description of this new consciousness, see Medard Kehl, *New Age oder Neuer Bund?* (Mainz: Matthias Grünewald, 1988), 22.

consists in the knowledge of a universal unity and wholeness of God and the world, spirit and matter, humanity and nature, body and soul, I and you. Everything is interconnected and forms a big web of being. This wholeness and interdisciplinary thinking that has been successful in medicine, psychology, and biology will, according to the New Agers, be all-pervasive and will replace analytical thought. There is a powerful network operating that will bring radical change in the world. "This network is the Aquarian conspiracy."[93] Like a big earthquake it irrevocably comes toward us and, according to Ferguson, it is neither a new political, nor a religious, nor a philosophical system. There is a new spirit that allows us to break through the old limitations and opens up a richness of choice, freedom, and human interconnectedness. "You can be more productive, confident, comfortable with insecurity. Problems can be experienced as challenges, a chance for renewal, rather than stress. Habitual defensiveness and worry can fall away. *It all can be otherwise.*"

Ferguson refers to Thomas S. Kuhn (1922-96) and his book *The Structure of Scientific Revolutions* (1962), in which Kuhn showed that scientific revolutions are brought about by changes in paradigms. Such a revolution is now coming because the paradigm of conspiracy in the sign of Aquarius regards humanity as embedded in nature. We are no longer victims limited by conditions, but heirs of evolutionary riches and capable of imagination, invention, and experience that up until now we have hardly visualized. "Human nature is neither good nor bad, but open for continuous transformation and transcendence. It has only to discover itself."[94] We are noting here a central tenet of the new kind of thinking that serves as a precondition for continuous transformation and transcendence toward the new and better. Human nature is indefinitely malleable, neither tainted by original sin and sinful inclinations, nor already good in and of itself.

It is not surprising that theologians are cautious. Ted Peters (b. 1941) says, for example, "I have come to believe that the overall Gnostic thrust of the new age is a big mistake. It leads to a naive and excessively innocent view of reality. It fails to acknowledge the strength of the powers of destruction and evil that are at work in the cosmos and in our own personalities."[95] Exactly this kind of innocence allows us to reach for new heights and insights,

93. For this and the following quote, see Ferguson, *The Aquarian Conspiracy* (1987), 23f.

94. Ferguson, *The Aquarian Conspiracy* (1987), 29.

95. Ted Peters, *The Cosmic Self: A Penetrating Look at Today's New Age Movements* (San Francisco: Harper, 1991), 91.

and forms the basic presupposition for the dawning of the new age. In typical apocalyptic fashion we are told that we are at the eve of a new age, "the age of an open world, an age of renewal in which the fresh release of spiritual energy in the world culture may unleash new possibilities."[96] Referring again to Teilhard, the suggestion is made that a wider consciousness will be kindled, and humanity will regain the sublimation of the spiritual-sensual love as a new source of energy.[97] Omitted, however, is Teilhard's insight that it is not the crowding together of humanity that will warm the human heart but the Spirit of God that in an incarnate form is already at work in the world. Yet for Ferguson it is exactly the crowding together that makes the difference when she claims: "Rich as we are — together — we can do anything. We have it within our power to make peace within our torn selves and with each other, to heal our homeland, the Whole Earth."[98]

We do not live from the past but toward the future. As Ferguson states at the end of her comprehensive treatise, "Our past is not our potential. In any hour, with all the stubborn teachers and healers of history who called us to our best selves, we can liberate the future. One by one can we re-choose to awaken. To leave the prison of our conditioning, to love, to turn homeward. To conspire with each other and for each other."[99] We need teachers like Capra and Ferguson who can draw things together and who tell us that we have lived the wrong way and have understood things the wrong way. They appeal to a new way of seeing things and teach us that history can come out all right. All our problems and anxieties can be overcome. We have the potential not only for a new chapter in world history, but for a totally new age. Against modern skepticism and frequent doomsday scenarios, the present beginning age of Aquarius will provide rescue and salvation from the global crises, deliverance from personal crises and from everything that is threatening to us.[100] People like to hear the optimistic perspective that is found in New Age literature. The world, including each individual being, can be changed toward the good and toward salvation. This kind of thinking can be understood as a replacement for or even a perfection of the Christian promise of salvation. It can be regarded as *the* comprehensive world religion that brings us to a new age and a new future.

96. So Ferguson, *The Aquarian Conspiracy* (1987), 42, with reference to Lewis Mumford.

97. See Ferguson, *The Aquarian Conspiracy* (1987), 403.

98. Ferguson, *The Aquarian Conspiracy* (1987), 406.

99. Ferguson, *The Aquarian Conspiracy* (1987), 417.

100. For the following, see very perceptively Kehl, *New Age oder Neuer Bund?* 21f.

A central aspect of New Age religion is the belief in "paranormal" realities that can be freely accessed by human beings. There are a variety of means by which we obtain insight into our own selves and into the essence of things through the "contact with spirit guides, channeling, use of crystals, and interpretation of the legacy of past cultures."[101] Important are teachers of wisdom and persuasive personalities in whom one has unconditional confidence and who promise to lead their followers to a new future. Many of these various techniques and insights can be subsumed under the term "esoterics," which is basically a primal knowledge toward completion. We learn here, for instance, that the spirit is of prime importance, that matter is often regarded as secondary, and that if we employ the right techniques and have the appropriate insights we can secure for ourselves and the world around us a new and promising future.

The access to new realities can be obtained through altered states of consciousness at which we arrive through certain spiritual techniques or which can also appear spontaneously. There is a "remarkable similarity between these 'worlds of the mind' or 'inner realms,' on the one hand, and the realities which the soul is believed to enter after physical death, on the other."[102] This means that heaven can already be experienced on this earth. Therefore the world we believe in as our destiny must have a reality since it is already a present experience and not simply subjective fantasy. There is even a strong suggestion that present and future are one and the same. The next world is very much like the world to which we are accustomed though it is much more beautiful. There is an unresolved tension, however, with regard to the structure of this new world. On the one hand there will be a unified consciousness as the final goal of evolution, and on the other hand there exists an unlimited creative "unfolding." This corresponds on the one hand to the return to unity, and on the other hand is more influenced by evolutionary thought, that is, an unlimited cosmic expansion.[103]

It is a natural assumption of the New Agers that at the end of the journey there is reincarnation. While reincarnation is largely taken for granted

101. So Michael York, *The Emerging Network: A Sociology of the New Age and Neo-Pagan Movements* (Lanham, MD: Rowman & Littlefield, 1995), 36, who also mentions the social and spiritual dimensions of the New Age movement in relation to the occult aspect.

102. This is claimed by Wouter J. Hanegraaff, *New Age Religion and Western Culture: Esotericism in the Mirror of Secular Thought* (Albany: State University of New York Press, 1998), 259, in his comprehensive and insightful study.

103. See Hanegraaff, *New Age Religion and Western Culture*, 261, who calls these two strands "monistic pathos" and "evolutionary pathos."

as a universal element in New Age ideas, it is believed to be only a part of a *"progressive spiritual evolution . . .* which started before birth and will continue beyond death."[104] This means it is a crucial part of a larger process that is purported to be logical and rationally consistent with the prospect of life after death. In this kind of development it is seen as superior to the traditional Judeo-Christian belief in one final future reconstitution of dead bodies, meaning the resurrection. The spirit or the soul will survive bodily death and move forward to a new unfolding. Reincarnation also provides the foundation for a rational ethics because the uneven distribution of earthly goods and talents, happiness or suffering, is balanced out in another life. Particularly in combination with the belief in *karma* (i.e., the sum total of our present life) reincarnation is a mechanism that guarantees ultimate cosmic justice. Through reincarnation we do not just have one single life on earth that is then followed by eternal life in heaven or hell, as Christians teach, but there are always new beginnings and new advancements.

Often it is unclear whether there is a continuation of one's ego in another life or whether only one's real individuality is to survive death and provide the link of continuity between this life and former or future lives. There may also be just a succession of lives or realities of one's real individuality so that one's own spiritual evolution is furthered.[105] If there is so little emphasis on the ego and so much value accorded to interconnectedness and the web of life, the individual does not count much in the life hereafter. Only the true self is important, but even that must be seen in the context of the larger picture.

We encounter here a connection to some kind of Gnostic spirituality. The Gnostic salvation myth starts with the insight that we are entangled in the negativity of the present world.[106] Therefore an ambassador of the heavenly region must address us, reminding us that we are aliens in this world. Through this knowledge we are lifted out of our forgetfulness concerning our true higher origin and destiny. Recognizing our heavenly image and becoming one with it, we are led by our guide on the journey to a new and, at the same time, original future. In the end we return from estrangement to

---

104. So Hanegraaff, *New Age Religion and Western Culture,* 262.

105. See Hanegraaff, *New Age Religion and Western Culture,* 267, who points to the ambiguous assertions of what is actually continued beyond death.

106. See Hans-Jürgen Ruppert, *Durchbruch zur Innenwelt: Spirituelle Impulse aus New Age und Esoterik in kritischer Beleuchtung* (Stuttgart: Quell, 1988), 105f., who draws here the parallel between the Gnostic Song of the Pearl and the esoteric understanding of salvation in the New Age movement.

the place from which we originated. In order to arrive at our eternal destination, we cannot be bothered with insights from this world. We have our own guides who tell us with certainty what is true and right. Our consciousness is not just enlarged. It is intensified so that we regain the original archaic unity of humanity and the world and live in a continuous, undivided presence of the whole of the world and its origin. Living in the spirit is living in the present, not in the past or in the future, but it is a life outside of time according to life's real essence and its eternal principle.

These ideas show no sensitivity to human depravity, the need for God's undeserved grace, and a redeemer figure who demonstrates undivided solidarity with us. As Immanuel Kant claimed in his essay *What Is Enlightenment?* and as we have seen with other figures, such as Gotthold Lessing and even Karl Marx, who were imbued with the Enlightenment spirit, given the right insight we have enough potential to bring ourselves not just to new heights but to a new world. We can save ourselves. Indeed, the Enlightenment spirit has made possible immense progress. But also the most abominable atrocities in the history of humanity have been committed during the last 200 years. So we wonder whether humanity can really be its own savior. Perhaps we should heed Martin Luther's insight: he claimed that as little as we are our own creator, we can also not be our own savior.

The New Agers, however, believe otherwise. In his characterization of the New Age movement British sociologist Steve Bruce (b. 1954) states as his first point: "There is the belief that the self is divine."[107] Since the distinction between God and the created is collapsed, we can be our own redeemer. Second, "The New Agers are holistic." There is just one single essence and no fundamental distinction between body and spirit. We should heed our environment since we and our planet are deeply spiritual. Third, "there is no higher authority than the individual self." If something works for me then it is true and the same is conceded to everyone else. We will notice this conviction again in postmodernism. But this point also leads to a fourth one, "Eclecticism. As we differ in class, in gender, in age, in regional background, in culture, we will have different notions of what works for us." We can borrow from whatever sources are available.

But when we hear of T'ai Chi, Reiki and Feng Shui, reflexology, aroma therapy, and post-life regression, to name just a few New Age practices, we

---

107. Steve Bruce, "The New Age and Secularism," in *Beyond the New Age: Exploring Alternative Spirituality,* ed. Steven Sutcliffe and Marion Bowman (Edinburgh: Edinburgh University Press, 2000), 227, who gives these four characteristics.

wonder whether the movement does not have strong Neo-pagan leanings. Yet it borrows just as freely from Christian sources as from non-Christian sources. By contrast Neo-pagan cults or movements generally exhibit much less "of an overlap or compatibility with Christianity."[108] Still it is difficult to keep the two apart. They are new and non-Christian ways to help people cope with their own problems and those of modernity. Since they are new and have no long track record, they are often more attractive than the "old-time religion" of the Christian faith.

b. The Ambivalence of Secular Humanism

While representatives of the New Age movement do not want to confine themselves to the material base of life, *secular humanists* accept a worldview of philosophy called naturalism, in which the physical laws of the universe are not superseded by nonmaterial or supernatural entities, such as demons, gods, or other "spiritual" beings outside the realm of the natural universe. They show a commitment to the use of critical reason, factual evidence, and scientific methods of inquiry rather than faith and mysticism. But like New Age representatives their primary concern is with fulfillment, growth, and creativity for both the individual and humanity in general. They are also convinced that progress can be made in building a better world for ourselves and our children. Secular humanists describe themselves as atheist or agnostic and do not rely on gods or other supernatural forces to solve their problems or to provide guidance for their conduct.

c. Faith in Human Reason (Humanist Manifestos I and II)

In 1933, the same year Adolf Hitler (1889-1945) came to power in Germany, a group of thirty-four liberal humanists in the United States defined and enunciated the philosophical and religious principles that seemed fundamental to them. They drafted the *Humanist Manifesto I,* which for its time was a radical document and portrayed a thoroughgoing rationalistic approach to the world. Thesis 1 sets the tone when it declares: "Religious humanists regard the universe as self-existing and not created."[109] According

108. So York, *The Emerging Network,* 128, who tries hard to show the difference between the two movements.

109. *Humanist Manifestos I and II,* ed. Paul Kurtz (Buffalo, NY: Prometheus Books,

to the *Manifesto,* the nature of the universe depicted by modern science "makes unacceptable any supernatural or cosmic guarantees of human values."[110] Forty years later the *Humanist Manifesto II* is even more explicit when it states that "humans are responsible for what we are or will become. No deity will save us; we must save ourselves."[111] Thus we were told in 1933 that "man will learn to face the crises of life in terms of his knowledge of their naturalness and probability. Reasonable and manly attitudes will be fostered by education and supported by custom."[112] This faith in education and reason was expressed at the same time that Hitler was indoctrinating the Germans about the superiority of the Nordic race and the necessity of eliminating the Jews.

The *Humanist Manifesto I* was updated in 1973. **Paul Kurtz** (b. 1925), an American professor of philosophy and one of the leaders of the humanist movement, who drafted the update admitted in the preface that events since 1933 "make that earlier statement seem far too optimistic. Nazism has shown the depths of brutality of which humanity is capable. Other totalitarian regimes have suppressed human rights without ending poverty. Science has sometimes brought evil as well as good. Recent decades have shown that inhuman wars can be made in the name of peace."[113] Yet we are still assured that we are reasonable beings and have no need of religion since it would only divert people "with false hopes of heaven hereafter."[114] But the optimistic note still prevailing is now coupled to caution when we are told that the future is filled with dangers and that "reason must be tempered by humility."[115] Still there is no doubt that "human life has meaning because we create and develop our futures."[116] In secular humanism technology assumes salvific dimensions:

1973), 8. For a good introduction to the problematic nature of the secular humanistic approach to the future, see Ted Peters, *Futures — Human and Divine* (Atlanta: John Knox, 1978), 134-49, where he also examines the *Humanist Manifestos I and II* (137f.).

110. *Humanist Manifestos I and II,* 8.

111. *Humanist Manifestos I and II,* 16.

112. *Humanist Manifestos I and II,* 9.

113. *Humanist Manifestos I and II,* 13. Kurtz was editor of *The Humanist* from 1967 to 1977 and drafted *Humanist Manifesto II* in 1973 (reprinted in *In Defense of Secular Humanism* [Buffalo: Prometheus, 1983], 39-47); see Vern L. Bullough, "Foreword" to *Toward a New Enlightenment: The Philosophy of Paul Kurtz* by Paul Kurtz, ed. with an intro. Vern L. Bullough and Timothy J. Madigan (New Brunswick, NJ: Transaction, 1994), ix.

114. *Humanist Manifestos I and II,* 13.

115. *Humanist Manifestos I and II,* 17.

116. *Humanist Manifestos I and II,* 17.

Using technology wisely, we can control our environment, conquer poverty, markedly reduce disease, extend our life-span, significantly modify our behavior, alter the course of human evolution and cultural development, unlock vast new powers, and provide humankind with unparalleled opportunity for achieving an abundant and meaningful life.[117]

It seems ironic that this faith in "achieving abundant life" was expressed on the eve of the first Arab oil embargo against the Western countries, an action that sent economic shock waves around the globe.

This document, however, was not quite as convinced of its own optimistic predictions concerning the future as it might sound. That is especially noticeable in the closing comments on "humanity as a whole" when it interchanges quite frequently indicative statements and imperative demands. We are urged to use reason and compassion to produce the kind of world we want, a world in which peace, prosperity, freedom, and happiness are widely shared.

> Let us not abandon that vision in despair or cowardice. We are responsible for what we are or will be. Let us work together for a humane world by means commensurate with humane ends. Destructive ideological differences among communism, capitalism, socialism, conservatism, liberalism, and radicalism should be overcome. Let us call for an end to terror and hatred. We will survive and prosper only in a world of shared humane values. We can initiate new directions for humankind.[118]

While we certainly agree with the goals envisioned and may join secular humanists in pursuing them, we cannot but remain skeptical about their basis for attaining such goals and about humanity's power to achieve them. Even if we disregarded our finitude, could we ever assume that there is a basis for hope if we trust in ourselves as the grantors of the future? While we cannot afford the luxury of despair, it is historically wrong to join with the *Humanist Manifestos* in blaming traditional religion for the stifling of human initiative. Humanity's enterprising and progressive spirit is intimately connected with the Judeo-Christian tradition. Yet precisely when this spirit has been left to itself, when reason becomes the sole court of appeal, it turns against humanity itself. From the French Revolution (1789) to the Russian Revolution (1917), with many revolutions in between and since then, all too

---

117. *Humanist Manifestos I and II*, 14.
118. *Humanist Manifestos I and II*, 23.

often the achievement of humanistic revolutionary ends has been replaced with permanent terror. Thus, the big unresolved question remains: who should educate, or at least guide, the educators (or revolutionaries)? If there are no metaphysical values left, we are thrown back to our own instincts, which quite often means our own selfishness.

d. Humanist Manifesto 2000

The Humanist Manifesto II was not the final appeal for secular humanism. In 1980 there came *A Secular Humanist Declaration* to counteract right-wing and fundamentalist religious attacks, and in 1988 the International Academy of Humanism "offered *A Declaration of Interdependence* calling for a new global ethics and the building of a world community."[119] Finally, at the turn of the millennium there appeared the *Humanist Manifesto 2000*. It referred to the collapse of the Soviet Union and the end of the Cold War. Though it mentioned the serious problems of global warming, the rise of terrorism, and widespread poverty, it claimed again triumphantly: "For the first time in human history we possess the means — provided by science and technology — to ameliorate the human condition, advance happiness and freedom, and enhance human life for *all* people on the planet."[120] To that effect they propose *A Planetary Bill of Rights and Responsibilities* and call for developing global institutions to address our global problems. Important are thereby "free market initiatives" and a scientific naturalism that excludes "occult causes or transcendent explanations."[121] Again, humanity is supposed to save itself by employing scientific reasoning. The *Manifesto* forgets, however, that scientists increasingly encounter issues of value that call for non-scientific reflection. Here the synthetic approach of the New Agers is more realistic in allowing for a spiritual dimension of humanity.

Yet the deep-seated optimism about our own potential cannot be so easily discarded. Until very recently, and despite ethnic and class revolts in many countries and occasional shortages of energy and material resources, the overall picture in the Western world has remained one of optimism. German existentialist philosopher Karl Jaspers (1883-1969) summed up this

---

119. *Humanist Manifesto 2000: Call for a New Planetary Humanism,* drafted by Paul Kurtz (Amherst, NJ: Prometheus Books, 2000), 11.

120. *Humanist Manifesto 2000,* 13.

121. *Humanist Manifesto 2000,* 40 and 24.

sentiment well when he claimed that we are always capable of doing more and other things than anyone expected. Our future is never sealed. But he dampened this optimism considerably when he wrote these words in the same essay on "Premises and Possibilities of a New Humanism":

> Civilizations have perished before. What is new today is that all of mankind is threatened, that the menace is more acute and more conscious, and that it does not only affect our lives and property but our very humanity. If we consider the ephemeral nature of all undertakings, our way of living under a stay of execution, we feel as though anything we might do now would be senseless in the future.[122]

e. A Modest Assessment of the Future

Even Paul Kurtz himself and those who follow his lead sometimes seem quite ambivalent about the prospects of the future. Since there is no evidence that life which is characterized by the processes of metabolism, growth, and reproduction can survive the death of the organism, it is questionable for Kurtz whether consciousness, the "self" or the "body," can survive in some discarnate form and whether we can reify psychological functions. Even so-called near-death experiences are of no help at this point.[123] Of course, a person's descendants who carry his or her genetic endowment and his or her accomplishments may have an influence on society or culture for a period of time. Yet it is clear for Kurtz:

> The humanist considers the doctrine of immortality to be basically unrealistic and even morbid. It grows out of both fear of and fascination with death.... This mood of denial expresses a basic lack of courage to persist in the face of adversity. Immortality is a symbol of our agony before an unyielding universe and our hope for some future deliverance.[124]

The key to humanist virtue is existential courage.

Contrary to secular existentialists, it is not enough to merely survive in the face of adversity. Secular humanists do not accept the status quo. They

122. Karl Jaspers, *Existentialism and Humanism: Three Essays,* ed. Hanns E. Fischer, trans. E. B. Ashton (New York: Russell F. Moore, 1952), 83.

123. Paul Kurtz, "Near-Death Experiences: A Skeptical View," in *Toward a New Enlightenment,* 349.

124. See Paul Kurtz, *The Transcendental Temptation: A Critique of Religion and the Paranormal* (Buffalo, NY: Prometheus Books, 1986), 415f., for this quote and the following.

are summoned to remake their lives constantly in spite of all the forces of nature and society that seek to overwhelm them. "The humanist is not content with simply discovering and accepting the universe for what it is, in an act of piety; he seeks to *change* it. Nor is the task of life to discover what our nature is (whether God-given or not) and to realize it, but to *exceed* our nature." The task before secular humanists is twofold: analytical and transformative. Life again is seen as an opportunity that can be grasped and changed toward the better.

As individuals secular humanists are aware of their interrelatedness with each other. It is important that a human being continually unfolds his or her selfhood in the community and continually strives to become human.[125] This also means self-actualization of the person in the quest for the good life. Kurtz has called this approach "eupraxophy," meaning a good way of doing things.[126]

> Self-actualizing people are gratified in all their basic needs embracing affection, respect, and self-esteem. They have a feeling of belongingness and rootedness. They are satisfied in their love needs because they have friends, feel loved and love-worthy. They have status, place in life, and respect for other people, and they have a reasonable feeling of worth and self-respect.[127]

Modern humanists hold that the shaping of humanity lies in our own hands. Our self-determination in connectedness with others can both enrich personal existence and provide a directive for association with others. Humans live in community and human achievement depends on social culture. There is progress in freedom of choice, and this freedom is naturally connected with justice as equity of choice.[128]

In this development and progress, evil, sorrow, and death are not de-

125. See Khoren Arisian, "Ethics and Humanist Imagination," in *The Humanist Alternative: Some Definitions of Humanism,* ed. Paul Kurtz (Buffalo, NY: Prometheus Books, 1973), 172.

126. See Paul Kurtz, "In Defense of Eupraxophy," in *Toward a New Enlightenment,* 276.

127. A. H. Maslow, "The Good Life of the Self-Actualizing Person," in *Moral Problems in Contemporary Society: Essays in Humanistic Ethics,* ed. Paul Kurtz (Englewood Cliffs, NJ: Prentice-Hall, 1969), 67.

128. See J. van Praag, "The Humanist Outlook," in *A Catholic Humanist Dialogue: Humanists and Roman Catholics in a Common World,* ed. Paul Kurtz and Albert Dondeyne (Buffalo, NY: Prometheus Books, 1972), 8.

nied since they are the natural dark sides of our aspirations. Yet modern science has made it possible for the continued introduction of novel and unexpected dimensions of explanation and understanding in the world around us and also in our psychological behavior and our social and cultural institutions. Progress of science, however, has its pluses and minuses. We therefore face a crisis unprecedented in human history because having discovered the key to a rich and bountiful life we find in the very process of our emancipation new forms of enslavement and destruction. But we cannot retreat to ignorance. We can only move forward. Even Paul Tillich's "courage to be" is invoked since "what is clear is that he [modern humanity] cannot afford the luxury of delay. For issues press in on him, and the terrible problems he faces will not wait for him to catch up to them. For the scientific humanist the option is clear. We should not retreat from scientific intelligence, but extend its range."[129] The reason for this optimism is also evident. For the first time the technological revolution allows us to develop a world community and to have a new global moral vision.

The vision of secular humanists is focused on this earth and not on heaven. In this respect they are quite optimistic: "Given dependence on intelligence and willingness to use our powers to solve our problems, human beings can still be saved in this life and we can discover and create a rich and meaningful existence. If we are to be saved, however, it is only by using our own resources, believing in *Man*, not depending upon overbelief, faith or mystery."[130] For secular humanists it is not sufficient just to reject religious beliefs but to put in their place "humanist values and principles, which have been tested by human experience."[131] For instance, in the face of global warming the basic human imperative is "to strive to preserve the natural ecology of this planet." While we generally agree with this tenet, we wonder what "natural ecology" means. There is hardly any place on this planet where there is a natural ecology. It has all, in some way or other, already been modified by human civilization. Moreover, we have seen especially in terms of global warming, how national and industrial interests will militate against what others see as wholly mandated by reason. Here Martin Luther was right when he quipped that though human reason is a gift of God, it

---

129. Paul Kurtz, "Crisis Humanology," in *A Catholic Humanist Dialogue,* ed. Kurtz and Dondeyne, 52.

130. Kurtz, "Crisis Humanology," 58.

131. Paul Kurtz, *Multi-Secularism: A New Agenda* (New Brunswick, NJ: Transaction Publishers, 2010), 135.

can also be a whore going to the highest bidder. But secular humanists are optimistic and shun ambiguity.

They also know that "men cannot live without hope. Men cannot live without faith. Hope has to do with the sense that something better is possible."[132] Yet how can such hope be engendered and such faith be maintained if, at the same time, humanism "does not hold that man is perfect or perfectible"? It even concedes that no one who has ever lived has lived a perfect life nor will such occur in the future. Therefore the sober admission: "Perhaps it is man's fate to strive even though he knows that he will never fulfill his dream of self and his dream of society."

What has been accomplished after so much effort, after so much pulling on one's own boot straps? The dream of a good life may never become reality. Ultimately, it is a sober estimate that secular humanists provide, without pretentiousness and usually without undue claims. At the same time there is very little actual hope. We are thrown in on ourselves and the possibilities we have. Actual hope does not come from us or the world we live in. At the most, we can somewhat improve it. If there is hope, it must come from beyond, from outside ourselves and our environment, from the one who created and sustains us.

f. The Postmodern Turn

While secular humanists emphasize that insight gained through natural reason is an unfailing instrument to obtain truth, postmodern thought asserts an emphatic relativism in all spheres of knowledge and value. Postmodernism focuses on a tendency in contemporary culture characterized by the problem of objective truth and inherent suspicion toward global cultural narrative or meta-narrative. It involves the belief that many, if not all, apparent realities are only social constructs, as they are subject to change inherent to time and place. Postmodernism has been primarily advanced by French philosophers such as Michel Foucault (1926-84), Jacques Derrida (1930-2004), and **Jean-François Lyotard** (1924-98). The term "postmodernism" became prominent with Lyotard's 1979 publication of *The Postmodern Condition: A Report on Knowledge* (English trans. 1984).

Lyotard defines "*postmodern* as incredulity toward meta-narratives.

---

132. Algernon D. Black, "Our Quest for Faith: Is Humanism Enough?" in *The Humanist Alternative,* ed. Kurtz; for this and the following quotes see 75, 76, and 77 respectively.

This incredulity is undoubtedly a product of progress in science: but that progress in turn presupposes it."[133] As Lyotard points out, science has sought to distinguish itself from narrative knowledge communicated through myths and legends. Science, however, requires that one language game, that of denotation, be retained to the exclusion of all others.[134] It displaces narrative knowledge, including the meta-narratives of philosophy. This is due, in part, to what Lyotard characterizes as the rapid growth of techniques and technologies in the second half of the twentieth century, where the emphasis on knowledge has shifted "from the ends of action to its means," with the emphasis on material prosperity.[135] As a result, new, hybrid disciplines develop without connection to old epistemic traditions, especially philosophy, and this means that science too only plays its own game and cannot legitimate others, such as moral prescription.

Inventing new codes and reshaping information is a large part of the production of knowledge, and in its inventive moment science does not adhere to performative efficiency. By the same token, the meta-prescriptives of science, its rules, are themselves objects of invention and experimentation for the sake of producing new statements. In this respect, says Lyotard, the model of knowledge as the progressive development of "consensus has become an outmoded and suspect value."[136] In fact, attempts to retrieve the model of consensus can only repeat the standard of coherence demanded for functional efficiency.

The compartmentalization of knowledge and the dissolution of epistemic coherence are a concern for researchers and philosophers alike. As Lyotard notes, "lamenting the 'loss of meaning' in postmodernity boils down to mourning the fact that knowledge is no longer principally narrative."[137] Knowledge is so diversified that there is no unity and therefore no master narrative by which one can orient oneself. This also has drastic consequences for theology. "The postmodern denial of a master narrative refuses the privileging of any particular revelations or metaphysical formulations that reside outside the textual experience."[138] This means there is no

---

133. Jean-François Lyotard, *The Postmodern Condition: A Report on Knowledge,* trans. Geoff Bennington and Brian Massumi, foreword Frederic Jameson (Minneapolis: University of Minnesota Press, 1993), xxiii.

134. See Lyotard, *The Postmodern Condition,* 25.

135. Lyotard, *The Postmodern Condition,* 37.

136. Lyotard, *The Postmodern Condition,* 66.

137. Lyotard, *The Postmodern Condition,* 26.

138. Charles Winquist, "Theology," in *Encyclopedia of Postmodernism,* ed. Victor E. Taylor and Charles E. Winquist (London: Routledge, 2001), 399f.

universal authority but only relative authorities. In the case of theology they are tied to textual experience. Anything beyond the text is covered with silence.

Postmodernism radically questions the grounds on which knowledge claims are made. There are no longer universals since they deny cultural and historical differences. History is no longer a description of the way things really were. Though there is a residual factuality, history could always have been written otherwise. It reflects to a large extent the writer and his or her preferences. Of course, postmodern relativity has invited severe criticism. German philosopher Jürgen Habermas (b. 1929), for instance, agrees with the postmodernists that the Western patterns of communication have had a colonizing effect, especially since they are often accompanied by material and symbolic goods. One may take Windows and McDonalds as examples. Yet Habermas reminds the postmodernists that "not only by Western standards are Western science and technology convincing and successful."[139] From the fact that often universal discourses have served as the medium of social, political, epistemic, and cultural violence it does not follow that a universal discourse is a priori suspect.

We also agree with Habermas that we cannot dispense with the employment of reason to construct that which we perceive as reality. At the same time we must be aware that we are always children of our own time and culture and dare not claim universal validity for our insights. Yet scientific progress has been characterized by reformulating old insights on account of new discoveries and by replacing that which was no longer tenable with new proposals. The principle of "valid until proven otherwise" is characteristic of all scientific endeavors. Only if superstition of science creeps in does one make claims that are "valid forever." But then science has transgressed its boundaries.

139. Jürgen Habermas, "Konzepte der Moderne: Rückblick auf zwei Traditionen," in Habermas, *Philosophische Texte: Studienausgabe in fünf Bänden* (Frankfurt am Main: Suhrkamp, 2009), 1:387.

II. Human Freedom

"Freedom" is the catchword of modernity, starting with the Declaration of Independence in North America, reverberating through the French Revolution in continental Europe, and surfacing again in the various theologies of liberation. Yet are humans actually free? We have already noticed that from a biological perspective humans are predisposed in many ways, their wings are clipped, and their strides are fettered. When we now look at that which humans often consider their inner sanctum, their brain and their psychic makeup, the answer is not very different. We are not actually beings who pursue our very own path. And if Frank Sinatra (1915-98), at the end of his life, sang, "I did it my way!" he was just telling half the truth. Only within certain limits can we really pursue our own way. This is of course most evident for those who suffer from bodily or psychic handicaps, and are severely challenged in pursuing their lives. Even those without such problems have difficulties pursuing their own path or even discerning what that path ought to be.

4. The Perspective of the Sciences

From a scientific perspective human freedom is challenged by the neurosciences, which have allowed us to peek deeper and deeper into the human brain. The brain is the most complex organ we have and it can be likened to a vast network of wires and switches. It is tempting, therefore, to understand the functioning of the brain in purely materialistic terms. When certain areas of the brain are stimulated by outside influences, predictable actions can be induced. Moreover, psychoanalysis perceives human behavior as governed by drives that humans can hardly harness. What if anything is then left of human freedom?

1. The Perspective of the Neurosciences

With the research into the functioning of the human brain the notion of "free will" has been severely challenged. Exploring the physical and chemical functioning of the brain and its relatedness to sense impression, body movements, and even emotions, the question must be raised as to what extent humans are still in charge of themselves if such essential human actions are governed by mechanical or chemical reactions. Perhaps Frank Tipler may have overstated the case when he claimed that "a human being is nothing but a particular type of machine, the human brain only an information processing device and the human soul a program run on a computer called the brain."[1] But if the brain is an organism subject to physical and chemical reactions, how can we arrive at free decisions?

1. Frank J. Tipler, *The Physics of Immortality: Modern Cosmology, God and the Resurrection of the Dead* (New York: Doubleday, 1994), xi.

a. The Ambiguity of Freedom

In his book *On Aggression* Konrad Lorenz has shown that instinctive drives no longer significantly govern the behavior of human beings. For instance, in an experiment done with rats it was discovered that 65 percent of their drinking following water deprivation is due to cellular dehydration, and about 25 percent is due to blood volume reduction. The percentage rate is similar in other animals.[2] This shows that there is a strong drive or motivation in animals to correct the water deficit by drinking. One can even measure how hard an animal will work in order to correct the fluid deficit. Yet with humans daily water intake is guided by other factors. Of course, we drink heartily to quench our thirst after exercise or heavy work, but we also drink fluids with our meals, have a coffee break in the morning, drink on social occasions, and sometimes drink simply for the enjoyable taste. This means that our intake of liquids is also culturally conditioned.

These different reasons for drinking or not drinking depend on different kinds of receptors: "taste receptors in the mouth and pharynx, somatosensory receptors in the mouth, pharynx, and esophagus, stretch receptors that sense the amount of distention in the stomach and duodenum; stretch receptors and osmoreceptors in the hepatic portal veins that return blood from the liver to the heart." If something tastes good, we drink more. But if something does not taste good, we drink little or nothing. Similarly, if we feel full, we stop drinking or, to the contrary, if something tastes especially good, we will continue drinking, even if our stomach tells us to stop. For humanity, then, there are many signals that determine when, what, and how much we will drink.

While we respond to and anticipate presumed needs, our freedom from instinctive drives no longer guards us against possible mistakes in our behavior. Indeed, our instinctive drives are at the most suggestive and obliterated by many other signals, including those from the environment, culture, our bodies, and our intentions. Excessive drinking, for instance, can damage our liver and our cardiovascular system and can distend our abdomen. This illustration merely demonstrates that while we have the chance to shape our own life, we can also destroy it. Therefore, as Jean-Paul Sartre contended, the freedom of our will can be part of human dignity as well as a curse.

2. For the following, including the quote, see Gordon M. Shepherd, *Neurobiology,* 3rd ed. (New York: Oxford University Press, 1994), 584.

b. The Functioning of the Human Brain

In the last few decades, extraordinary progress has been made in a variety of scientific fields that together constitute the neurosciences. These disciplines attempt to understand the biological basis of human behavior as it expresses itself in the functioning of the brain. But the interpretation of the results of this research is often highly controversial, if not emotional.[3]

There are basically three philosophical theories that deal with the relationship of the mind and the brain: dualism, pluralism, and monism. In dualistic theories, mind and brain are treated as separate and distinct entities that in some way interact with each other, but neither one is reducible to the other. In pluralist theories there are separate and distinct realities suggested, such as the subjective world of the mind, the physical world of the brain, and the objective world of scientific knowledge. This so-called three-worlds-theory was first proposed in 1978 by Austrian philosopher Karl Popper (1902-94) and then adapted by Australian neurophysiologist John Eccles (1903-97). Finally, monism asserts that mind and brain are actually the same and psychological processes can ultimately be explained in terms of underlying neural events.

Within the complex organ of the brain "the ultimate explanation of both mental life and behavior must be sought."[4] This view, the psychoneural identity hypothesis, reflects the belief that mental and brain processes are one and the same. Without a brain there can be no mind and the mental events are processes of a physical functioning brain. But this need not result in a monistic view since the whole can always be understood to be more than its constituent parts.

In order to understand human behavior, brain science must be reductionist, breaking down complex phenomena into simpler underlying mechanisms that produce these phenomena. To understand the biological basis of behavior means to specify the neural determinants of that behavior. Three areas appear to be especially important for the experience and expression of emotion: the hypothalamus, the amygdala, and the septal area.[5]

3. See John Eccles, *How the Self Controls Its Brain* (Berlin: Springer, 1994), in which he analyzes many different approaches.
4. Jackson Beatty, *Principles of Neuroscience* (Madison: Brown & Benchmark, 1995), 4.
5. See Beatty, *Principles of Neuroscience,* 339, including figure 1.

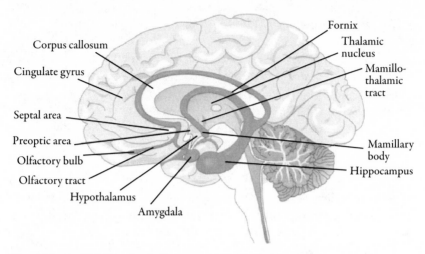

Fig. 1 Principal Midline Brain Structures Involved in Emotions

Lesions of the hypothalamus or of the amygdaloid nuclei have profound effects on emotional behavior, but are far from simple to explain.[6] While lesions in some areas of the brain have parasympathetic effects, others have sympathetic effects; in some regions they produce fear and depression with occasional outbursts of aggression, in other areas these effects are reversed. Lesions in the septal area of the brain lead to hyper-emotionality in many species, including human beings. Electrical stimulation of the hypothalamus can also lead to differing emotional consequences; fear and anxiety if one area is stimulated, and the opposite effect if other regions are stimulated. Stimulation of the amygdala or the septal area also produces profound emotional effects. This means "external" disturbances in certain parts of the brain brought about by disease, electrical stimulation, or drugs can alter our emotions.

It is especially the hypothalamus that "generates the visceral part of emotion and is itself influenced by limbic entities that in turn receive input from the cortex, particularly the frontal lobes."[7] Since emotions are rather complex states that involve perception, affect, cognition, drive, judgment, and action, and since various parts of the brain come together in generating emotions, our knowledge of emotions is still rather limited.[8] The complex nature of

6. Beatty, *Principles of Neuroscience,* 344.

7. Richard E. Cytowic, *The Neurological Side of Neuropsychology* (Cambridge, MA: MIT Press, 1996), 285.

8. See Cytowic, *The Neurological Side of Neuropsychology,* 294.

emotions is compounded by the elusiveness of self-awareness. "The physical brain has no sensory nerves and is not aware of its own physical substance."[9] Regardless of how we influence the brain, manually or with an electric current, the sensation is never felt in the brain, but rather in the peripheral body part, for instance, if the heartbeat is accelerated or a finger is lifted. We may conclude that there is no identity between the actual neurons being stimulated and the spatial occasion of the subjective experience that results from it. Therefore American neurologist Richard Cytowic (b. 1952) cautions that "we must be aware of abstractions that claim to capture the whole picture."[10]

One kind of emotive behavior that has received widespread attention is aggression. "Aggression is a part of the normal behavioral repertoire of humans and animals. Appropriately applied, it is necessary for the survival of both species and individuals. Inappropriately applied, aggression can become destructive to persons and property."[11] We may even compare appropriately applied aggression to the theological concept of the law since it establishes and maintains social boundaries and cohesion ("Thou shall not steal," "thou shall not commit adultery," and so on). Inappropriately applied aggression can then be likened to sin since it is destructive of both boundaries and social cohesion.

It has been shown through animal and human studies that serotonin plays an important role in the central nervous system with regard to balanced behavior. "Decreasing serotonergic functioning is conducive to aggressive and impulsive behaviors; increasing it reduces such behaviors."[12] This is supported by a study conducted by Finnish psychiatrist Matti Virkkunen (b. 1943) and others who checked fifty-eight violent offenders approximately three years after they were released from prison for repeat crimes.[13] Thirteen of them had again been sentenced for violent crime. These repeat offenders had significantly lower CSF 5-HIAA (cerebrospinal fluid 5-hydroxyindoleacetic acid) concentrations and blood glucose nadirs

---

9. Cytowic, *The Neurological Side of Neuropsychology,* 297.

10. Cytowic, *The Neurological Side of Neuropsychology,* 312.

11. Markku Linnoila and Dennis S. Charney, "The Neurobiology of Aggression," in *Neurobiology of Mental Illness,* ed. Dennis S. Charney et al. (New York: Oxford University Press, 1999), 855.

12. Linnoila and Charney, "The Neurobiology of Aggression," 861.

13. Matti Virkkunen et al., "Relationship of Psychobiological Variables to Recidivism in Violent Offenders and Impulsive Fire Setters," *Archives of General Psychiatry* 46 (July 1989): 600-603; and Linnoila and Charney, "The Neurobiology of Aggression," 863, who also relate the research by Virkkunen.

during the oral glucose tolerance test than those who were not repeaters. Yet American psychiatrist Emil F. Coccaro cautions that it is unrealistic to think "that only central serotonin system function is relevant to impulsive aggressive behavior in humans."[14] While serotonin functions as a behavioral inhibitor, other neurotransmitter or modulator systems may interact with serotonin and with each other to affect the inhibition or activation balance, which results in increased or decreased aggressive behavior. Therefore he calls for further studies regarding the neurotransmitter basis of human aggression.

Another dimension involved in emotive responses is individual differences in electro-physiological measures of the prefrontal activation of the brain. "For example, the lack of remorse and failure to plan ahead that are characteristic of antisocial personality disorder may be a function of decreased activation in the right prefrontal regions that have been implicated in aversive motivation and behavioral inhibition. The inhibition and fear of criticism that are hallmark signs of avoidant personality disorder may be associated with hyperactivation in the circuitry subserving the aversive motivation system."[15] Again, certain areas of the brain seem to indicate in their increased or decreased function specific emotive states. It is not surprising, therefore, that even diseases, such as schizophrenia or major depression, can be pinpointed to specific changes in the brain.[16]

If the brain processes are highly disturbed through disease, manipulation, or injury, then it is much easier to correlate brain activity, or the lack of it, with certain emotive behaviors. But the situation is much more difficult if such disturbances do not exist. Moreover, we must remember that the brain consists of at least 15 billion interconnected nerve cells. Each of these cells can have up to 10,000 synapses, namely, significant connections to other nerve cells. Therefore an exact description of the brain, including a complete tracing of brain activity, is virtually impossible and we cannot make accurate predictions as to how the brain will act or react in each instance. It is here that we reach the limits of our technical possibilities.

---

14. E. F. Coccaro, "Central Neurotransmitter Function in Human Aggression and Impulsivity," in *Neurobiology and Clinical Views on Aggression and Impulsivity,* ed. Michael Maes and Emil F. Corraro (Chichester: John Wiley, 1998), 163.

15. Richard A. Davidson, "The Neurobiology of Personality and Personality Disorders," in *Neurobiology of Mental Illness,* ed. Charney et al., 852.

16. See Paul M. Churchland, *The Engine of Reason, the Seat of the Soul: A Philosophical Journey into the Brain,* 3rd printing (Cambridge, MA: MIT Press, 1995), 151-84 ("The Brain in Trouble") for the possibilities of correlating diseases with changes in the brain.

Yet there has been a breakthrough of sorts at least in one direction. There seems to be a time interval between "deliberation" and the "decision" to do something. In 1965 German neurologist Hans Helmut Kornhuber (1928-2009) published experiments in which he recorded the electrical potentials in the brain before and after the physical movement of the hand. He discovered that almost one second before the subject makes a conscious decision to move a finger, there is a build-up of brain activity, the so-called readiness potential.[17] American physiologist **Benjamin Libet** (1916-2007) refined Kornhuber's experiment in 1979 by trying to establish the following: (1) when a person decides to move a hand, (2) when the brain prepares for that activity, and (3) when this activity is executed. He noticed that the brain becomes active before that person (consciously) decides to move the hand. This would mean that the brain acts independently of our will. Yet in another experiment he stimulated the skin with a pin prick and noticed that this stimulation reaches the brain in 10 to 20 milliseconds.[18] But there is a delay of around half a second during which the brain activity builds up before the pin prick is consciously perceived. Yet the subject notices no delay. Libet explains that the initial pin prick is almost immediately conveyed by the cortex to the brain. This initial signal then acts as a time marker. After half a second of neural "deliberation," the experience is referred back to the time marker and therefore the subject experiences no delay in his or her own mind between the occurrence and the bodily (brain) sensation. The delay could involve the possibility of a conscious response to the stimulus, while "a quick response to a stimulus would have to be made unconsciously."[19] A conscious response could then involve a "free will." One should be cautious, however, with such a conclusion since the experiments conducted by Kornhuber and Libet were clearly "reductionistic" in the sense that they took place in the lab and not in a natural, much more com-

17. L. Deecke, H. Eisinger, and H. H. Kornhuber, "Comparison of Bereitschaftspotential, Pre-motion Positivity and Motor Potential Preceding Voluntary Flexion and Extension Movements in Man," in *Progress in Brain Research,* vol. 54, ed. H. H. Kornhuber and L. Deecke (Amsterdam: Elsevier/North-Holland Biomedical Press, 1980), 171-76; and Cytowic, *The Neurological Side of Neuropsychology,* 298, who reports on earlier work by Kornhuber, whom he consistently refers to as "Kornhüber."

18. See for the following Benjamin Libet, "Subjective and Neural Time: Factors in Conscious Sensory Experience, Studied in Man, and Their Implications for the Mind-Brain Relationship," in *Mind and Brain: The Many-Faceted Problems,* 2nd ed., ed. John Eccles (New York: Paragon, 1985), 187; and Cytowic, *The Neurological Side of Neuropsychology,* 299, for the diagrams of the build-up of brain activity.

19. Libet, "Subjective and Neural Time," 188.

plicated environment. Whether they actually tell us something about an "act of (free) will" is still debatable.[20]

While the neurological sciences can trace physical and chemical activities in the brain, an exact correlation between emotive behavior and brain functions is not that simple. We may conclude that if our body is wounded, this is immediately registered in the brain. After some delay, an awareness of pain follows which, mostly on the subconscious level, releases defense mechanisms, and to which also a conscious defense reaction will be added.[21] The situation is similar with fear. Once we freeze with fear and express physiological responses to a dangerous stimulus, the rest is up to us. "On the basis of our expectations about what is likely to happen next and our past experiences in similar situations, we make a plan about what to do."[22] In this subconscious and conscious process different areas of the brain are involved: the amygdala, the hippocampus, and the hypothalamus, plus the connections between them. We notice here a complexity of responses on various levels, one of which clearly shows causal connections, while others would allow only tenuous causal inferences. But in talking about conscious defense reactions, we assume a certain consciousness. What does this actually mean and to what extent does that allow for a free will, assuming that only a conscious being is free to decide and to act and therefore to assume responsibility for the consequences of its decisions and actions?

For an action to be free or voluntary it presupposes that we could also decide to perform some other action.[23] This means it should not simply be a reflex. It should also not just be a reaction to an internal or external cue and therefore the result of certain stimuli. Furthermore, a free or voluntary action should be performed with directed attention, not automatically (like shifting a car from one gear to another). Finally, we should be

---

20. See Jeff Coulter and Wes Sharrock, *Brain, Mind, and Human Behavior in Contemporary Cognitive Science: A Critical Assessment of the Philosophy of Psychology,* foreword P. M. S. Hacker (Lewiston, NY: Edwin Mellen, 2007), 65, who claim that these results do not cast any light on "what would conceivably be involved in 'acts of will' or in 'willing.'"

21. See Erhard Oeser and Franz Seitelberger, *Gehirn, Bewußtsein und Erkenntnis,* 2nd enl. ed. (Darmstadt: Wissenschaftliche Buchgesellschaft, 1995), 87.

22. So Joseph E. LeDoux, "Emotions: A View through the Brain," in *Neuroscience and the Person: Scientific Perspectives on Divine Action,* ed. Robert John Russell et al. (Notre Dame, IN: Notre Dame University Press, 1999), 113f.

23. For the following, see R. E. Passingham, *The Frontal Lobes and Voluntary Action* (Oxford: Oxford University Press, 1993), 1f.

able to compare alternative courses of action and not habitually follow one or the other, but make an actual free decision. But do humans really have such freedom?

c. Consciousness, Free Will, and the Brain

While animals have the capacity to adapt to new or changed circumstances, humans need not try out certain actions but can evaluate potential actions beforehand by employing a mental trial-and-error strategy. "The prefrontal cortex is critically involved in the process by which the human brain generates and selects actions."[24] Humans can select between ideas and thereby plan future actions by setting goals and devising strategies to attain them. This means they are capable of free or voluntary actions. Moreover, free will is a subjective phenomenon of human consciousness. We feel that we are free in our actions as German poet Friedrich Schiller (1759-1805) claimed: "Humans are created free; they are free even if they were born in chains."[25]

Over the last decades a consensus has developed that consciousness is also a scientific object.[26] While a complete view of the neural basis of consciousness is still unattainable, it is clear that consciousness is not a separate faculty, "but a certain activity mode of basic cognitive functions — memory, perception, action planning."[27] Consciousness can be described in at least three different ways: (1) as a state, such as in drowsy, alert, or altered states of consciousness; (2) as an architectural concept, namely, as the executive system at the center of cognition that seems to receive input, allocate attention, set priorities, generate imagery, and initiate recall from memory; and (3) as an indicator of representational awareness in becoming conscious of some specific idea or event.[28] While there is no evidence for a single integrated anatomical structure in the brain that functions as the head of a fixed hierarchy of processors, "human consciousness has special memory retrieval features that set it apart from animal consciousness; it can voluntarily recall items from its own memory store . . . without needing further specific cues

---

24. Passingham, *The Frontal Lobes and Voluntary Action*, 236f.

25. Friedrich Schiller, "Der Taucher," stanza 2.

26. So Jean Delacour, "An Introduction to the Biology of Consciousness," *Neuropsychologia* 33 (July 1995): 1061.

27. Delacour, "An Introduction to the Biology of Consciousness," 1070.

28. So Merlin Donald, "The Neurobiology of Human Consciousness: An Evolutionary Approach," *Neuropsychologia* 33 (July 1995): 1087.

from the environment."[29] Only in bird vocal mimicry and in the use of symbols by acculturated apes do we find such a limited voluntary recall.

British psychologist Jeffrey A. Gray (1934-2004) suggests that the contents of consciousness consist of the output of a comparative process that takes place in the limbic forebrain, especially in the hippocampal system.[30] In this output the perceptional descriptions of events that were predicted are compared with any further events not so predicted, and result in the degree of match or mismatch detected by the comparator system. This would account for certain features of the contents of consciousness, for instance, that "these occur too late to affect the processes . . . to which they appear to be linked; that conscious events take place on a time scale that is about two orders of magnitude smaller than neural events; that one has conscious awareness, not of motor programming processes, but only of their outcomes; that consciousness is selective; that it is closely linked to memory," and the like. Of course, Gray knows that this is only speculation, though it can explain certain features of our consciousness. The reason for the hypothetical nature of this claim is that the neural processes that constitute consciousness do not reflect on themselves. They only consider the external world of our body or our environment. Therefore we cannot determine whether this kind of comparative activity, which would point to a free will, goes on in the brain.

Neurobiology shows us that we are not free to do whatever we want. We are first of all determined in our emotive actions by our psychic makeup. If we are aware of our psychic constitution, we can influence this constitution to some extent and with it our emotive inclinations. Second, we are restricted in our emotive actions by that which encounters us both within and outside our body. Again, if we are conscious of the interdependence between the brain and its environment, we are able to determine our emotive actions. But being part of this empirical world, both our brains and its neuron cells act and react according to the biochemical conditions in which they find themselves.

What does this mean for the freedom of the will? It means that there is freedom to choose how to reach a certain self-determined goal. Freedom does not mean that there is no causality at work, but that we evaluate and

---

29. Donald, "The Neurobiology of Human Consciousness," 1090.

30. See for the following, including the quote, J. A. Gray, "Dopamine Release in the Nucleus Accumbens: The Perspective from Aberrations of Consciousness in Schizophrenia," *Neuropsychologia* 33 (July 1995): 1151.

determine a possible action according to our own knowledge and our own volition. Rational, emotional, and cognitive elements come together. The causality that is subjectively assumed is not identical with the causality of cerebral functions through which our choices are inaugurated.[31] There is a subjective emotive sequence and an objective causal sequence. While these processes are neither identical nor parallel to each other, they can only alternatively rise to our consciousness, which then suggests to us the notion of causality. Therefore neurobiology does not eliminate the freedom of the will by correlating brain activities with certain emotive behavior, but it makes us aware that freedom is not without boundaries and not without a neural substratum out of which freedom is possible. This means there is no basis for some kind of physicalism, which claims that a human being is nothing but a very complicated biological apparatus. As philosopher Nancey Murphy and neuropsychologist Warren S. Brown contend, through their investigations of the brain the cognitive neurosciences "help us to understand *how* humans succeed in acting reasonably, freely and responsibly."[32] Since the neural sciences have been able to an astounding degree to correlate physical-chemical neural processes with certain behaviors, we may use these insights to direct our behavior in a commonly acceptable and beneficial direction. As German behavioral physiologist Gerhard Roth (b. 1942) states: "The demonstration that subjective consciousness is neurologically conditioned does not preclude that such consciousness does indeed exist."[33] We may not be as free as we think we are but we are not simply without a will of our own that can be enacted.

d. Religious Consciousness

Since people are conscious of God and their experiences with God, this consciousness can also be related to certain activities in parts of the brain. How complicated the situation is in locating these activities in the brain is shown by the following. According to present calculations, "real-time human ac-

---

31. See Oeser and Seitelberger, *Gehirn, Bewußtsein und Erkenntnis,* 101.

32. Nancey Murphy and Warren S. Brown, *Did My Neurons Make Me Do It? Philosophical and Neurobiological Perspectives on Moral Responsibility and Free Will* (Oxford: Oxford University Press, 2007), 3. For a discussion of physicalism, see 7f.

33. Gerhard Roth, "Wir sind determiniert: Die Hirnforschung befreit von Illusionen," in *Hirnforschung und Willensfreiheit: Zur Deutung der neuesten Experimente,* ed. Christian Geyer (Frankfurt am Main: Suhrkamp, 2005), 222.

tion reflects one hundred billion neurons firing and processing information at one hundred trillion operations per second. The amazing fact highlights the challenge that neuroscientists face when investigating religious and spiritual behavior or any other complex behavior."[34] Though not all of them function simultaneously, tracing these activities is still enormously complicated.

It has long been noted that people who have certain brain disorders often exhibit striking intensification of religious experience. In schizophrenia, bipolar disorder, and partial-complex epilepsy these religious experiences occur without external stimulation. This provides neuroscientists with the opportunity "to investigate neural correlates of religion and spirituality."[35] So far, however, one can only gather from data provided by neuroscience which brain regions are likely unconsciously impacting conscious experience, but one cannot designate "a particular brain region the God Spot, nor can we designate which specific brain region produces religious or spiritual tendencies."[36] Neurologist **Patrick McNamara** (b. 1956) states: "As far as I can see none of the extant cognitive or neuroscience models of human nature of the Mind/Brain can adequately account for the range of behavioral and cognitive phenomena associated with religion."[37] This means that religious experience has something to do with the brain but does not evolve from the brain.

In the last decade new functional neuroimaging techniques have provided additional insights into how the brain supports religiosity, for instance, what brain activity occurs when we pray or meditate. The interesting conclusion is that the brain sites identified as crucial for religiosity in clinical patients "also appear consistently in neuroimaging findings of healthy persons performing religious practices. . . . There is a network of brain regions that consistently are activated when persons perform religious acts."[38] This means there are certain areas in the brain that are activated in persons who have brain disorders to produce religious experiences and that are also activated in healthy persons when they perform religious practices.

---

34. So psychiatrist Stephan Carlson, "The Neuroscience of Religious Experience: An Introductory Survey," in *Neuroscience and Religion: Brain, Mind, Self, and Soul*, ed. Volney P. Gay (Lanham, MD: Rowman & Littlefield, 2009), 161.

35. Carlson, "The Neuroscience of Religious Experience," 165.

36. Carlson, "The Neuroscience of Religious Experience," 168.

37. Patrick McNamara, *The Neuroscience of Religious Experience* (New York: Cambridge University Press, 2009), x.

38. McNamara, *The Neuroscience of Religious Experience*, 127.

There are also certain neurotransmitters, such as serotonin — LSD and mescaline act on the serotonin system — that are crucially involved in religious experience. The level of these neurotransmitters is higher in religious exercises and experiences and too high in certain brain disorders. Therefore religious experiences in healthy persons are reflected in the level of these transmitters and in the activities of certain brain regions.

McNamara also shows that "there is considerable anatomical overlap between the brain sites implicated in religious experience and the brain sites implicated in the sense of Self and self-consciousness."[39] Religious practices often support the transformation of the self so that it becomes more like the ideal self for which the individual strives. Therefore religious practices can contribute to the creation of a unified self-consciousness and an ideal executive self that can in a coherent and assured way approach the future. Small wonder neurologist Andrew B. Newberg (b. 1966) advocates a neurotheology for which he sees four foundational goals:

1. to improve our understanding of the human mind and brain
2. to improve our understanding of religion and theology
3. to improve the human condition, particularly in the context of health and well-being
4. to improve the human condition, particularly in the context of religion and spirituality[40]

Neuroscience helps us to understand how religious experiences are activated and express themselves in both sick and healthy persons. It also makes us aware that religion and the human self are closely associated with each other, perhaps indicating that when we exclude religion from our personal and public spheres we damage ourselves and others. It is not by accident that surveys consistently show that religious persons are healthier, happier, and more content in life.

2. Freedom from a Psychoanalytic Perspective

When we now consider human freedom with regard to the human psyche, we recognize that this can be done from different angles. We realize, for in-

39. McNamara, *The Neuroscience of Religious Experience*, xi.
40. Andrew B. Newberg, *Principles of Neurotheology* (Burlington, VT: Ashgate, 2010), 18.

stance, how deeply childhood experiences influence adult behavior and how dramatic experiences, such as war crimes or accidents, can haunt people for years. Even the break-up of parental marriages can influence offspring even into adulthood with regard to the establishment of stable marriage relationships. It is also not surprising in our fast-changing times, where people are under more pressures than ever, that although they deem themselves to be free, psychotherapists and counseling services are in increasing demand. Even the burnout syndrome of highly successful people shows that humans are not as stable as their outward appearance may portray. As every educator knows, human beings are extremely vulnerable.

In addition to these various milieu factors that influence people in their psychic makeup and in their decision-making, psychoanalysis has shown that in human beings themselves there is a continuous battle going on about which direction they ought to turn. There seem to be a destructive drive in people even to the extent of self-destruction, and also an affirmative drive that rises above the present situation and maps out the way to the future. The classical representatives of psychoanalysis, Sigmund Freud, Carl Gustav Jung, and Erich Fromm, have perceptively mapped out this intrinsic struggle within the human person. Although Freud's psychoanalysis has been perhaps overly criticized by feminists and "hard" psychologists, Freud's enduring legacy was to suggest new ways of understanding those things and relations that make up our lives.[41]

a. The Intrinsic Form of Evil (Freud)

Sigmund Freud, the founder of modern psychoanalysis, recognized, as did Karl Lorenz after him, an aggressive drive in humanity. This recognition, however, did not come easily for Freud. For twenty years, Freud, in his analysis of human behavior, resisted recognizing an independent aggression drive that was equated with destruction.[42] Only through the impact of World War I was he ready to accept the existence of such a drive. Thus he

---

41. See the sympathetic description of Freud by Pamela Thurschwell, *Sigmund Freud,* 2nd ed. (London: Routledge, 2009), 1, and her chapter "After Freud," 110-34, esp. 131ff. For a well-researched biography, see Ronald W. Clark, *Freud: The Man and the Cause* (New York: Random House, 1980).

42. So Helmut Nolte, "Über gesellschaftstheoretische Implikationen des Aggressionsbegriffs," in *Kritik der Anthropologie: Marx und Freud, Gehlen und Habermas über Aggression,* ed. Wolf Lepenies and Helmut Nolte (Munich: Hanser, 1971), 104f.

wrote in his 1915 work, "Thoughts for the Times on War and Death," that evil could not be eradicated. "Psychological — or, more strictly speaking, psycho-analytic — investigation shows instead that the deepest essence of human nature consists of instinctual impulses which are of an elementary nature, which are similar in all men and which aim at the satisfaction of certain primal needs."[43] To be sure, these primitive impulses can be culturally transformed so that they lose their effective reality. It must, nevertheless, be admitted that "our unconscious is just as inaccessible to the idea of our own death, just as murderously inclined towards strangers, just as divided (that is, ambivalent) towards those we love, as was primeval man" (299). Through war the cultural transformations are stripped away and primitive humanity, which encountered the foreigner with murderous intent, comes once again to light. Instinctive drives, though inherently neither good nor bad, contain hidden within them the potential for evil, which repeatedly breaks out into the open.

In *Beyond the Pleasure Principle* (1920) Freud presents the aggression drive as the externally oriented, secondarily autonomous variant of the self-destruction drive. Important in this regard is the concept of narcissism. Freud wrote in 1925: "The ethical narcissism of humanity should rest content with the knowledge that the fact of distortion in dreams, as well as the existence of anxiety dreams and punishment dreams, afford just as clear evidence of his moral nature as dream interpretation gives of the existence and strength of his evil nature."[44] According to Freud, human behavior is largely determined through sexuality, which consists of both good and bad tendencies. Alongside *eros,* the drive that supports the living substance and embraces ever greater numbers of individual units, there exists another, opposing drive: the death instinct. Unlike the *eros* instinct, the death instinct breaks apart the individual units and is bent on returning them to their primordial, inorganic condition.[45] In the cooperation and opposition of these two instincts Freud sought to explain the phenomena of life. In this collab-

43. Sigmund Freud, "Thoughts for the Times on War and Death" (1915), in *The Standard Edition of the Complete Psychological Works of Sigmund Freud,* ed. James Strachey (London: Hogarth, 1966-74), 14:281.

44. Sigmund Freud, "Moral Responsibility for the Content of Dreams" (1925), in *Collected Papers,* ed. James Strachey (London: Hogarth, 1950), 5:157. A good introduction to Freud's interpretation of the human condition and the Christian understanding of original sin is offered by Sharon MacIsaac, *Freud and Original Sin* (New York: Paulist, 1974).

45. For this and the following, see Sigmund Freud, *Civilization and Its Discontents* (1930), trans. Joan Riveriere, in *The Standard Edition,* 21:119.

oration the two instincts seldom appear in isolation from one another, but have varying levels of intensity and are often intermingled with each other so that from our perspective they are indistinguishable.

Freud admits that in the beginning he advocated the existence of these two instincts only hesitantly and tentatively, but then became increasingly convinced of their reality. That he also encountered opposition regarding this view he indicated when he wrote: "For 'little children do not like it' when there is talk of the inborn inclination to 'badness,' to aggressiveness, and destructiveness, and so to cruelty as well" (120). Freud establishes that the inclination toward aggression "is an original, self-subsisting instinctual disposition in man" that finds in civilization its strongest impediment. Civilization is a process in the service of *eros* that seeks to gather together not only isolated human individuals, but also families, tribes, peoples, and nations into a great union in order to bind them to one another through their *libidos,* thereby resisting the natural aggression drive of humans in which the hostility of the one is directed against the whole and that of the whole against the one. The aggressive instinct "is the derivative and the main representative of the death instinct which we have found alongside of Eros and which shares world-dominion with it" (122).

The battle between *eros* and death, between the drive toward life and the drive toward destruction, is, according to Freud, the essential content of life and is indicative of the human struggle for survival. We are not dealing here, however, with a simple dualism, for "it is very rarely that an action is the work of a single instinctual impulse (which must in itself be compounded of Eros and destructiveness). In order to make an action possible there must be as a rule a combination of such compounded motives."[46] For this reason it is difficult to isolate the two instincts in their manifestations. Moreover, the destruction drive only becomes such in that the death instinct "is used against the objects with the help of special external organs. The life form protects its own life, so to speak, through the destruction of that which is foreign." But a part of the death instinct remains always active within a living being and shows itself in normal as well as in pathological phenomena. Nevertheless, the external expression of these destructive, driving forces is judged to be exculpable and beneficial. Humans and their community are therefore seriously jeopardized. Yet in order to fathom fully the human predicament, we must, along with Freud, distinguish between the id, the ego, and the superego.

46. For this and the following quote, see Sigmund Freud, "Why War?" (1932), in *The Standard Edition,* 22:210.

The foundation of all psychic life is the id, which consists primarily of chaotic and unconscious drives. Prominent among these drives is the reproduction drive, or libido. But in all affirmations of life the libido is mixed with the death wish, the goal of which is to once more achieve a state of lifelessness. In conformity with its source and development the libido is closely bound to the body, in which it strides forward from the oral phase of nursing and the anal phase, which has to do with the control of the excretion organs — both of which phases are known as pre-genital — to the Oedipus phase, which is characterized by the death wish against the father and the incest wish toward the mother.[47] Connected with the libido is the threatening power of the death instinct, which is primarily directed against humanity itself.

If humans do not wish to destroy themselves, they must direct the death instinct to the outside in the form of aggression or destruction. In this regard Freud said: "It really seems as though it is necessary for us to destroy some other thing or person in order not to destroy ourselves, in order to guard against the impulsion to self-destruction."[48] Yet it would be wrong to describe the death wish as something entirely negative, for together with the libido it serves life. It leads the *eros* to be in control of the objects of its pleasure and helps us to achieve control over nature. But the death wish can erupt at any time in its naked power as aggression and destruction and endanger the culture that was made possible through the libido. Freud acknowledges that "in consequence of this primary mutual hostility of human beings, civilized society is perpetually threatened with disintegration."[49]

To comprehend the entire structure of being, however, we must go beyond the id and turn to the ego. The ego emerges from the id as that part of the id that is oriented toward the external world. It functions in such a way that it recognizes internal and external stimuli, orders them, and initiates reactions to these stimuli. Thus the task of the ego can be described as that of a mediator. This does not rule out, however, the fact that the ego also pursues its own interests. Freud alludes to this when he says, even if the death instinct "emerges without any sexual purpose, in the blindest fury of destructiveness, we cannot fail to recognize that the satisfaction of the in-

47. Sigmund Freud, "Two Encyclopedia Articles" (1923), in *The Standard Edition,* 18:242ff.

48. Sigmund Freud, *New Introductory Lectures on Psychoanalysis* (1933), in *The Complete Introductory Lectures on Psychoanalysis,* trans. and ed. James Strachey (New York: W. W. Norton, 1966), 569.

49. Sigmund Freud, *Civilization and Its Discontents,* trans. and ed. James Strachey (New York: W. W. Norton, 1962), 59.

stinct is accompanied by an extraordinarily high degree of narcissistic enjoyment, owing to its presenting the ego with a fulfillment of the latter's old wishes for omnipotence" (68). But the ego must also represent the demands of the external world over against those of the id. This corrective function of the ego is facilitated by the superego.

The superego originates through the internalization of external authority, by means of which one is able to identify with this authority. This is especially important for humans as social creatures. According to Freud, the ideals and laws of a society are nothing other than a collective superego (89). The superego of the individual is formed through education by the collective superego and becomes the "vehicle of tradition and of all the time-resisting judgments of value which have propagated themselves in this manner from generation to generation."[50] The superego binds together families and societies through the submission of the interests of the individual to those of the parents and of society. Yet the superego also has its negative side. It can assume cruel and demonic features that drive one to neurosis, melancholy, and even death. The "conscience" of the superego can lead to a sense of guilt, or to aggression, or even to suicide.

Regardless of the direction in which we look, we notice that humanity is continually struggling to find its way between life and death, between the creation and protection of life and its destruction. One is, therefore, practically forced to the conclusion that Freud presents a dualistic understanding of humanity that is torn "between the life and death instincts."[51] Yet it is not only within individuals that these instincts are seen. Cultures are also torn between life and death.[52] Freud broadens his perspective event wider when he says:

> And now, I think, the meaning of the evolution of civilization is no longer obscure to us. It must present the struggle between Eros and Death, between the instinct of life and the instinct of destruction, as it works itself out in the human species. This struggle is what all life essentially consists of, and the evolution of civilization may therefore be simply described as the struggle for life of the human species.[53]

50. Freud, *New Introductory Lectures,* 531.

51. See Sigmund Freud, "Beyond the Pleasure Principle" (1920), in *The Standard Edition,* 18:53.

52. See Paul Ricoeur's detailed analysis of Freud in *Freud and Philosophy: An Essay on Interpretation* (New Haven, CT: Yale University Press, 1970), 302ff.

53. Freud, *Civilization and Its Discontents,* 69. This would mean that Freud does not ac-

If this dichotomy is so all-pervading, one could conclude that it is not possible "to transcend the limits of the human condition or to change the psychological structural conditions that make humanity possible."[54] These are precisely, however, the limits of psychoanalysis. As Ernest Becker has convincingly shown, "psychoanalysis failed therapeutically where it fetishized the causes of human unhappiness as sexuality, and where it pretended to be a total world-view in itself."[55] In this context Carl Gustav Jung blazed a path different from that of Freud. Jung deviates from Freud's primary subject of analysis, namely, human sexuality, and breaks through to a more comprehensive and differentiating view of humanity.

b. The Integration of Evil (Jung)

Swiss medical doctor and psychologist **Carl Gustav Jung** distinguishes between the conscious and the unconscious aspects of the human psyche.[56] The conscious part of the human psyche is oriented toward the external world and has as its center the ego. The unconscious part of the human psyche is divided into two distinct realms, the personal unconscious and the

cept a (destructive) death instinct in humanity, but rather, he describes the intrinsically human awareness of finitude and the resulting effort to overcome this finitude.

54. So Ernest Becker, *The Denial of Death* (New York: Free Press, 1973), 277. As we have seen in this convincing book Becker follows largely the thought of Freud by means of a heavy reliance on Otto Rank, a student of Freud, and he shows that the human fear of death provides the primary stimulus for human actions. In a posthumously published book, *Escape from Evil* (New York: Free Press, 1975), a sequel to *The Denial of Death,* Becker attempts to demonstrate that "man's natural and inevitable urges to deny mortality and achieve a heroic self-image are the root causes of human evil" (xvii). In other words: the attempt of humanity to become like God and deny its finitude is not only the stimulus to heroic acts but also the cause of all evil. Of course one must ask whether our activities are really only a reflection of our fundamental denial of what we are not, namely, God, or whether these activities can and should be understood as an attempt on our part to desire to live as we ought to live, as representatives of God. The Pauline recognition, for example, that humanity knows what is good, but does what is evil, indicates that human actions cannot be simply attributed to a single stimulus. When Becker in the final analysis expresses a hope for "that minute measure of reason to balance destruction" (*Escape from Evil,* 170), he seems implicitly to admit this because "reason" can serve as a means of self-preservation or as something that allows humans to live as they ought to live.

55. Becker, *The Denial of Death,* 194.

56. For a well-researched biography of Jung, see Ronald Hayman, *A Life of Jung* (New York: W. W. Norton, 1999).

collective unconscious. The personal unconscious contains that which one has forgotten, suppressed, and unconsciously perceived, thought, and felt, provided that these things reveal a close relationship to the experiences of the individual.[57] The collective unconscious consists of the collective memory of humanity, as, for example, conditions and situations indicative of human nature such as anxiety, danger, struggle against insurmountable odds, relationships between the sexes, attitudes toward father and mother figures, and experiences of the powers of light and darkness.[58]

Jung discovered the collective unconscious in his work with people whose dreams contained picture motifs that were not related to any of their concrete life experiences. These motifs, however, were related to religious symbols that were not consciously known by these individuals. Jung called these potent picture motifs of the collective unconscious "archetypes." "The archetype is, so to speak, an 'eternal' presence, and it is only a question of whether it is perceived by consciousness or not."[59] Like Freud's id, the archetype has a unique, ambivalent aspect. According to Jung, this is already seen in the picture of the serpent in Genesis 3 when it becomes the picture of either the tempter or the savior. Similarly, the great mother can be either the threatening Tiamat of the Babylonian creation myth or Mary, the saving queen of heaven. Also, the image of the father is divided between that of the violent, castrating demon and the benevolent sage who leads us to the realm of the spirit.

In contrast to Freud, Jung does not dwell so exclusively on the negative side of the collective unconscious, but emphasizes its positive powers that give new impulses to life.[60] While in the collective unconscious the antitheses are

---

57. Carl Gustav Jung, *Psychological Types* (1921), trans. H. G. Baynes, rev. R. F. C. Hull, in *The Collected Works of C. G. Jung*, ed. Wm. McGuire, 2nd ed. (Princeton, NJ: Princeton University Press, 1967-78), 6:377 (par. 625).

58. For the following, see Murray Stein in his intro. to *Encountering Jung on Evil*, selected and intro. Murray Stein (Princeton, NJ: Princeton University Press, 1995), 3, who also writes there: "Jung spent much of his adult life investigating the bewildering contents and tempestuous energies of the unconscious mind."

59. Carl Gustav Jung, *Psychology and Alchemy* (1935/1936), trans. R. F. C. Hull, in *Collected Works*, 12:211 (329); see also 11f. (12ff.), where Jung points out that it is important, especially for Christians, to bring the archetype into harmony with the conscious mind, lest the Christian faith become simply an external, religious veneer and the inner person remain unchanged.

60. See Jung's criticism of Freud when he says that Freud overemphasizes "the pathological aspect of life" and interprets "man too exclusively in the light of his defects." So Carl Gustav Jung, "Freud and Jung: Contrasts" (1929), in *Collected Works*, 4:335 (773).

not yet distinguished from one another, the situation is different when the ego emerges and these things move into the realm of consciousness. The paradise of primordial unity and wholeness is then irrevocably lost. Thus Jung believes that "there is deep doctrine in the legend of the fall: it is the expression of a dim presentiment that the emancipation of ego-consciousness was a Luciferian deed."[61] As the ego seeks to achieve cognition it encounters insurmountable antitheses and is torn between opposing forces such as spirit and matter, male and female, good and evil, life and death. Although we cannot return to the primordial unity, we are able to overcome the inner strife through individuation. This means that we become "a single, homogeneous being, and, insofar as 'individuality' embraces our innermost, last, and incomparable uniqueness, it also implies becoming one's own self."[62] Individuation is therefore equated with "coming to selfhood" or "self-realization." This process of individuation is guided by what Jung calls the "archetype of the self." The individual now comes to its self as well as to the collective self since in its wholeness the individual also reflects the cosmos. "The individuated ego senses itself as the object of an unknown and superordinate subject" (238 [405]). Does this mean that we finally come to a point at which the dichotomy is overcome and ego-consciousness ceases?

If we wish to determine to what extent we can achieve wholeness, we must accompany Jung one step further in his analysis of the person, for he distinguishes still another aspect of the ego which is directed toward the external world and which he calls the "persona." The persona can be understood as similar to a mask in Greek theater, for through it we play a role in society and it filters out everything that does not belong to this role. What the ego considers to be irreconcilable with its persona is relegated to the unconscious as a "shadow" (see 183f. [225] and 156 [246]). Thus the shadow contains the undeveloped, the inferior, and the suppressed, as well as wild drives, the immoral, the evil, and the destructive. Jung desires to achieve an integration of the shadow as a part of the individuation process since "mere suppression of the shadow is as little of a remedy as beheading would be for a headache."[63] We should rather love our shadow, just as Jesus called us to

---

61. Carl Gustav Jung, "The Phenomenology of the Spirit in Fairytales" (1948), in *Collected Works*, 9/1:230 (420). Jung continues his comments on the fall when he perceptively says: "Man's whole history consists from the very beginning in a conflict between his feeling of inferiority and his arrogance."

62. Carl Gustav Jung, "The Relations Between the Ego and the Unconscious" (1916), in *Collected Works*, 7:171 (266).

63. Carl Gustav Jung, "Psychology and Religion" (1938), in *Collected Works*, 11:77.

love our enemies.[64] Like the way in which God integrates in some ways his own shadow, evil, we are summoned to overcome moral suffering through the integration of our shadow.[65] Of course, Jung realizes that we cannot overcome evil by ourselves, but "we hope to put our trust in the higher powers."[66] The attempt at self-redemption wins humanity nothing.

Clearly, Jung goes beyond Freud's dualistic picture of humanity. While Freud saw a deep chasm within humanity between good and evil, Jung admits that there are evil traits within and beyond us that are sometimes not reconcilable with one another. But Jung insists that everything ultimately serves the good. This is to be seen most clearly when Jung suggests that the "shadow" of God will be taken up into the Trinity, making it a quaternity. This positive relationship to evil in Jung's thinking is to be explained by the fact that his view of the biblical portrayal of evil is highly idiosyncratic.

Jung is "indeed convinced that evil is as positive a factor as good."[67] According to Jung, it would be a logical contradiction for a quality to be able to exist without its opposite. When something is good, something bad must also exist for one cannot maintain that something is good when it cannot be distinguished from something that is its opposite. The same applies to the affirmation of the existence of good. Thus, good cannot be identified with being, and evil with a deficiency of being. When something is good and a little evil is added to it, say 5 percent, one could not for this reason reduce its existence to 95 percent, so that the 5 percent simply vanishes. Jung believed that the classical Christian definition of evil as a *privatio boni,* that is, as a

---

64. See Carl Gustav Jung, "Psychotherapists or the Clergy?" (1932), in *Collected Works,* 11:340f. (522f.).

65. Carl Gustav Jung, "A Psychological Approach to the Dogma of the Trinity" (1942/1948), in *Collected Works,* 11:196ff. (290ff.). Since Jung wants to maintain human responsibility for evil he is careful not "to impute all evil to God." He is even convinced that "through the intervention of the Holy Spirit, however, man is included in the divine process, and this means that the principle of separateness and autonomy over against God — which is personified in Lucifer as the God-opposing will — is included in it too." We must ask, however, whether the biblical promise that God will be all in all may be interpreted as to indicate a hope in a possible unification of good and evil. The eschatological hope of the New Testament shows that evil is beyond integration and can only be overcome through elimination.

66. Carl Gustav Jung, "Good and Evil in Analytical Psychology" (1959), in *Collected Works,* 10:467 (883). See also 465 (879), where Jung, in reference to evil, or the devil, says: "I personally find it hard to believe the idea of the *privatio boni* still holds water," that is, evil is not simply a deficiency of the good, as Augustine supposed.

67. Carl Gustav Jung, "Answer 5," in H. L. Philp, *Jung and the Problem of Evil* (New York: Robert M. McBride, 1959), 18. For the following, see 18ff. in the same work.

diminution of the good or a deficiency of being, is to be accounted for by the desire to avoid the introduction of a dualism. The *privatio boni* theory, however, is for Jung in itself contradictory. According to this theory, even the devil, as evil incarnate, must be good inasmuch as he exists. Because, however, he is evil through and through, he simply has no business existing.

In the conflict between the early church and the Gnostics, God and Christ could have only a single meaning, which they hold to this day, namely, that God and Christ are good without qualification.[68] In order to escape any hint of dualism Christ must not possess a shadow side that actually belongs to him. When one begins with the premise that God is the *summum bonum,* that is, the highest good, one could never reach the conclusion that God created evil (52f. [94-97]). God simply created that which is good and that which is less good, whereby the latter is seen as the worse of the two. Jung believes, however, that this type of argumentation is dangerous, for there are things which, seen from a certain perspective, are so evil that one can be deluded by such arguments into a false security. Also, in human nature there are things that are so dangerous that they simply cannot be explained with the concept of a *privatio boni.* "Human nature is capable of an infinite amount of evil, and the evil deeds are as real as the good ones so far as the psyche judges and differentiates between them" (53 [97]). Only in the unconscious does there exist no differentiation between good and evil. Therefore it is important that the danger of evil not be overlooked.

Jung summarizes his misgivings to the effect that the doctrine of evil as a *privatio boni,* or a deficiency of the good, provides an overly optimistic view of evil in human nature and an overly pessimistic view of the human soul. In order to counter evil, early Christianity balanced Christ against the anti-Christ since one cannot speak about height if there is no depth, or about good if there is no evil. Together with Christ, therefore, the devil comes into the world as the adversary of God. In early Christian circles, according to Jung, Satan was even viewed as the older brother of Christ (61 [113f.]). Along with the doctrine of evil as a deficiency of good another danger made its way into in the early church, for evil appeared to exist only as

---

68. See Carl Gustav Jung, *Aion* (1951), in *Collected Works,* 9/2:44f. (79f.). The problem of evil, especially with regard to the "missing shadow of Christ," is elaborated well in John P. Dourley, "Trinitarian Models and Human Integration: Jung and Tillich Compared," in *Carl Gustav Jung: Critical Assessment,* ed. Renos K. Papadopoulos, vol. 4, *Implications and Inspirations* (London: Routledge, 1992), esp. 217-20. Yet his own solution stemming from Jung's idea that through the full absorption of the shadow Christ can be seen as both truly human and reunited with God sounds less convincing.

an omission that one could effectively deal with by a change of attitude. This psychological interpretation of evil, however, attributes an ominous power to the psyche or soul since God himself must intervene to deliver humanity from the curse of evil.

For Jung, as psychologist, the Christ symbol is of highest importance, for it is probably the most highly developed and differentiated symbol of the self.[69] While one encounters within one's own self an amazing unity of contrasts, Christ, on the other hand, represents only the good, and the devil, as his adversary, only the evil. This opposition, according to Jung, is the real problem of the world, which remains to this day unresolved. The reality of evil and its incompatibility with the good keep the two opposites apart and lead unavoidably to the crucifixion and neutralization of everything living. Jung even understands Gnosticism in a positive manner when he says, "The dualism of the Gnostic systems makes sense, because they at least try to do justice to the real meaning of evil. They have also done us the supreme service of having gone very thoroughly into the question of where evil comes from."[70] Jung rightly notes that in this regard the biblical tradition, as well as the early church, says very little.

According to Jung, in a monotheistic religion everything that turns against God must ultimately be traced back to him. Moreover, it is difficult within a Trinitarian understanding to allocate a place for the devil. As the antagonist of Christ, for instance, the devil would have to receive an appropriate, opposing position as a son of God. But this would lead to a Gnostic view in which, according to Jung, the devil, or "Satanael," is called the first son of God, and Christ the second. A logical result of the incorporation of Satan would then be the expansion of the Trinity to a quaternity, which was already strongly attacked by the church fathers. Jung, on the other hand, seems to have no problem with a quaternity since even in the Old Testament Satan was one of the sons of God. Of course, it is strange for us to imagine that in God both good and evil could be united, or that God could even perhaps desire such a thing. Yet for Jung the legend of Lucifer is just as little an absurd fairytale as the story of the serpent in the Garden of Eden.[71] Life as an energy process needs opposites, without which there would be no energy. Good and evil are, therefore, simply moral aspects of a natural polarity.

---

69. So Carl Gustav Jung, "Introduction to the Religious and Psychological Problems of Alchemy," in *Collected Works*, 12:19 (22).

70. Jung, "A Psychological Approach," 169 (249).

71. For this and the following, see Jung, "A Psychological Approach," 196f. (291).

In the story of Job one finds a very clear association of evil with God. It is remarkable, according to Jung, how quickly Yahweh gives in to the proposals of Satan.[72] Neither does God bring Satan to account when Job's innocence is proven. One must, therefore, assume that Yahweh plays along with Satan. God's willingness, according to Jung, to deliver Job into the murderous hands of Satan shows that God's own tendency toward unfaithfulness is projected onto Job as a "scapegoat." Jung writes:

> We have plenty of evidence in the Old Testament that Jahwe is moral and immoral at the same time, and Rabbinic theology is fully aware of this fact. Jahwe behaves very much like an immoral being, though He is a guardian of law and order. He is unjust and unreliable according to the Old Testament. Even the God of the New Testament is still irascible and vengeful to such a degree that He needs the self-sacrifice of His son to quench His wrath. Christian theology has never denied the identity of the God of the Old Testament with that of the New Testament.[73]

Yet Jung does not simply equate the Old and New Testaments on this matter, for he notices a curious metaphysical phenomenon to which Christ points: he saw Satan fall from heaven like lightning.[74] In this vision, according to Jung, a metaphysical event becomes temporal, the final separation of Yahweh from his son of darkness. Satan was banned from heaven and no longer had the opportunity to drag his father into questionable enterprises. He therefore also no longer had a relationship of personal trust with Yahweh. He was deprived of the affections of his father and sent into exile. Jung finds the explanation for this punishment in the fact that the story of Job had, for Satan, finally reached its conclusion, even if in a strangely limited form. He had, indeed, no longer access to the heavenly household, but continued to exercise dominion over the earth. Only at the end of time will he be made forever powerless. Yet he cannot be blamed for Christ's death, for this sacrificial death was decreed by Yahweh.

As a result of the partial neutralization of Satan, Yahweh identified himself with his luminous side and became the good God and loving father. "He has not lost his wrath and can still mete out punishment, but he does it with justice. Cases like the Job tragedy are apparently no longer to be ex-

---

72. See Carl Gustav Jung, *Answer to Job* (1952/1967), in *Collected Works*, 11:390 (616).

73. Jung, "Answer 5," 19f.

74. For this and the following, see Jung, *Answer to Job,* 410 (650f.), and for the following citation, see 410 (651).

pected. He proves himself benevolent and gracious. He shows mercy to the sinful children of men and is defined as Love itself." Although Christ had the full trust of his father and felt himself one with him, he nevertheless included in the Lord's Prayer the petition "and lead us not into temptation but deliver us from evil." With this petition he asks God not to drag us into evil, but to deliver us from it. This means, therefore, that the possibility still exists that Yahweh might revert back to his earlier ways, and that we must guard ourselves against this possibility. For this reason Christ wishes to make his father aware of this destructive tendency and asks him to refrain from it.

While Jung seeks to recognize a development within God, we will, in contrast, when the question of evil is taken up from the perspective of the biblical witness, point out that the actual change is not to be found in God but in our understanding of God. To be sure, Jung is correct when he says that "the God of the Old Testament is both good and evil."[75] We must disagree with him, however, when he continues by saying that God "is just as much the father or creator of Satan as of Christ." Jung comes to his solution of the mystery of evil in the contemporary world through his lifelong work in psychology and from his own experience. In this way he came to recognize that God, too, had a dark side. We must agree with Jung that evil cannot be restricted to a simple *privatio boni*. But even Augustine, as we shall see, had not done this. The alternative to a *privatio boni,* however, is not to be found in the localization of evil in God. Neither is it to be found in the manifestation of evil in humanity itself, for God's creation includes more than just humans. This means, then, that the power that aligns itself against God cannot be located in the human consciousness.[76]

As can be seen in his "Answer to Job," Jung has projected a great deal into the biblical tradition that the texts themselves do not justify. This is because Jung sought to solve the mystery of evil with these projections, a mystery that is described but not solved in the Christian tradition. Whether he does justice thereby to the Judeo-Christian tradition, with the exception of its fringes, is doubtful. For Jung, the attribute of holiness in relation to God plays almost no role. Had he emphasized God's holiness more, much, if not all, that he attributes to the subjective evil actions of God would have been

---

75. Jung, "Answer 5," 20.

76. Thus rightly Wallace B. Clift, *Jung and Christianity: The Challenge of Reconciliation* (New York: Crossroad, 1988), 145, who points here to the "angelic world" in a broad sense, thereby referring to Paul Tillich, among others, as supporters of this view.

explainable. The holiness of God requires, for example, when God does not wish to stop being God, that everyone who opposes him be correspondingly punished. This makes God neither a wrathful demon nor unpredictable. Rather, God expects that the honor due him be given without hesitation or ulterior motives. Precisely with regard to the holiness of God, however, is the evident desire of human beings to be in God's place.

c. The Tragedy of Evil (Fromm)

German-American psychoanalyst **Erich Fromm** (1900-1980) "always lived and worked in the name of Life"[77] and was deeply influenced by the psychoanalysis of Freud and Jung as well as by evolutionary thought. Fromm claims that "the growing process of the emergence of the individual from his original ties, a process which we may call 'individuation,' seems to have reached its peak in modern history in the centuries between the Reformation and the present."[78] Of course, the beginning of modernity is not the cause of all our problems, although it did magnify them since the existence of humanity itself has become a problem.[79]

Whereas animals, living completely within nature, are guided by instinctive behavior, humans have lost such instinctive mechanisms. Although living within nature, they transcend it at the same time and are conscious of themselves. In setting themselves over against nature they have lost their unity and feel unbearably alone, lost, and powerless. This same process can be seen in the development of individual human beings. Each of us initially feels at one with our environment, but then becomes gradually more aware of our individuality. Fromm determines, therefore, that "on the one side of the growing process of individuation is the growth of self-

77. So fittingly Daniel Burston, "Erich Fromm: A Brief Biography," in *A Prophetic Analyst: Erich Fromm's Contribution to Psychoanalysis,* ed. Mauricio Cortina and Michael Maccoby (Northvale, NJ: Jason Aronson, 1996), 424. Similarly Edward S. Tauber and Bernard Landis, "On Erich Fromm," in *In the Name of Life: Essays in Honor of Erich Fromm,* ed. Bernard Landis and Edward Tauber (New York: Holt, Rinehart and Winston, 1971), 1. In this collection are found excellent essays on various aspects of Fromm's work.

78. Erich Fromm, *Escape from Freedom* (1941; New York: Holt, Rinehart and Winston, 1960), 24.

79. For this and the following, see Erich Fromm, "Psychoanalysis and Zen Buddhism," in D. T. Suzuki, Erich Fromm, and Richard De Martino, *Zen Buddhism and Psychoanalysis* (New York: Harper, 1960), 86f.

strength," but on the other side of this process is a "growing aloneness."[80] Human existence implies "freedom from instinctual determination of . . . actions" that is prerequisite for the development of human culture. The troubling fact, however, is that the two sides of this development, growing power and increasing individuation, are not balanced. Consequently, the history of humanity is littered with conflict and strife and "each step in the direction of growing individuation [has] threatened people with new insecurities."

If the human being is self-conscious, maintains Fromm, "he realizes his powerlessness and the limitations of his existence. He visualizes his own end: death."[81] Yet we cannot go back to the pre-human state of harmony with nature without giving up our humanity. Fromm claims, therefore, that a human being "must proceed to develop his reason until he becomes the master of nature, and of himself." But can a human being really achieve this? Fromm appears to give a partial answer when he admits that the short lifespan of humans does not allow, "under even the most favorable conditions," the full development of their potential.[82] Furthermore, instead of responding to their freedom with dedication and work in solidarity with nature, humans often seek to escape from their freedom through a sadistic domination of, or a masochistic submission to, the object to which they are supposed to relate. Or perhaps they attempt to rid themselves of the object through its destruction.[83] Yet, according to Fromm, "the intensity of destructive strivings by no means implies that they are invincible or even dominant."[84]

According to Fromm, evil is a specifically human phenomenon. It manifests itself in the "syndrome of decay," which consists of the love of death, narcissism, and symbiotic fixation on incest. It prompts people to destroy for destruction's sake and to hate for hatred's sake. Yet this decay syndrome, which is symbolic of regression, is countered by a growth syndrome

---

80. This and the following citations are taken from Fromm, *Escape from Freedom,* 29, 32, and 36.

81. Erich Fromm, *Man for Himself: An Inquiry into the Psychology of Ethics* (1947; New York: Holt, Rinehart and Winston, 1959), 40.

82. Don S. Browning, in his book *Generative Man: Psychoanalytic Perspectives* (Philadelphia: Westminster, 1973), 115f., rightly warns that it is hardly fair to accuse Fromm of "glib utopianism and perfectionism."

83. Fromm, *Escape from Freedom,* 173 and 179.

84. For this quote and the information in the following paragraph, see Erich Fromm, *The Heart of Man: Its Genius for Good and Evil* (New York: Harper, 1964), 22f.

that is symbolic of progress and expresses itself in the love of life, humanity, and independence.

While Fromm admits that the human heart can become hardened and inhumane, he contends that it can never become non-human. "It always remains a man's heart."[85] Even the followers of Hitler or Stalin, Fromm insists, began their lives with the chance to become good people. Human nature in its essence is neither good nor evil, although a contradiction is rooted within the very condition of human existence. This conflict requires a resolution for which there are only two possibilities: either to regress or to progress. Even if these possibilities create new contradictions, humans should be able to resolve these problems either progressively or regressively. In the struggle between the love for life (biophilia) and the love of death (necrophilia), neither tendency is ever present in its pure form, that is, holiness or insanity. In most cases there is to be found a mixture of both forms of love, and our spirit orients itself toward whichever one dominates. For Fromm, of course, the question of which form will ultimately gain the upper hand is largely settled since unlike Freud he contends that there is an inherent, qualitative predisposition toward life to be found in all living substances. Thus he labels as the "death instinct" "a malignant phenomenon which grows and takes over to the extent to which the Eros does not unfold."

In contrast, for instance, to Konrad Lorenz, Fromm desires to show that the problem of human life does not lie in a reduction of instinctive reactions, but rather, that human aggression is conditioned by society and works in collaboration with the biological necessities of humanity.[86] As the works of Fromm repeatedly show, the fundamental problem of humanity is indeed grounded in its character, but not in (deficiently) instinctive behavior. This is also to be seen in Fromm's denial of the existence of original sin.[87] "The Bible leaves no doubt that it does not consider man as either good or evil, but endowed with both tendencies. . . . Yet it is very significant that in the story of the 'fall' the Bible never calls Adam's act a sin."[88] What

85. For this and the following, see Fromm, *Heart of Man,* 150 (quote), 138, 120f., 48, 45 and 50 (quote).

86. See "Erich Fromm: Some Biographical Notes," in *In the Name of Life,* ed. Landis and Tauber, xiv.

87. See the extensive treatment by Ramon Xirau, "Erich Fromm: What Is Man's Struggle?" in *In the Name of Life,* ed. Landis and Tauber, 152.

88. So Erich Fromm, *You Shall Be as Gods: A Radical Interpretation of the Old Testament and Its Traditions* (New York: Holt, Rinehart and Winston, 1966), 159.

Adam can be reprimanded for, however, according to Fromm, is his disobedience. If, therefore, disobedience is sin, admits Fromm, then Adam and Eve sinned. Yet for Fromm disobedience is virtually a liberating act.

> The act of disobedience set Adam and Eve free and opened their eyes. They recognized each other as strangers and the world outside them as strange and even hostile. Their act of disobedience broke the primary bond with nature and made them individuals. "Original sin," far from corrupting man, set him free; it was the beginning of history. Man had to leave the Garden of Eden in order to learn to rely on his own powers and to become fully human.[89]

Fromm offers with these comments an idealistic interpretation of the fall that leaves no place for the concept of original sin. He believes he is supported in this interpretation by the Old Testament tradition since even the prophets confirm the idea that humans have a right to be disobedient. Only after their disobedience can human beings establish a harmony between themselves, other persons, and nature through the forces of reason and love. Fromm even believes that humanity, through new acts of disobedience, has progressed in its development. This applies to humans' spiritual as well as intellectual development since they liberate themselves from authorities that would not tolerate any new thoughts or any new freedoms for the individual.

For Fromm the biblical witness portrays a humanity that is not sinful and in its very nature depraved, but rather a humanity that simply has evil inclinations and therefore a tendency toward evil. One must consequently take into account that while "the Bible acknowledges the fact of man's 'evil imaginings,' it also believes in his inherent capacity for good."[90] Thus, for example, Israel is called a "holy nation." Fromm, however, does not overlook the fact that the Israelites, together with their kings, sinned. According to the Jewish understanding of humanity, all people are born with the capacity to sin, but are able to change their ways, rediscover themselves, and through their own efforts, apart from any gracious act of God, redeem themselves. "Man, in the biblical and post-biblical view, is given the choice between his 'good and evil drives'" (162). Because humans have, in many ways, the freedom of choice, they can sometimes go too far and forfeit this

---

89. For this and the following, see Erich Fromm, *On Disobedience and Other Essays* (London: Routledge & Kegan Paul, 1981), 1f.

90. Fromm, *You Shall Be as Gods,* 161.

freedom. This can be seen, for instance, in the story of the exodus from Egypt, in which, according to the biblical understanding, God hardened the heart of Pharaoh. Also, in the prophetic writings, according to Fromm, it is emphasized that humans can lose their ability to choose. For this reason the prophets pressed the people so often to exercise their ability to choose and not to fall into the misfortune of a lost freedom of choice (165).

According to Fromm, we do not need any self-accusation or penance in order to be accepted by God after we have sinned. According to the Jewish view, a person is free and independent. When we sin, thereby straying from the right path, we can always show remorse, which means that we are returning to the right path.[91] In our changes and conversions we are not dependent on God, for our sin is our own sin and our repentance is our own repentance. There is, therefore, no ground for self-accusing submission. There is also no collective or original sin; rather, we all share a common human nature. "Because we all share in the same humanity, there is nothing inhuman in sinning, hence nothing to be ashamed of, or to be despised for. Our inclination to sin is as human as our inclination to do good and as our capacity to 'return'" (175f.). In Fromm's thinking, human beings stand on their own two feet and need neither a savior nor a God who shows them grace.

As we now seek to summarize Fromm's position we notice that the antagonistic conflict that Freud found within humanity is interpreted by Fromm as a positive possibility for life. Does this mean that for Fromm no radical evil exists, either internal or external to humanity? We receive from him no direct answer to this question. Fromm characterizes evil as the human being's loss of the self "through the tragic attempt to rid himself of the burden of his humanity."[92] Therefore we are confronted here with something tragic that could well be identified with that which is fateful, and thereby, also with something for which humanity is not ultimately responsible. This unaccountability cannot be undone by the fact that Fromm speaks within the same context of a lesser evil and a greater evil, in which the greater evil is always directed against life itself whereas the less significant evil merely reveals a deficiency. The fateful character of evil is also addressed by Fromm when he argues that one needs a "rational faith in man's capacity to extricate himself from what seems the fatal web of circumstances that he has created."[93]

---

91. For this and the following, see Fromm, *You Shall Be as Gods,* 169.

92. Fromm, *Heart of Man,* 148.

93. Fromm, *The Anatomy of Human Destructiveness* (New York: Holt, Rinehart and Winston, 1973), 438.

Within human life Fromm observes that which is fateful. Yet he does not feel comfortable with identifying anything external to humanity from which evil summons its threatening power. It is, however, doubtful whether Fromm's hope will prove correct that humanity can turn back from this fate in order to build a society "in which no one is threatened: not the child by the parent; not the parent by the superior; no social class by another; no nation by a superpower" (435). This, however, is also not a "rational faith," but rather wishful thinking that up until now has not been fulfilled. As Fromm demonstrates, we must, on the one hand, affirm that humanity possesses a potential for life, and, on the other hand, we must not forget that which is essentially evil, that is, that which threatens to destroy the potential for life. While we welcome and affirm Fromm's passion for life, we must at the same time point out that the realization of this passion in humanity is inadequately grounded.

d. An Inborn Inclination for Evil

How shall we assess human freedom? Does human existence really, as British philosopher and mathematician Thomas Hobbes (1588-1679) asserted, consist of a war in which everyone is against everybody else? Sigmund Freud resurrected this notion by juxtaposing *eros* and *thanatos* when he was confronted with the destructive human forces unleashed by World War I. Konrad Lorenz, too, emphasized that there is an aggressive drive in nature, perhaps reflecting Herbert Spencer's insistence on the survival of the fittest. In sociobiology that struggle for survival is seen on the level of genes where altruistic behavior is essentially egotistical, assuring the survival of one's own genetic material against foreign material. In neurobiology we detect the notion that violence results from neurobiological defects that are either inborn or acquired. But neurobiology, as we have seen, also shows that humans are not just biologically determined, but have a "faculty of deliberation." This human faculty of deliberation can be used in a destructive way. While on the one hand humanity had no chance of surviving unless individuals cooperated and helped one other, as can be seen in the organization of the family, humans have at the same time become more belligerent and more cruel than any other species when it comes to inflicting harm on, or even killing, its own kind. We need only think here of Adolf Hitler and the cunning way in which he attempted and to a large extent succeeded in eradicating those he thought were inferior or detrimental to the Aryan race. Joseph Stalin (1878-1953), also without any moral qualms, wiped out millions of people in order to reach his goals. There is indeed an immensely destructive possibility in each human being that may or may not be activated. Yet it is interesting that when we look at the biblical creation accounts, it is consistently affirmed that everything was very good once God had created it.

5. The Biblical View of Human Evil

According to both creation stories at the beginning of the Bible, God gives a command to human beings. Since a command only makes sense if one can obey it or resist it, this would imply that from the very beginning humans had a certain freedom of volition and were not completely determined by their instinctive behavior. Since the story of the fall is situated after the creation narratives, this would imply that when humans were created they exhibited an initial consonance with God's aims. It was after God had created humans that evil emerged when humans alienated themselves from God and subsequently from each other.

1. The Old Testament Sources

As Gerhard von Rad noted: "The contents of Gen., ch. 2, and especially ch. 3 are conspicuously isolated in the Old Testament. No prophet, psalm, or narrator makes any recognizable reference to the story of the Fall."[1] Indeed, the story of the fall itself in Genesis 3 is isolated from the rest of the Old Testament. Walter Brueggemann (b. 1933) even claims: "In general, the Old Testament does not assume such a 'fall.'"[2] Yet Robin C. Cover reminds us that there are more than fifty words for human evil or "sin" in biblical Hebrew. "The plethora of Hebrew terms and their ubiquitous presence in the

1. Gerhard von Rad, *Genesis: A Commentary,* rev. ed., trans. John H. Marks (Philadelphia: Westminster, 1972), 102.

2. Walter Brueggemann, *Genesis* (Atlanta: John Knox, 1982), 41, in his comments on Genesis 2:4b–3:24.

Hebrew Bible testify to the fact that sin was a dominant concern of the Israelite theologians."[3]

While evil in the Old Testament can have a qualitative connotation as something that is simply bad or worthless, it can also be used in a moral and spiritual sense as the designation for immorality and unfaithfulness to the covenant that God made with his people. We hear that human hearts are continually evil (Gen. 6:5), and they "call evil good and good evil" (Isa. 5:20). Humans can also bring evil on themselves. In nearly every book of the Old Testament we read about human disobedience, divine punishment, and forgiveness of sin. The human situation is so bad that God even regretted having created humanity (Gen. 6:6). Then we hear the sobering words from God: "The inclination of the human heart is evil from youth" (Gen. 8:21). Yet how did that all-pervading sinfulness or that evil inclination of humanity get started? While everything that God had created was good, sin and evil occurred right at the beginning with the first woman (Eve) and the first man (Adam). While "adam" was initially a generic term for a human being, it is understood as a proper name in the latter part of Genesis 3. By talking about Adam as a specific person, the Yahwist wants to point to the exemplary character of this event. The sin committed in Genesis 3 is not simply a violation of God's command not to eat from the tree of the knowledge of good and evil. Rather, the distrust of God is at the center of the fall account. The condition depicted in the Yahwist creation account is characterized by innocence. Israeli scholar Umberto Cassuto (1883-1951) puts it well: "When man was created he was simple like a new-born child; and like a babe of a day, who receives his food without toil, he was happy in the garden that his God had prepared for him. . . . [But] He did not wish to remain in the position of a child who is under the supervision of his father and is constantly dependent on him."[4] Now the harmony between God and human beings is broken. The intention of connecting creation and fall so intimately is not to show how the once good creation turned so bad. Even after the fall the world, including humanity, is still God's good creation. But the Yahwist wants to demonstrate the reason for our present human predicament.

---

3. Robin C. Cover, "Sin, Sinners," in *The Anchor Bible Dictionary,* ed. David Noel Freedman, 6 vols. (New York: Doubleday, 1992), 6:31.

4. Umberto Cassuto, *A Commentary on the Book of Genesis,* part 1, *From Adam to Noah,* trans. Israel Abrahams (Jerusalem: Magnes Press, 1989 [1944]), 113.

a. The Mysterious Cause of Evil

It has often been claimed that the disruption of the initial harmony is actually beneficial because it leads to the actualization of the human potential. German philosopher Georg Friedrich Wilhelm Hegel (1770-1831), for instance, understands sin as the logical necessity to recognize the good since if man "does not know about evil, he also does not know about good."[5] He characterized the fall "as the eternal myth of man through which he becomes man."[6] German poet and philosopher Friedrich Schiller thought along similar lines and concluded that the alleged disobedience against God's command was actually the fall of humans from their instinct, which brought moral evil into creation, but only to enable the moral good within creation. Therefore without doubt it is the happiest and greatest event in human history. From this moment onward human freedom is inscribed; here the first and remote foundation was laid for human morality.[7]

This idealistic notion of human sinfulness is affirmed by many psychoanalysts. For instance, 175 years after Schiller, Erich Fromm claimed: "This first act of disobedience is man's first step toward freedom." Man was expelled from paradise and is now able "to make his own history, to develop his human powers, and to attain a new harmony with man and nature as a fully developed individual instead of the former harmony in which he was *not yet* an individual."[8] As noted above, Carl Gustav Jung was a little more restrained when he wrote: "There is deep doctrine in the legend of the fall: it is the expression of a dim presentiment that the emancipation of the ego-consciousness was a Luciferian deed."[9] Pursuing a different perspective, Pierre Teilhard de Chardin also came close to this idealistic notion when he asserted that evil is a necessary byproduct of

5. Georg Friedrich Wilhelm Hegel, *Vorlesungen über die Philosophie der Religion,* vol. 1 in *Sämtliche Werke* (Glockner), 15:285.

6. Georg Friedrich Wilhelm Hegel, *Vorlesungen über die Geschichte,* vol. 1 in *Sämtliche Werke* (Glockner), 11:413.

7. Friedrich Schiller, *Etwas über die erste Menschengesellschaft: Übergang des Menschen zur Freiheit und Humanität* (1789), in *Gesammelte Werke in fünf Bänden,* ed. Reinhold Netolitzky (Gütersloh: C. Bertelsmann, 1959), 103.

8. Erich Fromm, *The Heart of Man: Its Genius for Good and Evil* (New York: Harper, 1964), 20.

9. Carl Gustav Jung, "The Phenomenology of the Spirit in Fairytales," in *The Collected Works of C. G. Jung,* ed. Wm. McGuire, vol. 9/1, 2nd ed. (Princeton, NJ: Princeton University Press, 1971), 230 (420).

evolution through which in manifold errors and trials nature progresses on its evolutionary course.[10]

The idealistic interpretations of the fall argue on the basis of an evolutionary process, in which a later stage of the process is perceived as more highly developed and therefore better. There are two objections, however, that have to be voiced. First, it is difficult to assert on strictly biological grounds that an evolutionary development toward a higher stage is necessarily better. Biologically speaking, humans are not better than fish though humanity represents a higher evolutionary development of life. The same case can be made for the cultural development of humanity. A highly developed culture is not necessarily better than a less developed one. On the contrary, it can be more vulnerable especially with respect to natural disasters and terrorist attacks. Second, while the account of the fall is not incompatible with evolutionary theories, it is not amenable to any kind of evolutionary interpretation. This becomes evident in two ways.

First, "the sudden appearance of sin does not derive causally from God's good creation according to Genesis 3."[11] When Adam is questioned by God about his behavior, he tries a causal inference, saying, "The woman whom you gave to be with me, she gave me fruit from the tree, and I ate" (Gen. 3:12). In other words, he wants to excuse himself by blaming God as the cause of evil. The woman tries a similar causal inference, though not as daring, when she replies to God: "The serpent tricked me, and I ate" (Gen. 3:13). Again the excuse is made that the cause of evil comes from outside. Yet none of these attempts suffices before God to account for the gravity of the situation. Second, there is also no causal connection between this first sin and the emergence of subsequent sins. We concede that the Yahwist demonstrates in the chapters following the account of the fall that evil spread like a forest fire. But he does not mention anywhere that the emergence of new sin is connected with prior sin and thus can be used to excuse the significance of each case.

Evil came into the world with the first appearance of man and woman

10. See Pierre Teilhard de Chardin, *The Phenomenon of Man,* trans. Bernard Wall, intro. Julian Huxley (New York: Harper Torchbook, 1959), 301f., where he says: "The involuting universe . . . proceeds step by step by dint of billion-fold trial and error. It is this process of groping, combined with the two-fold mechanism of reproduction and heredity . . . which gives rise to the . . . tree of life." See also 310, where he picks up the same terminology in talking about the "evil of disorder and failure" as a necessity in the evolutionary process.

11. So Walther Zimmerli, *Old Testament Theology in Outline,* trans. David E. Green (Edinburgh: T&T Clark, 1984 [1978]), 168, and see 169 for the following.

and it continued to erupt with every further appearance of man and woman. It is important to remember here what behavioral psychology has told us about the phenomenon of aggression. In many ways aggressive drives are present already on the animal level. Yet there they are usually displayed to help and further the species instead of destroying it. This is true for aggression activated against other species (defense, hunting, and the like) as well as within their own species (rank and order, mating, and the like). However, once humanity emerged and began to dominate its environment and members of its own kind through the introduction of more and more sophisticated tools (and weapons), the aggressive drives became increasingly ambivalent. At the same time they furthered the potential good and the potential evil. There went hand in hand with this the extinction of some species and the domestication of others, genocide of parts of humanity and the unification of others through regional cultures. As psychoanalysis rightly tells us, the activities of humanity are highly ambivalent, pursuing life and spreading death at the same time.

But the emergence of evil cannot be compared with a fateful decree against which humanity has no choice. We should not overlook the fact that not a human being but the serpent is introduced as the tempter in the fall account. Yet it is an over-interpretation of the temptation story to conclude that the woman has more immediate access to the dark sides of life than man because she is seduced first and in turn seduces the man.[12] What is emphasized is that the essence of human beings was not sinful from the beginning, but that temptation had to come from the outside. Yet the cause of evil is not an anti-Godly principle outside of God's creation, as in Gnostic thought. We remember that the serpent is explicitly introduced as an animal and as part of God's creation, and not as part of the heavenly court.[13] Why this part of God's good creation becomes the tempter is beyond the interest of the Yahwist since the answer to this question does not contribute anything to the description of human sinfulness. There are two things, however, that still need clarification: what was the object that tempted humans, and what were the consequences for them once they succumbed to sin?

The first couple was tempted to be like God, knowing good and evil. It is difficult to assume that God had created a creature that would become

---

12. See von Rad, *Genesis*, 90, in his exegesis of Genesis 3:6, who presents this interpretation.

13. See Johannes Fichtner, "*ophis* (Gen. 3)," in *TDNT*, 5:573, who emphasizes the creational aspect of the serpent.

God's potential challenger since man "carries potential Godhead within himself."[14] While it is also absurd for the Yahwist to surmise that anybody could be like Yahweh, it is much easier for him to suggest that a human being wanted to become like the *elohim,* that it wanted to become divine.[15] When humanity was tempted to know good and evil, it was not just tempted to know the distinction between good and evil. As German Old Testament scholar Claus Westermann (1909-2000) says, humanity set into action that urge "which is always part of human existence whenever and as long as it is lived, namely, that people have the urge to transcend themselves by overstepping the limits set for them."[16] This human *hubris* to do more than what was actually good and allowed for them effectively destroyed humanity's relationship with God.

However, God did not respond to humanity's sinful pride like an insulted tyrant. Admittedly, the harmonious unity with God was gone, and the couple was sent forth from the garden. But the threat that if they ate from the tree of knowledge of good and evil they would die (Gen. 2:17) was not actualized once they had sinned. They were only reassured that they would return to the dust from which they had been taken (Gen. 2:7; 3:19). Almost as if in defiance to the original threat, Adam now dares to call his wife Eve, that is, the mother of all living beings. Not even the obligation to work can be understood as the actual curse of the fall (Gen. 2:15). However, once the harmonious relationship with God was broken so was the harmonious relationship between humanity and nature, and between man and woman. Life now, confesses the Yahwist, is drudgery, filled with hatred and passion, and longing for harmony. Yet life does not come to an end because "the Lord God made garments of skins for the man and for his wife, and clothed them" (Gen. 3:21). Instead of lamenting evil the Yahwist points to signs of grace that are given to the first couple on their wanderings through life, the coats of skins and God's help in clothing them. This compassionate act of God is much more likely understood as the first sign of the gospel than the verdict that there would be constant animosity between the snake and humanity.[17] As Westermann perceptively comments: "The last action

14. This assumption is advanced by Erich Fromm, *You Shall Be as Gods: A Radical Interpretation of the Old Testament and Its Tradition* (New York: Holt, Rinehart and Winston, 1966), 24.

15. Similarly, von Rad, *Genesis,* 89, in his exegesis of Genesis 3:4f.

16. Claus Westermann, *Genesis 1-11,* trans. John J. Scullion (Minneapolis: Fortress, 1994), 249, in his commentary on Genesis 2:4b–3:24.

17. For the interpretation of Genesis 3:15, see Fichtner, "*ophis* (Gen. 3)," *TDNT,*

of the creator towards his creature before expelling him from the garden is an action of care and concern."[18]

Why is it that humans fall so out of line with God's will? We should remember here that humans (Adam) are closely associated with *adamah* (dust, or clay). Therefore we read in Job 4:17-19: "Can mortals be righteous before God? Can human beings be pure before their Maker? Even in his servants he puts no trust, and his angels he charges with error; how much more those who live in houses of clay, whose foundation is in the dust, who are crushed like a moth." Humans are made of clay, of dusty substance, and therefore are frail and impure and much more prone to sin than celestial beings, which also fall into error. In terms of the Israelite cultic law both conception and birth are connected with impurity, so that a woman after childbirth must undergo purification (Leviticus 12). Every newborn human being, having come in contact with impurity at birth, has therefore this fragile beginning. Since pregnancy and childbirth at that time were much more dangerous to both child and mother than they are today in Western societies, human frailty was much more a problem than it is today. Yet one ought to be careful not to misread statements such as Psalm 51:5, where we read: "Indeed, I was born guilty, as sinner when my mother conceived me." This is not a statement about original sin, but about the pervasiveness of sin that starts at the very beginning of a human being.[19] Humans have feet of clay and when they are not aligned with God, they are indeed lost as Isaiah in confrontation with God realizes and exclaims: "Woe is me! I am lost, for I am a man of unclean lips, and live among a people of unclean lips" (Isa. 6:5). Yet humans are not so alienated from God that they could never live in harmony with God. Their mouth as that vessel from which often unclean and evil things proceed can be cleaned by God and then they can become God's messengers.

5:574f. At this point no indication is made yet that the animosity between snake and humanity will be overcome. But such animosity will no longer exist in the messianic time. Then the original harmony will be re-established; see Isaiah 11:1-8.

18. Westermann, *Genesis 1–11*, 269, in his comments on Genesis 3:21.

19. See Hans-Joachim Kraus, *Psalms 1–59*, trans. Hilton C. Oswald (Minneapolis: Fortress, 1993), 503, who states in his exegesis of Psalm 51:5 that this "total depravity" is something very different from what the church asserts with the notion of original sin.

b. Human Responsibility for Sin

In the Old Testament we hear of sin in the context of disobedience, rebellion, and disloyalty. Yet something evil, such as David sending Uriah on a death mission so he can have Uriah's wife Bathsheba as his own spouse, only became sin when God's prophet Nathan confronted David. Then the king confessed: "I have sinned against the Lord" (2 Sam. 12:13). But sins can also be just sins committed out of ignorance, for instance, when the psalmist asked God, "Do not remember the sins of my youth or my transgressions" (Ps. 25:7). Yet usually sins are committed as an act of disobedience against God. This is true for Israel as a whole as well as for the individual Israelite. Though especially in the intertestamental period, the figure of Satan is introduced as the one who tries to lead humans astray, humanity has no excuse for its own sinful behavior. The same is true when sin can be traced all the way back to Adam's fall (Apoc. Abraham 23 and 26). Neither Satan nor the fall is the cause of sin. Each human being must shoulder his or her own responsibility. This is clearly expressed in 2 Baruch 54:15, 19:

> For, although Adam sinned first and has brought death upon all who were not in his own time, yet each of them who has been born from him has prepared for himself the coming torment. And further, each of them has chosen for himself the coming glory. . . . Adam is, therefore, not the cause, except only for himself, but each of us has become our own Adam.

While it is mentioned here that through Adam's fall physical death came into the world, an understanding that is taken up by Paul in the New Testament, the fall is not yet seen as the cause of spiritual death (this latter idea is only occasionally expressed in the intertestamental period; see 2 Bar. 48:42f., 4 Ezra 3:21). At times Adam is understood as the cause of perdition of the whole human race. But there is never a clear connection between Adam's sin and the sin of his descendants.[20] We read, for instance, in 4 Ezra:

> For the first Adam, burdened with an evil heart, transgressed and was overcome, as were also all who were descended from him. Thus the disease be-

---

20. It is interesting that in 2 Enoch 31:6 and in the Apocalypse of Moses the fall is attributed to Satan. Especially in the latter book the significant observation is made that, after being expelled from heaven because of disobeying God's orders, Satan speaks through the mouth of the serpent and entices Eve and causes her to sin (Apoc. Moses 17:4). This identification of Satan with the serpent is then picked up in the New Testament book of Revelation (see Rev. 12:9).

came permanent; the law was in the people's heart along with the evil root, but what was good departed, and the evil remained. (4 Ezra 3:21f.)

This means that the free will of humanity is significantly weakened after the fall. But when we read "what was good departed," then this is "in clear contradiction to Rabbinic theology which emphasizes the power of the Law to keep evil tendency in check and overcome it."[21]

The main tenor of the intertestamental period, however, is expressed in the admonition "So understand, my children, that two spirits await an opportunity with humanity: the spirit of truth and the spirit of error" (Test. Judah 20:1). Humanity then must choose between "light or darkness, the Law of the Lord or the works of Beliar" (Test. Levi 19:1). In the Qumran writings the command for a personal decision takes on cosmic dimensions. World history is perceived as a battle between light and darkness.[22] There is no neutral ground between the sons of light and the sons of darkness who fight in this world for their ultimate victory. But humanity does not become a tool in the struggle between the two "spirits." It receives its destiny from the hands of God. In the intertestamental period Satan, Beliar, Mastema, or Azazel, as the evil one is called, is understood as raging against God and rivaling his dignity.[23] Being confronted with a time of immense political and spiritual crises, the perspective of the intertestamental writers was certainly appropriate. But they did not simply surrender the world to an indefinite dualistic struggle. They still held God to be in control.

When we read the Old Testament we notice that Israelite history ended with the destruction of Jerusalem and the Babylonian captivity and that, despite the promising beginnings with the conquest of a promised land and the kingship of David and Solomon, Israel's history ended in failure. Indeed, sin, whether corporate or individual, is never belittled in the Old Testament. Though the path to forgiveness by God "through repentance and cultic ritual might be complicated, though compensation and expiation might be costly, and though some natural consequences of sin might be irreversible, the hope of a restored relationship with God found an equally important place in the Hebrew Bible."[24]

---

21. So G. H. Box in his translation of 4 Ezra in *The Apocrypha and Pseudepigrapha of the Old Testament in English,* ed. R. H. Charles, vol. 2 (Oxford: Clarendon, 1963), 563.

22. See for the following Foerster, *"satanas,"* in *TDNT,* 7:156.

23. See D. S. Russell, *Divine Disclosure: An Introduction to Jewish Apocalyptic* (London: SCM, 1992), 109f., who talks here about a "cosmic dualism."

24. Cover, "Sin, Sinners," 6:39f.

Starting with the oldest traditions of Israelite history, we notice that God does not simply condemn Israel, though judgment and reprimands are there, but that God always makes promises to Israel. Here Jürgen Moltmann (b. 1926) distinguishes between the Israelite history of promise and the static epiphanic religions in the environment of Israel. After the Israelites' conquest of Palestine, Yahweh still appeared as the promising God who pointed to a new future. This meant that the Old Testament promises were never superseded by historic events, but were constantly modified and expanded toward the future. Of course, some of these promises were realized in history. These "fulfilled" promises to which Israel owed existence (the exodus, the promised land, David's kingship) proved, amid all the upheavals of history, to establish a continuity in which Israel was able to recognize the faithfulness of its God. Yet the promises were never completely resolved in any one event, but there remained an overflow that pointed to the future. "The tension between promise and fulfillment was not left behind by the simple progression of history, but was much more strongly creative of Israel's historic progress."[25] When we read the promise in Ezekiel 11:19f., "I will give them a new heart, and put a new spirit within them; I will remove the heart of stone from their flesh and give them a heart of flesh, so that they may follow my statutes and keep my ordinances and obey them," then we see again that the turn-around from sinfulness to obedience is not a human accomplishment. God takes the initiative to change humanity so that they can again walk in his ways instead of going astray. This means that while there is the human possibility of either living in conformity with God or abandoning God, once the choice against God has set in, it takes more than human efforts to return to God.

2. The New Testament Outlook

In Judaism, there occurred a differentiation between mortal sins, such as idolatry, licentiousness, and bloodshed, and venial sins that were committed unknowingly. For the former one attained satisfaction only through death, while for the latter one could atone through rites of purification, good works, and sufferings. Sin was mainly understood as a transgression of the divine law, behind which God was still discernible. Following Jewish us-

25. Jürgen Moltmann, *The Theology of Hope: On the Ground and the Implications of a Christian Eschatology*, trans. J. W. Leitch (New York: Harper & Row, 1967), 112.

age, the New Testament authors considered sin to be an activity or stance that is opposed to God. Since God loves humanity and commands that humans love one another, sins against humans are also sins against God. The general Jewish view, accepted throughout the New Testament, was that all people sin and in that sense are entangled in sinfulness.

a. Humanity's Intrinsic Sinfulness

The Sermon on the Mount shows us Jesus' deep awareness of the extent to which each person is hopelessly entangled in sinfulness. But Jesus did not just acknowledge humanity's sinfulness; he tackled sin in an unprecedented way. First, we remember that his whole ministry must be understood as a continuous battle against the anti-Godly powers. His victories over the anti-Godly powers were not sporadic impacts on the domain of evil. They were manifestations that the time of salvation had commenced and that the destruction of these powers had started.[26] This means that Jesus emphasized humanity's thoroughgoing sinfulness and, through his ministry, even eliminated the very cause of sin, checking the anti-Godly powers that tempt to sin. But Jesus did not stop there.

As the bringer of the kingdom of God, Jesus also established table fellowship with sinners and pronounced forgiveness of sin (Mark 2:5-16). "Jesus claims for himself what seems to have been reserved as God's own prerogative."[27] He did not separate himself from sinners, but as the one who stands in the place of God, he established a new communion with them. These acts signal the beginning and foreshadowing of the eschatological communion of God with his people when he will no longer hold their sins against them. In Jesus the promise of the servant of Yahweh is fulfilled: "I, I am He who blots out your transgressions for my own sake, and I will not remember your sins" (Isa. 43:25). The forgiving of sins constitutes an eschatological moment; the new creation is proleptically anticipated in which no one will any longer turn away from God. However, the proclamation of the kingdom of God and the forgiving of sins cannot be taken lightly. They demand a response and ask for acceptance. Those who reject that God's Holy

---

26. See Mark 1:24, and Joachim Jeremias, *New Testament Theology*, trans. John Bowden (New York: Scribner, 1971), 94, in his interpretation of this verse.

27. So Udo Schnelle, *Theology of the New Testament*, trans. M. Eugene Boring (Grand Rapids: Baker, 2009), 105, on this passage. See also for the table fellowship of Jesus, 106ff.

Spirit is present in Jesus' life and destiny have forfeited their chance to return to God; they have brought judgment on themselves and have committed an unforgivable sin (Matt. 12:31f.).[28]

The life and destiny of Jesus is the great crisis for sin, as seen especially in the Gospel of John. When Jesus confronts the people with his words and deeds, they realize that they are sinners. They also know that in him they are offered the chance to return to God. Jesus says, "If I had not come and spoken to them, they would not have sin; but now they have no excuse for their sin" (John 15:22). In the confrontation with Jesus occurs the separation between those who accept him and those who reject him. By rejecting God in Christ the latter are judged and their sins stand against them. Therefore we encounter the threatening and at the same time the comforting pronouncement "Whoever believes in the Son has eternal life; whoever disobeys the Son shall not see life, but must endure God's wrath" (John 3:36).

b. Humanity's Unnatural Nature

When we come to Paul we notice a distinct difference between his understanding of sin and that of both the Old Testament and the Gospels. Though Paul builds on many of the Old Testament insights, his understanding of sin is determined by his own experience, which in turn is shaped through his confrontation with God's self-disclosure in Jesus Christ. Because of his experience with God through Christ, sin became such a dominant theme for Paul that for him sin seems to be humanity's second nature. In following Jewish thinking Paul universalizes human sinfulness by saying that "sin came into the world through one man, and death came through sin, and so death spread to all because all have sinned" (Rom. 5:12). As German New Testament scholar Walter Grundmann (1906-76) shows, Paul differed from Judaism since for him "sin does not consist only in the individual act. Sin for him is the state which embraces all humanity."[29]

Adam is the "gate" through which sin came into the world, and sin is the "gate" through which death reached all people. Paul does not want to put the blame on Adam for the emergence of sin and death. For Paul sin *(he hamartia)* assumes almost anthropomorphic features, personifying the anti-Godly destructive powers that found their way into our human world

---

28. See Walter Grundmann, *"hamartanō* (Sin in the NT),*"* in *TDNT,* 1:304.

29. Grundmann, *"hamartanō,"* in *TDNT,* 1:308.

through this first human being. However, Paul does not just talk about the emergence of the age of death in a biological way. Symbolically, this age had Adam as its head whose antitype is Christ, the head of the age of life and the bearer of the new eon.[30]

Many Western theologians, however, concluded from Paul's remarks that humanity had once been in an integer, or original, state in which human beings had the possibility of not sinning and consequently of not dying.[31] Death, sorrow, and pain were thought to have come into the world through human sinfulness.[32] Only those outside the confines of the orthodox faith dared to assert the first human being would have died, whether he or she had sinned or not.[33] Today most theologians rightly refrain from speculation about a pre-mortal, original state of humanity. Yet they, too, acknowledge that there is something peculiar about human death. Human death is not only a biological phenomenon, as it is with the death of an animal.

We learned above that a human being is the only living species that has an acute self-awareness, while humanity's predecessors had only rudiments of self-awareness or lacked it altogether. Russian-American geneticist Theodosius Dobzhansky (1900-1975) made the important observation that

> self-awareness has, however, brought in its train somber companions — fear, anxiety, and death-awareness. . . . Death-awareness is a bitter fruit of man's having risen to the level of consciousness and of functioning ego. Self-awareness has developed as an important adaptation; death-awareness is not obviously adaptive, and it may be biologically detrimental.[34]

30. See Anders Nygren, *Commentary on Romans,* trans. C. C. Rasmussen (Philadelphia: Fortress, 1949), 210f., for his exegesis of Romans 5:12. This is picked up again by Joseph A. Fitzmyer, *Romans* (New York: Doubleday, 1993), 406, who quotes Nygren.

31. Augustine, *Treatise on Rebuke and Grace* (33), in *NPNF,* first series, 5:485.

32. See W. Rohnert, *Die Dogmatik der evangelisch-lutherischen Kirche* (Braunschweig: Hellmuth Wollermann, 1902), 198, who recites a whole catalogue of qualities that humanity enjoyed prior to the fall. Francis Pieper, *Christian Dogmatics* (St. Louis, MO: Concordia, 1950), 1:551ff., even ponders whether original sin caused immediate death or only started the process of dying, which results in complete separation of body and soul. For the discussion of the "original state" in the history of the church, see *Chr. Ernst Luthardt's Kompendium der Dogmatik,* ed. Robert Jelke, 14th ed. (Leipzig: Dörffling & Franke, 1937), 200-203.

33. So Pelagius according to Mari Mercator, "Commonitorium de Coelestio" (2.2ff.), in *Patrologiae Cursus Completus: Series Latina,* ed. J.-P. Migne (Paris, 1844-64), vol. 48, col. 85.

34. Theodosius Dobzhansky, *The Biology of Ultimate Concern* (New York: New American Library, 1967), 68f.

Humanity can never completely control this death-awareness. Contrary to animals in which it often arises at the end of life, in humans it can emerge at any moment, even in the prime of life. It reminds human beings that they are mortal, that their efforts are ultimately in vain. While we can say that very likely death-awareness is an outgrowth and a necessary concomitant of self-awareness, and that it may be genetically conditioned, Dobzhansky warns us not to assume that there is a single genetic unit responsible for death-awareness.[35] There is not a special gene for death-awareness, but it is a basic human capacity derived from the whole of the human genetic endowment. Why is it, then, that human beings make death one of their primary concerns, as Ernest Becker pointed out? Why is it that from the earliest times of philosophical speculation, one of the primal concerns was the issue of death? Does this not indicate that Paul was correct when he asserted that the first human being was the gate through which sin and death-awareness entered the human world? Once humanity had alienated itself from the primordial conformity with its creator, death as God's condemnation of this sinful lifestyle threatened humanity and reminded human beings of their ultimate dependency that they refused to accept.

Like us Paul is not so much interested in the condition of the first human being. He wants to convey that we are born into the sinful context that the first human being ever to move on this earth initiated. As Rudolf Bultmann states with reference to Romans 5:13f.: "At the base of the idea of inherited sin lies the experience that everyman is born into a humanity that is and always has been guided by a false striving."[36] Nobody starts from the beginning, for we are all influenced in our self-assessment by the sins of the human family. This is what Paul means when he says, "By the one man's disobedience the many were made sinners." And "one man's trespass led to condemnation for all" (Rom. 5:18f.). We rightly must talk here about sin as a hereditary affliction. At the same time, however, Paul appeals to personal accountability because he suggests that everyone knows about God and his word, in one way or another. He states that even the pagans, who do not have the (Old Testament) law, have the law written on their hearts and they have a conscience that convicts them (Rom. 5:18f.). We are reminded here of Luther's insight that there is not a special law for Christians, but the same "natural" law applies to both Christians and non-Christians.[37] As

35. Dobzhansky, *The Biology of Ultimate Concern,* 72.

36. Rudolf Bultmann, *Theology of the New Testament,* trans. Kendrik Grobel (New York: Charles Scribner's, 1951), 1:253.

37. So Paul Althaus, *The Ethics of Martin Luther,* trans. with a foreword R. C. Schultz (Philadelphia: Fortress, 1972), 30.

mentioned before, this understanding of common basic norms for human behavior is reaffirmed by the findings of behavioral research.

It is significant to find out how humanity expresses its sinful existence.
Paul asserts that sinful humanity exchanges the truth about God for a lie
and worships and serves the creature rather than the creator (Rom. 1:25).
This means that at the center of human sinfulness lies the abandoning of
humanity's administrative position. The human family abandoned its position as God's administrators of the world and wanted to rule the world in
autonomy. Since humanity is aware of itself, it recognizes its finitude and
attempts to overcome it. There are two main ways in which humanity tries
to accomplish this. Either it wants to expand its dominion to ever further
horizons, an attitude that leads to self-glorification, or it is willing to surrender to that which surrounds it, a mindset leading to religious idolatry. In either case, humanity prides itself for being in control of the situation.[38]

But humanity is deceiving itself, for it is not actually in control of its
own situation. Instead of trusting the infinite God as humanity should,
with an attitude that would enable it to have dominion over the world as
God's administrator, humanity wants to have dominion over life as a whole
and consequently trusts the finite world.[39] Thus humanity wants to dominate what it should trust, and trusts what it should dominate. Can we, however, agree that this perverse attitude results from humanity's own choice;
that it lives by its own intentions contrary to the way it ought to live?

When we come to chapter 7 of Paul's Letter to the Romans we get the
impression that sin has a "demonic character."[40] In confrontation with
God's law, the nascent desires are awakened (v. 5). These desires or passions
are not primarily sensual desires, but the whole gamut of sinfulness, from
basic pride to actual individual sins. Even the good and holy will of God is
used to increase the power of sin (v. 13). In its natural (fallen) state human
freedom is reduced to that of a slave (v. 14). Before its physical death hu-

---

38. Reinhold Niebuhr, *The Nature and Destiny of Man* (New York: Charles Scribner's,
1941), 186, rightly states that pride is one of the basic sins if not the basic sin. It is even more
basic than sensuality since the latter is, in some way, derived from the former.

39. Wolfhart Pannenberg, *What Is Man? Contemporary Anthropology in Theological
Perspective,* trans. Duane Priebe (Philadelphia: Fortress, 1970), 36, rightly speaks here of a
"perversion of the relation between control and trust that expresses the perverseness of man
himself."

40. So Grundmann, *"hamartanō,"* in *TDNT,* 1:311. For the historical and theological
problems of Romans 7, see Otto Michel, *Der Brief an die Römer,* 11th ed. (Göttingen:
Vandenhoeck & Ruprecht, 1957), 156ff.

manity is already sold to sin and therewith to eternal death. Remembering his own situation prior to his conversion, Paul can identify with human sinfulness and exclaim:

> I do not understand my own actions. For I do not do what I want, but I do the very thing I hate. . . . So then it is no longer I that do it, but sin which dwells within me. For I know that nothing good dwells within me, that is, in my flesh. (vv. 15-18)

Significantly, Paul does not identify flesh and sin, but only insists that human existence in the flesh is also an existence in sin. The human sphere of the flesh is the sphere of sin and is dominated by sin. We can even draw the conclusion that humanity is living according to the human sphere, and, living in it, is enslaved by sin. Though humanity knows what to do and even intends to do it, it just cannot accomplish it. Actually, this should not come as a surprise. We have just seen that as long as humanity lives in and from its "self," it lives in sin and pride, and so is turned away from God. That it still wants and wills the good attests to the unnatural status of this behavior. Thus human nature has not changed, but humanity lives, however, in a totally unnatural way, so to speak, with its back toward God.

It is evident that humanity's unnatural attitude need not affect the penultimate quality of its doings. Very often we find high moral standards among pagans and among deliberate atheists. Augustine observed early on that the virtues "are themselves vices rather than virtues, if the mind does not bring them into relation with God."[41] The relationship to God is the deciding factor that determines theologically, but not phenomenologically, between virtue and vice. As soon as this relationship is broken, human action is sin against God, regardless of how "good" this action is. Sin is aversion from God and must always be measured against this background.

Paul knows, however, that we are not condemned to live according to the flesh; we can also live according to the Spirit. Right after the admission "Wretched man that I am! Who will rescue me from this body of death?" Paul exclaims: "Thanks be to God through Jesus Christ our Lord!" (Rom. 7:24f.). The Christ event is the event that liberates us from the bondage of

---

41. Augustine, *Concerning the City of God against the Pagans,* trans. Henry Bettenson, intro. G. R. Evans (London: Penguin Books, 2003), 891 (19.25). The more popular wording: "The virtues of the pagans are splendid vices," however, is apocryphal and wrongly attributed to Augustine. See Friedrich Loofs, *Leitfaden zur Dogmengeschichte,* ed. Kurt Aland, 6th ed. (Tübingen: Max Niemeyer, 1959), 333n.4.

sin (Rom. 5:21). The New Testament authors believed that Jesus came to save people from their sins and consequently faith in him was required for the remission of sin. In the Gospel of John we even hear Jesus say that when the Paraclete, that is, the Spirit, comes, "he will prove the world wrong about sin and righteousness and judgment: about sin because they do not believe in me" (John 16:8f.). In the Gospel of John, not believing in Jesus is equated with sin. Jesus saw it as his mission to call back to God those who were sinners. In the Synoptic Gospels Jesus singled out the tax collectors as sinners par excellence, meaning "that their manner of life was basically antithetical to the will of God."[42] Yet Jesus associates with sinners, with tax collectors, who had the reputation of being dishonest and greedy, and also with others who transgressed against God's will. Jesus told these sinners that if they repented, God would forgive them. Repentance, however, did not mean the usual confession to a priest and atoning sacrifice, but rather believing in Jesus and in God's grace, which was shown through Jesus accepting sinners.

Once we follow Jesus, we live according to the Spirit, meaning we no longer live on our own and for our own. Paul can therefore say that we are no longer our own (1 Cor. 6:19). We are Christ's and belong to Christ. In the trusting relationship with Christ, enabled through the Spirit, our basic alienation from God is overcome. Like the basic sinfulness of natural humanity, however, this new status is not brought about through a biological or genetic change. It is achieved through God's grace. Therefore it is open to mistreatment, and Paul constantly summons his readers to realize that which they already are.[43] Since Christ has gained the victory over the anti-Godly powers for those who claim Christ on their side, sin is no longer dominant. Yes, there are still daily battles with sin, battles that sometimes even end in defeat, but those struggles with sin also foreshadow Christ's victory over sin.

---

42. E. P. Sanders, "Sin, Sinners (NT)," in the *The Anchor Bible Dictionary*, 6:43.

43. When Handley C. G. Moule, *The Epistle to the Romans* (Cambridge: Cambridge University, 1952), 202, says with reference to Romans 7 that "there is a conflict in the Christian man, regenerate, yet taken, in a practical sense, apart from his Regenerator," Moule seems to be too pessimistic. The victory is gained, yet the full disclosure of the victory is not yet attained. See Bultmann, *Theology of the New Testament*, 1:330ff., in his excellent treatment of the relationship between the Pauline imperative and indicative. Bultmann here recognizes that "the *imperative*, 'walk according to the Spirit,' not only does not contradict the *indicative* of justification (the believer is rightwised) but results from it." In other words, salvation though still outstanding is not just in the future.

6. The Understanding of Sin in the Tradition of the Church

The basic issue in the understanding of sin throughout the centuries was whether there is still some goodness in humanity or whether humanity is a totally corrupt entity. If the latter is true, then human freedom is also considerably restricted if not eliminated. Yet if the first is true, then the question arises as to what extent humans can contribute toward their own salvation. In either case, one needs to assess to what extent humans have a free will to do what they actually want and also to lead a God-pleasing life. The issue of freedom and responsibility twice gained unprecedented prominence in the history of the church — once in the formative years of Western theology, climaxing in the struggle between Augustine and Pelagius, and then during the emergence of the Protestant Reformation.

1. The Extent of Evil in Human Beings

Augustine (354-430), later bishop of the North African city of Hippo Regius, which is present-day Annaba in Algeria, joined the Manicheans at age nineteen, although he was already a catechumen, or candidate for baptism, in the Christian church. The young Augustine found the Manicheans' rational understanding of evil especially attractive. According to Mani (ca. 216–ca. 276), the founder of Manicheism, matter is evil and was created by an evil creator God, while the true God, untainted by any material blemish, is the source of everything good. In this dualistic proposal the world is seen as a battlefield between the principles of good and evil in which humanity is caught in the middle. This freed young Augustine from any personal responsibility for committing evil or for sinning. Yet after about ten years he no longer found the Manichean doctrine satisfying. He came under the influence of Bishop Ambrose of Milan and was greatly impressed by Ambrose's understanding of the Old Testament. He finally broke free of Manicheism in 385 and the following year decided to once again become a catechumen in the Catholic Church. Late in the year 386, he wrote a dialogue in two books with the title *De ordine* (On order), which, on the basis of its content, one might better translate: "Divine Providence and the Problem of Evil."[1] In this work Augustine tackled the problem of evil, and along with this the issue of theodicy, which attempts to answer the question as to why a gracious God can allow evil in the world.[2]

a. The Problem of Evil (Augustine)

Augustine is confronted immediately with the dilemma that, if evil is real, then God is either not almighty or God wills evil. In the face of these alternatives Augustine admits that he would rather portray God as limited in his sphere of activity than label God as the author of evil and thereby as cruel. Augustine next distinguishes natural evil, as it is manifest, for example, in natural catastrophes, from moral evil, which is seen in the human will.[3] Evil within nature can, according to Augustine, have either a goal or be completely senseless. Since many natural occurrences surpass the limits of human ingenuity, one cannot simply attribute them to chance. They must fulfill some purpose that transcends humanity. Yet Augustine admits, on the other hand, that many natural occurrences appear to be completely senseless. Augustine suggests, however, that we probably have too anthropocentric a starting point to easily perceive a divine purpose within such events. Rather than occupy ourselves with detailed questions that could be painful for us, we should seek to view our own misfortune in light of a universal plan.

The perfection of the universe postulated by Augustine is not easily reconciled with his unmerciful openness to the reality of evil. Another

---

1. For the dating of this work, see the edition in *Patrologiae Cursus Completus: Series Latina,* ed. J.-P. Migne (Paris, 1844-64), 32:977-1022.

2. Jörg Trelenberg in his comprehensive study, *Augustins Schrift De ordine: Einführung, Kommentar, Ergebnisse* (Tübingen: Mohr Siebeck, 2009), vii, writes: "These are the central issues of theodicy to which the young philosopher of Cassiciacum is seeking an answer."

3. For a summary of this dialogue, see David E. Roberts, "The Earliest Writings," in *A Companion to the Study of St. Augustine,* ed. Roy W. Battenhouse (New York: Oxford University Press, 1969), 100-103.

problem is his assumption that God is always just. In light of the fact that there is injustice in the world it is a short step to the conclusion that evil exists eternally alongside of God. Neo-Platonism appears to offer a solution to this dilemma that Augustine follows in locating the origin of evil in non-being. The solution is that God did not cause evil since no positive reality exists outside of divine providence. Yet the examples given by Augustine are not convincing. He mentions, for instance, the example of cock-fighting and believes that beauty is to be found even in this brutal sport since it occurs in accordance with the laws of nature. In another place he brings forward the example of the gruesome office of executioner, which is indeed something negative, yet contributes to the order of a well-functioning state. He similarly describes prostitution as evil, yet suggests that its elimination could lead to even greater evils. Everything evil, according to Augustine, contributes to perfection since its non-occurrence would destroy perfection. At this point one is tempted to ask why evil should be resisted at all when it contributes so much to the good.[4]

Although not completely satisfying, this dialogue is Augustine's first attempt to free himself from a Manichean type of dualism. Evil is allowed no place of its own but must rather always contribute to the good. Augustine does not remain, however, with the enigmatic character of evil, probably out of fear that this could once again be interpreted dualistically.

In another dialogue, begun two years later and completed in Africa, Augustine made a further decisive step. In his *Retractations* at the end of his life he wrote in order to refute the Manichean objection against the Christian belief that evil is ultimately attributed to God.[5] This work, *De libero arbitrio* (On Free Will), was highly rated by Augustine as well as by his contemporaries. He commented in a letter to Jerome: "A few years ago I wrote some books on free will — which have gone out into many hands and are possessed by many more. . . . [I opposed] with all my might those who were trying to prove that nature was endowed with its own principle of evil in conflict with God. These were the Manichaeans."[6] This relatively short work, in the form of a dialogue between Augustine and Evodius, a youth from his hometown of Tagaste, begins with the fundamental question: "Is not God the cause of evil?"[7]

4. See Roberts, "The Earliest Writings," 106, who asks this same question.

5. Augustine, *The Retractations* (1.8.2), in *FC*, 60:32.

6. Augustine, *Letters* (166.7), in *FC*, 30:12f.

7. For this and the following, see Augustine, *The Problem of Free Choice* (1.1.1), in *ACW*, 22:35.

Augustine distinguishes between committing evil and suffering from evil. Since God is good, he can commit no evil. Yet because God punishes evil and this punishment is itself experienced as something evil, God is the cause of suffering from evil in the sense of a divine punishment. The evil that we do is done by us freely; otherwise it could not be justly punished. Augustine goes a step further and maintains that the evil deeds of humans are not learned since learning and teaching are good. In response Evodius asks from whence evil comes if it is not learned (1.2.4). Augustine replies that this question had driven him into heresy since he wanted to find an answer to it. Finally, he came to the following explanation: "We believe that everything which exists is created by one God, and yet that God is not the cause of sin. The difficulty is: if sin goes back to souls created by God, and souls go back to God, how can we avoid before long tracing sin back to God?" (1.2.4). In order to avoid this conclusion we must, according to Augustine, assume that God is almighty and completely immutable. God is the creator of all good things, although God transcends these, and God is the perfectly just ruler over everything that God has created. God is self-sufficient and unassisted by any other being in the act of creation.

After clarifying his understanding of God, Augustine sought to establish his conception of evil. When something evil takes place, its dominant motive is to be located in the libido (Lat. *cupiditas*), that is, in human passion (1.4.9). Evil deeds such as murder, blasphemy, and adultery arise out of human passion. Even when one commits evil deeds out of fear, the motive is still to be found in covetous desires, namely, in the desire for a life without fear. Of course, human law can permit something that we perceive as evil so that passion is excluded from an evil deed. But such a law would be contrary to the eternal law, which consists of principles which, in contrast to human laws, never change. That which is correct in temporal laws is derived from the eternal law which alone should be our point of orientation. Augustine speaks next of the distinction between humans and animals and explains that humans possess a spirit that determines and directs all other elements within them so that they are directed according to the divine order (1.8.18). Human wisdom, then, consists in giving such place to the human spirit that passion cannot reign over humans, for apart from God there is nothing better than a sensible and wise spirit. The spirit is therefore rightly punished when it enslaves passion and sins.

At the beginning of the second book Evodius asks why God has given humans a free will, to which Augustine replies that without a free will humans could not live as humans. Evodius then asks why this decision of God was correct if we are able to misuse our free will. Augustine attempts to explain that the free will is good. According to Augustine, we possess three types of good things: virtues, which we cannot misuse; bodily things, which he does not regard as being of particular importance; and the power of the soul as a good of secondary status. This free will can be used either rightly or wrongly. It is used correctly when we place our trust in God for he is unchanging good, truth, and wisdom and humans can obtain a happy life through him. Evil consists of turning away from the unchanging good. Since we do this by our own free will, the consequent punishment is just.

In the third book Augustine takes up the subject of God's foreknowledge and declares that predestination is not implied here. Yet what Augustine says concerning natural evil is hardly convincing. He dismisses, for example, the problem of suffering among children by saying that there is no need to suffer any longer once suffering (along with this life) has come to an end. Additionally, one does not know what compensation God has in store for such children who suffer. There is also the question concerning the suffering of animals, which only shows that we understand nothing of the nature of the excellence of the supreme good, for animals are by nature mortal. We see also by the suffering of animals that the souls of all creatures "strive for unity in governing and animating their bodies" (3.23.69). They resist division and corruption and through their struggle against suffering point to the fact that they were created for unity. Finally, Augustine reflects on the possibilities possessed by the first human pair and claims that they had the means by which, if they had used them well, they could have risen to what they did not possess, that is, wisdom (3.24.72). There is a distinction between whether humans are wise or merely blessed with reason. Humans, however, have forsaken the heights of wisdom. For Augustine, Satan also comes into the picture here. He writes: "And that is 'pride, the beginning of all sin; and the beginning of the pride of man is to fall off from God' (Sir. 10:13). The devil added malevolent envy to his pride when he persuaded man to share his pride, through which he knew he was damned. So it was that man suffered a punishment designed to correct him rather than to destroy him" (3.25.76).

Finally, Augustine arrives at the conclusion that pride (Lat. *superbia*) is the beginning of all sin. This work, therefore, does not pursue the question of free will, although this topic is repeatedly touched on, but rather aims to demonstrate, as the opening sentence announced, that God is *not* the cause of evil. The problem of free will, however, cannot thus be passed over for it is closely bound with the problem of evil. When at the end of this work Augustine addresses once again the question of why there is not only good but also evil he cannot, in contrast to his earlier work *De ordine,* simply answer that evil belongs to the good. Rather, he must maintain that evil stems from the libido, *cupiditas,* and *superbia,* whereby God cannot be held directly or indirectly responsible for evil since God is immutable and essentially good. Yet Augustine has not yet understood evil dynamically enough as an actual opponent of God. Owing to his own Manichean past he did not have the courage to do this since he feared that he might lapse into "heresy." He viewed evil as something that contradicted *ratio* and was essentially connected with the will. It is the power that continually opposes and is separated from God, which sinks into corruption and base actions.

Only one side of reality is thus addressed, namely, that there is just one primal principle: God. This God is just and good. Everything that is evil has no causal relationship with God but exists on the basis of its own self and its opposition to God. As Augustine correctly admitted in his *Retractations,* there is yet another side: "For it is one thing to inquire into the source of evil and another to inquire how one can return to his original good or reach one that is greater. Hence the new Pelagian heretics who treat free choice of the will in such a way as not to leave a place for the grace of God, and they assert that it is given according to our merits, should not boast as though I have pleaded their cause."[8] Because Augustine said very little here about the necessity of grace for the attainment of salvation, the Pelagians sought, albeit unjustly, to cite him as a supporter of their own position. In this work Augustine dealt almost exclusively with the question of the origin of evil. This in turn raises the question of how evil can be overcome or avoided.

We have seen that Augustine argued for the unity of God over against the dualistic worldview of Manicheism. According to Augustine, there are not two separate principles, one good and one evil, nor is there a graduated order of reality in which, so to speak, good is stronger than evil so that it will ultimately prevail. Rather, there is only one God and one creation. When evil exists, and Augustine never entertained the slightest doubt as to its reality, then it exists only to the extent that a part of God's good creation has risen up against its creator and entered into conflict with him. Many questions, however, remain unanswered, such as issues concerning the origin and function of that within nature which is objectively bad. Likewise, despite Augustine's assertion that humans themselves are responsible for their sinfulness, this was not thought through so thoroughly as to overcome all contradictions in rela-

---

8. Augustine, *Retractations* (1.8.2f.), in *FC,* 60:33.

tion to human freedom and responsibility. It is no wonder, therefore, that there has been much conflict over the question of the relationship between freedom and accountability in the early church, at the start of the Reformation, and in many other periods in the history of the church.

At the beginning of this conflict Augustine himself brandished the banner of attack. His opponent Pelagius even imagined himself a confederate of Augustine until he was taught differently by Augustine and transformed by him into one of the most denounced heretics in the history of the Christian faith.[9] Even Karl Barth threw Pelagianism, fatalism, and heathenism together and wrote in his *Church Dogmatics:* "Pelagianism and fatalism are alike heathen atavisms in a Christian doctrine of God. They both ascribe to the creature an autonomy in relation to God's will which it cannot possess."[10] Yet Pelagius laid much stock in being an orthodox theologian of the entire church.[11] In his works he clearly separated himself from the Arians, Marcionites, and, of course, the Manicheans. In a positive sense he wanted to underline the moral responsibility of humans over against God and thus decisively distinguish the Christian position from Manichean anthropology. Without overlooking divine grace he appealed to human responsibility.

b. The Appeal to Human Responsibility (Pelagius)

We know "preciously little" about **Pelagius** himself.[12] He came from Britain, was ascetically influenced, and between 384 and 409 lived primarily in Rome, where he enjoyed a good reputation from all sides. Afterward he traveled with Celestius, a young man of aristocratic birth, first to Sicily, then to North Africa, and later to Asia Minor.[13] While Pelagius was re-

9. So Robert F. Evans, *Pelagius: Inquiries and Reappraisals* (London: Adam and Charles Black, 1968), 66.

10. Karl Barth, *CD,* II/1:562f.

11. For this and the following, see Evans, *Pelagius,* 92.

12. So rightly B. R. Rees, *Pelagius: Life and Letters* (Rochester, NY: Boydell Press, 1988), xii.

13. See John Ferguson, *Pelagius: A Historical and Theological Study* (Cambridge: W. Heffer & Sons, 1956), 39-49. It is uncertain, however, whether Pelagius was a monk, as claimed by Reinhold Seeberg, *Lehrbuch der Dogmengeschichte,* vol. 2 (Darmstadt: Wissenschaftliche Buchgesellschaft, 1965), 488. Celestius, on the other hand, desired to enter the priesthood and probably later achieved this goal.

served, Celestius took up his cause with zeal so that, indeed, without him the matter of free will and human responsibility would not have become a controversy so quickly, if at all. Celestius had a sharp, analytical mind and was in his element when in debate. The question was taken up for the first time at a synod in Carthage in 411. Celestius was accused there of holding to the following seven positions, which were considered false:

1. That Adam was created mortal and would have died even if he had not sinned.
2. That the sin of Adam injured himself alone and not the human race.
3. That infants at the moment of birth are in the same condition as Adam was before the fall.
4. That infants, even though they are not baptized, have eternal life.
5. That the race of man as a whole does not die by the death or fall of Adam, nor does the race of man as a whole rise again by the resurrection of Christ.
6. That the law has the same effect as the gospel in introducing men into the kingdom of heaven.
7. That even before the coming of Christ there were men without sin.[14]

Although Celestius skillfully defended himself through his eloquence at the proceeding, he was nevertheless excommunicated. Celestius, as a result, turned to Asia Minor while Pelagius went to Jerusalem where he made the acquaintance of Jerome.

For Pelagius himself the suspicion of heresy was a very serious matter. He wrote in his commentary on Colossians 4:6: "Other than the heathen, other than the Jews, other than heretics and anyone else who contradicts the truth: hence Peter says: 'always give a satisfactory answer.'"[15] He sought in his exegesis of the Pauline epistles to avoid every suspicion of heresy. At

14. Ferguson, *Pelagius,* 51. See also Carl Joseph Hefele, *A History of the Councils of the Church from the Original Documents,* trans. H. N. Osenham (Edinburgh: T&T Clark, 1883-96), 2:447. Hefele leaves out the fourth point, as does Marius Mercator. According to Augustine, this point comes not from Celestius but from Sicilian Pelagians. See Augustine, *On Original Sin* (12.11), in *NPNF,* 5:241; see also (3.3), *NPNF,* 5:237f., for Augustine's comments on the synod of 411.

15. According to the Latin edition of Alexander Souter, *Pelagius's Exposition of Thirteen Epistles of St. Paul,* vol. 2, *Text and Apparatus Criticus* (Cambridge: Cambridge University Press, 1926), 471; references in the following pages are to this edition, and the biblical passage discussed by Pelagius is given in brackets.

the center of his explanations one finds moral admonitions. In his exposition of Ephesians 4:27, for example, we read: "Sin is the gateway for the devil, but the Holy Spirit the gateway for righteousness" (370). He said the primary causes of vices are unrighteousness and an evil will as well as impurity and greed (see 317 [Rom. 1:29] and 373 [Eph. 5:3]). It is important that we reject evil desires and have a good conscience, by which Pelagius equates the conscience with the natural law that exists within our spirit (see 60 [Rom. 7:23]). When he comes to the subject of virtues it is clear for him that the greatest of all virtues is *caritas,* that is, love (337 [Gal. 5:22]). *Caritas* is the law of Christ, as Jesus himself said: I give to you a new law (339 [Gal. 6:2]). *Pax, caritas,* and *fides,* that is to say, peace, love, and faith, make for a perfect Christian, for love without faith is unfruitful just as faith without love and peace bears no fruit. Yet "love is greater than peace" (386 [Eph. 6:23]). From the high estimation of love it follows that faith does not become active through fear but rather through love, as Pelagius emphasizes in reference to the words from 1 John: "Whoever believes on God will keep his commandments" (333 [1 John 5:3]).

The concept of works righteousness finds no place in the exegesis of Pelagius. Indeed, he frequently stresses in agreement with Paul that one is justified through faith alone and not through the works of the law (12 [Rom. 1:17]). The unjust who repent are justified by God through faith alone and not through the good works they have done (36 [Rom. 4:5]). It is, however, important that faith be accompanied by deeds, "for the faith which proceeds purely through the mouth and is denied through deed is fabricated" (476 [1 Tim. 1:5]). Only the heathen conduct themselves so. We must not be Christians in name only, confessing God with our mouth while doing evil deeds. Rather, as far removed as the devil is from God, so clearly should the works of the children of God be distinguished from those of the children of the devil (367 [Eph. 4:17]). God must be glorified through our works according to the example of Christ (390 [Phil. 1:11]).

The exemplary behavior of Christians was an important concern for Pelagius. He therefore wrote at the beginning of his exposition of the epistles to the Thessalonians: "The Thessalonians had not only achieved personal perfection in every regard, but others had profited as well through their word and example. Therefore the apostle praised them and encouraged them and invited them to do still greater deeds" (417 [in the introduction to 1 and 2 Thess.]). The imitation of Christ is also important. Pelagius thus asks rhetorically: "If we are saved through the death of Christ, how much more will we be glorified when we have followed him?" (44f. [Rom. 5:10]).

More problematic, however, are comments such as "The example of Christ is sufficient for our life," or through his victory on the cross Christ "has given us an example that we should also be victorious" (458 [Col. 2:6] and 461 [Col. 2:15]). Although following Christ is important for believers, the redemption effected through Christ cannot be reduced to an example that we should follow. Though Pelagius never tired of pointing out that we are saved through the free grace of God and not our own efforts, it was very important for him that we make progress in a moral sense and move toward being just. Indeed, Pelagius correctly emphasized that grace was given to us through baptism apart from the works of the law. But he nevertheless maintained that "grace indeed justifies the unrighteous who repent" (32f. [Rom. 3:24] and 246 [2 Cor. 3:6]). In this manner he also emphasized human initiative. There must be something already present on which the grace of God works.

Also, on the question of baptism a shift of emphasis is discernible.[16] Pelagius emphasizes the validity and necessity of baptism since it is in baptism that we receive the forgiveness of all our sins. At the same time he qualified himself by stating that the water (of baptism) washes only the body, while teaching cleanses the soul (377 [Eph. 5:26]). Teaching can serve as admonition, which is not possible in the case of the sacrament.

Finally, Pelagius makes reference to the significance of Adam. It is obvious for him that death came into the world through Adam since he was the first one who died (217 [1 Cor. 15:22]). Through his sin death came into the world. Yet once again Pelagius qualifies himself by saying that through Adam's example offense and sin entered the world (45f. [Rom. 5:12-16]). It is unusual, however, that he quotes the inquiries of those who reject original sin *(tradux peccati)* without lending his approval to these. His intention seems to be to show that the doctrine of original sin is not meaningful since sin is passed along through imitation.

In regard to the question of what sort of theological presuppositions Pelagius brought into this discussion we must not overlook the social context of his time. The Roman Empire was internally and externally on the verge of political and moral bankruptcy. Even for the "Christian" emperors their words were often hollow and a human life had little meaning. The church had become a part of the establishment which, while enjoying many privileges, had largely forgotten its task of reforming society. Within this context Pelagius, who spent nearly twenty-five years in Rome, sought to remind people that each individual was responsible for his or her own life and

16. See also Ferguson, *Pelagius,* 135, in this regard.

sins. As British classics scholar Brinley R. Rees (1919-2004) writes: "He wanted above else to be a good Christian, working for the reform of the Christian church from within."[17] It would have been a complete reversal of emphasis had he stressed the context of original sin and the necessity out of which we continually commit new sins. Instead, he underlined the accountability of the individual and the possibility of human sinlessness.[18]

Pelagius did not view sin as a "substance" that could be passed on to others or could influence human nature. He saw it rather as a "form" or quality of individual human actions. Thus he addressed the issue of avoiding sin, for one can always improve a quality and can, therefore, always further repress sin. This is also to be seen in his contention that Adam's sin did not contextually or organically damage humans, but rather it is simply spread further through imitation. With this thought Pelagius had broken with the Western tradition. He probably would have felt more at home with theologians of the East such as Clement of Alexandria (d. 220) who, in his *Exhortation to the Heathen*, advised: "Wisely cultivate the fruits of self-command, and present thyself to God as an offering of first-fruits, that there may be not the work alone, but also the grace of God; and both are requisite, that the friend of Christ may be rendered worthy of the kingdom, and be counted worthy of the king-dom."[19] The Eastern tradition did not shy away from the idea of human initiative, as can still be seen today in the predominant idea of the divinization of humans *(theosis)* in the Eastern church. Human initiative and grace are not mutually exclusive; rather, both contribute to preventing evil from gaining the upper hand as well as toward God's ultimate overcoming of evil. This view, however, did not set well with Augustine.

c. Captive, Yet Responsible (Augustine)

Three phases in Augustine's understanding of evil can be distinguished:[20] first, the controversy over the Pelagian teaching in Carthage and Sicily (411-

---

17. Rees, *Pelagius,* 131.

18. See Ferguson, *Pelagius,* 159, who presents a similar contextual argument. See also Hans Schwarz, *Our Cosmic Journey: Christian Anthropology in the Light of Current Trends in the Sciences, Philosophy and Theology* (Minneapolis: Augsburg, 1977), 205f.

19. Clement of Alexandria, *Exhortation to the Heathen* (11.117.5), in *ANF,* 2:204.

20. See the fourfold division by Ekkehard Mühlenberg, "Dogma und Lehre im Abendland," in *HDT,* 1:447. Mühlenberg indicates four phases, the first of which we have already dealt with in the context of Augustine's controversy with the Manicheans.

415); then the direct attack on Pelagius himself which, together with the continuation of the battle through the dispute with Julian of Eclanum, represents the high point of the controversy (415-424); and, finally, the controversy with the so-called semi-Pelagians (425-429).

Phase 1

After the capture of Rome in 410 by Alaric, chief of the Goths, Pelagius found himself among the refugees fleeing to North Africa by way of Sicily. In Carthage he met up with Celestius, who had spread Pelagius's ideas among the people in pregnant form. At a synod in Carthage (411) six theses of Celestius were rejected. Augustine rose immediately to the challenge of this attack against the catholic faith and in 411-412 wrote *A Treatise on the Consequences and Forgiveness of Sins, and on the Baptism of Infants* and *The Spirit and the Letter.* We do not wish to give a detailed analysis of Augustine's doctrine of grace here, but rather to inquire to what extent, according to Augustine, the human is ensnared in evil.

Celestius claimed that Adam was mortal and would have died whether he had sinned or not. Augustine, too, admitted that the body of the first human was made from dust and was destined to return to dust. If, however, he had not sinned his body would have been transformed into a spiritual body with an incorruptible condition as had been promised to the saints and believers so that they would no longer be confronted with the possibility of death.[21] Had Adam not sinned, he would have become immortal and incorruptible. Adam's sin, however, not only pulled humanity into spiritual death but it resulted in the death of the body as well (4.4 [16]). Death, therefore, has nothing to do with earthly frailty but with sin. Before the fall the body was capable of dying but it was not destined to die (5.5 [16]). Sin and death pass via natural descent from one human to all humans and not through emulation. Augustine admits that all humans emulate the example of Adam, who through his disobedience violated the commandment of God (10 [18f.]). But Adam is not only the example for those who sin, but rather the ancestor of all who are born with sin.

Augustine distinguishes between many sins that humans commit themselves that are theirs alone and the one sin of one human being through which all have sinned (10.11 [19]). Augustine appears to assume a

---

21. So Augustine, *A Treatise on the Consequences and Forgiveness of Sins, and on the Baptism of Infants* (2.2), in *NPNF*, 5:16; references in the following pages are to this edition.

unity of all humans in the first human so that they, so to speak, all have a common genetic genealogy in Adam. This original or inherited sin is sufficient for the damnation of humans so that no additional personal sins are needed (12.15 [20]). This original sin cannot be escaped for one acquires it "by the generation of the flesh" (15.20 [22]). Of course, therefore, everyone born of the flesh is in need of spiritual renewal, that is, rebirth through baptism (21.30 [26]).

Since humans possess no superior merits that would earn God's grace, it is not problematic when seemingly unworthy individuals receive this grace or when those equally unworthy are denied it (23.33 [23]). On the basis of original sin we can, at any rate, only anticipate alienation from God. That which transcends this condition and changes our hopeless situation for the good is just as much unmerited as the retention of this condition would have been merited. Similarly, one also cannot inquire as to why one person may receive baptism and another may not and on this basis be denied the kingdom of God as well as eternal life and salvation. All such transformations are connected not with the behavior of the individual but rather with the unfathomable will of God, while the continuation in our condition comes from the fact that on the basis of original sin we deserve nothing other than death.

When children are not baptized, explained Augustine, they remain in darkness (see John 12:46), that is, in the state of punishment (35 [29]). Only through baptism can they escape from the sphere of the influence of sin and the anti-Godly, and gain access to the kingdom of God. Augustine was even of the opinion that the crying and screaming of infants at baptism demonstrated with what reluctance they accepted this sacrament for they are not aware of how important it is for them (36 [29]). It is not sufficient, however, that one simply be informed about the word of truth. Through the word one recognizes and knows that the law is true, but the spirit must be fed internally through the sacraments. For Augustine the word alone is not sufficient, for the power of God must be added to the word in order that it be understood. This takes place through baptism.

Humans are therefore completely incapable by their own selves to come to God. The reason for this is that humans do not stand within the sphere of God's influence but rather under the dominion of the devil who is "the author of sin" (26.39 [30]). The question as to whether two rival powers of light and darkness are thereby once more introduced must at this point at least be asked. Augustine appears to vindicate himself of this charge in that he views God as the all-encompassing power within whose sphere the devil has created an enclave of his own power. Augustine now juxtaposes two states of being. First, no one dies who is brought forth according to the will of the flesh except through Adam, in whom all have sinned. Second, no one is equipped with life who is born again through the will of the Spirit except through Christ, in whom all will be justified. Through one person all have been condemned and through one person all will be justified. There exists no neutral territory between the two. When individuals are not with Christ they are with the devil (28.55 [36]). There is no neutral territory in the world in which one is not either under the influence of evil or under the reign of God. This insight was further developed later by Martin Luther.

Human beings have no position of their own. Like iron shavings within a magnetic field they are oriented according to the structure of the field. Augustine thereby naturally rejects the Pelagian view that only one's own actual sins are forgiven at baptism. Already at the very beginning of our lives in this sinful world we stand within the realm of sin. It is primarily original sin that is forgiven at baptism. Through the grace of God original sin is canceled out. Yet *concupiscence,* that is, the sinful desire that lives in humans, is not destroyed to the point that it no longer exists. Even though a person is baptized he or she still lives within the sphere of influence of this world (39.70 [43]). Concupiscence is only restricted insofar as it must no longer necessarily lead humans to death since those baptized no longer live within the realm of death, but are able to overcome concupiscence with God's help. A similar transformation is to be seen in the case of adult baptism. Although the bonds of guilt through which the devil had taken the soul captive have been broken and the barrier that divided humans from their creator is removed, concupiscence nevertheless remains so we continue to give in to sin.

At the end of the first book of this inquiry Augustine asks whether, in light of this situation, there could ever be a person who already had or could live without sin. This in turn leads to the question of how free humans are, on the basis of their acceptance through baptism, to determine their own destiny for either better or worse. The genuine threat posed by evil is, for Augustine, already clear inasmuch as Christians are admonished to pray to God "Lead us not into temptation!"[22] Of course, Augustine does not contend that humans are condemned to absolute passivity. In order to over-

---

22. For this and the following, see Augustine, *A Treatise on the Consequences and Forgiveness of Sins* (2.3.3–2.4.4), in *NPNF,* 5:44f.

come our evil desires and misplaced fears we must put forward an effort and, indeed, sometimes employ the full power of our will. When we perform works of mercy after baptism, for example, Augustine holds these to be helpful against guilt and the bonds of sin. The concupiscence and the desires that are at work within humans must be overcome through a battle. When those who are baptized and blessed, with reason, go along with concupiscence and allow evil deeds to result, this is attributed to their own will. Every appeasement of these desires conceals within it a consent. New guilt is thereby accumulated when it is not removed from us through penance, works of mercy, or Christ's intervention. A second death and complete damnation would then occur. Therefore we pray in the Lord's Prayer "Forgive us our sins as we forgive those who sin against us, and lead us not into temptation, but deliver us from evil."

The evil that operates in us and remains in us cannot be blamed on our nature, which was given us by God at creation. It is our own will that is at work when we find it easier to sin than not to sin so we must be warned not to let sin reign within us. Augustine thus advises those who are baptized to make certain of God's assistance when they feel that concupiscence is welling up within them so that they are not without God's help, but are victorious over it and are not swept away into temptation. Finally, our hope is that at some point concupiscence will no longer exist in us and that our request, expressed in the Lord's Prayer, will become reality. Yet the hope for perfection, for the freedom from the predilection for concupiscence, is an eschatological hope (2.8.10 [48]). For the present we need the help "of divine grace assisting the human will," so that we can do what is right. When we do the opposite and act evilly, however, we act out of our own free will.

Augustine even believed that humans could live without sin in this life; otherwise the biblical admonition to live a sinless life would be senseless. Yet a life lived according to the will of God is not possible without God's help.[23] Nevertheless, no one can actually live a life free of sin for humans repeatedly go in the wrong direction. The necessity of daily renewal for the Christian also speaks against a completely sinless life. Augustine also puts the argument a different way and asks why it is that humans, though they are able to live without sin, do not do so. Augustine answers succinctly that humans are not willing to live sinlessly since they either do not want to do what is right because they do not know what is right, or because it is not ap-

---

23. For this and the preceding quote, see Augustine, *A Treatise on the Consequences and Forgiveness of Sins* (2.17.26–2.27), in *NPNF,* 5:55.

pealing enough to them. Humans have, therefore, a willful predilection toward evil's sphere of influence. The primary ground for this predilection is to be found in human pride, which lies behind all transgressions.

Through these explanations, which are repeated in various forms and are always supported by scripture references, Augustine seeks to show that humans are plunged into the realm of evil through original sin and can only escape through the grace of God. The grace is offered to humans in the first place in baptism. Yet even after their baptism humans do not fully escape evil's sphere of influence for they continue to sin willfully and deprive themselves of God's grace. Although Augustine also speaks of holiness and maintains that humans should strive to do good, there is little trace of this dynamic of human existence that was so prominent in the thought of Pelagius. Likewise, there is little emphasis on the imitation of Christ which ultimately, according to Augustine, could only be imperfectly accomplished.

Although Augustine continually addresses Pelagius's position, he only names him by name in the third part, which is appended to the work as a letter. There he characterizes Pelagius as "a holy man . . . who has made no small progress in the Christian life" (3.1.1 [69]). The reason Augustine only mentions Pelagius's name at the end and then in a very positive light becomes clear from his statement that he had hoped for a peaceful settlement of their dispute.[24]

In a work from the same period, *The Spirit and the Letter* (412), Augustine pursues the same question that he touched on in *A Treatise on the Consequences and Forgiveness of Sins, and On the Baptism of Infants*. He expressed the opinion there that it was indeed possible for humans to live without sin but that, with the exception of Jesus, there had not yet been anyone who had accomplished this. Almost the entire work is given over to addressing the question as to what extent the law leads to a righteous life. Only at the end does he come back to the original question, that is, why he maintained that a person could live a sinless life when this had never been accomplished by anyone. He concluded that one must only apply one's will sufficiently in order to achieve such a great accomplishment.[25] The fact that this never happens is not because it is impossible but is due to God's juridical activity. Humans could indeed achieve righteousness in this life, desisting from all that is forbidden. It is much more difficult, however, to genu-

---

24. Augustine, *The Retractations* (2.33), in *FC,* 60:188.

25. For this and the following, see Augustine, *A Treatise on the Spirit and the Letter* (35.62–36.66), in *NPNF,* 5:111f.

inely love God since God is hidden from us. Correct behavior is not only facilitated by the teaching of the law but also by the infusion of grace through the Spirit. God is able to lead the human will in such a way that it becomes righteous, not merely in regard to faith, but also so that it lives eternally in the presence of God. Why then, asks Augustine, does this not take place? He can only answer that with God nothing is indeed impossible, but God is also not unjust. There is a hidden depth to the righteousness of God that cannot be plumbed by humanity. Finally, Augustine humbles himself before the sovereignty of God, who has reserved the perfection of humans for the *eschaton*.

Phase 2

In the second phase of the dispute with Pelagius, beginning in the year 415, Augustine authored an entire series of works. With *On Nature and Grace* (415) Augustine sought to respond to a work by Pelagius in which human nature is so portrayed that humans are capable of being justified without the grace of God.[26] Once again Pelagius's name is not mentioned by Augustine for he continued to hope that Pelagius would return to the right path. Augustine once more emphasizes that humans were created without imperfections and without sin. Yet our nature is from Adam. Thus, all the gifts of nature we possess, such as life, mind, and understanding, are in need of enlightenment and healing because of Adam's sin.[27] All of humanity has rightly merited punishment because of original sin. It is pure grace that God sent Jesus Christ into the world in order to save the sinners whom God has foreknown and predestined, and whom he calls, justifies, and glorifies (5.6 [123]). Augustine raises here the subject of predestination, that is, the doctrine that certain individuals are chosen for salvation. This is not a problem for him since humans have nothing but condemnation awaiting them; therefore, if any are rescued out of the predicament of sin it is only by unmerited grace. Grace does not belong to the human constitution and its natural functions but is rather directed toward the restoration and justification of human beings (11.12 [125]).

God not only shows his grace to humans, but also makes use of "bad" things to help them. Augustine is thinking here in the first instance of the

---

26. See Augustine, *The Retractations* (2.42), in *FC*, 60:207.

27. Augustine, *On Nature and Grace* (3.3), in *NPNF*, 5:122; references in the following pages are to this edition.

death of Christ to which Christ submitted in order to rescue human beings from death and the power of darkness (24.26f. [130]). Alongside of this there are also "bad" things or experiences that humans encounter that can serve to help them overcome their pride. Even sin can contribute to the conquest of sin just as an operation may bring about pain in order to alleviate pain. As previously, Augustine speaks once more of pride *(superbia)*, which is the beginning of all sin. In order to conclude his argumentation, Pelagius, according to Augustine, confuses nature and grace. Pelagius believed that humans were so created that of their own will they had the power to either sin or not sin. Augustine argues in a very similar fashion. Yet, according to him, grace must also be added for us to be able to avoid sin (59.69 [145]). Falling from grace is possible for us only through our own free will. If we want to turn toward God, we need God's assistance.

Finally, Augustine's work from this period, *Marriage and Concupiscence* (418/20), must also be examined. In this work Augustine defends himself against the accusation that he rejects marriage on the grounds that original sin manifests itself in the sexual union of man and woman.[28] Of course, according to Augustine, everyone born of human parents is under the influence of the devil unless they have been "born again" in Christ and through his grace snatched from the powers of darkness and brought into the kingdom of God. Yet Augustine does not wish, for this reason, to condemn marriage since the person born within marriage is a work of God and not of the devil. Because of original sin marriage is a much greater good than that which comes out of adultery and sexual promiscuity. "For as sin is the work of the devil, from whencesoever contracted by infants; so man is the work of God, from whencesoever born."

In this work, therefore, Augustine distinguishes between the evil, fleshly concupiscence through which humans are set loose and by which they incur original sin and the good of marriage. According to Augustine, there would have been no shame caused by concupiscence if humans had not sinned. Marriage, however, would have existed even if humans had not sinned since bringing forth children is inherent to this life. Yet this would have taken place without the sickness which, in our present bodies, is death, that is, without concupiscence. For Augustine neither marriage nor the bringing forth of children is evil, rather, only the fleshly desire which, since the first human sin, is associated with procreation. Augustine views marital

---

28. For this and the following quote, see Augustine, *On Marriage and Concupiscence* (1), in *NPNF*, 5:263f.; references in the following pages are to this edition.

purity as a gift of God which, however, is not held in as high esteem by unbelievers as by believers since the former misuse this gift of God. One can only speak properly of marital fidelity when it occurs out of no other motive than as an act of devotion to the true God (4.5f. [265]). What is naturally good within marriage is the unity of man and woman in procreation. Yet this degenerates into animal passion when it takes place for the satisfaction of lust rather than out of the desire for children.

The fact that Augustine held a diminished view of marriage does not need to be belabored here. In his argument he is primarily concerned with whether marriage is something bad since it is bound to concupiscence. For Augustine the sickness of concupiscence is not the result of marriage but of sin. On account of fleshly desire, which is to be condemned, marriage itself cannot be condemned. The sickness of concupiscence is to be kept in check within marriage so that marital cohabitation is not a decision of the will but rather a necessity for procreation, even if the will cannot be switched off (8.9 [267]). As we have already seen, fleshly concupiscence is forgiven through baptism. It is, however, not simply eradicated but afterward is no longer counted as sin (25.28 [275]). The concupiscence remains a human weakness which, through progressive renewal of the inner person, can be healed to the extent that the outer person becomes imperishable (1 Cor. 15:53).

Concupiscence is neither substance nor body nor spirit; rather, it is much more an expression of an evil quality. Although concupiscence is closely bound with sexuality Augustine does not equate the two. The connection between them is made clear when Augustine asks rhetorically: "For why is the special work of the parents withdrawn and hidden even from the eyes of their children, except that it is impossible for them to be occupied in laudable procreation without shameful lust? Because of this it was that even they were ashamed who first covered their nakedness [see Gen. 3:7]. These portions of their persons were not suggestive of shame before, but deserved to be commended and praised as the work of God" (2.5.14 [288]). What is negative in regard to concupiscence is lust. Reason has no control over it so that humans react impulsively and even animal-like. If humans do not master their minds, they are delivered over to concupiscence, which can seduce them to do things to which, as beings blessed with reason, they would not normally consent. The reason that Augustine so often brings up the subject of sexual reproduction is probably that he can thereby best illustrate how it is that original sin is passed on since it is not something material but rather something intentional.[29] Since the Pelagians re-

---

29. See also the comments of Mühlenberg, "Dogma und Lehre," 460.

ject the doctrine of original sin, they can describe concupiscence within the act of reproduction as something good. Augustine, who calls the act of reproduction good and the will of God, distinguishes it from concupiscence, which he rejects as sinful. At the beginning of the life of a human, just as in the life of the Christian, we perpetually encounter a mixture of God-willed creatureliness and God-opposing sinfulness.

Phase 3

In the last phase of the dispute with the Pelagian teaching Augustine had to deal with questions that arose from the ranks of the church, as, for instance, from the monks of a monastery in Hadrumetum, the present-day Sousse on the east coast of Tunisia. In his *Retractations* Augustine reports that the monks there asked how the freedom of the will fit in with the grace of God and whether the one excludes the other.[30] By way of an answer to this question he wrote, along with several letters, *Grace and Free Will* (426 or 427).

Augustine once more argues that God has given us certain commandments and that these would be completely useless if we had no free will to enable us to follow them.[31] We are thus able to choose freely to live and behave as we should (4.7 [258f.]). Similarly, he also says that eternal life is not only a free gift of grace but also a reward for our service. He seeks to overcome this contradiction by maintaining that justification is a completely gracious act of God and our good life, and is, therefore, nothing other than God's grace at work within us. If a reward is given it is grace that is rewarded on account of its own merit and not because anyone has earned it (8.19f. [270ff.]). Even belief does not come from our own free will, for we pray that one who does not believe might believe. God is able, therefore, to transform the will that strives against him and to take away the hardness of the heart (14.29 [282]). God changes evil to good. Yet we also read in scripture that we should not harden our hearts (Ps. 95:8), which again brings to mind a free will. Augustine concludes from this, as earlier, that the free will acts of its own accord when it serves evil. When it does that which is good, however, this occurs through the grace of God.[32] Yet how should one separate the divine activity from the human? Augustine gives the following answer:

30. Augustine, *The Retractations* (2.66), in *FC*, 60:268.

31. See Augustine, *Grace and Free Will* (2.4), in *FC*, 59:253, and for the dating of the work, 245ff.; references in the following pages are to this edition.

32. For this and the following, see Augustine, *Grace and Free Will* (16.32f.), in *FC*, 59:285ff., and for the quote 289.

"God then works in us, without our cooperation, the power to will, but once we begin to will, and do so in a way that brings us to act, then it is that He cooperates with us. But if He does not work in us the power to will or does not cooperate in our act of willing, we are powerless to perform good works of a salutary nature." Augustine therefore follows the biblical insight that God works within us both the willing and the effect.

Augustine wants to emphasize God's complete dominance of the will. This is also clear when (in predestinarian manner) he claims that God turns humans when and whither he will, that he shows favor to some and punishes others according to his will, and yet remains just.[33] God makes use of both good and evil, as with Judas, that Christ might be betrayed, or with the Jews, that he might be crucified. "He even makes use of the devil himself, the worst of all, but does so in the best way possible to exercise and put to the test the faith and piety of good men; not for His own sake, since He knows everything before it happens, but for our benefit, since it was necessary that He should deal with us in this fashion." Like Martin Luther after him, Augustine maintained that God does what God wills in the hearts of evil humans but at the same time lets them continue in their own evil deeds. Despite this apparent contradiction we must hold fast to the fact that there is no unrighteousness with God, even when God's own judgments are not always comprehensible. When we read in scripture, for example, that people are hardened by God in their striving, we should never doubt that they suffer justly when they perpetrate evil deeds (21.43 [303]). When it comes to God's grace, however, everything is turned around. Here we do not receive what we earn but rather that which we have not earned. Nevertheless, Augustine suggests that even in evil persons the evil is not brought about by God but came originally from Adam and gained strength through his will. If God does not transform evil persons for the good, then he works within them according to their own desires.

Finally, Augustine addressed a second treatise to the monks of Hadrumetum, *On Rebuke and Grace* (426 or 427), in which he speaks of the gift of perseverance that is necessary for one to remain in faith until the end. No one can fall away who is elected and predestined since the grace of perseverance is always given to the end. Yet it belongs to the hidden counsels of God as to why one person should receive this gift but another should not. This was especially problematic in the case of Adam. Because he did not

33. For this and the following quote, see Augustine, *Grace and Free Will* (20.41), in *FC*, 59:297ff.

have the gift of perseverance evil came on him, as it were, out of necessity. Augustine argues in the following manner: God, who through his power created all things good, "foreknew that evil things would arise out of good." God knew that it was within the power of his almighty goodness to turn evil into good "rather than not to allow evil to be at all."[34] Adam was given a free will and, since he was not aware of his coming fall, he was content. He thought that it was within his power not to die and not to end in evil. If he had desired of his own free will, without the experience of death and misfortune, to remain in the condition of uprightness and freedom from sin, he would have thereby earned through his perseverance the fullness of the blessing that was also given to the angels. Then it would have become impossible for him to fall. Since he forsook God of his own free will, however, he received God's just condemnation. And with him the whole of humanity was condemned, which is identified with him and sinned in him.

Adam possessed a different grace from that which was given after the fall since he was not yet in a context of evil. He did not need divine assistance as do those who have been justified after the fall. Augustine distinguished, therefore, between the original freedom that was in every respect free and was not yet burdened with evil, and the freedom of fallen humanity that is fundamentally restricted since without divine assistance it continually turns away from God.[35] With Adam, however, a turning away was not something to be taken into consideration, even if God did foresee such a turning away. But predestination and the gift of perseverance are necessary for fallen humans if they are to escape from evil in the long run. So that no one becomes proud and self-confident Augustine points out that no one knows whether or not they will persevere to the end. The grace of perseverance and predestination is a divine mystery (13.40 [488]). We cannot empirically establish who belongs to those who will be accepted by God, or who belongs to those who will be left to their self-deserved fate.

It is extremely difficult to compare Pelagius's position with that of Augustine since both have different starting points and deal with different problems. For Pelagius, sin remains primarily the action of an individual

---

34. Augustine, *Treatise on Rebuke and Grace* (10.27ff.), in *NPNF,* 5:482f.

35. G. R. Evans, *Augustine on Evil* (Cambridge: Cambridge University Press, 1982), 148, notes: "In the last years of his life it became increasingly clear to Augustine that the way to the Highest Good he sought from his boyhood was not to be trodden by human effort, but only by the soul which allowed itself to be led by grace." It is not our doing but God's. But then we are back to theodicy where Augustine started unless we opt for a universal homecoming, which he certainly did not. Perhaps the issue of sin and grace transcends our rational means to solve it.

person that can either be carried out or avoided. Augustine, on the other hand, sees the individual as bound to the destiny of the corporate community, the orientation of which has been determined by the first human. The individual's activity is, therefore, pre-formed and his or her freedom already decisively qualified. In order for the individual to achieve and retain the ability of free choice, which is Pelagius's starting point, a prevenient grace is necessary. Since the individual can never completely escape the human context, a special act of grace, as occurs, for instance, in justification, is indispensable but is nevertheless insufficient. If humans are to act freely they need the continual support of God's grace. For Augustine, however, this poses a problem since it is apparent that not everyone has that support. Therefore some are, so to speak, predestined to salvation while others are not. Although Augustine insists on the accountability of the individual, it seems that ultimately God distributes good and evil and we do not know why some receive the one, and others the other.

Augustine consistently thought through this double predestination, yet the danger nevertheless exists that one might question the goodness of God. This danger was also recognized by the second Synod of Orange (529), which dealt expressly with the Augustinian heritage and the semi-Pelagians, who were especially active in France.[36] At the urging of Pope Felix IV this synod, which met on the occasion of the dedication of a new church in Orange in southern France, produced a series of basic articles that were largely extracted from Augustine. The prevenient grace of God was strongly emphasized by the synod so that, for example, all good thoughts and deeds are a gift of God (article 9) and that even the saints stand in need of divine assistance (article 10). It was also pointed out that when humans commit evil deeds they fulfill their own will; however, when they do good they freely fulfill the will of God (article 23). Yet we hear nothing of a double predestination. With these articles the problem of the relationship between God and evil was not explained, but only pushed aside. Although Augustine taught, based on a questionable exegesis of Romans 5:12, that all persons have sinned in Adam since they were all somehow present in him, he draws the right conclusions about the human situation.[37] Humans do not live in a vacuum but are always influenced by the context in which they live.

---

36. For information on this synod and the articles formulated by it, see Hefele, *A History of the Councils of the Church,* 4:152-67.

37. See Julius Gross, "Das Wesen der Erbsünde nach Augustin," in *Augustinus Magister: Congrès International Augustinien,* 3 vols. (Paris: Ètudes augustiniennes, 1954-55), vol. 2: *Communications,* 774.

The question about free will as well as the question about the extent to which we are given over to evil are questions that have always occupied theology, whether we think of Anselm of Canterbury, Bonaventure, or Thomas Aquinas. Especially in late Scholastic theology a position arose concerning human free will which, in its essentials, was very similar to that rejected by the Synod of Orange.[38] Martin Luther was one of the few theologians of the late Middle Ages who tenaciously defended the old catholic doctrine of Augustine and of the Synod of Orange.[39] The representatives of humanism, along with late medieval theologians like John Eck (1486-1543), were especially opposed to Luther on this issue. Finally, after much hesitation and under pressure from Pope Hadrian VI, Henry VIII of England, and other Catholic leaders, Erasmus of Rotterdam decided to take up the dispute against Luther and Luther's work *Assertio omnium articulorum M. Lutheri per bullam Leonis X. novissimam damnatorum* (Defense of all articles of Martin Luther which have been condemned through the latest bull of Leo X).

This defense presented by Luther was published in 1520 at the behest of his prince, the Elector Frederick the Wise of Saxony (1463-1525). It deals in detail with the accusations that were brought against Luther in the papal bull *Exsurge Domine*. Most of the forty-one theses treat the question of the extent of human freedom. Especially instructive is thesis 36, which is identical with thesis 13 of the *Heidelberg Disputation* (1518). It reads: "Since the fall of Adam, or after actual sin, free will exists only in name, and when it does what it can it commits sin."[40] As sinners humans do not have a free will but contribute only to their condemnation by their actions. With this position Luther stands in alignment with the Synod of Orange and Augustine. It is with this position that Erasmus takes issue. As we will see, however, he does not refute Luther's position but rather speaks past him.[41] We have here

---

38. See the detailed study by Harry J. McSorley, *Luther: Right or Wrong? An Ecumenical Theological Study of Luther's Major Work, "The Bondage of the Will"* (Minneapolis: Augsburg, 1969), 129-215, who provides a helpful historical-theological overview.

39. See McSorley, *Luther,* 293. Thus Ernst-Wilhelm Kohls, *Luther oder Erasmus,* vol. 1 (Basel: Reinhardt, 1972), 29, can rightly say that the conflict between Erasmus and Luther "was a renewal of the great conflict between Augustine and Pelagius." Unfortunately, the second volume of this work, which was to treat the dispute over *The Bondage of the Will* and was "promised" to appear soon, never appeared.

40. Martin Luther, "Defense and Explanation of All the Articles," trans. C. M. Jacobs, in *LW,* 32:92.

41. So McSorley, *Luther,* 284.

a situation like the conflict between Augustine and Pelagius in which the two disputants begin from very different starting points and are ultimately speaking of two entirely different matters.

d. Overcoming Evil through Human Willpower (Erasmus)

In his book *On the Freedom of the Will* (1524) **Erasmus** takes up the question of free choice. He begins with the assumption that, with the exceptions of Mani and John Wycliff (ca. 1330-84), no one had yet totally denied humans the power of choice.[42] Erasmus first discusses the biblical texts that support free choice, such as Sirach 15:17, where we read: "Before each person are life and death, and whichever one chooses will be given [to him or her]." Although this quote applies especially to the first humans, it is also important for us since we have the freedom to choose between good and evil. This freedom has admittedly been damaged by sin but it has not been destroyed by it (51ff.). Before we receive the grace of God we incline more toward evil than good, yet free choice is not completely absent. In the first place, according to Erasmus, there is freedom of choice in external things by which we can make decisions, for instance, whether to sit or stand, speak or remain silent, and the like. This freedom to choose cannot help us acquire eternal life and it was not destroyed through sin. The ability to make such decisions is the first gift of grace.

Erasmus distinguishes this from the second, or operative, grace through which we have the freedom to surrender ourselves to the will of God, for example, through prayer, study of the scriptures, or hearing the preached word. Erasmus seeks to support his contention that the human will is free through further quotations from the Bible such as Matthew 23:27 or John 14:15, texts that appear to presuppose a freedom of choice.

Erasmus next takes up those texts that seem to deny the freedom of choice. The most important example is the hardening of Pharaoh (Exod. 9:12), which is taken up by Paul in Romans 9:17. Erasmus explains that Pharaoh was given a will that was able to turn toward either good or evil (66). Of his own will Pharaoh chose evil and with his heart followed evil rather than God's commandments. God nevertheless took the depravity of Pha-

---

42. Erasmus of Rotterdam, *On the Freedom of the Will*, trans. E. Gordon Rupp, in *Luther and Erasmus: Free Will and Salvation*, ed. E. Rupp and S. Watson (Philadelphia: Westminster, 1969), 43; references in the following pages are to this edition.

raoh and used it for God's own glory and for the redemption of his people in order to make it clear that human attempts to strive against the will of God are vain. Similarly, according to Erasmus, a smart king or lord makes use of the cruelty that he hates in order to punish evil. Hardening is therefore a pedagogical measure of God but is not to be viewed as predetermined. Even the foreknowledge of God is not to determine, for God does not foreknow something so it will occur but because it occurs. Yet with God what God wills and foreknows coincide. But not every necessity involved in human events excludes the freedom of our will (68). God foreknew, for example, that Judas would betray the Lord. If one considers, however, the infallible foreknowledge of God and his unchangeable will, then one must conclude that Judas necessarily betrayed his Lord. And yet Judas could have changed his will. Thereby the foreknowledge of God would not have been compromised since God would have foreknown even this and changed his own will accordingly.

But what about the story of Jacob and Esau, where it is said that God loved Jacob but hated Esau?[43] Here also Erasmus claimed that God contains within himself no contradictions but loves and hates on just grounds and that this does not preclude human free will. When, for example, God hates one who is not yet born this is because God knows that this person will commit acts that will merit hate, and when God loves one who is not yet born this occurs on the same grounds, but based on deeds of an opposing nature. When Erasmus points to the Old Testament picture of humans as clay in the potter's hand so that God can do with us what he will (see Jer. 18:6), this is an expression of the fact that we should entrust ourselves to God just as a vessel is entrusted to the hands of the potter. "Yet in truth this is not to take away free choice wholly, nor does it exclude our will from cooperating with the divine will in order to attain eternal salvation." When Paul takes up this passage in Romans 9:21ff. he does so to silence the evil grumblings of the Jews against God, but not with the intention of completely excluding the freedom of choice.

If humans cannot do anything positive, then, according to Erasmus, there is no place for merits, and where there is no place for merits there is also no place for punishment or reward (73). On the other hand, if humans are able to do everything, then there remains no place for grace. When one views the effort of the human will together with the support of divine grace,

---

43. For this and the following, see Erasmus of Rotterdam, *On the Freedom of the Will,* 69ff.

then those scriptures that appear to oppose one another quickly lose their contradictory character.

When Erasmus comes to Luther's work he makes the criticism that not enough place is given to the human will. From statements such as "No one can receive anything except what has been given from heaven" (John 3:27), one cannot conclude, according to Erasmus, that there is no strength or use of our freedom of choice. The fact that fire warms comes from heaven just as much as the fact that we seek that which is advantageous for us and avoid that which is harmful to us. The fact that after the fall the human will was spurred on to seek better things is likewise from heaven. It is also from heaven that we find favor with God through tears, alms, and prayers, which make us acceptable before God. God, therefore, always goes before us as creator and sustainer so that we are able to make use of our free will.

Without the assistance of grace, according to Erasmus, we of course are unable to achieve even part of that which we seek (79). The situation here is like that of a ship's captain who, after a severe storm, does not say that he has saved the ship but rather that God has, although his own skill and effort were not completely useless. With reference to Philippians 2:13, "For it is God who is at work in you, enabling you both to will and to work for his good pleasure," and calling on the authority of Ambrose's interpretation of this passage, Erasmus concludes that "a good will cooperates with the action of grace" (81). The entire scriptures speak so often of help and assistance that one must here bring humans and God together. Over against those who claim that humans can do nothing without the grace of God and conclude therefore that no human work is good, Erasmus maintains that which seems to him much more probable: "There is nothing that man cannot do with the help of the grace of God, and . . . therefore all the works of man can be good" (85).

In his epilogue Erasmus again speaks against the idea that human merit remains completely worthless and that the works even of godly persons are sinful (87). He also rejects the claim that an absolute necessity be ascribed to everything we do or desire. He assures his readers once again that he readily admits that all human efforts are traced back to God, without meaning that we can do nothing. Our share of free will is very small and it is a part of divine grace that we can turn our souls toward that which leads to salvation and can cooperate with grace. Erasmus seeks in this way to establish that we are able to cooperate with God's grace and to contribute something toward our salvation. He also suggests: "After his battle with Pelagius, Augustine became less just toward free choice than he had been before. Luther, on the other hand, who had previously allowed something to free choice, is now carried so far in the heat of his defense as to destroy it entirely" (90).

In order once more to clarify his position for Luther, Erasmus distinguishes three stages in the efforts of humans toward salvation: beginning, progress, and end. Divine grace is ascribed to the first and last of these stages while the freedom of choice has its place in the stage of progress. Yet even here the grace of God is the primary factor while human freedom of choice remains a secondary cause. Although Erasmus attempted to explain his position to Luther through repeated entreaty, no new impetus was produced. Decisive for him is that humans themselves can contribute something to their salvation. Erasmus's goal was a virtuous life. German church historian Gustav Adolf Benrath (b. 1931) characterized Erasmus's position accurately as follows:

> External enemies such as the world, the devil, and death play no role in this battle as individual powers. The battle takes place within humans themselves. Reason must continually defeat the rebellious "outer person." . . . Being a Christian consists largely of the heart's desire to become a Christian. Everyone will be victorious; only those who do not want to be victorious will not achieve victory. The one who makes an effort will be brought along further by the Spirit, for everything depends on moral progress and advancement. Christ is thereby not only the teacher and leader into battle but also the goal toward which we must orient ourselves. . . . In this way the Christian way of salvation becomes for Erasmus a way of sanctification. Indeed, it would be a way of self-sanctification were it not for the Christian the sign of baptism at the beginning, the progress with the help of the Spirit, and the heavenly reward at the end.[44]

44. So Gustav Adolf Benrath, "Die Lehre des Humanismus und des Antitrinitarismus," in *HDT,* 3:29. Of course one can portray Erasmus in a more conservative light and make of him a representative of orthodox theology. Ernst-Wilhelm Kohls, *Die Theologie des Erasmus,* vol. 1, *Textband* (Basel: Reinhardt, 1966), 152-58, writes, for example, that "The Erasmian concept of sin rises above every legalistic or sociological-moral standardization. Such a standardization is likewise avoided through the fact that Erasmus ultimately views the battle of the Christian against actual sins as an extension of the battle between God and Satan. In this sense sin appears to him as nothing short of 'the power of the devil.' Nothing of this godly/anti-Godly dynamic, however, is to be detected in Erasmus's work against Luther. The accent is not upon an anti-Godly action or upon the aggravating severity of evil, but rather clearly upon the cooperation, the cooperation of humans in the salvation process." Also in this regard see the comment of E. Gordon Rupp in his introduction to the transla-

e. The Person as Torn between Two Powers (Luther)

Martin Luther waited more than a year before he responded to Erasmus with his *The Bondage of the Will* (1525), which numbers among one of the most impressive works ever produced by Luther. Luther's "response" was approximately four times the length of Erasmus's work. Erasmus answered back with a rejoinder titled *Hyperaspistes* (The Defender), which was longer than his original work and Luther's response put together. Although at the beginning Luther wrote very respectfully and congratulated Erasmus on having understood the essence of his teaching, thus making a response worthwhile, Erasmus was hurt by the intensity of Luther's response. Even a letter from Luther in which he sought to justify the passionate nature of his argumentation could not reconcile Erasmus (*LW,* 33:11).[45] This was not surprising, for Luther did not simply put forward his own position over against that of Erasmus, but rather took Erasmus's work apart almost sentence by sentence in order to refute it. At the very beginning Luther made clear that the main point of conflict between himself and Erasmus was the question of whether the human will is able to contribute something to the eternal salvation of humans.[46] This in turn raised the question of whether God foreknows something and we all act out of necessity, or whether a free will exists within us. Luther's conviction is clear, for he says, like Augustine before him, that it is fundamentally necessary for the salvation of the Christian to know that God does not foreknow contingently, but that he foresees, aims, and carries out all things through his immutable, eternal, and infallible will (37).

Luther begins with the presupposition that nothing takes place accidentally but that God's eternal plan and providence stand behind all things. The divine power is sovereign and it cannot be restricted. Salvation lies beyond our power and depends wholly on God. Luther concludes from this that when God is not present and at work in everything that we do, the result will be evil and we will necessarily do that which is of no avail for salva-

---

tion of *De libero arbitrio* "The Erasmian Enigma," in *Luther and Erasmus,* ed. Rupp and Watson, 8, where Rupp says of Kohls's evaluation: "One is bound to have reservations about a demonstration taken almost exclusively from the early writings [of Erasmus]."

45. For further literature on the dispute between Luther and Erasmus, see Bernhard Lohse, "Dogma und Bekenntnis in der Reformation: Von Luther bis zum Konkordienbuch," in *HDT,* 2:33.

46. Martin Luther, *The Bondage of the Will* (1525), in *LW* 33:35; in what follows, references to this work are to this edition.

tion (64). Luther does not mean, thereby, that without the Spirit of God humans do evil against their will as if they were physically forced to do it, but rather that they do evil out of their own obliging will. One is quite naturally reminded here of Luther's hymn "A Mighty Fortress Is Our God" (*Evangelical Lutheran Worship*, no. 503), where he writes: "No strength of ours can match his might! We would be lost, rejected."

Luther speaks of a necessity of unchangeableness, that is, that the will is not only unable to change itself and go in a different direction but is at the same time also inclined to continue in its original evil direction. As Lutheran theologian Gerhard Forde (1927-2005) explained: "We are under necessity but not forced. We are not puppets controlled by a transcendent puppeteer, yet the will cannot change itself. It goes on willing what it wills and will not change because it wills immutably. It cannot change itself, because it does not want to."[47] When God works graciously within us the will is changed and acts likewise out of its own inclination and its own willing and not out of coercion so that it cannot be changed toward another direction through an opposing will. Just as the will previously willed and found satisfaction in evil it now wills and rejoices in that which is good. Luther thus comes to the point that is most discussed and that he explains as follows:

> If we are under the god of this world, away from the work and Spirit of the true God, we are held captive to his will, as Paul says to Timothy [2 Tim. 2:26], so that we cannot will anything but what he wills. For he is that strong man armed, who guards his own palace in such a way that those whom he possesses are in peace [Luke 11:21], so as to prevent them from stirring up any thought or feeling against him; otherwise, the kingdom of Satan being divided against itself would not stand. And this we do readily and willingly, according to the nature of the will, which would not be a will if it were compelled; for compulsion is rather (so to say) "unwill." But if a Stronger One comes who overcomes him and takes us as His spoil, then through His Spirit we are again slaves and captives though this is royal freedom so that we readily will and do what he wills. Thus the human will is placed between the two like a beast of burden. If God rides it, it wills and goes where God wills, as the Psalm says: "I am become as a beast [before thee] and I am always with thee" [Ps. 73:22f.]. If Satan rides it, it wills and goes where Satan wills; nor can it choose to run to either of the two riders

---

47. Gerhard O. Forde, *The Captivation of the Will*, ed. Steven Paulson, intro. James A. Nestingen (Grand Rapids: Eerdmans, 2005), 56.

or to seek him out, but the riders themselves contend for the possession and control of it (65f.).[48]

The first impression of Luther's argument is that a dualism is here being introduced that divides the world into two spheres of influence. The two powers, God and Satan, however, are not the focus here, but rather humanity. Humans, according to Luther, never live in a neutral vacuum but always in a particular context that decisively influences them and from which and in which they live. If this context is formed by God, then they desire and do that which is of God. If, however, it is determined by the anti-Godly powers, then humans desire and do what the interests of these powers demand. Even when one takes both powers into consideration Luther leaves no doubt that God, as the stronger of the two, wins. Satan is not equal in power to God but is a creature, even if he has an anti-Godly rank and is ultimately dependent on God for his being. Humans only have freedom within a context that is determined either by God or by the anti-Godly powers. As creatures, humans do not have the freedom to choose their context but rather live within a context that they can only leave if they are transferred into that other context. The questions of the freedom of the will and freedom of choice are not thereby touched on but rather the question of whether humans can choose by their own power the sinful context, a possibility that Augustine always emphasized. Luther, however, appears to reject this possibility.

Luther next distinguishes between the preached and offered grace of God on the one hand, and the hidden and frightening will of God on the other. In the latter, God determines through his own counsel which persons will be the recipients of his preached and offered grace.[49] One can only worship the divine will in reverence but cannot penetrate it. This awesome aspect of the divine majesty is reserved for God alone.

> God must therefore be left to himself in his own majesty, for in this regard we have nothing to do with him, nor has he willed that we should have

---

48. For a discussion of the image of the beast of burden and the two riders as well as of the relevant literature, see McSorley, *Luther,* 335-40. McSorley's argument, that Luther does not discuss where Satan comes from, is not valid. Luther's intention is not to explain evil, but rather to show that humans do not have a free will when it comes to their own salvation. Therefore it is also not correct to say, with McSorley, that according to Luther God himself appears to be the author of evil (343). At this point McSorley has missed the actual intention of Luther, which focuses in a different direction.

49. For this and the following quotes, see Luther, *The Bondage of the Will,* in *LW* 33:138ff.

anything to do with him. But we have something to do with him insofar as he is clothed and set forth in his Word, through which he offers himself to us and which is the beauty and glory with which the psalmist celebrates him as being clothed. In this regard we say, the good God does not deplore the death of his people which he works in them, but he deplores the death which he finds in his people and desires to remove from them.

We must distinguish "between God preached and God hidden, that is, between the Word of God and God himself." Since God is all-working and there is no other power equal to him Luther must necessarily distinguish between two wills in God: the revealed will, out of which good comes to us, and the hidden will, which we ultimately cannot ground and which contains, so to speak, that which is cruel and evil. The latter also predestines certain persons to evil. It is through God's will, as it were, that it is decided whether certain persons come to stand under the sphere of the influence of God the redeemer, or whether they spend their lives under the reign of evil in alienation from God. Why someone would be excluded from salvation is not answered by Luther, who instead points to the hidden will of God, which we can ultimately only worship and honor but not fathom.[50]

Luther seeks to shed light on the evil that God works in still another way and gives the hardening of Pharaoh as an example. The starting point here is the assumption that God does not cause sin.[51] Luther begins with the efficacy of God and reminds Erasmus that he himself admitted that God works all in all (1 Cor. 12:6).

Now, Satan and man, having fallen from God and having been deserted by God, cannot will good, that is, things which please God or which God wills; but instead they are continually turned in the direction of their own desires, so that they are unable not to seek the things of self. This will and nature of theirs, therefore, which is thus averse from God, is not something nonexistent. For Satan and ungodly man are not nonexistent or possessed of no nature or will, although their nature is corrupt and averse from God. . . . Since, then, God moves and actuates all in all, he necessarily moves and acts also in Satan and ungodly man. But he acts in them as they

50. Philip S. Watson, "The Lutheran Riposte," in *Luther and Erasmus,* ed. Rupp and Watson, 23, rightly observes: "His doctrine of predestination, like Calvin's after him, is from one point of view a confession of ignorance and a very proper piece of Christian agnosticism."

51. Luther, *The Bondage of the Will,* 174; references in the following pages are to this work.

are and as he finds them. . . . When God works in and through evil men, evil things are done, and yet God cannot act evilly although he does evil through evil men because one who is himself good cannot act evilly; yet he uses evil instruments that cannot escape the sway and motion of his omnipotence. (175f.)

Because of the omnipotence with which God moves all things Satan is able to hold on to his followers. Yet God does not work in such a way that he himself brings about evil, a fact that Luther continually stressed, but he rather moves further along and hardens that evil that he finds already before him. Evil does not occur through a mistake of God but rather through our false behavior since we are by nature evil through our fallen nature. In accordance with the nature of God's omnipotence, evil persons are driven further along in their own evil activity although God, in accordance with his wisdom and for his glory and our salvation, can also use this evil for good.

Two points are here worthy of special consideration: first, Luther's statement that the evil will cannot do anything other than evil *(aliter facere non possit);* and second, that Satan became evil in that God forsook him and Satan sinned *(deserente Deo et peccante Satana malam factam)* (178). The fact that God made Pharaoh's will unrepentant can be derived from God's omnipotence. That he could not have changed Pharaoh's will, however, appears at the very least unusual and would seem to contradict God's omnipotence. Also, the fact that Satan became evil because God forsook him and he sinned seems to trace evil back to God, a consequence that Luther will not accept. He wishes rather to show that it is an aspect of God's omnipotence to move everything further along, whether good or evil, according to its own character. In this way he answers the question of why God does not transform evil into good but instead actually strengthens evil in its wickedness. Luther also advises that this belongs to the mystery of God's majesty, which we can only worship but cannot explain. When we ask, therefore, why God allowed Adam to fall and why he created all of us infected with the same sin since he could have protected Adam or created us with a different constitution, then we must not forget, according to Luther, that God is God. For God's will there is no cause or rule of reason that we could use as a measure since nothing is equal or superior to his will but his will is itself the ruler of all things (180f.). Hence God himself is the final rule and measure of his action and his judgment.

At the conclusion of his work Luther summarizes his argument once more in three points (293):

1. God foreknows and predetermines all things. He can make no mistakes in his foreknowledge nor be hindered in his predetermining. Nothing happens that he does not will to happen.
2. Satan is the ruler of this world who constantly battles against the kingdom of Christ with all his might. He would allow no one to escape the sphere of his power if he were not forced to do this through the divine power of the Spirit.
3. Original sin has so damaged us that it causes many problems in the fight against evil even in those who are led by the Spirit of God. Without the help of the Spirit of God, therefore, there is nothing in humans that is able to turn toward the good but rather only toward evil.

Luther understands humans as having a tendency toward evil placed on them by original sin and as turning themselves away from God and seeking to please themselves. If it were possible for humans to contribute something to their own salvation, then a certain amount of uncertainty would enter into and interfere with us being assured of salvation. Erasmus, on the other hand, interprets this perspective of Luther as determinism. He desires, therefore, despite the recognition that humans are sinful, to hold fast to the idea that humans can contribute at least something to their salvation. Luther, however, does not embrace determinism. This is clear when he concedes that there is a kingdom of the left in which humans can do through their own choice and counsel what they will, while in the other kingdom (of the right) things are directed by the choice and counsel of God (119). Erasmus makes no distinction between a kingdom of the left and a kingdom of the right. Worldly respectability leads simultaneously to heavenly acceptance for Erasmus. It is not surprising, then, that the key thoughts of *On the Bondage of the Will,* even if they appear to be extreme, are necessary for Luther's dispute "with a theology that is largely semi-Pelagian or has even become Pelagian."[52]

The basic statements of Luther on this subject were of such importance that they found their way into the *Formula of Concord* of the Lutheran Church. There, with reference to Luther, we read that "there is no cooperation of our will in our conversion and God must draw and give new birth to the human being."[53] Yet no mechanistic understanding of the Christian's

---

52. So Lohse, "Dogma und Bekenntnis," 39.

53. For this and the following quote, see "The Formula of Concord," in *The Book of Concord: The Confessions of the Evangelical Lutheran Church,* ed. Robert Kolb and Timothy J. Wengert, trans. Charles Arand et al. (Minneapolis: Fortress, 2000), 552 and 560.

transfer out of one sphere of influence into the other is thereby intended for the confessors also explain that "conversion is such a change in the human mind, will, and heart effected by the activity of the Holy Spirit that the human being, through this activity of the Holy Spirit, can accept the grace offered." Humans, therefore, are not wholly passive. If they wish to escape evil's sphere of influence, however, they are dependent on the grace of God. We continue to encounter here two spheres of influence, that of good and that of evil. It would be therefore profitable at this point to take a closer look at the structure of evil's sphere of influence. Yet before we do this, we should consider one more point.

f. Humanity's Shattered Image

In the discussion of the creation of humanity in chapter 5, we noted that humans were created in the image of God. Yet humanity has abandoned its God relationship. Therefore the issue must be pursued whether sinful humanity still resembles that image. Bishop Irenaeus of Lyons (120/140–ca. 202) introduced the distinction between image and similitude by which he attempted to assert both the sinfulness of humanity and its status as God's special creature. While the similitude is lost, the image is retained. This distinction goes back to Genesis 1:26 in which two different Hebrew words *(tselem* and *demut)* are used to express that humanity is created in the image of God.[54] These Hebrew words are virtually synonymous. Some of the dogmatic conclusions, however, drawn from these two different words have no scriptural basis. Irenaeus claimed that through Adam's fall the God-intended development of humanity, through which it was to become immortal, was interrupted. Humanity lost its similitude, that is, its relationship with God, while it retained the image of God, being a reasonable and morally free creature. This distinction enabled Irenaeus to affirm that human beings did not change physically but only relationally once they had become sinners.

---

54. For the following, see Irenaeus, *Against Heresies* (5.16.2), in *ANF,* 1:544; and see Gerhard von Rad, "*eikōn* (The Divine Likeness in the OT)," in *TDNT,* 2:391, who also remarks very interestingly, "In Gen. 5:1ff. reference is made to the physical progeny of the first man, and it is said of Seth, Adam's son, that he was begotten in the image and likeness of Adam. This statement is most important. It ensures the theological actuality for all generations of the witness to the divine likeness." See further Paul Althaus, *Die christliche Wahrheit: Lehrbuch der Dogmatik* (Gütersloh: Gerd Mohn, 1959), 336ff., for his very perceptive treatment of the issue of humanity being created in the image of God.

The distinction between similitude and image, however, could easily be interpreted to mean that sinfulness only affected part of humanity, while the rest remained in a state of original integrity. This hazard is especially noticeable when Augustine uses Neo-Platonic terminology and talks about evil as a deficiency of the good that results from a deficient cause or from a defect. As he writes: "It is not a matter of efficiency, but of deficiency; the evil will itself is not effective but defective."[55] Such a train of thought could lead to the notion that humanity only needs to improve in order to be no longer sinful.

In late medieval theology the deficiency aspect of sin was developed even further. Thomas Aquinas (1225-74), for instance, stated that "original sin is concupiscence, materially, but privation of original justice, formally."[56] Original justice, which Adam once enjoyed, is now missing and therefore humanity is plagued with sin. This "corrupt disposition," namely, the privation of original justice, is now called "original sin."[57] But it can be corrected through a supernatural gift that achieves a sublimation of the rational creature beyond human nature.[58] Human nature no longer needs a conversion, but an addition, a sublimation. Grace was then understood as something supernatural in humanity or a supernatural quality "infused by God into the soul."[59]

To perceive grace as a supernatural addition to humanity's natural state is as dangerous as the idea that a human being is not a totally corrupt and sinful entity, but only lacks the supernatural gifts of the similitude, that is, original justice and integrity.[60] But the Catholic Church thought differ-

55. Augustine, *Concerning the City of God against the Pagans* (12.7), trans. Henry Bettenson, intro. G. R. Evans (London: Penguin Books, 2003), 479.

56. Thomas Aquinas, *Summa Theologica,* literally trans. by Fathers of the English Dominican Province (London: Burns, Oates, and Benziger, 1912-25), Ia IIae.82.3.

57. Thomas Aquinas, *Summa Theologica,* Ia IIae.82.2.

58. See Thomas Aquinas, *Summa Theologica,* Ia IIae.110.3, where Thomas says that human virtues dispose man fittingly "to the nature whereby he is a man; whereas infused virtues dispose man in a higher manner and towards a higher end, and consequently in relation to some higher nature, i.e., in relation to a participation of the Divine Nature."

59. Thomas Aquinas, *Summa Theologica,* Ia IIae.110.2.

60. For the following, see the perceptive analysis by Helmut Thielicke, *Theological Ethics,* vol. 1, *Foundations,* ed. William H. Lazareth (Philadelphia: Fortress, 1966), 197-211, on the issue of the Roman Catholic ontological perception of humanity being created in the image of God. When he states that "Roman Catholic thinking is profoundly ontological, Reformation thinking profoundly personalistic," this is true for the time of the Reformation, but, as we will see, it is no longer true in this exclusive sense for our present time.

ently. Therefore the Council of Trent decided in the "Decree on Justification" that through God's grace humanity can assent, cooperate, and dispose itself to God's salvific activity.[61] This meant that the Catholic Church did not hold that humanity's sinful nature was really changed. Its properties as an image of God were still thought to be integral so that the lost similitude could be achieved through a supernatural addition.[62]

When we come to the Reformers, we note that the distinction between image and similitude has been abandoned. "Man must be an image," we hear Luther say, "either of God or of the devil, because according to whom he directs his life, him he resembles."[63] Humanity is perceived as an entity and if it is sinful, the whole of humanity is sinful. This reminds us of Luther's statement in *The Bondage of the Will* that a human being resembles an animal that is driven either by God or by the devil.[64]

John Calvin (1509-64), though asserting that there is nothing left in humanity of which it could boast, claimed that there are "some remaining traces of the image of God which distinguish the entire human race from the other creatures."[65] Perhaps a little more cautious, this was the line of thinking that Lutheran Orthodoxy took. Johann Gerhard (1582-1637), for instance, maintains that "with regard to these most minute particles . . . the image of God was not utterly lost."[66] These "most minute particles," however, are inborn moral principles, humanity's dominion over other crea-

---

61. "Decree on Justification" (5), in Henricus Denzinger, *The Sources of Catholic Dogma,* trans. Roy J. Deferrari (St. Louis: B. Herder, 1957), 250 (§797).

62. So rightly Thielicke, *Theological Ethics,* 1:207. Since he does not distinguish between image and similitude, he rightly says that the *"imago* qualities of man" are not affected by the fall.

63. Martin Luther, *Über das 1. Buch Mose. Predigten* (1527), in *WA,* 24:51.12f., in his exegesis of Genesis 1:27.

64. Luther, *On the Bondage of Will,* in *LW,* 33:65f.

65. John Calvin, *Institutes of the Christian Religion* (II.2.1 and II.2.17), ed. John T. McNeill, trans. Ford Lewis Battles, The Library of Christian Classics, vols. 20 and 21 (Philadelphia: Westminster, 1960), 1:255 and 277. See also T. F. Torrance, *Calvin's Doctrine of Man* (Grand Rapids: Eerdmans, 1957), 88ff., in his excellent analysis of this evident dichotomy. Torrance rightly claims that it is important to be aware of Calvin's distinction between the natural and the spiritual. While humanity is deprived of its spiritual gifts, it is only corrupted in its natural gifts. He also admits that "it is difficult to see how there can be any ultimate reconciliation between Calvin's doctrine of total perversity and his doctrine of a remnant of the *imago dei,* though the very fact that he can give them both in the same breath seems to indicate that he had no difficulty in reconciling them."

66. Johann Gerhard, "The Image of God," in *The Doctrine of Man in Classical Lutheran Theology,* ed. Herman A. Preus and Edmund Smits (Minneapolis: Augsburg, 1962), 62.

tures, its intelligence, and its free will concerning the things that are under its control. We must agree with German systematic theologian Paul Althaus (1888-1966) that something important was emphasized here, but with inadequate conceptuality.[67] As mentioned above, humanity did not suddenly become stupid, lazy, and unreliable once it was drawn into universal sinfulness.

Karl Barth was right when he emphasized that the fact that humanity was created in the image of God did not get lost through sin. Even as a sinner a human being is still God's creature and related to God.[68] The psalmist captured this insight very precisely when he exclaimed: "Whither shall I go from thy Spirit? Or whither shall I flee from thy presence?" (Ps. 139:7). As we have noted, Genesis 1:26 does not talk about an ideal state of the distant past.[69] Still today humans are called to be God's administrators. As Wolfhart Pannenberg (b. 1928) writes: "God's will as Creator is still the standard for dominion we exercise as God's image."[70] To fulfill this task humans are still endowed with the same gifts they always possessed. This does not mean that Luther was wrong when he stated that humanity has totally lost its status as being created in the image of God. We must remember that Luther was attacking the idea that some features in humanity were still integral while others were contaminated by sinfulness. Thus he insisted that the total human being was a corrupt entity. Emil Brunner (1889-1966) seems to make the same point when he says, "The breaking of man's relation to God means that the image of God in man has also been broken. This does not mean that it no longer exists, but that it has been defaced."[71] The same stand is taken by Dutch Reformed theologian Gerrit C. Berkouwer (1903-96) when, in attacking any cooperative view of humanity, he emphasizes the total corruption of humanity.[72]

Today most Roman Catholic theologians have abandoned an ontologi-

---

67. See Althaus, *Die christliche Wahrheit*, 340.

68. Barth, *CD*, III/2:324, opts for an analogy of relationship instead of an analogy of being between God and humanity.

69. Barth, *CD*, III/1:200, arrives at the same conclusions in his excellent comments on the *imago dei* issue. See also Walther Zimmerli, *Old Testament Theology in Outline*, trans. David E. Green (Edinburgh: T&T Clark, 1984 [1978]), 35f.

70. Wolfhart Pannenberg, *Systematic Theology*, trans. Geoffrey W. Bromiley (Grand Rapids: Eerdmans, 1994), 2:205.

71. Emil Brunner, *Man in Revolt*, trans. Olive Wyon (Philadelphia: Westminster, 1947), 136; see also Thielicke, *Theological Ethics*, 1:167, esp. n. 18.

72. G. C. Berkouwer, *Man: The Image of God*, trans. D. W. Jellema (Grand Rapids: Eerdmans, 1962), esp. 145ff.

cal understanding of humanity being created in the image of God, which so easily leads to the misunderstanding that part of a human being is still intact while the other part is corrupt. German Roman Catholic Michael Schmaus (1897-1993), for instance, maintains that the statement in the Genesis account that humanity is created in the image of God should be understood in a functional way.[73] Humans are called to exercise dominion over the world. Only with regard to the new creation in the *eschaton* can we talk about an ontological understanding of the image of God when we will fully participate in Christ's being, made in the image of God (see Rom. 8:29; 2 Cor. 3:18). Very interestingly, Schmaus also mentions that according to the church fathers the statement that humanity is created in the image of God means that God reflects himself in humanity.[74] This implies that people can only realize themselves if they realize themselves as being created in the image of God.[75] But we have seen that instead of reflecting God, people want to be like God. We misuse the creation instead of exercising dominion over it and managing it in gratitude to God. We are searching for ourselves in the creation instead of looking in it for the "footprints" of our creator. Therefore, in trying to discover the cosmos, we lose ourselves to the cosmos. Our world begins to resemble more and more a kingdom of sin rather than the kingdom of God.

2. The Kingdom of Evil

When we speak of a "kingdom of evil" or a "kingdom of sin," we are not thinking of a dualistically structured principle of evil or sin that stands in opposition to the good, but have in mind rather that individual manifestations of evil are derived from a communal existence. Humans never live in solitary isolation, but they always form communities. These communities are ruled according to certain precepts to which the individual existence complies either voluntarily or involuntarily.

The concept of a kingdom of evil addresses a genuine New Testament state of affairs. We read, for instance, in the Gospel of John of the "prince of this world" and of the "battle of darkness against the light." Also in the Syn-

73. For the following, see Michael Schmaus, *Der Glaube der Kirche: Handbuch katholischer Dogmatik,* vol. 1 (Munich: Max Hueber, 1969), 336.

74. Schmaus, *Der Glaube der Kirche,* 650.

75. The *Catechism of the Catholic Church* also affirms: "The divine image is present in every man" (1702). This means all human beings have the vocation to be God's representatives.

optic Gospels from beginning to end the destiny of Jesus stands in opposition to the anti-Godly powers. Even Paul writes of the "powers and authorities of this world." In Christianity the concept of a kingdom of evil was first systematically developed in Augustine's *The City of God against the Pagans* — a book that he wrote between the years 413 and 426. The immediate occasion for the writing of the book was the capture of Rome in 410 by Alaric I (ca. 370-410) and his Visigoths. Concerning this event Augustine wrote in his *Retractations:*

> Meanwhile, Rome was destroyed as a result of an invasion of the Goths under the leadership of Alaric, and of the violence of this great disaster. The worshipers of many false gods, whom we call by the customary name pagans, attempting to attribute its destruction to the Christian religion, began to blaspheme the true God more sharply and bitterly than usual. And so, "burning with zeal for the house of God" [Ps. 68:10 (69:9); John 2:17], I decided to write the book On the City of God in opposition to their blasphemies and errors.[76]

a. Jerusalem and Babylon in Conflict (Augustine)

Augustine made use of an image that was already familiar among African Christians and to which he was probably first introduced through Tyconius, a North African contemporary of Augustine and a Donatist bishop.[77] According to this view, since the fall of Adam humanity has been divided into two great cities or communities, that is, into two great camps of allegiance. The one city serves God and his faithful angels while the other serves the rebellious angels, the devil, and his demons. These cities appear to be inextricably mixed together within the church as well as in the world, but they will be separated from one another at the last judgment. When Christ passes judgment the two cities, Babylon and Jerusalem, will clearly emerge, one to the left and the other to the right.

Already before Augustine wrote *The City of God* he had spoken of these two communities. We read therefore in his work *The First Catechetical Instruction* (ca. 400):

76. Augustine, *Retractations* (2.43.2), in *FC*, 60:209.

77. For this and the following, see Peter Brown, *Augustine of Hippo: A Biography* (London: Faber and Faber, 1967), 314. See also Henry Chadwick, *Augustine of Hippo: A Life* (Oxford: Oxford University Press, 2009), 128, a posthumously published book for which Peter Brown wrote the preface.

There are two cities, one of the wicked, the other of the just, which endure from the beginning of the human race even to the end of time, which are now intermingled in body, but separated in will, and which, moreover, are to be separated in body also on the day of judgment. For all men who love pride and temporal dominion together with empty vanity and display of presumption, and all spirits who set their affections on such things and seek their own glory by the subjection of man, are bound together in one fellowship; and even though they frequently fight one with another for these ends, still they are flung headlong by an equal weight of desire into the same abyss, and are united to one another by the likeness of their ways and deserts. And again, all men and all spirits who humbly seek God's glory, not their own, and who follow Him in godliness, belong to one fellowship. And yet God is most merciful and long-suffering toward ungodly men, and offers them room for repentance and amendment.[78]

The two communities encompass not only humans but also spiritual beings. Their separation has existed since the beginning of humanity, that is, since the fall of Adam, and will last so long as the earth exists. Externally one cannot determine to which of the two communities a person belongs since only their wills are structured oppositely to one another. It is also difficult to distinguish the two groups since they are mixed together and there exists no visible dividing line separating the communities from each other.

In *The City of God* Augustine sought to divide history into seven epochs following the pattern of a seven-day schema.[79] The first epoch extends from Adam to the flood, the second from the flood to Abraham. The third epoch covers the period between Abraham and David, the fourth between David and the exile, and the fifth extends from the exile to the coming of Christ. Currently we find ourselves in the sixth epoch. Augustine rejects immediately the possibility of an exact prediction of the course of history since one cannot measure the length of these epochs according to a certain number of generations. "The seventh [age] will be our Sabbath, whose end will not be an evening, but the Lord's Day, an eighth day, as it were, which is to last forever, a day consecrated by the resurrection of Christ, foreshadowing the eternal rest not only of the spirit but of the body also." Augustine describes, then, a linear progression of history from the beginning to the end of this world.

Augustine explains that God originally chose to derive all humanity

---

78. Augustine, *The First Catechetical Instruction* (19.31), in *ACW,* 2:61.
79. See Augustine, *The City of God* (22.30), 1091, including the quote.

from one individual in order to unite humans into a community and to bind them together in a harmonious unity and a bond of peace.[80] According to this plan humanity would not have been subject to death. Yet the first humans brought death on themselves through their disobedience. This sin was so serious that human nature was altered and resulted in enslavement to sin and unavoidable death for all their descendants. This reign of death left such a mark on human beings that they ran directly into a second death, which was their well-deserved punishment, although no small number of persons were saved through the unmerited grace of God. We now have the result before us: a great number of different peoples who are spread over the entire world and who are distinguished through their various religious and moral practices and their different languages.

Nevertheless, there are really only two main groups within human society that one might call two cities. The one city prefers to live according to the principles of the flesh, the other according to the principles of the spirit. The citizens of these two different cities want to pursue their own peace and they achieve this goal. According to Augustine, the world does not disintegrate into two societies in which one is characterized by the power of Satan and the other by the power of God, but, rather, both exist through the unmerited grace of God. Both, however, organize their lives in contrasting fashion for they pursue either the goals of the spirit or those of the flesh, whereby Augustine takes up a Pauline distinction.

When Augustine distinguishes between spirit and flesh or spirit and body he in no way intends to place the blame for sin on the latter. As he expressly states, the flesh is not the cause of every kind of moral failure, but rather, the ground for evil behavior is to be found in the soul or spirit of humans. "It is in fact not by the possessions of flesh, which the Devil does not possess, that man has become like the Devil: it is by living by the rule of self, that is, by the rule of man. For the Devil chose to live by the rule of self" (14.3 [552]). If humans live according to their own criteria and not according to God's, Augustine asserts, they become like the devil. But if they live according to the criterion of truth, they do not live according to their own standards but according to those of God. There are "two cities, different and mutually opposed, [that] owe their existence to the fact that some men live by the standard of the flesh, others by the standard of the spirit. It can now be seen that we may put it this way: that some live by man's standard, others by God's" (14.4 [553]).

---

80. For this and the following, see Augustine, *The City of God* (14.1), 547ff.

In this way love of self is contrasted to the love of God. The love of self is at the same time the love of the flesh, that is, of one's own flesh. Those who love themselves are not concerned for the truth for this is not a human possession. Augustine characterized the two cities as follows:

> The two cities were created by two kinds of love: the earthly was created by self-love reaching the point of contempt for God, the Heavenly City by the love of God carried as far as contempt of self. In fact, the earthly city glories in itself, the Heavenly City glories in the Lord. The former looks for glory from men, the latter finds its highest glory in God, the witness of the good conscience. The earthly lifts up its head in its own glory, the Heavenly City says to its God: "My glory; you lift up my head." In the former, the lust for domination lords over its princes as over the nations it subjugates; in the other both those put in authority and those subject to them serve one another in love, the rulers by their counsel, the subjects by obedience. (14.28 [593])

We encounter here two entirely different and opposing types of conduct that characterize these two communities.

The earthly city is only able to live in peace when its life is not grounded on belief. A harmonious agreement among its citizens is achieved through the establishment and following of ordinances so that a certain compromise is reached between people concerning those things that are necessary for mortal life. Since the heavenly city has a pilgrim existence on the earth and must dwell here it makes use of this earthly peace. So it is that the heavenly city "leads what we may call a life of captivity in this earthly city" (19.17 [877]). The heavenly city, however, does not hesitate to obey the laws of the earthly city, for through these are regulated those things that serve toward the maintenance of this mortal life.

Christians live in the earthly city and are active within it so that their lives, to the extent necessary, can be provided with earthly goods. Although Augustine is no friend of the earthly city and criticizes it correspondingly, he views it nevertheless as necessary and lends it his support. The heavenly city, during its earthly pilgrimage, calls together citizens of every nation to form a community of foreigners. This does not, however, mean that the laws and ordinances of the earthly city are abolished. Rather, the heavenly city makes use of and defends these laws and seeks a compromise with the human will for those things that are important for the mortal nature of humans without compromising true religion or piety in the process. Even if the earthly city is called a city of the devil, it cannot be rejected. It is necessary for the material aspect of our humanness and requires our support. This is made easier by the fact that as a Christian one lives within this city and has a dual citizenship in both cities.

Augustine never portrays the evil world as being equivalent to the secular state. But since the city of God may be conceived of as the empirical, physical church, the reader might very naturally think of the city of the world as being equivalent to the (Roman) state.[81] Augustine's thought demands this equating of the two inasmuch as he recognizes and affirms the necessity of earthly laws, although everything that is truly and lastingly good is to be found only in the city of God. It must be asked, however, whether one may really bind the earthly city to the devil, as Augustine does, while at the same time attributing to it an important function for the earthly living together of humans. But the other side of this identification is also problematic. Augustine is able to mention together in one breath the city of God and the church, indeed, even in connection with the kingdom of God.[82] Yet the visible church is not, for Augustine, an ideal community. Within the visible church dwell the good and the lost "and both sorts are collected as it were in the dragnet of the gospel."[83] Within this net both swim together until the shore is reached. There the evil will be separated from the good.

Augustine knew that in his time many entered the church only because they hoped to gain personal advantage by doing so. It was therefore difficult to precisely identify the city of God and the world in regard to their members. Augustine's proposal is based simply on the assumption that humanity is only able to live on this earth because of God's grace. Two possibilities then present themselves: to live one's life either according to the will of God or according to one's own will. The latter is understood as sinful. Yet sin, as Augustine demonstrated in his dispute with Pelagius, is not an individual phenomenon. It has a social dimension, as do all things in the world that are evil. Therefore it is used for the self-glorification of humanity and is, at least potentially, self-destructive. Augustine is, however, aware that God can use even evil for good. In this way human self-interest also serves human self-maintenance, a fact from which even Christians benefit. We must not forget, however, that the *City of God* was written in the context of the destruc-

---

81. So Reinhold Seeberg, *Text-Book of the History of Doctrines,* trans. Charles E. Hay (Grand Rapids: Baker, 1954), 1:327.

82. So Augustine, *The City of God* (8.24), 335; (13.16), 524; and (20.11), 920.

83. Augustine, *The City of God* (28.49), 831.

tion of Rome by Alaric and his followers. Augustine therefore points clearly to the fact that human history, as a history of the earthly city, is a history of evil, behind which lies the judgment of God.

b. The Kingdom of the Devil (Luther)

It is not surprising that **Martin Luther**, who learned a great deal from Augustine, also adopts his distinction between the kingdom of God and the kingdom of the devil.[84] Luther writes:

> There are two kingdoms. The first is a kingdom of the devil. In the Gospel the Lord calls the devil a prince or king of this world [John 16:11], that is, of a kingdom of sin and disobedience. To the godly, however, that kingdom is nothing but misery and a vast prison. . . . Thus he who submissively serves the devil in sin must suffer much, especially in his conscience, and yet, in the end, he will thereby earn nothing but everlasting death. Now all of us dwell in the devil's kingdom until the coming of the kingdom of God. However, there is a difference. To be sure, the godly are also in the devil's kingdom, but they daily and steadfastly contend against sins and resist the lusts of the flesh, the allurements of the world, the whisperings of the devil. After all, no matter how godly we may be, the evil lust always wants to share the reign in us and would like to rule us completely and overcome us. In that way God's kingdom unceasingly engages in combat with the devil's kingdom. . . . The others dwell in this kingdom, enjoy it, and freely do the bidding of the flesh, the world, and the devil. If they could, they would always stay there. . . . The other kingdom is that of God, namely, a kingdom of truth and righteousness. . . . It is the state when we are free from sin, when all our members, talents, and powers are subject to God and are employed in his service. . . . That comes to pass when we are ruled not by sin, but only by Christ and his grace.[85]

The kingdom of the devil, therefore, is the world in which everyone lives, whether Christian or non-Christian. Luther takes up here, along with Augustine, the testimony of John 16:11, which tells us that Satan is the prince of this world.

84. On the distinction between the two kingdoms, see Cargill Thompson, *Studies in the Reformation: Luther to Hooker*, ed. C. W. Dugmore and Philip Broadhead (London: Athlone, 1980), 45, who also traces the distinction of the two kingdoms back to Augustine.

85. Martin Luther, *An Exposition of the Lord's Prayer for Simple Laymen* (1519), in *LW*, 42:38ff.

In his familiar, realistic manner Luther does not glorify the world as the already in-breaking kingdom of God, but rather characterizes it as a place plagued by many problems and evils. In this kingdom of the devil we must persevere and defend ourselves for we are constantly in conflict with the devil. Luther indicates much the same thing in his *Small Catechism* when he says that the old Adam within us must daily be drowned by sorrow and repentance and that a new person must daily rise up. The kingdom of God struggles with the kingdom of the devil although the former is, in a strict sense, an eschatological phenomenon that only fully breaks into the world when the latter passes away. Luther also points out that the kingdom of God does not come with outward signs but is already present inside of humans and that we should pray that it will be established and increase within us and grow strong. God's grace and his kingdom together with all virtues will come to us just as "Christ came to us from heaven to earth; [for] we did not ascend from earth into heaven to him."[86] While the kingdom of the devil manifests itself outwardly, the kingdom of Christ is an inner power active in Christians.

Christians and non-Christians differ from one another in that the latter follow the will of the devil. They seek to advance his kingdom and to destroy the kingdom of God. Therefore they do not come out of the kingdom of the devil into the kingdom of Christ but, according to their own desire, remain eternally in the kingdom of the devil. Humanity is then divided into two kinds of persons: one belongs to the kingdom of God but must live in the kingdom of the devil while the other not only lives within the kingdom of the devil but belongs to it as well.

One cannot simultaneously belong to both kingdoms. Luther expressed this clearly in *The Bondage of the Will* when he wrote:

> For Christians know there are two kingdoms in the world, which are bitterly opposed to each other. In one of them Satan reigns, who is therefore called by Christ "the ruler of this world" [John 12:31] and by Paul "the god of this world" [2 Cor. 4:4]. He holds captive to his will all who are not snatched away from him by the Spirit of Christ, as the same Paul testifies, nor does he allow them to be snatched away by any powers other than the Spirit of God, as Christ testifies in the parable of the strong man guarding his palace in peace [Luke 11:21]. In the other kingdom, Christ reigns, and his Kingdom ceaselessly resists and makes war on the kingdom of Satan. Into this Kingdom we are transferred, not by our own power but by the grace of God, by which we are set free from the present evil age and deliv-

---

86. Luther, *An Exposition of the Lord's Prayer,* in *LW,* 42:41.

ered from the dominion of darkness.... We are bound to serve in the kingdom of Satan unless we are delivered by the power of God.[87]

If the kingdom of God or the kingdom of Christ did not exist, all humans would be delivered over to the kingdom of Satan. There is no escape from this kingdom unless Christ liberates us so that we are freed from its sphere of influence and transferred into that of the other kingdom. We remember that in *The Bondage of the Will* Luther compared the individual to a beast of burden that is ridden either by God or by Satan. The members of the kingdom of God follow Christ and are one with him and he with them, whereas the members of the kingdom of the devil follow him and are one with him. In contrast to Augustine an individual and existential perspective is clearly to be seen in Luther. He does not stress so much the opposing structure of the two kingdoms as he does the opposing manner in which Christians and non-Christians conduct themselves.

If Satan is indeed the prince of this world, as Luther continually emphasizes in agreement with John 12:31, then should one not simply write off this world as evil? Should we not hope to be taken out of this world and should we not lead a life of withdrawal and detachment from the world? In regard to Luther one can confidently answer these and similar questions in the negative for he was no proponent of either Manicheism or of Platonic philosophy. For Luther this world was God's creation and therefore the place in which we were placed by God. It would be a distortion of Luther's position if the world were simply given over to the devil. It is rather the other way around for the devil's power in this world is limited. He is a created being for he was originally a part of God's good creation. As such he cannot be equal to God. Although Luther sometimes dramatizes the devil dualistically, for him, the devil does not stand primarily beside God and over humanity but rather between God and humanity.[88] The devil, so to speak, obstructs the view of God so that humans mistake the devil for God and in presumed obedience to God serve the devil.

In Luther's view angels are the soldiers, keepers, guides, and governors of God's creation.[89] It is their task to watch over and lead us and the crea-

---

87. Luther, *The Bondage of the Will*, in *LW*, 33:287f.

88. See in this regard the comments of Hans-Martin Barth, *Der Teufel und Jesus Christus in der Theologie Martin Luthers* (Göttingen: Vandenhoeck & Ruprecht, 1967), 208, on the place of the devil in Luther's theology.

89. For this and the following, see Martin Luther, *Lectures on Genesis* (1535-45), in *LW*, 6:87f.

tures of this creation whereby they do battle not only for the pious but for all people. Of course Satan, in Luther's view, since he is the god of this world, has under him many other devils, that is to say, evil angels. These evil angels govern everyone, from the pope and the emperor to the princes and to those in private homes. Through them the works of the devil are produced which we see and experience but which the world does not recognize for what they are.

As experience shows, the good angels contend with the evil angels. Yet we should not let ourselves be too intimidated. Even if Christ calls Satan the prince of this world it is God who is the creator and ruler of all. Satan cannot even harm a hair on our head "except by God's will and permission."[90] Luther even says consolingly:

> The power of the devil is not as great as it appears to be outwardly; for if he had full power to rage as he pleased, you would not live for one hour or retain safe and intact a single sheep, a crop in the field, corn in the barn, and, in short, any of those things which pertain to this life. . . . You will find more good than bad things and you will also see that a very small part is subjected to the power of the devil. For he is compelled to leave the fish in the rivers, the birds in the air, the men and animals in the villages and cities, which he would not do if it were not for the protection of the angels. At times, however, he causes great disturbances, brings kingdoms and monarchies into conflict with each other, and throws provinces, states, and households into confusion. To be sure, he causes disturbance, and yet he is not able to carry out what he most desires, to overthrow all things and to mingle heaven with earth. So strong are the walls, fortifications, and hedges of the angels round about us and all things.[91]

If, when considering evil, we disallow that which occurs through God when he leads us, for example, into temptation or punishes or chastises us because we have fallen away from him, then, according to Luther, considerably more good than evil occurs. The kingdom of evil on this earth is sharply curtailed through God's all-encompassing activity. It is not able to destroy the foundational orders of God that belong to his creation and its preservation. These orders can be impaired and even brought into question, but the kingdom of evil and the devil are not able to transform this world into chaos.

90. Luther, *Lectures on Genesis*, in *LW*, 6:90.
91. Luther, *Lectures on Genesis*, in *LW*, 6:90f.

But why does God, if he is ultimately the creator and preserver of all things, tolerate at all the kingdom of evil, which seeks to transform the good creation into a sea of blood and tears and injustice? Luther's answer is that there should be no discussion about the wisdom of the counsels of God.[92] He speaks of the goodness of God that is not limited as is ours but that remains unlimited and unfathomable. One should let God govern as he does and praise God for the great mercy that even with evil persons more good than evil occurs. If God and his angels would cease only for a single day to rule the world, the devil would bring everything to an end in a terrible chaos. Luther therefore avoids theodicy, that is, the question of God's righteousness, and points instead to God's unfathomableness and to the fact that, seen as a whole, God is merciful and good. Luther realistically recognizes that there is evil in the world. He does not explain this evil individualistically inasmuch as he would trace it back to humans. Yet he also does not view evil as simply an outgrowth of human society. For Luther there is a metaphysical power that stands in the background and battles against God's creation, seeking to destroy it.

For the preservation of temporal order God has established the worldly regiment or kingdom. According to Luther's categorization, humans belong either to the kingdom of God or to the kingdom of the world. "Those who belong to the kingdom of God are all the true believers who are in Christ and under Christ, for Christ is the King and Lord in the kingdom of God."[93] These persons do not, in principle, need the temporal law or sword, that is to say, the worldly force that is exercised against persons who do not observe the law. Since the Holy Spirit works in their hearts and teaches them that they should do no one injustice and love all people they do of their own accord what is required of them. But there are also those persons in this world who belong to the kingdom of the world. "The unrighteous do nothing that the law demands; therefore, they need the law to instruct, constrain, and compel them to do good."[94] For non-Christians, who actually belong to the kingdom of the world and do not just live within it as do Christians, temporal law is necessary for the preservation of law and order. Luther, exhibiting his typical realism, said that if it were not for temporal authority,

---

92. Luther, *Lectures on Genesis,* in *LW,* 6:91.

93. Martin Luther, *Temporal Authority: To What Extent It Should Be Obeyed* (1523), in *LW,* 45:88.

94. Luther, *Temporal Authority,* in *LW,* 45:89.

men would devour one another, seeing that the whole world is evil and that among thousands there is scarcely a single true Christian. No one could support wife and child, feed himself, and serve God. The whole world would be reduced to chaos. For this reason God has ordained two governments: the spiritual, by which the Holy Spirit produces Christians and righteous people under Christ; and the temporal, which restrains the un-Christian and wicked so that no thanks to them they are obliged to keep still and to maintain an outward peace.[95]

The temporal regiment of God, through which he keeps the world from self-destruction, is a divine order of preservation that is implemented, as it were, through the law, that is, through temporal law and corresponding punishment. All persons are subject to this regiment of God whether Christian or non-Christian, the Christian willingly and the non-Christian often unwillingly. From this regiment is to be distinguished God's government through the gospel, that is, through grace and consolation, through which humans find entry into the kingdom of God. Law and force have no place here, for faith cannot be forced on anyone but is rather God's own work. Hence there is a necessary connection between Luther's "two kingdoms doctrine," that is, Luther's conviction that there is a kingdom of God and a kingdom of the devil, and the "two regiments doctrine," his view that God governs differently in the temporal sphere than he does in his very own kingdom of the gospel.[96]

Luther thus goes a decisive step beyond Augustine. With Augustine it was difficult to understand how the ordinances of the city of the world could be affirmed since its purpose and its citizens were earthly and estranged from God. For Augustine the ultimate home of humans is in heaven, while on earth they are only pilgrims.[97] For Luther, however, Christians have a task here on earth. Therefore he distinguishes between the temporal kingdom of the devil and God's kingdom through which God battles

95. Luther, *Temporal Authority*, in *LW,* 45:91.

96. Thompson, *Studies in the Reformation,* 47f. has convincingly demonstrated a necessary connection between the two kingdoms and the two regiments. He writes: "Luther's concept of the two divine orders or regiments is profoundly influenced by his doctrine of the eschatological conflict between the kingdom of God and the kingdom of the Devil." Yet he concedes that Luther does not always strictly distinguish between "kingdom" and "regiment."

97. So Bernhard Lohse, *Martin Luther's Theology: Its Historical and Systematic Development,* trans. and ed. Roy A. Harrisville (Minneapolis: Fortress, 1999), 316, who also provides an extensive treatment of the "doctrine of the two kingdoms."

the devil's kingdom. With this notion he made it unmistakably clear that although the kingdom of evil exists and reigns in the world, it is not identical with the good ordinances of God which also exist in the world. These ordinances, or orders, are subsumed under God's regiment of the left. The devil always has the goal of destroying God's regiment and holding all persons bound within his kingdom. The result is that Luther not only sees a dynamic power struggle between the sphere of influence of God and that of the anti-Godly powers, but he is also able to affirm God's creation as an unqualified good that cannot be usurped even by the greatest efforts of the anti-Godly powers. Additionally, the kingdom of God, in contrast to the city of God, is not a *corpus permixtum,* a mixture of good and evil, but is rather a community of those sanctified by Christ. The kingdom of God, therefore, cannot be confused with the church.

c. The Kingdom of Sin (Kant, Ritschl)

In the person of Albrecht Ritschl (1822-89) we encounter a representative of modernity who greatly influenced German Protestant theology during the second half of the nineteenth century. We are not taking Ritschl into consideration here because of his stature, however. His significance for us is to be found in the fact that on the one hand he saw himself as building on the tradition of Luther, while on the other hand he was influenced by the ethics of Immanuel Kant, which led him especially to the idea that a kingdom of sin stood in opposition to the kingdom of God.[98]

In his book *Religion within the Limits of Reason Alone* (1793) **Immanuel Kant** treats in detail the problem of human sinfulness and the kingdom of evil. He begins his treatment of evil by asking how it expresses itself in humans and from whence it comes. According to Kant, persons are not called evil because they carry out activities that are contrary to the law and are accordingly seen as evil. Rather, these activities appear to be of such a nature that we can conclude that evil maxims or precepts exist in humans.[99] That means that one can sometimes see how it is that activities will end in opposition to the law and one is fully aware that they are illegal. Neverthe-

98. This is especially pointed out by David L. Mueller, *An Introduction to the Theology of Albrecht Ritschl* (Philadelphia: Westminster, 1969), 69.

99. Immanuel Kant, *Religion within the Limits of Reason Alone* (BA 5,6), trans. with intro. and notes Theodore M. Greene and Hoyt H. Hudson, and a new essay by John R. Silber (New York: Harper, 1960), 16; references that follow are to this edition.

less, the maxims themselves are not always observable. According to Kant, humans are by nature neither morally good nor evil but they are only in certain respects good and in others evil (BA 8, 9 [17f.]).

The human capacity to do evil can be demonstrated in three ways. First, it is part of the weakness of the human heart to not consistently observe accepted precepts. A frailty of human nature manifests itself here.[100] Second, there is a tendency in humans to mix morally and non-morally motivated causes, hence a so-called impurity of motivation. Third, Kant speaks of a tendency of humans to take up evil whereby they demonstrate a wickedness of human nature or of the human heart. The latter is present in all persons, even the best, so that one can say that a general tendency toward evil exists in humans. Humans are understood to be evil to the extent that they are aware of moral laws but nevertheless incorporate occasional deviations from these laws into their maxims (B27f., A25 [27]). Kant speaks of a radical, inborn evil in human nature which originates, however, through our own selves.

According to Kant, the cause of evil can be seen in the nature of human thinking and in the natural inclinations that arise out of it. But this would restrict evil too much since humans would be degraded to the level of animals. If one would locate this depravity in the moral, lawgiving reason, so as to imply that reason could destroy the authority of the law out of which it comes, this would be to attribute too much to evil. We would be confronted with a reason that is wicked and humans would be turned directly into demons. If there is an inclination to evil in human nature it must be sought in the human free will, which is capable of becoming morally evil. Evil is radical, then, for it perverts the foundation of all maxims through the human will (B36, 37, A33 [32]). Hence Kant guards human free will and neither degrades humans into sub-humans nor elevates them into super-humans. Nevertheless, it is difficult for him to adhere to a traditional doctrine of original sin, a deficiency for which he seeks to compensate with his doctrine of the kingdom of evil.

Kant relates the biblical story of the fall, including the appearance of two opposing principles with the prince of this world as the leader of the kingdom of evil.[101] The evil principle is not overcome through Christ for

---

100. For this and the following, see Kant, *Religion within the Limits of Reason Alone* (B21, A19), 24f.

101. For this and the following, see Kant, *Religion within the Limits of Reason Alone* (B106-115, A99-106), 73-78.

the kingdom remains standing. Before it can be defeated a new epoch must begin. Yet the power of the kingdom of evil is broken so that it can no longer hold people against their will as it had previously done. Another kingdom, one that is moral, is offered to humans as an asylum, a place where they can find support for their morality if they desire to leave the sphere of influence to which they previously belonged. Humans must stand under one lordship or the other. According to Kant, there is no salvation for humans when they do not thoroughly adopt genuine moral principles in their character. Yet Kant entertained doubt as to whether humans could conduct themselves correctly, not because of their sensual nature, but because of a certain self-afflicted perversity, or however one wishes to describe this wickedness that humans have brought on themselves, and through which evil came into the world.

Kant summarizes:

> Now man is in this perilous state through his own fault. . . . When he looks around for the causes and circumstances which expose him to this danger and keep him in it, he can easily convince himself that he is subject to these not because of his own gross nature, so far as he is here a separate individual, but because of mankind to whom he is related. . . . Envy, the lust for power, greed, and the malignant inclinations bound up with these, besiege his nature, connected within itself, as soon as he is among men. And it is not even necessary to assume that these are men sunk in evil and examples to lead him astray; it suffices that they are at hand, that they surround him, and that they are men, for them mutually to corrupt each other's predisposition and make one another evil. (B128f., A120f. [85])

In order to counter this situation one must build an alliance against evil and promote the good in the human. Kant therefore proposes an ethical commonwealth as an explicit effort to establish social relationships that assure eternal peace.[102] Of course, humans are continually at risk of falling back under the sway of evil.

In order to unite individual humans, who by themselves are unable to resist evil, in the pursuit of this common goal, the concept of a higher moral being is necessary. Through this concept the insufficient powers of individuals are united. In this way one can resist the evil that is to be found within one's self and within all others (B137-42, A129-34 [90ff.]). Kant sets the

---

102. See Philip Rossi, *The Social Authority of Reason: Kant's Critique, Radical Evil, and the Destinies of Humankind* (Albany: State University of New York, 2005), esp. 87ff.

kingdom of sin, therefore, over against the kingdom of God, which is exemplified in the church. Sin is not an individual offense but rather manifests itself in the community through which it is continually strengthened and set anew into motion. As an individual one cannot resist this sin but needs the community and the goal toward which this community is directed. Kant understands evil neither atomistically nor as a mystery that plagues human nature. He rejects every natural understanding of sin and maintains a deliberate, intentional deviation of the human will. As a child of the Enlightenment, however, he hopes in the prevailing of reason to overcome evil in the long run. In what manner, then, does Ritschl, who was strongly influenced by Kant's ethics, take up these ideas?

Albrecht Ritschl, like Kant, assumes that the kingdom of sin, as he calls it, "is a substitute for the hypothesis of original sin" that expresses that which the idea of original sin was meant to describe.[103] He thus distances himself from Augustine and Luther inasmuch as he accuses them both of having succumbed to a false exegesis. Luther saw the doctrine of original sin revealed in scripture while Augustine, in his well-known exegesis of Romans 5:12, was of the opinion that all humans have sinned in the person of Adam. Paul, however, was not speaking here of the relationship between cause and effect, as was the case with the law and the chain of natural descent. Rather, Paul recognized the divine decision as the interceding factor, even if he had spoken of sin coming into humanity through Adam's single transgression (344f.). If we view the concept of original sin as the background against which sin stands out, one cannot, according to Ritschl, adequately understand sin in the life of the individual or in humanity as a natural species. "The subject of sin, rather, is humanity as the sum of all individuals, in so far as the selfish action of each person, involving him as it does in illimitable interaction with all others, is directed in any degree whatsoever towards the opposite of the good, and leads to the association of individuals in common evil" (335).[104] Ritschl felt himself here to be in formal agreement with Friedrich Schleiermacher in opposition to Pelagius and Augustine.

---

103. Albrecht Ritschl, *The Christian Doctrine of Justification and Reconciliation: The Positive Development of the Doctrine*, trans. H. R. Mackintosh and A. B. Macaulay (New York: Charles Scribner's, 1900), 344f. (§41); references that follow are to this edition.

104. Karl Barth, *Protestant Theology in the Nineteenth Century: Its Background and History*, trans. Brian Cozens and John Bowden, new ed. (London: SCM, 2001), 645, correctly states: "The existence of a realm of sin, i.e. by the mutual effect of sinful conduct of all men upon one another, which with Ritschl takes the place of original sin."

According to Ritschl, Pelagius made the will of the individual exclusively responsible for sin, which meant for him that sin was passed along through example and imitation. Imitation, however, in Ritschl's view, becomes more infrequent in the later years of one's life, something that is not true, however, of sin. If one were to start with the "example" nature of sin, sin would not go beyond the limits of the individual will. The cooperation of humans in sinful deeds, therefore, is testimony against the example theory. Augustine views humanity as a natural race as the subject of sin so that all persons, as descendants of the first human pair, are burdened with the highest level of sin. Humans are therefore equal in regard to sin. With this deduction, however, Augustine, according to Ritschl, overlooks the interaction of actual sins. Additionally, justice is not done to the phenomenon of the will in the case of the actions of humans, which one could trace back to a common source, for the will disappears from the picture in the natural interpretation of sin.

Ritschl, on the other hand, claimed:

> If we discover in the individual action the proof-mark of the independence of the will, can we ascribe to ourselves, not merely individual actions, but likewise evil habit or evil inclination? . . . Even if we find radical evil working within us to the extent affirmed by Kant, responsibility for it can only be vindicated if it is assumed to be the result of the empirical determination of the will, for it can be derived neither from the natural origin of every man, nor from the pretended intelligible act of freedom. (337)

Important for Ritschl, as well as for Kant, is evil's determination of the will. With Ritschl this is also grounded on the fact that he wishes to overcome evil through education. This is only possible, however, when persistent bad behavior or evil inclinations are understood as the results of acts of the will. If one assumes a doctrine of original sin that is passed on from one generation to the next, then education would be of little help. Ritschl further maintained that one must distinguish among sinful transgressions according to their severity. With the concept of original sin, however, this is hardly possible since original sin is seen as a universal constant (337f.).

In order to take into consideration the various degrees of habitual sin and to view them as facets of sinful activity Ritschl introduces the idea of the kingdom of sin. Guilt can only be shared when one not only owns up to one's own sinful deeds but also recognizes how these cause other sins, although one cannot always precisely say how far this effect extends. This sinful federation with others does not exclude anyone so that we are all burdened with sin. Ritschl thus reaches the conclusion that, from the perspective of a discerning conception of guilt, original or hereditary sin can no longer be understood as the primary form of the concept of sin (341f.). Nevertheless, Ritschl did not feel that he was betraying his Lutheran heritage but sought to show that his understanding of sin, in rudimentary form, was already to be found in the Lutheran confessional writings and especially in Philipp Melanchthon. Finally, he even sought to find support in Paul when he wrote: "And finally, since Paul neither asserts nor suggests the transmission of sin by generation, he offers no other reason for the universality of sin or for the kingdom of sin than the sinning of all individual men" (348).

When we compare Ritschl's concept of the kingdom of sin with Luther's kingdom of the devil we notice that Ritschl's conception produces an unusually static effect. This is somewhat moderated in that sin is not viewed as an end in itself but as the opposite of universal good. Sin always strives, desires, and acts against God; the kingdom of sin finds its counterpart in the kingdom of God. "This whole web of sinful action and reaction, which presupposes and yet again increases the selfish bias in every man, is entitled 'the world,' which in this aspect of it is not of God, but opposed to Him" (350). We are, so to speak, caught up in a dragnet of evil, which is created and strengthened through us. Yet Ritschl claims that it is not inevitable that each individual be caught in this sinful web and make his or her own contribution to wickedness and untruthfulness. Moreover, one can act egotistically when one appears to be fighting for the kingdom of God and, for example, for certain goods like family pride, class feeling, patriotism, or loyalty to the confession of the church. Ritschl made it clear, therefore, that the church, as it manifests itself on this earth, must not be equated with the kingdom of God. The church belongs to the world and must be distinguished from the kingdom of God.

If we wish to do justice to Ritschl, we must take into consideration the context from which he argues. Optimism reigned supreme in the nineteenth century. It is therefore of no surprise that Ritschl should claim that "there exists in the child a general, though still indeterminate, impulse towards the good" (337). There is no place here for a doctrine of original sin with which humans are burdened from birth on. Humans are capable of improving. At the same time, however, Ritschl emphasizes that humans are not isolated individuals but always live within a context that necessarily influences them. This is made especially clear in his *Instruction in the Christian Religion* (1875) where he writes:

The unified action of many individuals in these forms of sin leads to a reinforcement of the same in common customs and principles, in standing immoralities, and even in evil institutions. So there comes to be an almost irresistible power of temptation for those who with characters yet undeveloped are so much the more exposed to evil example because they do not see through the network of enticements to evil. Accordingly, the kingdom of sin, or the (immoral human) world, is reinforced in every new generation. United sin, this opposite of the kingdom of God, rests upon all as a power which at least limits the freedom of the individual to good. This limitation of the freedom of the individual by his own sin and by connection with the common condition of the world is, taken strictly, a lack of freedom to do good. This, however, outside of the kingdom of God, is the common condition of all men.[105]

The recognition and emphasis of the super-individual form of sin and evil, clearly expressed in the preceding quotation (Ritschl used "sin" in the theological sense, whereas "evil" represented the morally bad), was a needed corrective in the nineteenth century. At least in the case of theologians this did not go unheard, as is shown by Walter Rauschenbusch and later Reinhold Niebuhr in the United States as well as by the religious socialists Leonhard Ragaz and Hermann Kutter in Switzerland at the beginning of the twentieth century. They took up Ritschl's terminology and spoke of a kingdom of evil that perverts humans and institutions.[106] One could, thereby, no longer push sin and evil off onto the individual and seek to convert the individual in order to make possible better living conditions on the earth. One must, therefore, concern oneself with the structures of injustice and evil and seek to reform them.

d. Evil as Societal Power (Rauschenbusch, Reinhold Niebuhr)

Walter Rauschenbusch (1861-1918), one of the most prominent representatives of the Social Gospel in America and a person influenced by his experience working with the innumerable immigrants who flooded New York at the end of the nineteenth century, recognized better than many the real-

---

105. Albrecht Ritschl, *Instruction in the Christian Religion,* trans. Alice Mead Swing, in Albert Temple Swing, *The Theology of Albrecht Ritschl, together with Instruction in the Christian Religion* (London: Longmans, Green, and Co., 1901), 206f. (§30).

106. So also Mueller, *An Introduction to the Theology of Albrecht Ritschl,* 73.

ity of sin in its far-reaching, societal context. In his 1912 book, *Christianizing the Social Order,* he wrote:

> Sin is a social force. It runs from man to man along the lines of social contact. Its impact on the individual becomes most overwhelming when sin is most completely socialized. Salvation, too, is a social force. It is exerted by groups that are charged with divine will and love. It becomes durable and complete in the measure in which the individual is built into a social organism that is ruled by justice, cleanness, and love. A full salvation demands a Christian social order which will serve as the spiritual environment of the individual.[107]

Sin is a societal power that stands in opposition to redemption, which is likewise described as a social force. In this and other works Rauschenbusch mentions sin only infrequently while his primary attention is directed toward societal structures and their problems. It is first in his *A Theology for the Social Gospel* (1917) that more space is given to a discussion of sin. This book also contains a chapter on "The Kingdom of Evil."[108] Although Rauschenbusch was never entirely content with Ritschl since he supposedly gave too little attention to social analysis, this work is nevertheless clearly influenced by Ritschl.[109]

In *A Theology for the Social Gospel* Rauschenbusch distinguishes between three forms of sin; sensuousness, selfishness, and godlessness, in which we sin against our higher self, against the good in humans, and against the universal good.[110] With remarkable unanimity theology has essentially categorized sin as selfishness and thereby provided an ethical and social definition that manifests itself in the irrepressible social spirit of Christianity. When theology, however, characterizes sin as an assault against God, this is foreign to reality for we seldom sin against God alone. This can be seen already in the Ten Commandments. If we describe sin,

107. Walter Rauschenbusch, *Christianizing the Social Order* (New York: Macmillan, 1915 [1912]), 116.

108. For a brief summary, see the detailed biography, *Walter Rauschenbusch,* by Dores Robinson Sharpe (New York: Macmillan, 1942), 328-34.

109. Paul M. Minus, *Walter Rauschenbusch: American Reformer* (New York: Macmillan, 1988), 145 and 221 (n. 11). See also Walter Rauschenbusch, *A Theology for the Social Gospel* (Nashville: Abingdon, 1978 [1917]), 138f. (n. 1); references that follow are to this edition.

110. For this and the following, see Rauschenbusch, *A Theology for the Social Gospel,* 47-50.

however, more as selfishness, then this definition fits better with the Social Gospel than with an individualistic type of religion. A sinful spirit is unsocial and antisocial.

In contrast to many of his contemporaries, Rauschenbusch defended the doctrine of original sin for he claimed that this was one of the few attempts of an individualistic theology to achieve a collective view of its field of study.[111] The doctrine of original sin views humanity as a unity that descended from a single individual and has been held together through the centuries through the unity of its origin and its bond of blood. Natural science, according to Rauschenbusch, confirms this view, for evil flows through the generations in the channels of biological connections. Yet conventional theology goes too far when it makes original sin responsible for such an all-encompassing corruption of humans. The evil that arose out of the sin of the individual was trivial and irrelevant in contrast. Rauschenbusch also doubted whether one could achieve a responsible freedom when original sin is so strongly emphasized. Theology forgot that sin is transmitted along the lines of community tradition, a channel that is, however, much more accessible to religious influence and religious control than is nature.

The persistent depravity and transgressions of adults are not transmitted through genetics but they are instead socialized. Sin resides in social practices and institutions and is taken up by the individual as well as by the individual's social group. According to the theology of the Social Gospel, original sin is for this reason partly conditioned by society and partly biologically inherited. This not only has something to do with the instinct for imitation, as Pelagius thought, but also with the spiritual authority of the community over its members. The emphasis on the biological transmission of evil, as is almost exclusively stressed in the doctrine of original sin, distracts attention from the power of societal transmission, from the authority of the social group that justifies, stresses, and idealizes that which is bad, and from the decisive influence of economic profit, all of which can defend and spread evil (67). Yet these aspects are just as important as the doctrine of creation or traducianism — doctrines that are often coupled with original sin. When one speaks of sin one cannot speak only of the community but must also speak of spiritual power and of the value of the combined, super-personal powers in the community such as governments or society's many

111. For this and the following, see Rauschenbusch, *A Theology for the Social Gospel*, 57-61.

groups and organizations. These "organizations are rarely formed for avow-edly evil ends. They drift into evil through sinister leadership, or under the pressure of need or temptation" (72).

If one considers the various aspects of sin it is but a short step to a dis-cussion about the kingdom of evil. "The life of humanity is infinitely in-terwoven, always renewing itself, yet always perpetuating what has been. The evils of one generation are caused by the wrongs of the generations that preceded, and will in turn condition the sufferings and temptations of those who come after" (79). While destructive insects are unable to change natural constellations in order to increase damage, this is possible for destructive humans. They can gain control of legislation, police, mili-tary, and religion and alter the constitutions of nations in order to in-crease the damage that they are capable of inflicting. Our theological con-ception of sin remains fragmentary if we do not recognize that all persons in their natural groups are bound together in a solidarity of all times and places and bear the yoke of evil and suffering (81). The understanding of the kingdom of evil, according to Rauschenbusch, is not new. "But while our modern conception is naturally historical and social, the ancient and mediaeval Church believed in a Kingdom of evil spirits, with Satan at their head, which is the governing power in the present world and the source of all temptation" (82).

According to Rauschenbusch the belief in a satanic kingdom exists to-day only where religious and theological traditions keep this belief alive. Yet in Rauschenbusch's view we cannot deny that Satan and his angels are in-creasingly disappearing today and that an actual belief in demonic powers is in conflict with modern life. We can no longer view the kingdom of evil as a demonic kingdom. Rauschenbusch saw the Social Gospel as the only influ-ence that could "renew the idea of the Kingdom of Evil in modern minds, because it alone has an adequate sense of solidarity and a sufficient grasp of the historical and social realities of sin" (87). This modern form would then offer religious values that were comparable to the old ideas since both, ac-cording to Rauschenbusch, were of a similar kind. The belief in a satanic kingdom, to the extent that this was not pure theology but rather living reli-gious belief, has always been related to societal realities. One sees this in Ju-daism as well as in the early church and in the Middle Ages.

When the collective consciousness of sin and evil, which Rauschen-busch holds to be important for the religious spirit, continues to disappear, our understanding of sin as well as our understanding of the necessity of re-demption will become increasingly shallow. The societal conception of the kingdom of evil is meant to battle this loss of reality. If we accept this understanding we can no longer restrict redemption to the soul and its personal interests but must conceptualize redemption societally. Walter Rauschenbusch impressively demonstrated that evil cannot be understood individually but must rather be understood trans-personally and thereby also societally. He saw the kingdom of evil in opposition to the kingdom of God and stressed that one cannot appropriately describe the kingdom of evil when one does not understand the kingdom of God since the latter is hindered in its coming-to-be through the kingdom of evil. We would agree with Rauschenbusch that evil has a societal dimension. Today one would expand this perspective in order to include the natural realm as well since it, too, is a creation of God that has not escaped the corruption-causing activity of humans. Yet one must still ask whether the kingdom of evil can be merged with the unjust structures of society, as does Rauschenbusch, or whether perhaps these structures point beyond themselves to a first cause of evil that is not simply the first manifestation of evil.

Reinhold Niebuhr taught for many years with Paul Tillich at Union Theological Seminary in New York City. Although he did not make use of the designations "kingdom of evil" or "kingdom of sin" it is clear from books such as his *Children of Light and Children of Darkness* that he recognized that evil was rooted societally in the world.[112] He proceeds from the biblical viewpoint that "the 'mystery' of 'original sin' . . . has the merit of being true to the facts of human existence."[113] Original sin is not an inertia of natural impulses that stand in opposition to the purer impulses of the spirit; rather, it is a perversion that exercises a universal reign over all persons even though humans do not sin by nature but in freedom. This "mystery" of original sin, which makes it impossible to expect redemption through the development of human power or freedom, will always be an intellectual insult for rationalists.

"The Christian doctrine of sin in its classical form offends both rationalists and moralists by maintaining the seemingly absurd position that man sins inevitably and by a fateful necessity but that he is nevertheless to be held responsible for actions which are prompted by an ineluctable fate."[114] Niebuhr does not reject this doctrine but rather, after a detailed cri-

---

112. Reinhold Niebuhr, *Children of Light and Children of Darkness* (New York: Charles Scribner's, 1945).

113. Reinhold Niebuhr, *Faith and History: A Comparison of Christian and Modern Views of History* (New York: Charles Scribner's, 1949), 122.

114. Reinhold Niebuhr, *The Nature and Destiny of Man: A Christian Interpretation,*

tique of the Pelagian and Augustinian interpretations, comes to the conclusion that "we cannot . . . escape the ultimate paradox that the final exercise of freedom in the transcendent human spirit is its recognition of the false use of that freedom in" action (260). The majority of Pelagians and many Augustinians did not take these paradoxes sufficiently into consideration, the former having emphasized too much the integrity of human freedom. For this reason they were unable to recognize that the discovery of human freedom brought along with it the discovery of human guilt. The representatives of the Augustinian tradition, on the other hand, were overly concerned to hold fast to the insight that human freedom was perverted by sin. They therefore almost entirely overlooked the fact that the discovery of this sinful characteristic must be attributed to human freedom. Niebuhr, in contrast, maintained that humans can only recognize that they are not free because they are free. Therefore one must emphasize human freedom and responsibility along with classical theology.

In viewing human sinfulness, however, it should not be overlooked that evil is not to be traced back to the individual but to the collective behavior of humanity. That is the reason Niebuhr wrote about "collective egotism" in his treatment of the doctrine of sin. For Niebuhr it was important to distinguish between the egotism of the individual and the pride of the group since the claims of a collective or societal self far transcend those of the individual "I." "The group is more arrogant, hypocritical, self-centered and more ruthless in the pursuit of its ends than the individual. An inevitable moral tension between individual and group morality is therefore created" (208f.). Strains similar to Rauschenbusch are here detectable. According to Niebuhr, it is clear that the egotism of racial, national, and societal economic groups is the most constant in the national state since this exhibits a collective identity in the minds of individuals. Even here he is able once again to point to a biblical example when he says that the prophetic religion of Israel stood from the very beginning in conflict with national self-deification.[115] Israel wanted to identify God and Israel with one another so that God would be the exclusive property of Israel. But only the prophetic faith, which rejected such nationalism, had a future. This faith allowed Augustine to withstand the collapse of the Roman Empire without despair and to confront the charge

---

vol. 1, *Human Nature* (New York: Charles Scribner's, 1953), 241; references that follow are to this volume.

115. For this and the following, see Niebuhr, *The Nature and Destiny of Man,* 1:214f.

that Christianity was responsible for its destruction with the assertion that its downfall was, to the contrary, the result of sinful pride. Niebuhr offers, therefore, an interpretation of history and society with a biblical basis that especially stresses the societal dimension of evil.

One might expect that the thoughts of Rauschenbusch and Niebuhr would be echoed by those European theologians who were especially concerned with social questions, like the Swiss religious socialists. Yet such a parallel or a mutual dependence of thought forms is difficult to demonstrate. Leonhard Ragaz (1868-1945) had indeed developed sympathies for American ideas of progress and brotherhood, but not for the emphasis on a societal dimension of evil. He wrote, for example, about the League of Nations proposed by President Woodrow Wilson: "We remain with the choice between the destruction of the world and the League of Nations, yet the bow of peace of the League of Nations has appeared to us in the clouds as a promise that it is not the destruction of the world but its renewal which is coming."[116]

Ragaz's involvement in socialism was not prompted by the knowledge that the world is threatened by evil but stemmed rather from an intensive hope and certainty concerning the kingdom of God.[117] Ragaz saw in the appearance of socialism, social democracy, and, to a certain extent, also communism, "a knocking on the gates of the world, and especially Christianity, by the living God of judgment and promise."[118] Important for him is not so much the dimension of evil, but rather that through its onslaught the "forgotten truth of the kingdom of God is being brought once again to remembrance." This salvation-optimism did not demand an extensive analysis of evil. Where such an analysis was made, as by Hermann Kutter, the result was a clearly optimistic perspective.

The interpretation of Kant by Hermann Kutter (1869-1931), *Am Anfang war die Tat* (In the Beginning was the Deed), contained a chapter on "radical evil." Kutter's direction is immediately clear when we read: "But we of course know that all human suffering stems from denial. The sickness of humanity is relative, human life is absolute."[119] The absolute,

116. Leonhard Ragaz, *Die Bedeutung Woodrow Wilsons für die Schweiz und für die Welt,* Schriften der Schweizerischen Vereinigung für den Völkerbund, 2 (Weinfelden, 1924), 18.

117. So also Arnold Pfeiffer, ed., *Religiöse Sozialisten* (Olten: Walter-Verlag, 1976), 152.

118. For this and the following quotation, see Leonhard Ragaz, *Die Erneuerung der Schweiz* (Zürich, 1933), 191.

119. Hermann Kutter, *Im Anfang war die Tat: Versuch einer Orientierung in der*

God, or the good is set over against the relative, or the evil. Since evil is understood as being only relative, there is no life-threatening power that can actually harm us. This is made clear when Kutter explains further: "How then should we understand evil differently if not as a break with the absolute? What is the good within the good? The absolute. What is evil within evil? The opposite of the absolute. A powerless counterpart, an evil will that seeks, within the absolute — in which we always remain enclosed — to make its own self absolute."[120] Seen from the perspective of the good, evil is simply powerless. It can oppose the good only in deluded self-overestimation. In another place Kutter even describes evil as nothing, "as the power, the nothing, which we must think, feel, and desire, which has empowered our existence. We know that it is something, but we also know that it is nothing. We recognize it as our guilt, that we have loved something that is nothing, and as our weakness, that we have sought something within nothing. This nothing is the imprisoned reality of averted will, which we could also call unwill."[121]

With this statement one encounters not only a terminological but also a clearly substantial connection to Karl Barth, who also characterized evil as nothing, or nothingness. On the basis of this interpretation of evil, therefore, it is justified to describe Kutter as a father of dialectical theology.[122] In this connection, however, we are not so much interested in the genetic dependence between the religious socialists and dialectical theology as we are in the fact that the religious socialists placed the certainty of the victory of the kingdom of God so much in the center of their reflections that they no longer had a proper grasp of evil in its profound depth and in its societal context. When the analysis of the context is neglected, the danger arises that the proposed therapy will also overlook reality and provide little remedy for solving the problem of evil. This is precisely the situation in which contemporary theology finds itself today.

Philosophie Kants und den von ihr angeregten höchsten Fragen. Für die denkende Jugend (Basel: Kober, 1924), 237.

120. Kutter, *Im Anfang war die Tat,* 238f.

121. Hermann Kutter, *Das Unmittelbare: Eine Menschheitsfrage* (Basel: Spittler, 1921), 82.

122. See in this regard Pfeiffer, *Religiöse Sozialisten,* 89.

3. Sin in Contemporary Discussion

This chapter subhead seems to be a contradiction in itself because there is no contemporary discussion of sin. Already in 1973 Karl Menninger (1893-1990) wrote a book entitled *Whatever Became of Sin* where he stated: "The popular leaning is away from notions of guilt and morality. Some politicians, groping for a word, have chanced on the silly misnomer, permissiveness. Their thinking is muddy but their meaning is clear. Disease and treatment have been the watchwords of the day and little is said about selfishness or guilt or the 'morality gap.' And certainly no one talks about sin!"[123] Indeed in a postmodern time of political correctness it is unwise to call certain behaviors sinful. In a time of extreme individualism where "I'm okay and you're okay," evaluative distinctions are difficult to make. Yet Menninger will not that easily abandon the concept of sin. He contends:

> Lots of sins have disappeared; nevertheless, I believe there is a general sentiment that sin is still with us, by us, and in us — somewhere. We are made vaguely uneasy by this consciousness, this persistent sense of guilt, and we try to relieve it in various ways. We project the blame onto others, we ascribe the responsibility to a group, we offer up scapegoat sacrifices, we perform or partake in dumb-show rituals of penitence and atonement. There is rarely a peccavi, but there's a feeling.[124]

Indeed, there is a feeling of uneasiness and there is also a shift in the allocation of responsibility for evil. The situation is like that in Genesis 3, where Adam pointed to Eve and Eve then pointed to the snake. I am not responsible for my sin, but the devil made me do it. Yet as American psychiatrist Scott Peck (1936-2005) contends, "evil people resist the awareness of their own condition."[125] This would mean that we are so much mired in sinfulness that we avoid facing up to our own sinful nature. But this "laziness is original sin," as Peck tells us.[126] This means we try to avoid looking in the mirror since that would make us discover who we really are.

Since sin is a deeply theological term, denoting our alienation from God and the concomitant human behavior, some theologians even suggest

---

123. Karl Menninger, *Whatever Became of Sin?* (New York: Hawthorn, 1973), 228.
124. Menninger, *Whatever Became of Sin?* 17.
125. M. Scott Peck, *The Road Less Traveled: A New Psychology of Love, Traditional Values and Spiritual Growth* (New York: Simon & Schuster, Touchstone Book, 1987), 218.
126. Peck, *The Road Less Traveled,* 277.

that such looking in the mirror would only lead us astray. For instance, Karl Barth (1886-1968) points out that by nature humans have no knowledge of their sinfulness. By looking at themselves and the world around them, they pursue some kind of natural theology and are led astray in their assessment of reality. "The access to the knowledge that he is a sinner is lacking in man because he is a sinner."[127] We can only know about sinfulness by looking at Jesus Christ and comparing ourselves with him. "Only when we know Jesus Christ do we really know that man is a man of sin, and what sin is, and what it means for man."[128]

a. The Enigmatic Shape of Nothingness (Barth)

In his *Church Dogmatics* **Karl Barth** develops the doctrine of sin in negative correspondence to developing the doctrine of Christ. Sin is understood as *superbia* (arrogance) and the fall as laziness and misery, and as lie and condemnation. These terms are opposites to that which Christ has accomplished in his salvific activity. Therefore salvation in Christ serves as that which allows us to recognize and fathom the doctrine of sin. Sin, therefore, always comes into view as that which is already judged and forgiven. "It is only of forgiven sin that we know that it is recognized as sin, that it is sin."[129] Since sin is subsumed under atonement, it also has no ontological status, meaning that it is not a constitutive phenomenon of reality. Against the background of the accomplished atonement in Christ sin is seen as "nothingness."[130]

In the context of God's election of humankind, God as the reconciler allowed for sin but has overcome it in Jesus Christ. Yet we should not minimize sin since it manifests itself in evil, which is contrary to God "in its concrete opposition to the will of God active and revealed in Christ Jesus."[131] Sin is always seen as that which is overcome and that which is destined to disappear. Karl Barth calls sin "the concrete form of nothingness because in sin it becomes man's own act, achievement and guilt."[132] Barth follows thereby the biblical model, for despite the accountability of humans for

127. Barth, *CD*, IV/1:360f.
128. Barth, *CD*, IV/1:389.
129. Barth, *CD*, II/2:768.
130. Barth, *CD*, III/3:305.
131. Barth, *CD*, IV/3.1:177.
132. Barth, *CD*, III/3:310.

their behavior sin as an action is continually described in the Bible as succumbing to a foreign power. Sin is on the one hand human action, but on the other hand it is a result of nothingness. According to Barth, however, nothingness does not exhaust itself in sin, for then it would simply be a part of creation.

What, then, is this nothingness? According to Barth, one cannot say of nothingness that it "is," as one might say, for example, that God or a created being "is."[133] Yet it would be playing down the significance of this nothingness if one concluded that nothingness is simply nothing. Rather, God takes account of it, is occupied with it, struggles against it, bears it, and overcomes it. It is not simply identical with that which does not exist, and it is also not the counterpart to God, nor is it a created being, but it is rather the other "from which God separates Himself and in the face of which He asserts Himself and exerts His positive will." Nothingness, according to Barth, has no existence or recognizability except as the object of God's activity. This means that God's affirmation implies a "No" toward that to which he does not say "Yes," that is, to nothingness. God is Lord both on the right hand and on the left. Precisely because he is also Lord of the left, "He is the basis and Lord of nothingness too." Nothingness is not merely an accident, an oversight of God, but rather under his "No" it is the object of his wrath and judgment. "Nothingness 'is,' therefore, in its connection with the activity of God. It 'is' because and as and so long as God is against it" (*CD* 3/ 3:353). A lively debate has been spawned over this statement about the being of nothingness, for it is incomprehensible to our "common logic" and it appears to such common logic that Barth comes very close to declaring God to be the cause of nothingness.[134]

Barth, as we have seen, declined to ascribe to nothingness a self-sufficient existence independent from God. He also denied, however, that one could derive nothingness from the activity of God alone, in which God has the role of one who foreknows and permits. Finally, nothingness does not simply represent a deficiency of good or perfection since it is not thereby ascribed a ground of being and is thus not an active power. But how can one then still rule out that nothingness comes from God himself? If nothingness corresponds with the divine non-willing, then the divine non-

133. For this and the following, see Barth, *CD*, III/3:349ff.; quotations, 351.

134. Regarding this assessment and for references to further literature, see Wilfried Härle, *Sein und Gnade: Die Ontologie in Karl Barths kirchlicher Dogmatik* (Berlin: Walter de Gruyter, 1974), especially his chapter on "Das Nichtige," 227-69.

willing is, as it were, the archetype for nothingness. Nothingness would then have its final parallel in God, namely, in God's negative will.[135] Despite all the attempts at interpretation, one must agree with Barth that we have to do here with the "ontic peculiarity" of nothingness.[136]

The gracious will of God is so strongly emphasized by Barth that that which strives and works against God cannot approach a genuine existence. Ultimately, everything will be received into the salvific scope of God. Barth always argues from the standpoint of the grace of God, from God's covenant with humanity. Evil is the opposite of that which God wills. Nevertheless, it becomes the object of his *opus alienum,* that is, the work that is not proper to him, that of anger and judgment. The negation of the grace of God is "chaos, the world which He did not choose or will, which He could not and did not create, but which, as He created the actual world, He passed over and set aside, marking and excluding it as the eternal past, the eternal yesterday. And this is evil in the Christian sense, namely, what is alien and adverse to grace, and therefore without it." Nothingness opposes the grace of God inasmuch as it offends God and threatens God's creation and breaks into the creation as sin, evil, and death and produces chaos.

Barth emphasizes that one cannot deal with nothingness in a frivolous manner. It is such a threatening power that the conflict with it, its conquest, removal, and settlement, is primarily a matter for God. Nothingness, therefore, is above all God's own problem (*CD,* 3/3:355). Humans are only affected by nothingness insofar as they fall willingly victim to it and thus become sinners. In this way suffering, want, and destruction come to humanity. Yet Barth is optimistic in the face of the destructive power of nothingness since the "kingdom of nothingness" has already been destroyed. "But its dominion, even though it was only a semblance of dominion, is now objectively defeated as such in Jesus Christ. What it still is in the world, it is in virtue of the blindness of our eyes and the cover which is still over us, obscuring the prospect of the kingdom of God already established as the only kingdom undisputed by evil."[137]

In his triumph of grace, Barth also does not want to talk about original sin (Ger. *Erbsünde*) since the fall is not a once and for all event. What Adam did and has been doing is also done by every human being.[138] Adam was a

135. See in this regard Härle, *Sein und Gnade,* 241.
136. For this and the following quotation, see Barth, *CD,* III/3:353.
137. Barth, *CD,* III/3:367.
138. See Barth, *CD,* IV/1:509ff. On the issue of "original sin," see 501. But *Ursünde* is

sinner just as we are sinners; he was just the beginner. At the same time, the name Adam is that predicate through which God brings together the grace that appeared in Jesus Christ for the world and for the whole of humanity, making atonement for all others.[139]

While we certainly concur with Barth's emphasis on the efficacy of Christ's atoning activity, we wonder at the same time whether Barth does justice to the phenomena of the negative and perverse within our world. Sin is not just an accompanying apparition of the salvific activity of God. It is a phenomenon that is within each of us and all around us. Therefore it is even easier to believe in the sinful and corrupt stature of humanity than in its eventual or already accomplished redemption.

b. Estrangement and Self-Destruction (Tillich)

Paul Tillich (1886-1965) covers in volume 2 of his *Systematic Theology* both sin and Christology. Yet to expound the term "sin" he needs just a little more than two pages because he wants to perceive sin under the concept of estrangement. However, Tillich does not want to abandon the term "sin" altogether because it conveys something that is not contained in the term "estrangement." The term "sin" contains "the personal act of turning away from that to which one belongs. Sin expresses most sharply the personal character of estrangement over against its tragic side. It expresses personal freedom and guilt in contrast to the tragic guilt and the universal destiny of estrangement."[140] Sin points to the personal responsibility contained in the phenomenon of estrangement. When "sins" are spoken of, as quite often occurs, one must remember that these are always manifestations of sin. It is the expression of the estrangement of humans from God, from the neighbor, and from themselves. Therefore, Tillich notes, Paul calls everything sin that does not proceed from faith, from unity with God.

Like Karl Barth, Tillich rejects the term "original sin" since it is often connected with absurd ideas, especially in terms of a hereditary sin. Rightly understood, it expresses the "universal character of estrangement." Tillich also recognizes that "the symbol of 'the Fall' is a decisive part of the Chris-

---

not exactly translated by the English term "original sin." A better term would be "primal sin."

139. See Barth, *CD*, IV/1:512.
140. See Paul Tillich, *ST*, 2:46, for this and the following quote.

tian tradition," whereby a symbol is understood as something that participates in the reality of that which it represents.[141] Although this symbol is
usually bound to a specific biblical story, its meaning goes beyond Adam's
fall and has universal, anthropological significance. We find here a symbol
that has to do with the entire human situation, for it expresses the transition from essence to existence. This is a matter of fact and not some derived
dialectical step. Tillich thus seeks not only to separate himself from ideal-
ism, which points toward an ideal through which human freedom can be
achieved, but also from naturalism, which takes existence for granted and
denies its negativity (*ST,* 2:29f.).

Before the fall — if one can even make use of such a temporal expression — humanity was in a condition of "dream-like innocence." The possibility of a fall is grounded in the fact that humanity alone possessed finite
freedom. Humans can deny their essential nature and destroy their own humanity. Nevertheless, the freedom of human beings is not absolute, for it
can only come to fruition within the context of universal destiny. Although
this "event" concerns only the fall of a human being it has cosmic significance. Freedom awoke within humanity and chose not to preserve the
"dream-like innocence" but to seek "self-actualization." The transition
from essence to existence bears both a moral and a tragic character. It is not
itself an event within space and time, but rather has trans-historical significance for all events that take place within space and time.[142] According to
Tillich, there is no state before the fall from which one could begin. "The
actual state is that existence in which man finds himself along with the
whole universe, and there is no time in which this was otherwise." Tillich
finds it "absurd" to speak of a moment in time in which humanity and nature were transformed from good to evil. Thus Tillich maintains that nature is included in the fall because one cannot separate human beings from
nature, for "man reaches into nature, as nature reaches into man. They participate in each other and cannot be separated from each other" (*ST,* 2:43).
If the intimate connection between time and the fall is problematic for
Tillich, it is just as problematic when one, with Tillich, correlates so closely
the concepts of creation and the fall.

Reinhold Niebuhr charged that Tillich's view of creation and the fall as
coinciding was an ontological speculation that portrayed the fall as unavoidable. Tillich countered that the unavoidability of the fall is indeed de-

---

141. Tillich, *ST,* 2:29; and see 1:239.
142. See Tillich, *ST,* 2:40f. for this and the following quotation.

rived "from a realistic observation of man, his heart, and his history."[143] Later he expanded on his statement to the effect that "creation and the Fall coincide in so far as there is no point in time and space in which created goodness was actualized and had existence" (*ST,* 2:44). Actualized creation and estranged existence are essentially identical for Tillich. Also, when he argues that existence cannot be derived from essence one must at least inquire to what extent God is the author of this estranged existence. At this point Tillich's logic is not clear. He wishes to explain the origin of estranged existence instead of allowing it to remain a mystery as most theologians do. Tillich calls the state of existence one of estrangement. "Man is estranged from the ground of his being, from other beings, and from himself. The transition from essence to existence results in personal guilt and universal tragedy" (*ST,* 2:44f.). Tillich thus appears to prefer the word "estrangement" to the concept of "sin" since estrangement shows to what humanity actually belongs — to God, to one's own self, and to the world. Sin is therefore viewed from the vantage point of estrangement.

Tillich next characterizes estrangement as unbelief — a definition of sin that is also found in article 2 of the Lutheran Augsburg Confession. Interesting here is that Tillich takes over from article 2 "without faith" [*Unglaube*] and "with concupiscence," but passes silently over the phrase "without fear of God" and in its place introduces the concept of *hubris* or "pride" (*ST,* 2:47). Because he always speaks of the "ground of being" instead of God, he is probably uncomfortable with the phrase "without fear of God." Along with unbelief, that is, the lack of trust in God, Tillich lists *hubris,* which he interprets as the temptation of humans to make themselves existentially the center of their own selves and the world instead of having their center in God. Finally, he speaks of concupiscence, which he characterizes as the unbounded striving after knowledge, sex, and power.

Tillich rejects the view that through Adam's fall the entire human race was corrupted so that we all live in estrangement and no one can escape sin.[144] He calls the supposed connection between the destiny of humanity and an entirely free act of Adam illogical and "absurd" since through a human being, Adam, freedom is imputed apart from destiny. One must view Adam instead as the essential human and as the one who symbolizes the transition from essence to existence. Original or hereditary sin is neither

---

143. Paul Tillich, "Reply to Interpretation and Criticism," in *The Theology of Paul Tillich,* rev. ed., ed. Charles W. Kegley (New York: Pilgrim, 1982), 388.

144. For the following, see Tillich, *ST,* 2:55f.; quotation, 2:56.

original nor hereditary but is the universal destiny of estrangement that applies to every person: "Sin is a universal fact before it becomes an individual act." It is questionable, however, whether the same is meant here as what Augustine expressed when he spoke of humanity as a *massa perditionis,* a depraved mass, a description with which Tillich agrees. Sin as a universal fact need not affect the individual in the way expressed by the concept of original sin. That gold is a valuable metal, for example, can also lay claim to being a universal fact. Yet this need not affect me as an individual when I neither purchase nor possess any object that is made from gold. Original sin as a universal fact, on the other hand, is understood as something hereditary that we cannot elude.

According to Tillich, humans find themselves, along with their world, in a context of existential estrangement, unbelief, *hubris,* and concupiscence. "Each expression of the estranged state contradicts man's essential being, his potency for goodness. It contradicts the created structure of himself and his world and their interdependence. And self-contradiction drives toward self-destruction" (*ST,* 2:59f.). Sin becomes "evil," as Tillich terms it, through its self-destructive consequences. Evil is the consequence of the state of sin and estrangement, so that the doctrine of evil is derived from the doctrine of sin (*ST,* 2:61). In the condition of estrangement humans contradict their essential self and destroy the structure of their being. This destruction results, then, in evil, in the structures of destruction. Because the individual exists within the polarity of freedom and destiny as well as of dynamic and form and individualization and participation, these polarities are destroyed by estrangement.[145] Through *hubris* freedom is no longer related to destiny but to an indeterminate number of contingent objects. Thus freedom becomes caprice and destiny degenerates into mechanical necessity. In a similar way the polarity of dynamic and form is destroyed so that dynamic without form becomes a formless search for self-transcendence, whereas form without dynamic is transformed into an oppressive, external law.

Individualization without participation becomes isolation in which humans become turned in on themselves. We encounter the most isolated and lonely individuals in Western industrial society and notice at the same time the loss of individuality that is becoming an increasingly frequent phenomenon in this society. Tillich summarizes his position in the following way: "Estranged from the ultimate power of being, man is determined by

---

145. For this and the following, see Tillich, *ST,* 2:62-66.

his finitude. He is given over to his natural fate. He came from nothing, and he returns to nothing. He is under the domination of death and is driven by the anxiety of having to die. This, in fact, is the first answer to the question about the relation of sin and death" (*ST,* 2:66). Humans are left in this world with the inevitability of death and the angst of non-being, which leads to the fear of death. The angst for non-being is present in all finite creatures. Human beings, therefore, have wandered from dream-like innocence into alienation from God and estrangement from their own existence and are increasingly threatened with self-destruction. Tillich is in agreement with Martin Luther's assessment of the bondage of the will when this attests to the human inability to break out of the state of estrangement. "In spite of the power of his infinite freedom . . . [man] is unable to achieve the reunion with God" (*ST,* 2:79). Only God, who in Jesus Christ relinquishes essence for existence and overcomes the latter, can lead human beings back to God's own self and to true humanness.

Tillich paints a picture of a humanity that has failed itself and God and is thus caught in the clutches of its own failure so that it is choked by the noose that it has thrown around its own neck. Evil is not rooted in God or in any anti-God, but alone in humanity itself that has misused and continues to misuse its freedom. Even when Tillich frequently speaks of the demonic he does not thereby indicate any anti-Godly power external to the structures of existence. According to Tillich, the symbol of the demonic represents "antidivine forces in individual and social life" (*ST,* 3:102). Tillich can speak of the demonic self-elevation of one nation over others or the demonic persecution of Christians. Powers, however, which strive against God and, so to speak, seek to force God's abdication, are not thereby mentioned. The demonic remains limited to the level of that which is existence-bound. In Tillich's thought evil, and whatever stands behind it, is a part of human existence that includes nature within its context. It is no longer this power that always only denies, but ultimately humans themselves who in their power or powerlessness deny themselves and their existence.

c. The Self-Centeredness of Humanity (Pannenberg)

With the term "estrangement" Paul Tillich connected sin with reality via psychology. **Wolfhart Pannenberg** does the same with exocentricity via anthropology. He does not want to present a *dogmatic* anthropology because "traditional dogmatic anthropology presupposes the existence of God when it speaks of the image of God in human beings. Furthermore, it develops this concept on the basis not of anthropological findings, but of what the Bible says."[146] Pannenberg wants to develop a fundamental theological anthropology focusing on two central themes: humanity created in the image of God and human sinfulness. In so doing, he does not argue from dogmatic presuppositions, but turns to the phenomena of human existence "as investigated in human biology, psychology, cultural anthropology, or sociology and examines the findings of these disciplines with an eye to implications that may be relevant to religion and theology."[147] It is important for him that what is qualified as sin can also be empirically demonstrated. Already in his 1962 book *What Is Man?* Pannenberg writes: "Where the ego falls into contrast with openness to the world — which happens, for example, through the greed that is enslaved to the things of the world — then the ego comes to be closed off toward God and thereby toward its own human destiny. This state of being closed up within itself is the essence of sin."[148] We are reminded here of Augustine's observation that as a sinner a human being is focused on itself *(homo incurvatus in se ipsum)*.

In his comprehensive *Anthropology in Theological Perspective,* Pannenberg takes up a concept from German philosopher and sociologist Helmuth Plessner (1892-1985) and speaks of the exocentricity of human beings in contrast to a centered position with its dependence on a here and now.[149] By use of the term "exocentricity" Pannenberg points to the fact that for human beings the center of their expressions of life lies not only in themselves but at the same time outside of themselves. This means that the human being displays a typical openness toward the world and toward God. In humans themselves there exists a tension between a centered position and an exocentricity that leads to a breach in the relationship of humans with their own selves and an inner conflict (80f.). While normally the ego, which seeks its identity within itself, stands in tension with an exocentric self-transcendence, that is, with the search of the self outside of its own self, it sets itself against this external relationship so that everything becomes a means to the self-assertion of the ego (85). This leads to a distorted ego-

146. Wolfhart Pannenberg, *Anthropology in Theological Perspective,* trans. Matthew J. O'Connell (Philadelphia: Westminster, 1985), 21.

147. Pannenberg, *Anthropology in Theological Perspective,* 21.

148. Wolfhart Pannenberg, *What Is Man? Contemporary Anthropology in Theological Perspective,* trans. Duane Priebe (Philadelphia: Fortress, 1970), 68.

149. See Pannenberg, *Anthropology in Theological Perspective,* 37; references in the text are to this book.

constitution that Pannenberg equates with sin. Thus it is no surprise that Pannenberg affirms the Augustinian interpretation of human sinfulness as concupiscence (90f.).

Sinful desire, which arises from the human relationship to the world, can, according to Pannenberg, be designated by the Augustinian concept *superbia,* that is, pride, the false self-glorification and egocentricity of humanity that produces a turning away from God and a turning toward one's own self (93f.). Pannenberg sees this reflected in the actual life-experience of human beings. The distortion of human behavior does not begin with a conscious turning away from God, but rather the estrangement from God takes place in various and often barely noticeable ways as distortions of our relationship to the world and to our own selves. Now, however, the centrality that culminates in ego-centeredness has become an existential structural moment of humanity. We each experience our own selves as the center of our individual world.[150] Pannenberg questions, then, how one can avoid viewing human nature as such as sinful. If one accepts the Augustinian analysis of sin and understands it as unrestrained love of self and concupiscence, then the natural life of human beings is sinful. Yet Pannenberg cautions that one must not characterize human nature in its essence as sinful, but rather only in the sense of the conditions of its existence by means of which human nature alters its natural living conditions. On the one hand sin is willed by human beings, yet on the other hand sin is rooted within the natural conditions of human existence. This unity of the two aspects, as Pannenberg points out, has not always been recognized by theology.

Pannenberg raises the additional question of why one speaks of sin only in regard to human beings if humanity shares an ego-centeredness with other life forms that are also guided in their behavior by an ego center. For Pannenberg the answer is to be found in the fact that only in the case of humans is their own identity made a central theme for their behavior. Humans are aware of their own self and find this self-awareness to be both a gift and a challenge. While animals live in an environment without feeling a tension between this environment and their ego, humans remain open to the world around them and exist in a relationship of tension with it. Thus arise the possibility and actuality of a distortion between ego-centricity and exocentricity. The result is the responsibility of humans for their sinful be-

---

150. For this and the following, see Pannenberg, *Anthropology in Theological Perspective,* 105-10.

havior, for sin does not come on them as an alien force to which they are helplessly handed over. It is much more the case that the concept of sin is inseparably bound with the ideas of accountability and guilt. Responsibility, however, can only be taken up when humans accept their actions as their own and assume liability for them. Thus Pannenberg can say in regard to human sinfulness that humans are of such a character that they

> can find pleasure in what is objectively evil (not only in itself but even for themselves). The observation that such is the case need not stir others to moral outrage. Such a reaction has its place, of course, especially when the structures of social life are being endangered. But those who realize that a failure to achieve the good is always a failure of the self as well will feel sadness more than anything else. In addition, there is little they can do to bring about a change. Good advice is of little avail in such cases since deception with regard to the good is not simply an intellectual matter. The bondage of the will calls, therefore, for a liberation and, in the radical case, for a redemption that will establish the will's identity anew. (118f.)

Pannenberg speaks of a bondage of the will that on the one hand rules out the possibility that humans can once again find their own way back to the original balance of tension between exocentricity and ego-determination, and on the other hand encompasses the recognition that human beings follow willingly the path of evil. The bondage of the will, according to Pannenberg, has left intact the ability to choose, but it has reduced the scope of this ability and points toward a structure of motivation that precedes the decisions and actions of the individual and that is the cause of the failure of the human self. This structure, which always restricts human beings since they are never able to reach high enough and wide enough, Pannenberg calls "original sin." For Pannenberg it is clear that human beings do not become sinners first through their actions and the imitation of the evil actions of others but that they are already sinners before they commit a single action of their own. This absoluteness of original sin leaves no place for human uprightness.

While Pannenberg accepts the traditional doctrine of original sin he does not view Adam as the historical forebear of humanity through whom original sin is passed on to us. Rather, Adam is to be seen in Judaic and Pauline tradition as "the prototype of all human beings, as their embodiment, as the Human Being pure and simple. In every individual, Adam's journey from sin to death is repeated as a copy" (122). Pannenberg notes, however, that the doctrine of original sin came under increasing disrepute within

Protestantism and that in its place one spoke of a kingdom of sin or evil (125). Concerning this criticism from Pannenberg it should be noted that behind the concept of a kingdom of sin or evil lay a protest against an excessive individualization of the idea of original sin. As we have seen, this is especially evident in the thought of Walter Rauschenbusch.

For Pannenberg it is important to demonstrate the empirical universality of sin. He contends that the universality of sin as such is just as much illumined in light of the revelation of human destiny through the law as it is through the crucified and resurrected Christ.[151] What is shown here in regard to content can likewise be empirically demonstrated, even if not specifically under the name "sin." A hint in this direction is seen by Pannenberg in the universality of death. Even the content of sin comes to light in the universality of concupiscence as a distinguishing feature of human behavior. Pannenberg no longer needs the historical person of Adam since the universality of sin can be empirically demonstrated. Following Paul, Augustine already recognized that concupiscence and its consequences are empirically discernible as a universal actuality. How, then, does Pannenberg formulate this empirical proof today? First, he follows Tillich, who maintained that sin led to the self-destruction of human beings. In this way Tillich had sought to demonstrate that the attempt of humans to ground their self-centered existence in their own selves, by which means they make themselves the center of their own world, produces precisely the opposite effect, leading to the loss of one's own self and to the failure of self-integration. He saw sickness, for example, as the dissolution of self-integration. There exists, therefore, a connection between sin and death in the collapse of the self-integration that is indispensable for the fulfillment of human life.

Regarding the empirical proof of the universality of sin, Pannenberg argues from the phenomenon of aggression.[152] He points to angst as a motif for aggressive behavior in which angst participates in the experience of the ego in the process of the development of the self. As a result of angst the ego can be thrown back on itself, so that it clings to its own finiteness and loses itself. This clinging and losing express themselves in the form of aggression

---

151. For this and the following, see Pannenberg, *Anthropology in Theological Perspective,* 138-42.

152. For the following, see Pannenberg, *Anthropology in Theological Perspective,* 142-51. The English version of the following quotation, which is found on p. 150, translates the German phrase "sowohl die (destruktive) Aggression als auch Flucht und Depression" inaccurately and somewhat amusingly as "both (destructive) aggression and flight depression."

or depression. In both cases a failure of willpower occurs as well as a breakdown in the formation and preservation of an independent and genuine ego. While angst is the basic form in which sin manifests itself in human self-consciousness, "(destructive) aggression . . . [as well as] flight [and] depression are also to be seen as expressions of human sinfulness." Pannenberg concludes his considerations by commenting that "If we understand the doctrine of sin as functioning in the context of a still unfinished process which has human identity as its goal, we will not misinterpret this doctrine as a product of aggression turned inward. The consciousness of the failure of the self — that is, of sin — is a necessary phase in the process whereby human beings are liberated to become themselves" (152).

Sin, therefore, is seen to have a positive side. Despite the immense discussion with tradition, especially with Augustine, Pannenberg cannot completely avoid an idealistic understanding of sin. It is thus no surprise that the concept of the kingdom of evil is, as it were, passed over. Sin and its evil consequences always revolve around the ego in the thought of Pannenberg. A societal component of evil is hardly mentioned. One must certainly agree with Pannenberg that sin is egocentricity and thereby a denial of the potential openness of human beings to the world and to God. Yet this narrowing of the concepts of sin and evil must be elucidated with much more clarity in regard to its consequences for human society and for the entire creation. At this point liberation theology has chosen to follow an entirely different path which too, however, unless it is understood as a corrective, produces a one-sided view.

d. Sinful Social Structures (Liberation Theology)

This section looks at the theology of liberation only in regard to the Latin America scene. There, as in other regions, the emphasis is not on the experience of the sins of an individual, or on the interior side of humanity, but on the sociopolitical dimension of sin and the concrete historical sociocultural context. This means emphasis on sin that is basically structural. Liberation theology argues primarily from a contextual angle and endeavors to thematize the contextual experience of sin and grace in the different societal situations that, as it claims, result from a global capitalistic and materialistic mindset. In the Latin American context it is especially sin against the poor that receives prominent focus and that is manifested by the fact that the poor are disenfranchised through the objective structures of evil, meaning through exploitation, oppression, and often torture.[153] Nevertheless, sin and evil are only implicit themes. As we can see in the 1972 classic by **Gustavo Gutiérrez** (b. 1928), *Theology of Liberation,* there is the socio-cultural description of the situation, the call for change, but then the main emphasis theologically speaking is on the creation of a new humanity and on liberation as a central concept of the Christian message. We hear that "sin — a breach of friendship with God and others — is according to the Bible the ultimate cause of poverty, injustice, and the oppression in which persons live." Yet understandably Gutiérrez focuses more on liberation from sin than on what sin actually means.[154] This is different from Jean Luis Segundo (1925-96), a Jesuit priest and theologian who together with Gustavo Gutiérrez was one of the initiators of liberation theology. The last volume of his five-volume-work, *A Theology for Artisans of a New Humanity,* bears the title *Evolution and Guilt.* When Segundo describes sin from a biblical perspective, he relies primarily on the Gospel of John. There we learn that Jesus has come in order to overcome and take away the sin of the world (John 1:29).[155] Sin is not a free act, but rather a condition of bondage from which Christ liberates. Liberation therefore is not a theory but a matter of *praxis.* But why, then, does the entire godless world stand under the power of evil (1 John 5:19)? From whence does this structural deficiency or this determinism come that turns the world into an anti-Godly entity? By way of an answer to this question Segundo refers to a social mechanism that is essentially conservative. From the comment in 1 John 4:5, "They are from the world; therefore what they say is from the world, and the world listens to them," Segundo deduces that the powers that rule the world, in a maliciously circular argument, reject all that is new. A conservative ideology suppresses all other possible interpretations through a circular argumentation by means of which everything is already decided and predetermined.

In Segundo's description we discover, although he does not say so explicitly, a portrayal of Latin American societal reality as it is characterized by most liberation theologians. Thus Gustavo Gutiérrez writes: "But in the liberation approach sin is not considered as an individual, private, or merely interior reality — asserted just enough to necessitate a 'spiritual' redemp-

---

153. See Christine Axt-Piscalar, "Sünde VII," in *TRE,* 32:427.

154. Gustavo Gutiérrez, *A Theology of Liberation: History, Politics, and Salvation,* trans. Caridad Inda and John Eagleson, preface Christopher Rowland (London: SCM, 2001 [1973]), 74.

155. For the following, see Jean Luis Segundo, *A Theology for Artisans of a New Humanity,* vol. 5, *Evolution and Guilt,* trans. John Drury (Maryknoll, NY: Orbis, 1974), 52, 54.

tion which does not challenge the order in which we live. Sin is regarded as a social, historical fact, the absence of brotherhood and love in relationships among men, the breach of friendship with God and with other men, and, therefore, an interior, personal fracture. When it is considered in this way, the collective dimensions of sin are rediscovered."[156] Sin, according to Gutiérrez, is clearly to be seen in structures of oppression; in the exploitation of one person by another; and in the conquest and enslavement of nations, races, and social classes. Sin is a fundamental alienation and the root of all injustice and exploitation. Yet one does not encounter sin directly as such but only in concrete examples of alienation. It is impossible, however, to recognize the concrete manifestations of sin without understanding how they came about.

It is telling that the "Instruction on Christian Freedom and Liberation" of 1986 by the Vatican Congregation for the Doctrine of the Faith under its prefect Joseph Cardinal Ratzinger, the present Pope Emeritus Benedict XVI, declared: "The sin which is at the root of unjust situations is, in a true and immediate sense, a voluntary act which has its source in the freedom of individuals, only in a derived and secondary sense is it applicable to structures, and only in this sense can one speak of 'social sin.'"[157] This means individual sin is primary and corporate (social) sin is secondary. Yet structures designed by individuals can be more pervasive than individual sins. When we look at the bygone era of apartheid in South Africa, the structures of segregation forced individuals by the threat of sanctions to sin.[158] Voluntary acts of not sinning would have been sanctioned by the existing law. Structures are as much in need of redemption or rather correction as are individuals. And this is exactly the direction in which liberation theology goes.

As Gutiérrez states, sin necessitates a radical liberation, including political liberation. By participating in the historical process of liberation one can demonstrate the fundamental alienation that is present in each individual case. This radical liberation, however, is not something that we ourselves earn, but it is rather a gift brought to us by Christ. Through his death and resurrection Christ has liberated human beings from sin and all its conse-

156. Gutiérrez, *A Theology of Liberation,* 174.

157. Congregation for the Doctrine of the Faith, "Instruction on Christian Freedom and Liberation" (March 22, 1986), in *Liberation Theology: A Documentary History,* ed. Alfred T. Henneley, with intro., commentary, and trans. (Maryknoll, NY: Orbis, 1990), 485.

158. See the comments by Alfred T. Henneley, "The Red-Hot Issue: Liberation Theology" (May 24, 1986), in *Liberation Theology,* ed. Henneley, 511, on this point.

quences as well as from all oppression and injustice. This liberation, which Christ has made possible through his own destiny, is realized through the progress and growth of the kingdom of God. "The growth of the Kingdom is a process which occurs historically *in* liberation" (175). Although it is a liberating event, the growth of the kingdom of God cannot be equated with its coming; neither is it our entire redemption. Rather, it is a historical realization of the kingdom and thus announces its consummation.

Sin, as a rupture of the friendship with God and other persons, is in the biblical view, according to Gutiérrez, the ultimate cause of the poverty, injustice, and oppression in which humans live.[159] By designating sin as the ultimate cause of these conditions Gutiérrez in no way intends to bring into question the structural grounds and objective determinants that have led to these conditions. He wishes to point out, however, that these things have not come about coincidentally. Behind the unjust structures a personal or collective will or force bears responsibility for the present situation, a will or force that rejects God and neighbor. Thus a societal transformation, regardless of how radical, cannot automatically achieve the suppression of everything evil. How then can this "sinful will" be stopped that expresses itself in sinful or evil constellations of poverty, injustice, and oppression? To begin with Gutiérrez points to the death and resurrection of Jesus Christ as facilitating the kingdom of God and the overcoming of sin, for God has, through God's own self, taken away sin and announced the beginning of a new era.

For Gutiérrez, however, the church is also important. Since evil has been sanctioned by society, its removal can only be achieved societally. Thus he welcomes the fact that the church has now declared its solidarity with the Latin American situation rather than elevating itself above this situation. The church is attempting to accept responsibility for the injustice that it has supported through its solidarity with the establishment and its silence about the evil that resulted from this arrangement (115).[160] Because God himself in the fullness of time sent Christ into the world to liberate all people from bondage to which they had been subjected by sin, it is now necessary to point to sinful injustice and oppression and to declare that the rejec-

---

159. For this and the following, see Gutiérrez, *A Theology of Liberation*, 34.

160. Of course, this was written before the Congregation for the Doctrine of the Faith issued its two "Instructions" of 1984 and 1986 about liberation theology, and also before more and more conservative bishops were appointed in Latin America. For how bishops were treated who were more favorable to liberation theology, see the moving report by Bishop Pedro Casaldáliga, "Letter to Brazilian Bishops" (June 1988), in *Liberation Theology*, ed. Henneley, 532-40.

tion of peace, which is furthered by social, political, economic, and cultural inequality, is an offense against God. The church in Latin America must make its presence felt in a new way and must prophetically label as sin the serious injustices that are overall present in that context. Through the denunciation of social injustice the church expresses "the intention of disassociation from the existing unjust order" (129).

The church must separate itself from the state so that it can free itself from this compromising relationship and be able to fulfill its own mission and to rely on the strength of its Lord rather than on earthly powers. The prophetic task of the church is at the same time constructive and critical. The church must point to elements within the process of liberation that lead to greater humanness and justice, while at the same time rejecting those elements that continue to produce injustice and oppression. Liberation theology, therefore, recognizes the fundamental human sinfulness that expresses itself in unjust structures. It also realizes that a fundamental transformation is only possible because God has taken up the forgiving and transforming initiative in Jesus Christ. It remains, however, unclear how one should relate the activity of establishing a just society to the values of the kingdom of God. Will the kingdom of God be confused here with revolution? Gutiérrez rejects this suggestion when it arises accusingly from the context of a comfortable, establishment Christianity. Yet he has himself no simple answer and admits that the Latin American church does not speak with a single voice on the process of liberation.[161]

One must concede the possibility that genuine societal change does not originate with the church but is born by other forces. It must also be admitted that liberation, revolution, and the advance of the kingdom of God are often viewed as parallel developments. However, when it is possible to live a Christian existence in a world that is characterized and threatened by evil then this existence must not be allowed to atrophy into a matter of private religiosity but must shine forth in the world and in society. To the extent that liberation theology has recognized the societal roots and structure of evil and has responded with an active call for liberation from these structures, it has freed us from the privatization of sin and recovered salvation for society.

161. For this and the following, see Gutiérrez, *A Theology of Liberation*, 134ff.

e. Against a Lop-sided Understanding of Sin (Feminist Theology)

Since feminist theology can be considered as a branch of liberation theology, it betrays considerable affinity to Latin American liberation theology. Oppression and exploitation are high on the agenda. Yet it is the oppressive and destructive patriarchal ideology of dominance that has had its deleterious effects on women. Moreover, the traditional doctrine of sin has been constructed predominantly from the perspective of men and therefore the experience of women (sexual exploitation, economic dependence, and patriarchal dominance) has largely been omitted. Yet these feminine experiences are adduced to show the dimension of sinfulness. Also, the connection between female sexuality and the temptation to sin by understanding sin primarily as concupiscence demonized women in their sexuality and their bodily experience.

Judith Plaskow (b. 1947), a Jewish feminist theologian and past president of the American Academy of Religion, in her Yale University doctoral dissertation *Sex, Sin, and Grace: Women's Experience and the Theology of Reinhold Niebuhr and Paul Tillich,* examines some of these points in detail. Having analyzed Reinhold Niebuhr and Paul Tillich's doctrines of sin and grace, she concluded that "although the two men claimed to speak to and from universal human experience in formulating those theologies, in fact . . . neither of them addresses the situation of women in Western society."[162] For instance, when Tillich wants to demonstrate the actualization of estrangement, he uses examples of unbelief, *hubris,* and concupiscence, thereby translating *hubris* as "self-elevation." Yet these characteristics, according to Plaskow, are more likely to be associated with men than with women in Western society (see 236). Similarly, when Niebuhr talks about the religious dimension of sin, he defines it as man's rebellion against God, his effort to usurp the place of God. Again, Niebuhr fails to convey with this definition the nature of women's sin and actually turns it into virtue since for women self-centeredness is not sin, but *"women's sin' is precisely the failure to turn toward the self"* (238). Women fail to take responsibility for their own self-actualization.

It is, however, not only the problem of sin that is seen from a limiting male perspective. Behind this there looms a one-sided conception of God.

---

162. Judith Ellen Plaskow, *Sex, Sin, and Grace: Women's Experience and the Theologies of Reinhold Niebuhr and Paul Tillich* (diss., Yale University, 1975; published: Lanham, MD: University Press of America, 1979), 234.

Plaskow, therefore, raises the following questions: "Are the images of God as male and as person inseparably related? Does the image of God as male person necessarily involve a hierarchical model of the divine/human relation? Does a hierarchical model require that sin be defined as pride, and grace as judgment and obedience?" (268). A male image of God leads to a male image of sin and of that which is evil and therefore excludes women from that kind of experience. Plaskow finds another problem with Niebuhr and Tillich, namely, that they speak of sin "in almost exclusively individual terms" (269). Yet women's sins, the way they treat themselves, are a product of social experience. "Through consciousness raising, women become aware of both the social context of sin and their own collusion with it" (275). The behavior of women is imposed by society and up until recently has been largely accepted by women and not challenged. Plaskow, however, recognizes that her own experience as a woman comes from the perspective of a white, Western, middle-class woman (281).

Plaskow is certainly correct that male theologians, such as Niebuhr and Tillich, reflect on evil from their own societal perspective. In this way, their perspective is limited by their own makeup and by the influence of society on them. Yet can one really call "the failure to take responsibility for self-actualization" a "sin" since such behavior has hardly been actively destructive of others? The same, however, cannot be said of what has been characterized by Plaskow and others as "male pride."[163] Plaskow's claims seem to border on a position that Patricia Wilson-Kastner (1944-98) associates with that of radical feminism. According to Wilson-Kastner, "radical feminists have insisted that male and female humanism is indeed radically different. . . . Women are fundamentally good, they insist, though women are the victims of male oppression."[164] But before we associate Plaskow with representatives of this position, we should not overlook her own admission that she argues from a white, middle-class, female context.

Susan Thistlethwaite (b. 1948) has observed that white feminist theology often finds process theology, and its ancestor in faith, Protestant liberalism, quite congenial. "Many aspects of process theology make sense to white, middle-class women."[165] While no black female theologian has so far

163. The question is rightly posed by Daphne Hampson, *Theology and Feminism* (Oxford: Basil Blackwell, 1990), 123.

164. Patricia Wilson-Kastner, *Faith, Feminism, and the Christ* (Philadelphia: Fortress, 1983), 55.

165. Susan Brooks Thistlethwaite, *Sex, Race, and God: Christian Feminism in Black and White* (New York: Crossroad, 1989), 87.

chosen a process perspective for her work, white feminist theologians claim that "feminism and [the] process God have commonalities both in their respective critiques of the classical tradition and their basic presuppositions."[166] The traditional worldview is seen as inadequate by both. "The classical tradition's way of conceiving self, world, and God is clearly dualistically defined and hierarchically patterned." This worldview draws dichotomies such as mind-body, spirit-nature, God-evil, being-becoming, subject-object, and activity-passivity. In each of these sets, one is given priority over the other and considered to be more valuable. Feminists add to this also the male-female dualism and the association of male with being superior. Both feminism and process thought come together in striving for a holistic worldview emphasizing becoming instead of being and relatedness and interdependence instead of self-completeness and independence. They assign limited active and passive power to all subjects and the interdependence of all things. "No subject is considered to be absolutely dependent or independent" (209). God is no longer conceived of as absolutely superior to everything else. The same kind of power is being attributed to God and to creatures; "the difference between the two is merely quantitative" (214). Thereby the traditional connotations of power, those of domination and control, are avoided. But God is not simply a human fabrication. Since "God is unfathomable mystery, the vastness of God's glory and holiness and power is too great for the human mind to grasp" (231). Therefore, all our concepts of God are human creations and we should seek the best constructions that are coherent and religiously viable for the honor of God and for promoting the welfare of creatures. In classical liberal fashion we find omitted here the fact that God disclosed God's self to the Israelite community and ultimately to all of humanity in the human form of Jesus of Nazareth. If one acknowledges God's self-disclosure, the issue of reconceptualizing God may be more difficult than some feminist theologians and proponents of process theology have envisioned.

Rosemary Radford Ruether (b. 1936) is one of the few feminist theologians who explicitly reflects on the phenomenon of evil and in so doing picks up the dichotomy of good and evil, albeit with some significant modifications. She claims that some feminists feel that this dichotomy should be rejected since it denotes the "evil" side as "female." Therefore, "sexism is the un-

---

166. See Anna Case-Winters in her published dissertation, *God's Power: Traditional Understandings and Contemporary Challenges* (Louisville: Westminster, 1990), 205, for this and the following quote.

derlying social foundation of the good-evil ideology."[167] According to Ruether, feminism claims that a most basic expression of the human community, the relationship between men and women, has been distorted through all known history. It has been turned into an oppressive relationship that has victimized women and turned men into tyrants. The relationship between male and female has been transformed into a dualism of superiority and inferiority. Ruether claims that this is "fundamentally a male ideology and has served two purposes: the support for male identity as normative humanity and the justification of servile roles for women. However much women may be socialized into these myths of female inferiority and evil and are induced to collaborate with them, women are neither their originators nor their primary perpetuators" (165). This means that women were simply drawn into this without having been able to extricate themselves from their lot. Once sexism is recognized as wrong, evil, and sinful, it brings about the total collapse of the myth of female evil. "Once a breach in the wall of sexist ideology and deep realization of woman is made, the entire ideological and social superstructure built up over thousands of years of sexism and justification of sexism is open to question. Every aspect of male privilege loses its authority as natural and divine right and is re-evaluated as sin and evil" (173).

The fundamental problem with sexism, according to Ruether, lies in the fact that it is based on a distorted relationality. There can be no I-Thou relationship where there is no authentic self that is allowed to stand over against and respond to another. The basic humanity of both men and women is fundamentally truncated when the one has no access to public power and skills whereas the other controls all power and resources. Consequently, the male regresses in those areas in which he depends on the woman to serve him, while the woman is helpless in the public realm to which she is denied access. Ruether realizes that sexism leads to "a disproportionate stigmatization of males as responsible for evil and the consequent exculpation of women. Sin becomes something that males alone have done. Women have only been victims."[168] While she concedes that no male as an individual is expected to carry the total burden of guilt for sexism since both males and females have been shaped by a pre-existing system of male privilege and female subordination, females are at present in a better position in regard to being accountable for evil. "Their opportunities to do

---

167. Rosemary Radford Ruether, *Sexism and God-Talk: Toward a Feminist Theology* (Boston: Beacon, 1983), 160.

168. See Ruether, *Sexism and God-Talk,* 180, for this and the two following quotes.

evil have been generally limited to the subsystem relationships within this overall monopoly of power and privilege by the male ruling class." This means that women can be accomplices to evil just as much as men if given the opportunity. They can be "racist, classist, self-hating, manipulative toward dominant males, dominating toward children." This admission by Ruether is quite revealing. According to her own analysis, this would mean that at present the domination and exploitation of one class of people by another, primarily females by males, must certainly be termed as evil and sinful. Once true emancipation and interdependence between men and women have been achieved, both will exhibit the same capacity for evil. When we now return to Plaskow's analysis of the shortcomings of such male descriptions of evil as exhibited by Tillich and Niebuhr, we must affirm that her criticism is correct when understood in the present context of latent or overt sexism. Tillich and Niebuhr were not, or did not want to be, cognizant of the present situation. Yet their analysis is correct when we go beyond the present lop-sided arrangement and consider that which is at the heart of every human being, the capacity for evil.

Ruether correctly points out "that the Genesis 3 story of the Fall of Adam through Eve does not become a normative story of the origins of evil in the Hebrew Bible."[169] Since the liberation of Israel from Egyptian bondage and the covenant at Mount Sinai are the key to Israel's identity, "the greatest evil, therefore, is the deliberate choice to reject this emancipation from Egyptian bondage, to long to be back in the land of slavery and idolatry." As the story of the golden calf suggests, evil is first equated with an apostasy from God whereby the Israelites reject their own liberation. According to Ruether, this implies for feminist theology that "sin is a fear of freedom, a longing for the security of bondage." According to Ruether, sin is similar to what Martin Heidegger called "inauthentic existence," that is to say, not wanting to live for yourself but living like everybody else. While Christians are certainly called to live their lives in responsibility before God, guided by the liberating word of the gospel and not tied to the law, Ruether's interpretation does justice neither to the story of the golden calf nor to the immense perversity of evil. The story of the golden calf does not just show the perverse longing for the flesh pots of Egypt, but also the introduction of gods of one's own making and the rejection of the one living God. As Austrian theologian Susanne Heine (b. 1942) rightly cautions: "With the prohibition against images the biblical tra-

169. For this and the preceding quote, see Rosemary Radford Ruether, *Woman Guides: Readings toward a Feminist Theology* (Boston: Beacon, 1985), 82.

dition also rejects all attempts to gain control of God as an 'object' that can be manipulated and to claim him for all possible interests."[170] While Ruether's interpretation of evil is certainly a needed perspective coming from feminist theology, it dare not obliterate the fact that God is neither a God of feminism nor a God of male domination, but one who calls to judgment both feminists and male chauvinists if they forsake loyalty to God in the pursuit of a mistaken loyalty to themselves.

Angela West arrives at the issue of the feminist concept of sin from a very different angle. From Judith Plaskow's analysis of sin she gathers that the female temptation to sin is a lack of self-assertion and the underdevelopment or negation of the self.[171] For the male, however, sin is primarily pride and self-assertion. Yet West questions whether the female is really more innocent, only needing more of what the male has in excess. For instance, when we talk about the use of modern technology, presumably a field in which males exert their power, we note that females use it just as much.[172] Peace and justice for one sex or the other cannot be attained simply by turning the victimizer into the victim or by reversing the order of scape-goating. Instead, the Christian feminist theologian in particular must be able to acknowledge that sin poisons not only males in power but that women also have their own part in violence and injustice. Therefore West defends the Augustinian notion of original sin, saying, "The ways in which we are sinful are historically and culturally conditioned . . . and sin is patterned according to race, gender, and class."[173] Though we should always strive for equality and mutual recognition between the sexes, humans form indeed a community of sinful beings, both male and female, who express their alienation from God in different ways.

f. Feet of Clay

What should we make of these contemporary analyses of sin that could be examined even further? First of all, we must acknowledge that sin is a theological concept and signifies the wrong relationship of humanity to God

170. Susanne Heine, *Matriarchs, Goddesses, and Images of God: A Critique of Feminist Theology,* trans. John Bowden (Minneapolis: Augsburg, 1989), 34.

171. See Angela West, *Deadly Innocence: Feminist Theology and the Mythology of Sin* (London: Cassell, 1995), 1.

172. See West, *Deadly Innocence,* 106f.

173. West, *Deadly Innocence,* 110.

which in turn results in a wrong relationship to oneself and the world around us. Sin never occurs just between me and my God and it never occurs just between me and some other person. Sin is not just an individualistic event, but has communal implications. What occurs between me and God always has an impact on individuals and the world around me. Therefore it is only consequential that liberation theology and feminist theology have pointed to the communal and structural aspects of human sinfulness. There is a web of warped relationships in which others get caught because of our actions and in which we ourselves get entangled. It is actually the deepest insight of the so-called doctrine of original sin that from the very beginning we are born, raised, and live in a sinful world that draws us into its fangs and to which we willingly succumb. As the "Confession and Forgiveness" in the *Evangelical Lutheran Worship* states at the beginning of the church service: "We confess that we are captive to sin and cannot free ourselves. We have sinned against you [God] in thought, word, and deed, by what we have done and by what we have left undone."[174] This means that on the one hand we are caught in this web of sinfulness, and on the other hand we contribute to it through our own doings or omissions.

We cannot free ourselves from this web and from our inclinations. As Thomas Hobbes wrote in his *Leviathan,* there is "a general inclination of all mankind, a perpetual and restless desire of power after power, that ceases only in death. And the cause of this, is not always that a man hopes for a more intensive delight, than he has already attained to; or that he cannot be content with a moderate power; but because he cannot assure the power and the means to live well, which he has presently, without acquisition of more."[175] The picture portrayed by Hobbes characterizes in a nutshell the human potential and its sinful shortcomings. Since human beings are finite, they can never be assured that their strivings will not be thwarted by someone or something else. Without the salvific covenant that God extends to humanity, human beings cannot be certain that they will succeed in the end in ridding themselves of sinfulness. There is a restless striving for power or, in other words, an egotistical self-centeredness in humans that uses everyone and everything else as a means and not as an end. Does this then imply that human beings are so enslaved by their sinful self-centeredness that they have no freedom whatsoever?

174. *Evangelical Lutheran Worship* (Minneapolis: Augsburg Fortress, 2006), 95.
175. Thomas Hobbes, *Leviathan,* ed. and abridged with an intro. John Plamenatz (Glasgow: William Collins, Fontana Books, 1962), 123.

No, even Hobbes would not agree to that. Admittedly, humans have no power beyond that which is in their immediate vicinity. They cannot achieve their own salvation. But through enlightened self-interest they can renounce some of their struggle for power so that there is peace and the possibility of communal coexistence. While Hobbes is not optimistic enough to assume that a human being could fulfill the golden rule, to love one's neighbor as oneself, humans possess the insight to refrain from doing to others what they do not want others to do to them. Since we are humans and not God our peaceful existence and coexistence on earth is never firmly assured. Our intrinsic sinful inclinations leave us with feet of clay.

III. Humanity as a Community of Men and Women

In the so-called priestly creation account, we read factually that when God created humans, he created them as man and woman. In the same way we read in the Yahwistic creation account in Genesis 2 that man was created by God and then the woman was created. While this twofoldness of man and woman has been there from the very beginning of humanity, we should also note that God did not create husband and wife. That man and woman come together in a marital union is only subsequently expressed when we read in Genesis 2:24: "Therefore a man leaves his father and his mother and clings to his wife, and they become one flesh." While marriage was very important in Old Testament times, it was not portrayed as having been given with the creation of man and woman, but as a result of that creation. As Claus Westermann writes, this verse "points to the basic power of love between man and woman" and it does so "in contrast to the established institutions and partly in opposition to them. . . . There is a basic love between man and woman."[1] This is more than just a community of men and women; it is a mutual attraction. Yet man and woman are not identical. Because they are different they are attractive to each other. Even in homosexuality the mutual attractiveness is not constituted by sameness, but by complementary difference.

---

1. So Claus Westermann, *Genesis 1–11: A Commentary,* trans. John J. Scullion (Minneapolis: Augsburg, 1984), 233, in his explanation of Genesis 2:24.

7. Distinction and Unity of Man and Woman

In some German universities in the early 1970s, women's studies were inaugurated that were supposed to investigate scientifically the role of women in a society dominated by men. The difference between the male view of women and the female reality experienced in society was supposed to be thematized with the goal of asserting that men and women are of equal value and therefore should have equal rights. Since many feminists maintained at the same time that there is also a specific culture of women, gender studies evolved in the middle of the 1970s to analyze the difference and the relationship between biological gender and the sociocultural role attributed to one sex or the other. The main point of these gender studies is that there is no cause-effect relationship between biological gender and the role this gender plays in society. While biological gender is usually fixed, the role in society is variable and can change. This means that the relationship between the sexes is changeable and not unchangeably set. That the roles of men and women have always been in flux can be traced throughout history. For instance, in the German state of Bavaria it was not until 1903 that women were allowed to study at universities. This made it possible for Amalie "Emmy" Noether (1882-1935) to study mathematics and to obtain a Ph.D. at the University of Erlangen in 1907. When she was called as a post-doc to the University of Göttingen, which then belonged to the Prussian state, it was not possible for a woman to do a second thesis there. It was not until 1919 with the changed situation in the Weimar Republic that she was able to do a second thesis and was promoted to associate professor in 1922 at the University of Göttingen. This paradigmatically shows how the role of a woman had changed at the beginning of the twentieth century.

One must also remember the often very heated discussions that many mainline denominations had in the last quarter of the twentieth century regarding the ordination of women to the ministry. Today, most mainline Protestant denominations accept women into the pulpit the same as they do men. We could also look at the changing situation in many families, where it is not just the mother who cares for the infant, but increasingly also the father. Does this mean that men and women are identical and that specific gender-related characteristics are only due to social conditioning?

1. Difference and Equality of Men and Women: The Issue of Gender

Since humans are social beings, the question has often been raised as to whether many of the specifically human characteristics are inborn or are the result of social conditions. Lately the issue as to whether male and female modes of human behavior are the result of social conditioning has especially gained prominence. We have already noted the verdict of Ashley Montagu from 1973: "The notable thing about human behavior is that it is learned. It is nonsense to talk about the genetic determinacy of human behavior."[2] Categorical statements like this, however, seldom hold up against scientific scrutiny. We might think here, for instance, of the impact of certain hormones that enhance or diminish sex-specific behavior. Since we already mentioned some characteristics of sex-specific behavior (see chapter 2) under behavioral aspects, we will briefly review the results of gender studies.

The term "sex" designates the different aspects of human biology between male and female human beings. The term "gender," however, refers to the culturally and historically based differences in the roles, attitudes, and behaviors of men and women. The notion of gender mainstreaming does not want to abolish the biological differences between men and women but to give both men and women equal access to all functions in daily life, from professional opportunities to domestic matters. While the notion of equal opportunity is primarily one of fairness, it may also be one that could enrich the human community. Since both men and women introduce their own sexually determined viewpoints or preferences into their respective sphere, a synergistic effect might evolve.

But the question is "whether gender really is separate from sex or

2. Ashley Montagu, ed., in his intro. to *Man and Aggression,* 2nd ed. (New York: Oxford University Press, 1973), xvii.

whether instead, the roles and functions we associate with gender actually grow out of biological differences."[3] Here the debate is far from over. Some deny that a woman's positioning in history and society is simply due to her sex; others insist that at least part of her position is due to her sex "because of hormones, brain structure, and other biological features."[4] Indeed, "there is general agreement that there are several sex differences in what is commonly viewed as gender role behavior."[5] These include juvenile play behavior, specific cognitive abilities, personality characteristics, and manifestations of neural asymmetry. In order to assess the significance of these differences we must note the following:

1. These differences do indeed exist and they seem to express themselves in different pursuits in life.
2. These differences, however, are not overwhelming. With respect to some aspects of behavior (e.g., physical aggression) they are small; with respect to others (e.g., leadership effectiveness) they are near zero.[6]
3. The brain has a certain plasticity that can be affected by many factors, including experience. "For example, a repeated experience that results in a particular set of synapses can lead to long-term potentiation (or alternately, depression) of the activity of those synapses."[7] This means that certain things can be learned and once learned they become part of oneself.

Still another thing is worth considering. While the brains of men and women are different, both retain "sex-atypical abilities, albeit on a diminished level."[8] With regard to the brain there is no justification for relegating a person to a (sex-)specific role since abilities of the other sex are still some-

3. Georgia Warnke, *Debating Sex and Gender* (Oxford: Oxford University Press, 2011), 1.

4. Warnke, *Debating Sex and Gender,* 118.

5. Melissa Hines, "Gonadal Hormones and Sexual Differentiation of Human Behavior: Effects of Psychosexual and Cognitive Development," in *Sexual Differentiation of the Brain,* ed. Akira Matsumoto (New York: CRC, 1999), 266, who also provides more details for the following.

6. For the exact statistics, see Janet Shibley Hyde, "New Directions in the Study of Gender Similarities and Differences," in *Current Directions in Gender Psychology,* ed. Wendy A. Goldberg (Boston: Allyn & Bacon, 2010), 181.

7. So Hyde, "New Directions," 185.

8. James C. Woodson and Roger A. Gorski, "Structural Sex Differences in the Mammalian Brain: Reconsidering the Male/Female Dichotomy," in *Sexual Differentiation of the Brain,* ed. Matsumoto, 233.

what present. Psychologist James C. Woodson and neurobiologist Roger A. Gorki claim: "Even in adulthood, the female brain appears to retain much of its inherent bipotential."[9] We may conclude that from the neurological side there is a fundamental gender equality that mitigates against any discrimination. It allows for equal opportunities for both men and women and does not dictate which actual roles they must play in public and private life.

While the gender-specific differences may predispose men and women to certain behaviors, they are not necessarily determinative for a certain behavior. The same can also be said for most bodily differences. In most cases, men are taller and heavier; have deeper voices; use up more calories; have a shorter life expectancy; and have more muscle cells, longer legs, and heavier brains. Women have a better connection between both sides of the brain and a better blood supply in the brain. Women also are less prone to virus and bacterial infections since they produce more antibodies on account of having two X-chromosomes over against one X-chromosome in men (information for the immune system is contained in the X-chromosome). Then there are some specifically sex-related differences. Women have a menopause while men are fertile even at old age. Puberty usually sets in earlier with girls than with boys. On account of the male hormone testosterone men are more aggressive than women and are more easily prone to bodily violence, while women fight more easily with words. Men have their fatty deposit usually in the stomach region, while for women it is around the lower abdomen and the hips, perhaps to protect the embryo during pregnancy. Yet all of these sex-specific characteristics are not strictly determinative. The only biologically given is that only women bear children.

Therefore Wolfhart Pannenberg pointed out many years ago that the right distribution of tasks between men and women is exclusively derived from the point of how the relationship between man and woman in the corresponding situation of society can be most profitably arranged for both partners, keeping in mind "that only women bring children into the world. It must also include an appropriate regulation of the education of the children."[10] Indeed, the roles of men and women can be quite flexible. For instance, in farm communities it is most common that a farm is run by the farmer who is a man and who may also be responsible for hiring any necessary farm workers. When we think of the Reformer Martin Luther and his

---

9. Woodson and Gorski, "Structural Sex Differences in the Mammalian Brain," 247.

10. Wolfhart Pannenberg, *What Is Man? Contemporary Anthropology in Theological Perspective,* trans. Duane Priebe (Philadelphia: Fortress, 1970), 92.

wife Katharina (1499-1552), then the situation was quite different.[11] Luther saw his role as a teacher and reformer, whereas his wife brewed beer, tended to the house and the garden, and acquired a little farm, the Bora family estate, in Zöllsdorf near Leipzig. We never hear that Luther himself was involved in hiring servants for either the house or the farm. This was all Katharina's duty, according to the arrangement that had evolved from their different interests and corresponding needs.

2. Men and Women in the Bible

a. The Old Testament Account

When we look at the Bible we also note different arrangements in the relationship between men and women. In the Old Testament "women appear for the most part as minor or subordinate figures; yet they play an essential role in the record of Israel's faith and include some of the best remembered actors in the biblical story."[12] Nevertheless, the economic and legal position of the woman is severely restricted within Israelite society as was customary in the ancient Near East. At the same time the dignity and also the right of the woman are given considerable attention. While an unmarried young woman lived within the kinship of her father, once she was married she was transferred into the family of her husband and lived under its juridical power. To compensate the father of the bride for the loss of his daughter, he received a bride price from the husband. In terms of inheritance, the main emphasis was on family and kinship and not on the woman (see Numbers 36). It was believed that whatever happened in terms of marriage or death, the integrity and strength of a tribe should not be weakened. This is the reason why a wife did not inherit from her husband, or the daughters from their father, except when there was no male heir (Num. 27:8). The property remained in the family circle and the family strength was maintained through the male. Women married into a family, but not men.

While a woman could address her husband even as her lord, a wife of

11. For a good assessment of Katie, see Kirsi Stjerna, "Katie Luther: A Mirror to the Promises and Failures of the Reformation," in *Caritas et Reformatio: Essays on Church and Society in Honor of Carter Lindberg,* ed. David M. Whitford (St. Louis: Concordia, 2002), 27-39, esp. 31.

12. So, as we will see, very correctly Phyllis A. Bird, "Women (OT)," in *The Anchor Bible Dictionary,* ed. David Noel Freedman, 6 vols. (New York: Doubleday, 1992), 6:951.

an Israelite was by no means on the level of a slave. Even if the woman was taken captive in war, she could be taken in marriage, but she was not unprotected. In case the husband was not happy with her, the stipulation was: "You shall let her go free and not sell her for money. You must not treat her as a slave, since you have dishonored her" (Deut. 21:14). Though the main duty of a married woman was in the husband's household, looking after the flocks, working in the fields, and doing the household chores, "in exceptional circumstances, a woman could even take part in public affairs."[13] In the history of Israel, there are important women, such as Sarah, Rebecca, Leah, and Rachel, the wives of the patriarchs. There are also the prophetess Miriam (Exod. 15:20), Moses' and Aaron's sister, and Deborah the prophetess and judge in Israel (Judg. 4:4). The Moabite woman Ruth deserves mention too, to whom a whole book of the Old Testament is devoted, and last but not least, the widow Judith, who contrary to the usual image of widows was exceedingly rich. We read of her in the Apocrypha in the book that bears her name: "She was beautiful in appearance, and was very lovely to behold. Her husband Manasseh had left her gold and silver, men and women slaves, livestock, and fields; and she maintained this estate. No one spoke ill of her, for she feared God with great devotion" (Jth. 8:7f.).

While the Genesis account of the creation of the woman was narrated from the perspective of a man and his needs, nevertheless "all emphasis is laid on the point that the woman alone is the corresponding vis-à-vis, which means neither as just as a help for work or in sexual respect, but in a comprehensive partnership."[14]

b. The New Testament Account

When we briefly look at the New Testament, we note first of all that in contrast to the official Judaism of his time, Jesus addressed women with unprecedented openness. The Gospels portray Jesus as one "who accepted women both as followers and as traveling companions."[15] According to John 8:3-11, the scribes and the Pharisees brought a woman to Jesus who had been caught in adultery, expecting that Jesus would apply the Mosaic law,

13. Roland DeVaux, *Ancient Israel,* vol. 1, *Social Institutions* (New York: McGraw-Hill Paperback, 1965), 39.
14. So Jürgen Hebach, "Frau II. Altes Testament," in *TRE,* 11:423.
15. Ben Witherington III, "Women (NT)," in *The Anchor Bible Dictionary,* 6:958.

which commanded that such a woman should be stoned to death.[16] But he confronted the accusers with their own sinfulness and refused to condemn her. Jesus allowed a woman sinner (a prostitute) to anoint his feet and he even pronounced forgiveness of her numerous sins (Luke 7:47). He also healed a crippled woman on the Sabbath, breaking the law prohibiting any work on that day of rest, and called her "a daughter of Abraham" (Luke 13:16). Jesus also allowed an officially unclean woman to touch his clothes (Mark 5:27f.) and healed her. These are just a few incidents that showed Jesus' sovereignty over the cultic and cultural restrictions that were placed on women and their relationship to men.

We could also point to the significance of women in Jesus' own life history, for instance, the two sisters Mary and Martha, and Mary Magdalene, who may have had a questionable reputation. In Jesus' own genealogy Matthew mentions four women: Tamar, Rahab, Ruth, and "the wife of Uriah" (Matt. 1:3-6). We should also not forget that according to the Gospels the first witnesses to the resurrection were women and not men (John 20:11-18). Of course, when it comes to the testable assertion of Jesus' resurrection as the Christ, Paul excludes any women from the account (1 Cor. 15:1-8) because according to the then valid Jewish law women could not serve as legal witnesses. Yet in the narrative accounts in the Gospels, women are adduced as witnesses. This means that Jesus broke the legal and cultural restrictions of his time with regard to women. This attitude also set a precedent for the early church and its main agents.

c. The Account of the Nascent Church

The New Testament trend of asserting equality between the sexes was continued in the early church. For instance, we read that Philip the evangelist had "four unmarried daughters who had the gift of prophecy" (Acts 21:9). We hear of Tabitha, a female disciple of Peter, who "was devoted to good works and acts of charity" (Acts 9:36). We also read of the married couple Priscilla and Aquila who explained to the Jew Apollos "the Way of God . . . more accurately" (Acts 18:26). Paul also greets the couple who have "a church in their house" (1 Cor. 16:19). This means that a Christian couple instruct others in the Christian faith and also have a house church in their

---

16. Although John 7:53–8:11 is not found in the earliest manuscripts, it reflects actions that are in keeping with the historical Jesus.

home. Paul even mentions that they "work with me in Christ Jesus, and . . . risk their necks for my life" (Rom. 16:4). We should not forget Lydia, "a worshiper of God," meaning that she attended the Jewish worship service without being a Jew herself, and she was a well-to-do businesswoman.[17] She and her household became the first Christians in Europe and were baptized by Paul (Acts 16:14f.).

Another important supporter of Paul on his missionary journeys was Phoebe, "a deacon of the church at Cenchreae," near present-day Corinth (Rom. 16:1). Paul calls her a sister in the same manner as he talks about others as brothers, showing her equality with men in the church. When he mentions that she is a deaconess of the church, that may not necessarily imply a certain official position, but it may show that she was engaged in helping not only individuals, but the whole congregation and also carrying "his letter to the Romans."[18] That is perhaps the reason why Paul calls her "a benefactor of many and of myself as well" (Rom. 16:2). Evidently she had decided to travel to Rome and it seems that Paul asked her to take this letter to the Roman congregation with her and deliver it to the Christians in Rome. As the New Testament scholar Eduard Lohse (b. 1924) mentions in his commentary on that letter: "Phoebe must have been quite a courageous woman that she set out on that long journey all by herself."[19] Pliny the Younger (A.D. 61–ca. 112) mentions in a letter to Trajan two female slaves who called themselves *ministrae* (ministers or deaconesses).[20]

We notice that in various ways women were involved in spreading the gospel and in supporting the nascent Christian church. These women were by no means illiterate members of the lower class, but quite often representatives of the upper middle class. Keeping in mind the Jewish law that provided the socioreligious context of most Christians in the early Christian communities, this shows "a decisive step toward a partnership-relationship between man and woman."[21]

But what should we make of Paul's comment in 1 Corinthians 14:33b-36?

---

17. For more details on Lydia, see Lynn H. Cohick, *Women in the World of the Earliest Christians* (Grand Rapids: Baker, 2009), 307f.

18. Cohick, *Women in the World of the Earliest Christians,* 304. See 304f. about the issue of whether Phoebe was actually a deaconess.

19. Eduard Lohse, *Der Brief an die Römer* (Göttingen: Vandenhoeck & Ruprecht, 2003), 404, in his exegesis of Romans 16:1.

20. Pliny, *Letters and Panegyricus* (X.96.7), trans. Betty Radice (Cambridge, MA: Harvard University Press, 1969), 2:289.

21. So Hermann Ringeling, "Frau IV. Neues Testament," in *TRE,* 11:433.

As in all the churches of the saints, women should be silent in the churches. For they are not permitted to speak, but should be subordinate, as the law also says. If there is anything they desire to know, let them ask their husbands at home. For it is shameful for a woman to speak in church. Or did the word of God originate with you? Or are you the only ones it has reached?

Paul seems to argue here according to Jewish custom. Though in the Jewish synagogue there was no law that did not allow women to talk, it was customary for women to listen silently to the synagogue service. This is in line with the Roman and Hellenistic custom that women should not talk in public assemblies.[22] From a passage in Deuteronomy the rabbis then deduced that women did not have the right to talk where men were assembled.[23] If women wanted to learn something, then they should ask their husbands at home. Unmarried women and widows were not considered in that kind of decision. Since the gospel did not start in Corinth and since the Corinthian Christians are not the only Christians, they must adhere to tradition. This seems to be Paul's answer to the people in Corinth who had allowed women to speak in church. Yet if we accept this as Paul's position, what do we make then of Paul's comment in 1 Corinthians 11:5, where he says, "But any woman who prays or prophesies with her head unveiled disgraces her head — it is one and the same thing as having her head shaved." Without question, Paul presumes the active participation of charismatically gifted women in the church service. The same is true for men as he says in the preceding verse. In contrast to Judaism, Christian men and women could publicly pray and prophesy in the church service. Still there was a difference between the sexes: in line with ancient Near Eastern tradition, women with their hair uncovered were considered indecent, whereas for men this was not so.[24]

22. For the cultural context, see the comments by Andrew Perriman, *Speaking of Women: Interpreting Paul* (Leicester: Apollos, 1998), 144ff.

23. See Hermann Strack and Paul Billerbeck, *Kommentar zum Neuen Testament aus Talmud und Midrasch*, vol. 3, *Die Briefe des Neuen Testaments und die Offenbarung Johannis*, 2nd ed. (Munich: C. H. Beck, 1954), 467, where Billerbeck explains: "The Old Testament synagogue prohibited, not in principle but in fact, women from speaking publicly in cultic assemblies."

24. Philip H. Towner, *The Letters to Timothy and Titus*, New International Commentary on the New Testament (Grand Rapids: Eerdmans, 2006), 196, explains that the veil (head scarf) was the "symbol of the faithful Roman wife" in contrast to the "new woman" who made her entry into Roman society in the first century A.D.

Should Paul now have argued in one and the same letter for and against women's participation in the church? Even if we assume that 1 Corinthians actually contains two letters, Paul would still contradict himself. Therefore many exegetes assume that this passage in 1 Corinthians 14 in which Paul seems to tell the women to be silent in the church services is a later interpolation that is more in line with the later pastoral letters than with genuine Pauline letters.[25]

What, then, was Paul's actual position regarding the relationship and difference between men and women? On the one hand, since Paul was a Jew, his Jewish background informed his understanding; on the other hand, since he was now a Christian, he was informed by Jesus' own position. In the temple that King Herod (73-4 B.C.) built, there was a special court for women. In the synagogue men and women sat separately. Yet according to Rabbi Jehuda (ca. 150-220), a pious Jew must praise God every day that he had not been created a pagan, a woman, and ignorant of rabbinic teachings.[26] This shows that in Judaism at the time of Jesus women played certainly second fiddle. This was different from many pagan cults where women were sometimes active as priestesses. The famous Pythia at the oracle at Delphi supposedly foretold the future. Though we do not find any women among the twelve, Jesus, as we had mentioned, had female disciples among his wider circle of followers and broke through restrictions imposed on women by Jewish customs and law. Therefore Paul could also argue that "in the one Spirit we are all baptized into one body — Jews or Greeks, slaves or free — and we are all made to drink of one Spirit" (1 Cor. 12:13). All Christians, both men and women, are one in Christ and therefore are called to common service and to witness. In Christ, Paul argues, everyone is a new creation and all are made "ambassadors for Christ" (2 Cor. 5:20). As Paul writes: "There is no longer Jew or Greek, there is no longer slave or free, there is no longer male and female; for all of you are one in Christ Jesus. And if you belong to Christ, then you are Abraham's offspring, heirs according to the promise" (Gal. 3:28f.). There is no salvational difference between Christians. All expect the same destiny.

Paul follows in the footsteps of Jesus, emphasizing the commonality of men and women. Yet Paul was not an enthusiast and realistically assessed the culture of his time. While it was a matter of fact for him that women are

25. So even the Anchor Collins Study Bible in the comment to this passage.

26. Strack and Billerbeck, *Die Briefe des Neuen Testaments und die Offenbarung Johannis,* 611. Jacob Neusner, *An Introduction to Judaism: Textbook and Reader* (Louisville: Westminster John Knox, 1991), 176, states very tellingly about women in the Mishnah: women "are perceived as the indicative abnormality in a world in which men are the norm."

co-workers "in the work of the Gospel" (Phil. 4:3), he also urged Christians to hold on to "whatever is true, whatever is honorable, whatever is just, whatever is pure, whatever is pleasing, whatever is commendable" (Phil. 4:8). In the case of Corinth, he therefore emphasized the tradition of women covering their heads. In other words, he commended Christians to observe the cultural and societal relationships in which they found themselves. Along this line also is the following advice: "Wives, be subject to your husbands as you are to the Lord" (Eph. 5:22); this is because it was clear at that time that the husband was the head of the home. Yet with this advice the patriarchal domination of the husband is not sanctioned since it is introduced with the admonition: "Be subject to one another out of reverence for Christ" (Eph. 5:21). This means that men and women are dependent on each other and this mutuality is sanctioned through Christ.

Summarizing Paul's position, we could say that Paul neither advocated any Hellenistic striving for the emancipation of women nor did he regard women as inferior to men. He also did not advocate the total renunciation of one's sexuality or a fundamental change of the societal order of his time. With the expectation that Christ might come any time, such radical and fundamental change to society did not seem necessary.

Paul's hesitancy could also be interpreted as an advocacy of the status quo. In the pastoral letters, for instance, we read: "Let a woman learn in silence with full submission. I permit no woman to teach or to have authority over a man; she is to keep silent. . . . Yet she will be saved through childbearing" (1 Tim. 2:11, 12, 15). We might still concede that this restriction to silence was given to curb any enthusiastic exuberance that easily could fall prey to heresy (2 Tim. 3:6f.). The emphasis on child-bearing — strange as it may sound to us — did not simply sanction the Jewish notion that through the pains of childbirth women can compensate for the curse uttered against Eve in connection to her expulsion from Eden (see Gen. 3:16). Here it was much more an injunction against certain heretical teachers who "forbid marriage and demand abstinence from foods, which God created to be received with thanksgiving by those who believe and know the truth" (1 Tim. 4:3). Marriage and giving birth to children should not be shunned by women in favor of an enthusiastic, ascetic lifestyle. It could also be seen as an injunction against the new women's movement at that time that showed an aversion to having children and practiced abortion to pursue a free life unencumbered by pregnancy and giving birth to children.[27] Nevertheless, a

---

27. See Towner, *Letters to Timothy and Titus,* 234f., in his extensive comments.

passage such as the one in 1 Timothy 2 could be easily used to bar women from meaningful participation in leadership functions in the Christian community and in worship and suggest that their actual place is in the house and in the kitchen. Up to the present time 1 Timothy 2 has often been advocated as a "divinely sanctioned Christian lifestyle," though there have always been notable exceptions.

After having summarized the biblical findings, we realize that the distinction between men and women has never been done away with. Yet Jesus and Paul viewed men and women as a corporate unity working together and destined for the kingdom.

3. The Phenomenon of Human Sexuality

Sexuality is one of the vital forces that determines life and has a strong impact on all religions. It is the exclusive means of reproduction in higher living species. While through asexual reproduction organisms create a genetically similar or identical copy of themselves without contribution of genetic material from another organism, sexual reproduction creates descendants that have a combination of genetic material contributed from two usually different members of the same species. Bacteria and viruses divide asexually and most plants are capable of reproduction without seeds or spores. But plants can also reproduce sexually and bacteria can also exchange genetic information through conjugation/copulation. Then there is the phenomenon of parthenogenesis, which means the growth and development of an embryo or seed without fertilization by a male counterpart. This occurs naturally in some species of lower plants and lower invertebrates (water fleas and aphids). Even some vertebrates, such as reptiles, fish, and even birds, can have natural parthenogenesis. It can even be artificially induced in higher vertebrates.

a. The Peculiarity of Human Sexuality

For the human being, sexual reproduction, or the coming together in copulation of a man and a woman, is the exclusive means of producing offspring and assuring the survival of the human species. The same reproductive process is operative in the animals with which humans have had more intimate contact through hunting, agriculture, and animal husbandry. Since sexual procreation has been *the* means of human survival, the sexual organs of human beings and animals have always provided immense fascination for humanity. From the Paleolithic age we have depictions of the sexual organs of humans and animals since "phallus and vulva were the symbols of fertility, of vegetation, and the renewal of life among people, animals, and in the fields."[28]

Since procreation and its success were often shrouded to a certain degree in mystery, it is no surprise that in many religions fertility and sexuality have played an important role. In the Sumerian religion of Mesopotamia, for instance, a holy marriage was celebrated as a re-enactment of creation through which the fertility of the herds and of the fields could be assured.[29] Sometimes sexuality was virtually shunned, such as in early Buddhism. Since sexuality is connected with desire and, as Buddha had realized, all desires essentially lead to suffering and therefore to the cycle of death and rebirth, sexuality is viewed as undesirable. On the other hand, in tantric Buddhism, sexual union symbolized cosmic energy and so was seen to be analogous to the process of enlightenment. Either through suppression or enhancement sexuality was always integrated into the religious sphere in order to regulate and channel this basic drive in humanity.

Such regulative means of sexuality are appropriate for humans because in contrast to the animals in humanity's immediate environment, human sexuality is not limited to certain seasons or an annual rhythm. Many animals have certain mating seasons. It is then that males either fight with each other for superiority in order to copulate with females, or try to entice females through some kind of courtship behavior. But this instinctive behavior no longer works in humans. Humans can be sexually active at any given time and therefore the activation of human sexuality has always been subjected to social and cultural factors.

b. The Old Testament Assessment

In the priestly creation account the creation of humanity is intimately connected with their sexuality since once they were created as male and female,

28. Peter Gerlitz, "Sexualität. I. Religionsgeschichtlich," in *TRE,* 31:187.

29. See Richard M. Davidson, *Flame of Yahweh: Sexuality in the Old Testament* (Peabody, MA: Hendrickson, 2007), 82, who talks about a "Divinization of Sex in Pagan Worship."

they received the divine command to "be fruitful and multiply" (Gen. 1:28). Similarly, in the Yahwistic account, once the woman was created and the man recognized her, the narrative states: "Therefore a man leaves his father and his mother and clings to his wife, and they become one flesh" (Gen. 2:24). Yet the painful experience of childbirth and the patriarchal rule of the husband over the wife are only mentioned in connection with, and as a result of, the fall of humanity (Gen. 3:16). This means that both the priestly and the Yahwistic creation accounts lead immediately from sexuality to procreation.

There are also other avenues for sexuality which, however, do not find divine approval. For instance, if a woman is pretty she can easily become the sexual victim of men. This is true with Sarai, Abram's wife, who "was very beautiful" (Gen. 12:14) and therefore was taken into Pharaoh's house. Then we hear of David, who saw Bathsheba, a woman who "was very beautiful" (2 Sam. 11:2), and he seduced her. We are also told of Absalom, who had "a beautiful sister whose name was Tamar" (2 Sam. 13:1) whom her brother Amnon seduced by force. This means that the attractiveness of women can easily lead them into danger, but it cannot be exploited to manipulate men as it is quite often done today. Only in the Apocrypha do we read of Judith, who in the eyes of the Assyrians was "marvelously beautiful" (Jth. 10:14), who seduced Holofernes and decapitated him.[30]

The actual locus of sexuality in the Old Testament as well as in the New Testament is within the marriage of husband and wife. In that context there is the Song of Solomon, which is actually a collection of love songs. If Solomon were actually the author, one should know that "King Solomon loved many foreign women" (1 Kings 11:1) and "among his wives were seven hundred princesses and three hundred concubines" (1 Kings 11:3). Whether Solomon is indeed the author of this collection is very difficult to ascertain. In the traditional Jewish understanding, it is a religious allegory expressing God's love for Israel and narrating the story of their relationship to each other. With this kind of interpretation it was received into the Old Testament canon. In Christian circles it has been interpreted as an allegory of Christ's love for the church. Yet already Theodore of Mopsuestia (ca. 351-428) understood this book as a collection of secular love songs. In eight chapters it expresses the beauty of the woman and languish for the beloved. Neither an allegorical nor a mythological interpretation seems to suffice.

30. See Tikva Frymer-Kensky, "Sex and Sexuality," in *The Anchor Bible Dictionary*, 5:1144.

The main topic is the mutual attraction of the sexes, their desire for each other, and the longed-for sexual union. This "secular" love is placed in a world that is understood as God's divine creation. The Song of Solomon shows that humanity can find its fulfillment in the mutual love of two people before God as they encounter each other as partners. There is no indication of a dualism between body and soul. The bodily aspect of humanity is not shunned and the sexual attraction is neither profane nor something simply mechanical. It is a gift of God to be enjoyed. As Old Testament scholar Richard M. Davidson (b. 1946) states: "In a unified song, then, the love relationship between a specific heterosexual couple — man and woman — is extolled and celebrated."[31] That the Song of Solomon was accepted into the Old Testament shows that the people of Old Testament were down-to-earth people who knew how to enjoy sexuality as a gift of God.

c. The New Testament Assessment

The New Testament assessment provides in one sense a continuation of the Old Testament perspective. The same acts that were outlawed in the Old Testament still stand under divine verdict. Paul is very clear on this point when he tells the Christians in Corinth: "Do not be deceived! Fornicators, idolaters, adulterers, male prostitutes, sodomites, . . . none of these will inherit the kingdom of God" (1 Cor. 6:9). This is very much in line with Leviticus 18:22.[32]

However, when we hear Jesus mention with approval those "who have made themselves eunuchs for the sake of the kingdom of heaven" (Matt. 19:12), we might wonder whether he introduced a new standard with regard to sexuality. Paul, too, says about sexuality within the marital bond: "Do not deprive one another except perhaps by agreement for a set time, to devote yourselves to prayer, and then come together again, so that Satan may not tempt you because of your lack of self-control. This I say by way of concession, not of command. I wish that all were as I myself am" (1 Cor. 7:5ff.). And then he continues: "To the unmarried and the widows I say that it is well for them to remain unmarried as I am. But if they are not practicing

---

31. Davidson, *Flame of Yahweh,* in his extensive treatment of the Song of Solomon, 545-632, here 561.

32. See Davidson, *Flame of Yahweh,* 637.

self-control, they should marry. For it is better to marry than to be aflame with passion" (1 Cor. 7:8f.). Why is sexuality for married couples restricted by periods of abstinence? Why are there eunuchs for the kingdom? Why does Paul prefer that people remain unmarried?

With Jesus the story is relatively simple. As we can gather from the Sermon on the Mount, Jesus had a high regard for sexuality within the marriage bond (Matt. 5:27-32). Yet he started his ministry with the telling words: "The time is fulfilled, and the kingdom of God has come near; repent, and believe in the good news" (Mark 1:15). His message and his proclamation were eschatological. He did not spell out certain eschatological doctrines, but confronted the people with the radical decision for or against God. This demand for a decision became at the same time a decision for or against Jesus and his actions. "Follow me, and let the dead bury their own dead" (Matt. 8:22); "no one who puts a hand to the plow and looks back is fit for the kingdom of God" (Luke 9:62); "and blessed is anyone who takes no offense at me" (Matt. 11:6) — these are only a few of the passages that show the urgency of an immediate decision here and now. Jesus emphasized the in-breaking of the kingdom of God and thereby "the now" as the decisive point of history. Therefore even human sexuality, properly channeled, which had always been held in high regard among the Israelites and later within the Jewish community, was now no longer important. The kingdom of God and its in-breaking was all that mattered.

Since Paul was a close follower of Jesus and his most important theological interpreter, he, too, emphasized the nearness of the kingdom. He saw himself as "a man who has been appointed to a proper place and the peculiar task in the series of events to be accomplished in the final days of this world."[33] According to Paul, Christ is the end of the law (Rom. 10:4) and the end of history. The old covenant no longer applies since the new covenant has been established (2 Cor. 3:6). But we still live in a transitional period, in a time of faith (2 Cor. 5:7), destined for redemption (Rom. 8:23-25). This means that the Christian existence is a dialectical existence. It is lived in the world, but is not of this world. When the Lord is close at hand, as Paul assumed (Phil. 4:5), then it does not make much sense to marry and to engage in sexual activity. There are more important things on which to focus.

To accuse Paul of despising the body and promoting sexual abstinence per se would not do him justice. In contrast to Hellenism, where the body

---

33. Anton Fridrichsen, in his short but excellent study *The Apostle and His Message,* Uppsala Universitets Årsskrift (Uppsala: Lundae Questska Bokhandeln, 1947), 3.

was only the prison house of the soul, Paul did not hope for a redemption from the body but was convinced that "this perishable body must put on imperishability, and this mortal body must put on immortality" (1 Cor. 15:53). He knew that the body we presently enjoy has no permanence. But a disembodied existence was unthinkable for him. While Gnostics held that the body with all its natural functions is the work of an anti-Godly demiurge, Paul thought differently. In line with the Old Testament and also with Jesus, he held that the body is a creation of God. The body and its sexual function receive a positive valuation and are gifts to be accepted with thanksgiving.

Yet as a Hellenistic Jew, Paul knew the Greco-Roman world and its practices. As the historian Peter Brown (b. 1935) notes: "To sleep with a prostitute was natural enough for a young man in Corinth."[34] People developed in their hearts lusts of impurity "to the degrading of their bodies among themselves" (Rom. 1:24). "Their women exchange natural intercourse for unnatural, and in the same way also the men, giving up natural intercourse with women, were consumed with passion for one another" (Rom. 1:26f.). Since for Christians the body "is a temple of the Holy Spirit" (1 Cor. 6:19), the body must be treated as a gift of God and be kept in tune with God's own command, that is, in terms of sexuality, in the relationship between a man and a woman within the bond of marriage. Paul wanted the Christian community to demonstrate that it is a holy people — segregated from the pagan world. Paul distinguishes between God as the giver of the body and the body itself as God's gift, but does not separate the two. Neither would he condone the exaltation of the body, which is quite often seen in Greco-Roman art. Nor does he condone a rejection of the body as is frequently the case in Gnostic literature. For instance, the Mandeans, a Gnostic group of baptizers who have lived in the region of present-day Iran and Iraq since at least the eighth century A.D., teach a highly dualistic view of humanity. They maintain that the body of the first human being was created by a creator-god, whereas the inner and hidden Adam comes from the sphere of light. The body therefore belongs to darkness, whereas the soul is destined for the realm of light. Small wonder then that when the soul departs from this world, she is said to leave behind "the stinking body" in which she found herself.[35]

---

34. Peter Brown, *The Body and Society: Men, Women and Sexual Renunciation in Early Christianity* (New York: Columbia University Press, 2008 [1988]), 51.

35. So a Mandean text as given in Werner Foerster, *Gnosis: A Selection of Gnostic Texts,*

For Paul, the soul does not return to the realm of light, but to God the creator in order to receive its new imperishable resurrection body. Therefore bodily existence not only belongs to the old perishable world, but also to the new creation in Christ and its eschatological completion. Since the body is part of God's good creation and sexuality is intimately connected with the body, sexual activity is not in principle sinful and wrong. Yet Paul follows here Jesus' admonition in the Sermon on the Mount where not only sexuality, but also sexual desire is reserved for marriage only. In Judaism the woman is usually portrayed as the temptress who wants to seduce the man as is seen in Sirach 26, where we read: "The haughty stare betrays an unchaste wife; her eyelids give her away" (v. 9). Jesus turns the situation around and says, "But I say to you that everyone who looks at a woman with lust has already committed adultery with her in his heart" (Matt. 5:28). For Paul, both man and woman are in the same way in danger and therefore he points out: "Because of cases of sexual immorality, each man should have his own wife and each woman her own husband" (1 Cor. 7:2). Sexual activity is nothing casual and is not on the same level as eating and drinking, as some people in Corinth thought. It is the intimate encounter between two responsible persons and therefore it seems evident for Paul that "the body is meant not for fornication, but for the Lord, and the Lord for the body" (1 Cor. 6:13).

Like Jesus, Paul distinguishes between the belly and the body. Jesus said that what goes into the stomach leaves the belly again and goes out into the sewer. Yet what comes out of a person (body), such as fornication, theft, murder, adultery, and the like, defiles that person (Mark 7:18-22). Therefore any food that is digested in the belly will ultimately be destroyed. Yet the body in terms of bodily existence is more than belly or stomach. It is the representation of a responsibly thinking and acting human being. Moreover, as a corporate community, the bodies of Christians are no longer independent, autonomous entities. Therefore Paul reminds the people in Corinth: "Do you not know that your bodies are members of Christ?" (1 Cor. 6:15). Therefore sexual activity is the most intimate form of a bodily personal communion between two people and cannot be regarded as a thing or something that is simply transitional.

As Jesus pointed out in the Sermon on the Mount and as Paul reemphasized, all sexual activity should occur only within the bonds of marriage. Sexuality as a human constitutive and as executed within the marital

---

trans. and ed. R. McL. Wilson, vol. 2, *Coptic and Mandean Sources* (Oxford: Clarendon, 1974), 261.

bond can indeed be enjoyed without detracting from communion with Christ. But the dualistic worldview of Hellenism and Gnosticism took a different tack. It either condoned sexual licentiousness since the bodily and material was considered inferior and nothing executed there could tarnish the soul, or it advocated an ethical rigorism that saw the material as inferior and therefore to be shunned. While sexual licentiousness certainly had no foundation in the New Testament, ascetic rigorism quite often embraced Paul's statement "I wish that all were as I myself am" (1 Cor. 7:7), meaning unmarried or celibate, as some kind of self-justification for refraining from any sexual activity. Yet Paul speaks here "of both marriage and celibacy as gifts of God."[36]

d. Dualistic Asceticism

While for Paul body and soul belong together, there was a strong trend in the early church to separate the two and to regard the bodily as inferior and even evil. Most influential was Marcion (ca. 85-160), who even founded his own church. He came from Pontus in Asia Minor, was an influential and affluent merchant and ship-owner, and joined the Christian congregation in Rome around A.D. 140. As Tertullian (ca. 150–ca. 230) tells us: "He contributed money to the Catholic Church, which along with himself was afterwards rejected, when he fell away from our truth into his own heresy."[37] Perhaps it was also in Rome that there was an encounter between Bishop Polycarp of Smyrna and Marcion, whom the bishop strongly rejected.[38] It was then that Marcion founded his own church and, as Justin Martyr said, "And this man many have believed, as if he alone knew the truth."[39]

Marcion had a considerable following, which becomes evident from Justin Martyr (103-165) when he relates that Marcion was teaching "his disciples to believe in some other god greater than the Creator. And he, by the aid of the devils, caused many of every nation to speak blasphemies, and to deny that God is the maker of the universe, and to assert that some other being, greater than He, has done greater works."[40] In this quotation an essen-

---

36. So Joseph A. Fitzmyer, *First Corinthians* (New Haven, CT: Yale University Press, 2008), 282, in his exegesis of 1 Corinthians 7:7.

37. Tertullian, *Against Marcion* (4.4), in *ANF,* 3:349.

38. Irenaeus, *Against Heresies* (3.3.4), in *ANF,* 1:416.

39. Justin, *The First Apology* (1.58), in *ANF,* 1:182.

40. Justin, *The First Apology* (1.26), in *ANF* 1:171.

tial feature of Marcion's teaching becomes evident: namely, he denied that God was the actual creator of the universe. He talked about two gods, one who created the world and rules it with his law, and a redeemer god who out of his goodness has pity on people, which is a characteristic of the gospel. The god of the gospel was the god of light and of goodness, and the god of the law and of creation was the god of darkness and of severity.[41] Small wonder that Marcion rejected the Old Testament. But he also purged the New Testament from what he claimed to be later Judaistic additions. As a result, he allowed only one Gospel, that of Luke, and Paul's letters, excluding the pastoral epistles and the Letter to the Hebrews. As Marcion insisted regarding the New Testament corpus: "False apostles interpolated the true record."[42]

Since everything bodily is the result of an evil creator god, Marcion concludes that one ought to abstain as much as possible from the fruits of creation. His followers are "companions in misery, and associates in hatred" of the world since they are entangled in this bodily existence and in this world.[43] Contrary to Paul, there is no redemption "of the body" but redemption "from the body." In contrast to some Gnostic sects who approved of lust and luxury as a means of showing their disdain for the material, Marcion went to the other extreme. As Tertullian writes:

> The flesh is not, according to Marcion, immersed in the water of the sacrament, unless it be in virginity, widowhood, or celibacy, or has purchased by divorce a title to baptism, as if even generative impotents [people who are impotent by nature or castration] did not all receive their flesh from nuptial union. Now, such a scheme as this must no doubt involve the proscription of marriage.[44]

This means that Marcion did not allow for marriage or any other institutions or actions that could lead to sexual activity. But evidently such asceticism proved attractive and the Marcionite church grew rapidly into a rival movement of the emerging Christian church. By the fifth century, Christian teachers of the church still felt that it was a threat to their own faith.[45]

As Irenaeus (ca. 135-202) tells us, Marcion also influenced others, such

---

41. See Tertullian, *Against Marcion* (2.29), in *ANF*, 3:320.
42. Tertullian, *Against Marcion* (4.3), in *ANF*, 3:348.
43. Tertullian, *Against Marcion* (4.9), in *ANF*, 3:355.
44. Tertullian, *Against Marcion* (1.29), in *ANF*, 3:293.
45. Barbara Aland, "Marcion/Marcioniten," in *TRE*, 22:99.

as the so-called Encratites, who "preached against marriage, thus setting aside the original creation of God, and indirectly blaming Him who made the male and the female for the propagation of the human race. Some of those reckoned among them have also introduced abstinence from animal food, thus proving themselves ungrateful to God, who formed all things."[46] This means there were certain groups who shunned marriage and thereby shunned sexuality since this was too closely connected with bodily existence. Even refraining from animal products was advocated. A Gnostic, Saturinus, "ascribed the origin of marriage and generation to Satan."[47] Irenaeus also mentions Tatian (ca. 125–ca. 185), who initially had been a student of Justin, but after Justin's martyrdom "he separated from the Church ..." and "declared that marriage was nothing else than corruption and fornication."[48] The example of Tatian shows that ascetic tendencies were quite widespread and included not only refraining from the consumption of meat and wine, but also from sexual activity of any kind, including marriage.

Mani (216-76) should also be mentioned here. His father had joined a baptizing group at the lower Euphrates River in present-day Iraq and it was this baptizing group that reinforced the ascetic tendency for Mani. From his earliest youth he claimed to have received revelations and at age twenty-five he had gained full insight, which allowed him to start his own religious group. He perceives human existence as one strung between good and evil, and that light and darkness stem from two different realms. There are three symbols that are decisive for Mani: the mouth, the hands, and the breast. "By the mouth we are to understand all the organs of sense in the head; by the hands, all bodily actions; by the breast, all lustful tendencies."[49] What issues from the mouth, such as bad words and blasphemy, or enters into the mouth, such as impure food, is sinful. Similarly sinful is any activity that is connected with the earth, such as agriculture and handwork. Every sexual activity is also sinful, and of course, the production of offspring. This means that human beings are tied to sin through their very activities.

Through Jesus the old humanity is turned into a new humanity full of love, faith, patience, and wisdom. The old, however, is not simply gone, and

46. Irenaeus, *Against Heresies* (1.28.1), in *ANF,* 1:353.

47. Jaroslav Pelikan, *The Christian Tradition: A History of the Development of Doctrine* (Chicago: University of Chicago Press, 1971), 1:87, and Irenaeus, *Against Heresies* (1.24.2), in *ANF,* 1:349.

48. Irenaeus, *Against Heresies* (1.28), in *ANF,* 1:353.

49. Augustine, *On the Morals of the Manicheans* (10.19), in *NPNF,* first series, 4:74.

therefore new human beings often have to do penitence. Since flesh "is made up of pollution itself . . . [and] in sexual intercourse, flesh is formed," one avoids eating meat and refrains from fleshly desires in order not to be defiled.[50] Since the Manicheans had to renounce manual labor and marriage, they would have soon died out, but in order to prevent that Mani divided his followers into the Elect and the hearers. The first group lived totally according to Mani's precepts; the second could lead a worldly life, but had to care for the Elect. The purification and liberation of good from evil is also produced "by their Elect through the food they consume."[51] The hearers, or catechumens, however, are changed into the Elect through the migration of their souls.

Already during Mani's lifetime, missionaries were sent out into the West. This is how Augustine came in contact with them and even belonged to the Manicheans for nine years. In the East, they traveled all the way to the Chinese imperial court in the eighth century, and in Turfan in Central Asia there was an active congregation of Manicheans until the thirteenth century. In southern China Manicheism lasted until the sixteenth century. This shows how attractive these ascetic tendencies had become. Yet it was an asceticism that pitted in a dualistic fashion the body against the soul. The Christians, however, still regarded the world, though succumbing to sin, as God's good creation. This provided the milieu in which Augustine was writing.

e. Sexuality as Part of God's Created Order

As British ethicist Michael Banner tells us: "Augustine was by no means the first Christian theologian who dealt with that theme [of sexuality and marriage], but he has a key position for the definition and systematization of the characteristics of the emerging sexual ethical teaching norms of occidental Christianity."[52] Augustine's sexual norms are closely tied to his understanding of sin. He follows Paul in 1 Timothy 6:10 when he states that "covetousness is the root of all evils."[53] Since Paul means here greed, this has

---

50. Augustine, *On the Morals of the Manicheans* (15.37), in *NPNF*, first series, 4:79.

51. Augustine, *The Heresies* (46.5), in *The Works of Saint Augustine: A Translation for the 21st Century*, vol. 1, *Arianism and Other Heresies*, trans., intro., and notes Roland J. Teske (Hyde Park: New York City Press, 1995), 42.

52. Michael Banner, "Sexuality II," in *TRE*, 31:196.

53. Augustine, "Acts or Disputation against Fortunatus" (21), in *NPNF*, first series,

nothing to do with sexuality. Augustine also writes: "In their present extremity unhappy men are so placed that they allow their vices to lord it over them, and are condemned for their lust, pride or curiosity."[54] Then Augustine elaborates: "Three classes of men are thus distinguished; for lust of flesh means those who love the lower pleasures, lust of the eyes means the curious, and ambition of this world denotes the proud." The only connection to sexuality we could discern here is with lust, which Augustine defines as the love of pleasures. Yet this is not totally warranted because in the following paragraph he talks about the lusting after the splendor of this world.

Augustine's use of the term "concupiscence," however, is intimately tied to human sexuality. Augustine dealt extensively with the situation expressed by the term in his discussion with the Pelagians. As he explains in the very first sentence of his treatise *On Marriage and Concupiscence,* the Pelagians maintained "that infants born in the flesh have no need of the medicine of Christ whereby sins are healed" and these Pelagians also claim that people such as Augustine "condemned marriage and that divine procedure by which God creates human beings by means of men and women, inasmuch as we assert that they who are born of such union contract that original sin."[55] As we noted, Pelagius had come from Great Britain to worldly Rome and insisted there that people, if they tried hard enough, could lead godly lives even without the aid of baptism by which rite original sin is forgiven. In contrast, Augustine insisted that without divine forgiveness a human being always remains a sinner. As Augustine states here, the Pelagians accused Augustine and his followers of being principally against marriage and human sexuality because they taught that through sexual union original sin was handed on to the next generation via the offspring from that union.

Augustine explained at length that for him a rejection of human sexuality and of marriage was totally unwarranted. In his treatise *On the Good of Marriage* Augustine first of all points out that "The first natural bond of human society is man and wife."[56] Since one was created from the other,

---

4:120; in the New Revised Standard Version this passage is translated as "the love of money is a root of all kinds of evil," which makes the point even clearer.

54. See Augustine, "Of True Religion" (38.69), in *Augustine: Earlier Writings,* The Library of Christian Classics, vol. 6 (Philadelphia: Westminster, 1953), 261, for this and the following quote.

55. Augustine, *On Marriage and Concupiscence* (1.1), in *NPNF,* first series, 5:263.

56. See Augustine, *On the Good of Marriage* (1), in *NPNF,* first series, 3:399, for this and the following quote.

this was "a sign also of the power of the union." This means there is a natural affinity between man and woman. This affinity goes strictly beyond just marital union. Then, however, comes the blessing to increase and multiply in Genesis 1, and immediately the question emerges whether this is not tied to the sinful state since there was no human progeny before the fall. Yet Augustine argues with that which is before our eyes, namely, "that according to this condition of being born and dying, which we know, and in which we have been created, the marriage of male and female is some good."[57] Marriage is not only for begetting children, but, especially if the couple has grown old or if they never had given birth to children, there is an order of charity between husband and wife, and good faith of honor and services. The attraction between the sexes, according to Augustine, should transcend mere sexuality in owing faith to each other.

Sexual intercourse, according to Augustine, is for procreation. In this way it is also free from blame, meaning free from sin. As he explains:

> For necessary sexual intercourse for begetting is free from blame, and itself is alone worthy of marriage. But that which goes beyond this necessity, no longer follows reason, but lust. And yet it pertains to the character of marriage, not to exact this, but to yield it to the partner, lest by fornication the other sin damnably. But, if both are set under such lust, they do what is plainly not matter of marriage. However, if in their intercourse they love what is honest more than what is dishonest, that is, what is matter of marriage more than what is not matter of marriage, this is allowed to them on the authority of the Apostle, as matter of pardon.[58]

Augustine evidently thinks here of Romans 1:26f., and, of course, is in favor of avoiding that kind of immorality. Marriage for Augustine is also not a matter of sexual convenience, but has a certain sacramentality to it that does not allow its dissolution, even if no children can be procreated and though perhaps with other partners such procreation might be possible. Augustine states: "But a marriage once for all entered upon in the City of our God, where, even from the first union of the two, the man and the woman, marriage bears a certain sacramental character, can no way be dissolved but by the death of one of them."[59] For Augustine it is evident that human sexuality is not the result of the fall and it is not necessarily con-

57. Augustine, *On the Good of Marriage* (3), in *NPNF*, first series, 3:400.
58. Augustine, *On the Good of Marriage* (11), in *NPNF*, first series, 3:404.
59. Augustine, *On the Good of Marriage* (17), in *NPNF*, first series, 3:406.

nected with concupiscence. "Marriage would have been worthy of the happiness of paradise, and would have given birth to children to be loved, and yet would not have given rise to any lust to be ashamed of. . . . The man would have sown the seed and the woman would have conceived the child when their sexual organs had been aroused by will . . . and had not been excited by lust."[60] Augustine understands "lust" always as something negative, whether connected with sexuality or with other human actions. He does not see that "lust" need not be the opposite of "under control of reason" but that it can also be something for pleasure that enhances life, therefore "denying the possibility of good, life-enhancing sexual pleasure. Augustine denied the possibility that sexual love could be a legitimate and profound expression of one's desire for intimate connection with one's beloved."[61]

Marriage therefore is a good that is given with creation and the sexual union of husband and wife is something natural that again is given with the creation of the sexual differentiation within humanity. Sexuality is also something that has been a part of humanity from the beginning and not just from the fall. This is very different, for instance, from Gregory of Nyssa (ca. 335–after 394), who called marriage a "sad tragedy."[62] According to Gregory, there was no sexuality in paradise and such started only when the first couple was driven forth from the garden. Then, "as the compensation for having to die, marriage was instituted."[63] Of course, Augustine knows, too, that there was no human procreation before the fall. Yet it was also clear for him that such could undoubtedly have occurred since human sexuality had nothing to do with the fall. Also, his emphasis on the sacramentality of marriage showed that it could not have been tinged by human sinfulness. His emphasis on the mutuality between husband and wife transcended mere procreation.

Yet Augustine now encounters the problem that with the fall sinfulness has set in. He recognizes marriage and human sexuality are part of God's created order but, contrary to Pelagian assertions, he insists that they are tainted by the fall. While sexual intercourse for the sake of propagation is not sinful, there is still human lust. Augustine explains that the reason for

---

60. Augustine, *Concerning the City of God against the Pagans,* trans. Henry Bettenson, intro. G. R. Evans (London: Penguin Books, 2003), 585 and 587 (14.23f.).

61. So very fittingly Julie B. Miller, "To Remember Self, to Remember God: Augustine on Sexuality, Relationality, and the Trinity," in *Feminist Interpretations of Augustine,* ed. Judith Chelius Stark (University Park: Pennsylvania State University Press, 2007), 245.

62. Gregory of Nyssa, *On Virginity* (3), in *NPNF,* second series, 5:345.

63. Gregory of Nyssa, *On Virginity* (12), in *NPNF,* second series, 5:358.

lust is the fall. He asks: "For why is the special work of parents withdrawn and hidden even from the eyes of their children, except that it is impossible for them to be occupied in laudable procreation without shameful lust?"[64] Then he gives himself the answer: "Because of this it was that even they were ashamed who first covered their nakedness. These portions of their person were not suggestive of shame before, but deserved to be commended and praised as the work of God. They put on their covering when they felt their shame, and they felt their shame when, after their own disobedience to their Maker, they felt their members disobedient to themselves." Augustine argues here by using as examples Adam and Eve, who covered themselves in shame. He explains that the reason they covered themselves was that their sexual organs were no longer under their complete control. The point he wants to make is that before the fall Adam and Eve were in complete control of their wills and therefore lust did not yet exist. After the fall this control no longer exists and Augustine has to reckon with it.

Augustine argues:

> Since, however, the cohabitation for the purpose of procreating children, which must be admitted to be the proper end of marriage, is not sinful, what is it which the apostle allows to be permissible, but that married persons, when they have not the gift of continence, may require one from the other the due of the flesh — and that not from a wish for procreation, but for the pleasure of concupiscence? This gratification incurs not the imputation of guilt on account of marriage, but receives permission on account of marriage. This, therefore, must be reckoned among the praises of matrimony; that, on its own account, it makes pardonable that which does not essentially appertain to itself.[65]

While it is clear for Augustine that the proper end of marriage is the procreation of children, an act that is not sinful, there is also certain concupiscence in married people who do not strive for procreation. Because it occurs in marriage Augustine considers it venial, or forgivable. Sexuality is not just for the procreation of children and it is not sinful. This is quite different from what we heard from Gregory of Nyssa, who was much more influenced by the monastic and ascetic tradition.

Yet like Paul, Augustine had a clear preference: "Marriage and conti-

64. See Augustine, *On Marriage and Concupiscence* (2.14), in *NPNF,* first series, 5:288, for this and the following quote.

65. Augustine, *On Marriage and Concupiscence* (1.16), in *NPNF,* first series, 5:270.

nence are two goods, whereof the second is better. . . . On this account it is good to marry, because it is good to beget children, to be a mother of a family: but it is better not to marry, because it is better not to stand in need of this work, in order to human fellowship itself."[66] While he perceived human sexuality and marriage as given by God and at the same time emphasized the preference for virginity and continence, human sexuality and marriage could easily be seen as something inferior. In analogy to Paul, Augustine argues here in terms of salvation history that begetting children is no longer necessary since the end is near. It was once necessary to have numerous posterity even to the extent of marrying additional wives if one's own was barren, as is seen from the Old Testament. But such is no longer lawful. "There is not now necessity of begetting children, as there then was . . . for the difference that separates times."[67] At that time human sexuality was in the service of God to procreate children, but because we now live in the end time procreation is no longer needed as a service to God. Continence and virginity now express more appropriately dedication to God and the future life that God promises.

For Augustine the state of being unmarried has preference over marriage because he sees us moving toward a state in which human sexuality in marriage, though good, will be far surpassed. Augustine is reminded here of Jesus' saying according to Mark 12:25: "For when they rise from the dead, they neither marry nor are given in marriage, but are like angels in heaven." Human sexuality and marriage, though constitutive for life here on earth, have no permanence.

While Augustine wants to anticipate proleptically something of that which is already envisioned for life after death, the question remains whether this does not devalue marriage in the long run. We can see this already in Pope Gregory the Great (ca. 540-604):

> Husbands and wives are to be admonished to remember that they are
> joined together for the sake of producing offspring; and, when giving
> themselves to immoderate intercourse, they transfer the occasion of pro-

---

66. Augustine, *On the Good of Marriage* (8f.), in *NPNF*, first series, 3:403. See also Mathijs Lamberigts, "A Critical Evaluation of Critiques of Augustine's View of Sexuality," in *Augustine and His Critics: Essays in Honour of Gerald Banner*, ed. Robert Dodaro and George Lawless (London: Routledge, 2000), 186, who writes: Augustine's "troubled view of sexual desire was partly due to his reading of Paul (especially 1 Corinthians 7), and to his own experience with sexuality."

67. Augustine, *On the Good of Marriage* (17), in *NPNF*, first series, 3:406.

creation to the service of pleasure, to consider that, though they go not outside wedlock yet in wedlock itself they exceed the just dues of wedlock. Whence it is needful, that by frequent supplications they do away their having fouled with the admixture of pleasure the fair form of conjugal union.[68]

Human sexuality is only for producing offspring and not for pleasure. Otherwise, the married couple is enjoined to do penitence because they have "fouled with the admixture of pleasure the fair form of conjugal union." This goes together with what the pope says shortly afterward, namely, that single people "are therefore to be admonished that, if they suffer from the storms of temptation with risk to their safety, they should seek the port of wedlock."[69] Marriage is considered as an escape valve for temptation. Reference is made here to 1 Corinthians 7:9. Yet then Gregory adds, "they come, in fact, to marriage without blame, if only they have not vowed better things." The better things, of course, are continence and an ascetic lifestyle.

Jerome (ca. 347-420) then claimed that even if the Roman tradition did not forbid receiving communion, it is the better option to refrain from communion immediately after sexual intercourse since already marital intercourse and prayer impede each other.[70] While the milder view of Gregory the Great found entry into the penitential books and marital intercourse was not per se considered sinful, the impression was certainly advanced that it was in fact sinful.[71] Gregory was also somewhat pragmatic when, in response to a question from Bishop Augustine of Anglia, he cautioned "those who receive the Body of the Almighty Lord to keep purity of the flesh in themselves, lest they be weighed down by the greatness of the inestimable mystery!"[72] But then he added: "Still a man who after intercourse with his wife has been washed with water may receive even the mystery of sacred communion, since according to the opinion above expressed, it is allowable for him to enter the church." This means that after purification one could receive communion. Whether one was tarnished by human sexuality or not was left undecided.

---

68. Gregory the Great, *The Book of Pastoral Rule* (27), in *NPNF,* second series, 12:57.

69. See Gregory the Great, *The Book of Pastoral Rule* (27), in *NPNF,* second series, 12:58, for this and the following quote.

70. Jerome, Letter 48, in *NPNF,* second series, 6:75.

71. See Banner, "Sexuality II," in *TRE,* 31:200.

72. See Gregory the Great, Epistle 64, in *NPNF,* second series, 13:80, for this and the following quote.

Thomas Aquinas is the great master of medieval ethics. For him sexual lust is without problems because it is concomitant with the preservation of the species in the procreative act. He writes in his *Summa Theologica*:

> Wherefore it is no sin if one, by the dictate of reason, makes use of certain things in a fitting manner and order for the end to which they are adapted, provided this end be something truly good. Now just as the preservation of the bodily nature of one individual is a true good, so, too, is the preservation of the nature of the human species a very great good. And just as the use of food is directed to the preservation of life in the individual, so is the use of venereal acts directed to the preservation of the whole human race.[73]

Humans share with all creatures the desire for self-preservation. Therefore sexual lust cannot per se be sinful. But the desire for sexual lust can lead to sin if it leads us to act contrary to the human good and therefore to right reason. Concupiscence as a force is a consequence of sin and punishment for our disobedience, and therefore the virtue of chastity is needed to regulate the desire for sexual lust. While sexuality allows procreating offspring, virginity has the greater value since it is not directed toward human good but toward divine good and "divine good takes precedence over a human good."[74]

Thomas no longer argues along the same line as Augustine that virginity and continence are already anticipating something of the envisioned eschatological goal. He states that "the precept of procreation regards the whole multitude of men, which needs not only to multiply in body, but also to advance spiritually"; thus both duties are maintained.[75] Since Thomas starts with the reality of human nature, he also knows that if one of the two partners in marriage would never ask for the expression of sexuality, the marriage would be damaged. One also gets the feeling that the wife may, not in an expressed but unexpressed way, ask for sexuality.[76] Thomas is clear that through the good of the marriage sexual relations are legitimized.

Thomas also distinguishes between different levels of moral life. He distinguishes those who simply want to live their lives according to the di-

---

73. Thomas Aquinas, *Summa Theologica*, literally trans. by Fathers of the English Dominican Province (London: Burns, Oates, and Benziger, 1912-25), II-II, 153, 2c.
74. See Thomas Aquinas, *Summa Theologica* II-II, 152, 4.
75. Thomas Aquinas, *Summa Theologica* II-II, 152, 2 ad 1; see Supplement 41, 2.
76. Thomas Aquinas, *Summa Theologica,* Supplement 53, 1.

vine commandments from those who choose to obey the evangelical counsels. These counsels need not be adhered to by every Christian, but everyone can follow them. In this way one obtains Christian perfection. These counsels — poverty, perpetual continence, and obedience under a superior — are voluntary.[77] While these evangelical counsels can be obtained through monastic life, there is also outside that life the possibility of perfection, which means continuous love toward God. Though a monk is not morally better than a layperson, in principle he has entered a higher level of life by abandoning everything earthly, which is superfluous, and has dedicated his life totally to God. In this way, monastic life is a higher, more ideal, and more certain form of Christianity than the life of the laity. This means that sexual chastity is superior, and marriage, though eventually obtaining the status of a sacrament, is basically a secular institution that shows little promise except for procreating the human race.

At the height of the Middle Ages Hugh of St. Victor (ca. 1096-1141) harked back to Augustine when he claimed that "matrimony and the duty of matrimony were instituted before sin, and both were instituted for a sacrament, so that matrimony might be hallowed by the pure love of the mind, and also that the duty of matrimony might be fulfilled without pollution of the flesh."[78] After the fall, however, so Hugh of St. Victor claimed, "the intercourse of the flesh cannot take place without carnal concupiscence." The reason for this is very simple. He contends that God removed one member in the human body from the power of the human soul, namely, the one member through which the offspring was to be engendered in the flesh. Since this member does not obey the soul, human propagation is always done in disobedience, namely, through concupiscence. So we are again back to Augustine, who sees human sexuality tainted by original sin and therefore chastity is to be preferred.

f. A New Look at Human Sexuality

When we come to the former Augustinian monk, **Martin Luther**, on the one hand we are still in the Augustinian tradition, but on the other hand sexual

---

77. Thomas Aquinas, *Summa Theologica* II-II, question 186a 3-5.

78. Hugh of St. Victor, *On the Sacraments of the Christian Faith* (Book 1, part 8, chap. 13), in *A Scholastic Miscellany: Anselm to Ockham,* The Library of Christian Classics, vol. 10 (Philadelphia: Westminster, 1956), 317.

activity is no longer limited to the propagation of the human race. The new position that Luther claimed becomes evident when he writes in his *Large Catechism:* "Marriage is not a walk of life to be placed on the same level with all the others, but it is before and above them all, whether those of emperors, princes, bishops, or any other. . . . [It is] the most universal and noblest, pervading all Christendom and even extending throughout all the world."[79] There we find nothing suggesting that marriage should be in second place. Since marriages are maintained throughout the world, marriage is the principal station that any human being can assume. While with this insight Luther goes beyond Augustine, he did not abandon Augustine completely.

In "A Sermon on the Estate of Marriage" (1519), he still calls marriage a sacrament. He refers here to Paul (Eph. 5:32), who states that like the union between husband and wife in which they become one flesh, God and humanity are united in Christ. Since Christ and Christendom also become one body, marriage is therefore a wonderful sacrament. Only a year later Luther attacks the idea that marriage is a sacrament since he could detect no "word of divine promise" connected with marriage.[80] Marriage has existed from the beginning of the world. Since pagans are married too, marriage is not reserved for Christians but is a worldly thing. Luther writes in 1522 on *The Estate of Marriage:* "Know therefore that marriage is an outward, bodily thing, like any other worldly undertaking."[81] But it is not something secular in the modern sense of the word.[82] Since "God himself instituted it . . . the estate of marriage and everything that goes with it in the way of conduct, works, and suffering is pleasing to God."[83] Marriage belongs to the kingdom of the left, to God's worldly order. Therefore Luther also discusses at length in *The Estate of Marriage* the issue of divorce. Since marriage is not a sacrament, Luther says it can be dissolved on one of three grounds: impotence, adultery, and the refusal of sexual intercourse. Yet Luther is "reluctant to recommend divorce even when it is allowed."[84]

---

79. Martin Luther, *Large Catechism,* in *The Book of Concord: The Confessions of the Evangelical Lutheran Church,* ed. Robert Kolb and Timothy J. Wengert, trans. Charles Arand et al. (Minneapolis: Fortress, 2000), 414.

80. Martin Luther, *The Babylonian Captivity of the Church* (1520), in *LW,* 36:92.

81. Martin Luther, *The Estate of Marriage* (1522), in *LW,* 45:25.

82. See Scott Hendrix's enlightening essay, "Luther on Marriage," in *Harvesting Martin Luther's Reflections on Theology, Ethics, and the Church,* ed. Timothy J. Wengert, foreword David C. Steinmetz (Grand Rapids: Eerdmans, 2004), 169-84, esp. 175.

83. Luther, *The Estate of Marriage* (1522), in *LW,* 45:38.

84. So Hendrix, "Luther on Marriage," 176.

In line with Augustine, however, Luther discovers one problem with marriage. There is the conjugal love that does not seek its own, but looks only for the other to have the other completely. Luther writes: "If Adam had not fallen, the love of bride and groom would have been the loveliest thing. Now this love is not pure either, for admittedly a married partner desires to have the other, and it is this desire which corrupts this kind of love."[85] This means that what was once pure and without sin before the fall is now tarnished through human concupiscence. Again, along the lines of Augustine, Luther points out that since the marital station has such great significance, "the wicked lust of the flesh which nobody is without, is a conjugal obligation and is not reprehensible when expressed within marriage, but in all other cases outside the bond of marriage, it is mortal sin. In a parallel way the holy manhood of God covers the shame of the wicked lust of the flesh."[86] The fall, therefore, has tarnished sexuality and now it is not without concupiscence and lust. Yet within the marital bond sexuality is not sinful. Luther argues here using the doctrine of the incarnation, saying that if God assumed human flesh, then human flesh by itself cannot be tarnished by sin if it executes that which God has commanded. Of course, Luther presupposes marital faithfulness here because the foundation for marriage is for him that one gives oneself totally to the other and also remains faithful. This does not allow anybody to come between the two. In this way, Luther transcends the mere sexual union in favor of a union of the whole person.

This is also clear when Luther talks about procreation. Procreation is something that is not restricted to a Christian marriage; Christian marriage is unique in that children are brought up in the Christian faith. The bringing up of children, Luther says, is much more important than pilgrimages to Rome or any other good work by which one wants to assure salvation. "For bringing up their children properly is their shortest road to heaven. In fact, heaven itself could not be made nearer or achieved more easily than by doing this work."[87] Luther does not argue here from nature that it is a natural for humans to procreate and therefore there is a duty to do so, but instead argues from the goal of humanity, which is to obtain salvation. In that direction parents can and should do an important work.

For Luther it was no longer the priestly station or the sexual continence

---

85. Martin Luther, *A Sermon on the Estate of Marriage* (1519), in *LW,* 44:9.
86. Luther, *A Sermon on the Estate of Marriage* (1519), in *LW,* 44:10.
87. Luther, *A Sermon on the Estate of Marriage* (1519), in *LW,* 44:12.

of the marriage partners that stood in the foreground, but God's creative order in which humans exist in this world as male and female. God has ordered things so that man and woman are mutually dependent on one another. And the attraction and desire for the other, sexual love, is a work of God: "And that is the word of God, through the power of which in the human body seed becomes fruit and the intense natural attraction to the woman is created and preserved. This cannot be hindered either with vows or with laws, for it is God's word and work."[88] This has been true since the beginning of creation and remains unchanged today. Yet sexual love, as we noted, is no longer pure. This is true for Luther also through the words of Psalm 51:5: "indeed, I was born guilty, a sinner when my mother conceived me." Luther sees this as evidence of the transition of original sin, which is connected with the human act of procreation and not, as is common in modern exegesis, a statement concerning the historical fate of Israel.[89] Luther follows here the traditional Augustinian understanding of the transmission of original sin. Yet he rightly recognizes that there is a demonic element of egotistic desire in sexual love in which the one partner only uses the other, instead of, as Luther stated in his explanation of the sixth commandment, loving and honoring the other. This also affects his understanding of marriage. Since sexual desire continues within marriage, marriage is not without sin. But marriage is instituted by God and therefore a holy order that stands under God's blessing.[90]

John Calvin thinks along lines like Luther's. He states with regard to the commandment "You shall not commit adultery" that a human being is "created in this condition that he may not lead a solitary life, but may enjoy a helper joined to himself [Gen. 2:18]; then by the course of sin has been still more subjected to this necessity. Therefore, the Lord sufficiently provided for us in this matter when he established marriage, the fellowship of which, begun on this authority, he also sanctified by his blessing."[91] This means

88. Martin Luther, *Christliche Schrift an W. Reisenbusch, sich in den ehelichen Stand zu begeben* (1525), in *WA*, 18:275.25-28.

89. See Martin Luther, in a wedding sermon on Hebrews 13:4 from January 8, 1531, *Predigten des Jahres 1531,* in *WA*, 34/1:73.3-10.

90. See also Paul Althaus, *The Ethics of Martin Luther,* trans. and foreword Robert C. Schultz (Philadelphia: Fortress, 1972), 86, who writes that Luther "views sexual love in two perspectives: as God's good creation and as distorted by sin."

91. See John Calvin, *Institutes of the Christian Religion* (II.8.41), ed. John T. McNeill, trans. Ford Lewis Battles, The Library of Christian Classics, vols. 20 and 21 (Philadelphia: Westminster, 1960), 1:405, for this and the following quote.

that a human being has not been created as a solitary being but is part of a fundamental twofoldness. This is even more so because of sin and therefore God has instituted marriage as a help to channel human sexuality because, as Calvin states, sexual activity between man and woman outside of marriage "is accursed in his [God's] sight." Sexuality therefore should occur only within marital fidelity. Most important for Calvin is that "the companionship of marriage has been ordained as a necessary remedy to keep us from plunging into unbridled lust."[92] We are told that our whole life should be lived in chastity and decency. This means for Calvin that we exercise self-discipline whether in marriage or outside marriage, whether in the single state or in the marital state.

According to Calvin, some are exempted from marriage through a "special grace." "Let each man, then, see what has been given to him. Virginity, I agree, is a virtue not to be despised."[93] The unmarried state, and here Calvin means of course having voluntarily refrained from marriage, is a special act of grace. What if someone does not want to get married? In this case, too, chastity and refraining from sexual activity is mandatory. If one cannot hold to this, one ought to get married. But marriage is not a secondary option. One should not look down on marriage. Calvin writes: "We are informed by an open declaration [of scripture], that it is not given to every man to keep chastity in celibacy, even if he aspires to it with great zeal and effort, and that it is a special grace which the Lord bestows only on certain men, in order to hold them more ready for his work."[94] If someone does not want to get married, and can remain single without doing violence to his own sexual desires, this is a special gift of God and ought to be used in God's service.

Calvin is very skeptical of monastic vows. If one has the special grace to live in chastity, one should use it, and if one is disturbed by one's fleshly desires, one should seek help from God through whose power alone one can withstand those desires. If they do not benefit from celibacy, "let them not despise the remedy which is offered to them. For those who are denied the power of continence are called to marriage by God's clear word [1 Cor. 7:9]."[95] Calvin concedes that if someone has vowed celibacy and cannot keep it, that person should simply abandon the vow and seek mar-

---

92. Calvin, *Institutes* (II.8.41), 1:405.
93. Calvin, *Institutes* (II.8.42), 1:406.
94. Calvin, *Institutes* (II.8.43), 1:406.
95. Calvin, *Institutes* (IV.13.17), 2:1272.

riage. For Calvin celibacy is not just a bodily act, but an intentional act of the whole human being. There is unchastity in external matters and also an internal unchastity in the heart. If the vows are too difficult to keep, one should revoke them since initially there was also the possibility of returning to secular life. Calvin notes this by quoting Cyprian (ca. 200/210-258), who stated that if virgins "are unwilling or unable to persevere, it is better that they should marry, than that by their crimes they should fall into the fire."[96]

For Calvin the marital state "is a good and holy ordinance of God" but it is not a sacrament.[97] He attacks the Roman Catholic Church because, on the one hand, the Catholics call marriage a sacrament and, on the other, they devaluate it by calling it "uncleanness, and pollution, and carnal filth."[98] Moreover, they do not allow the priest to partake of this sacrament. The reason for this, Calvin states, is that the Catholics talk about the grace of the Holy Spirit being given in the sacrament of marriage but also claim that there is a fleshly use in this sacrament, from which a priest must abstain. Calvin questions how fleshly use and the grace of the Holy Spirit can be simultaneously present. He observes a half-hearted approach by the Roman Catholic Church.

When we summarize the position of the Reformers, then, to some extent, they stay in the Augustinian tradition, Luther more so than Calvin. But they also have a clear appreciation of sexuality within the marital station as something created by God. They are aware that marital fidelity and chastity have been violated during their time, but they adamantly affirm that sexuality is reserved for marriage alone. There was little consideration given to those who were unable to find a marriage partner and who had to live in involuntary chastity. Of course, homosexuality was a taboo, as it had been since biblical times.

A Sexual Revolution?

While the Reformation period is separated from New Testament times by 1,500 years, the views of the Reformers on human sexuality and its practice remained almost the same as Paul's. Paul's injunction against sexual immorality implicitly shows that his own perspective was a minority position,

---

96. Cyprian, *Epistle* (61.2), in *ANF*, 5:357.
97. Calvin, *Institutes* (IV.19.34), 2:1481.
98. Calvin, *Institutes* (IV.19.36), 2:1483.

both in the almost exclusively non-Christian environment and also frequently within the Christian community. This holds true for the approach by the Reformers. Though they lived in the Holy Christian Empire, the people there were neither holy nor very Christian in their approach to human sexuality. For instance, Pope Julius II (1443-1513) was the father of three daughters, and many priests had concubines.[99] The city council of Regensburg even warned young women not to come too close to the entrance of monasteries so they would not be snatched away by lusty monks.

When we come to the present day, we could also point to the discrepancy between the sexual perspectives advocated by the official church and the way many priests and laypeople actually live. But we must also consider that living conditions, at least in many parts of the world, have drastically changed. Until the middle of the twentieth century, heterosexual activities were always conducted under the threat of an unwanted pregnancy. With the availability of chemical contraceptives, such as the pill, this is no longer the case. Heterosexual intimacy need no longer result in an unwanted pregnancy. This has caused a "sexual revolution" by which many young people can "enjoy" sexual activity without procreative consequences.

Moreover, life expectancy has increased considerably in contrast to the Middle Ages. When Martin Luther died at barely sixty-two years old, his bodily strength was spent and having reached such "old" age he was even an exception. Most people who were less educated and materially less well off died in their forties. This also necessitated early marriages and, for those who could afford schooling, very early education. Philipp Melanchthon (1497-1560) became professor at Wittenberg when he was just twenty-one years old, and Martin Luther was a mere twenty-five years old when he was sent to the University of Wittenberg to teach there. Therefore young people could marry relatively early, and the time span between when they reached sexual maturity and when they married was relatively short. Today, however, there are often twenty or more years between the time of sexual maturity and the date of marriage, if a person marries at all. At the other end of the age spectrum, there are more and more older people who are widowed. If they were to get married again, the pension they receive from their

99. Hans Kühner, *Lexikon der Päpste* (Frankfurt am Main: Fischer, 1960), 108, and Janette Werner, "Promiscuous Priests and Vicarage Children: Clerical Sexuality in Late Medieval England," in *Negotiating Clerical Identities: Priests, Monks and Masculinity in the Middle Ages,* ed. Jennifer D. Thibodeaux (New York: Palgrave Macmillan, 2010), 166, who writes about a fourteenth-century visitation: "Regular and secular clerics had distinct patterns of sexual misconduct."

deceased spouse would be endangered. Therefore the channeling of sexual activity into marriage is severely tested on both ends of life.

When we consult the *Catechism of the Catholic Church,* however, no note is taken of this change. There it states: "*Fornication* is carnal union between an unmarried man and an unmarried woman. It is gravely contrary to the dignity of persons and of human sexuality which is naturally ordered to the good of spouses and the generation and education of children."[100] Human sexuality is seen here first of all as occurring within the conjugal bond of husband and wife and for the purpose of generating children. It also suggests that the children are corrupted through such activities. Yet, in this light, if we consider the sexual activity of older people, it is unlikely that their aim is the generation of children. Should older people simply refrain from human sexuality then, even if they are married, when they can no longer procreate? The close bond between human sexuality and procreation is again stated in the *Catechism* when we read: "Sexual pleasure is morally disordered when sought for itself, isolated from its procreative and unitive purposes."[101] Indeed, self-seeking sexual pleasure can often be morally disordered, if it excludes the partner. Yet especially with older married people, if one partner can no longer be sexually active for medical or other reasons, would this mean that the other partner must remain sexually inactive, even if he or she would not have to go outside the conjugal bond to engage in his or her sexual activity?

A different aspect is considered, however, when we read in the same *Catechism:* "*Sexuality* affects all aspects of the human person in the unity of his body and soul. It especially concerns affectivity, the capacity to love and to procreate, and in a more general way the aptitude for forming bonds of communion with others."[102] Sexuality is seen here as a very comprehensive human expression that comprises the whole human person. Indeed, a human person is always a sexual person and appears always as a male or a female. Where there is a genetic mismatch, the affected person feels unhappy regardless of whether he or she looks male or female according to anatomical appearance. Human sexuality, as any other sexuality, is there for the ability to procreate. Yet in humans it is also an expression of love, a concern and consideration for the other, and in this way a means for forming bonds of

---

100. *Catechism of the Catholic Church* (2353), rev. ed. (London: Geoffrey Chapman, 1999), 504.

101. *Catechism of the Catholic Church* (2351), 503.

102. *Catechism of the Catholic Church* (2332), 500.

communion and for deepening those bonds. In the Augustinian tradition the legitimate goal of sexual activity was procreation within the conjugal bond, and the concomitant pleasure, or lust, was then channeled into that conjugal arrangement. Now sexual activities are also seen as an expression of love and as a means of deepening the conjugal bond. Procreation is no longer the exclusive goal.

When the official Roman Catholic Church does not allow artificial means for protecting against unwanted pregnancy for married couples, this shows that it does not want to exclude pregnancy from sexual intimacy. Yet to advocate so-called natural means by observing those days on which it is most unlikely for the woman to become pregnant, the suggestion is that one try to trick nature, which is "unnatural." The distinction between natural and artificial means of birth control is artificial in itself. In the same way that sexual pleasure should never be just for one's partner, it should also not be just for husband and wife. In a responsible way sexual activity should also consider the next generation. The sexuality of human beings is no longer nature-guided by instinctive drives as in animals. There are also no special mating seasons for humans. Human sexuality can be activated at will. Therefore it needs cultural formation and channeling.[103]

Up until modern times sexual activity was focused on procreation because life expectancy was so short, infant mortality was so high, and pension plans were nonexistent. One depended on one's children in old age. But for people in modern industrialized societies this is different. Once we reach retirement, we usually have sufficient funds to live on. But given our long life expectancy and the resultant increasingly necessary care for the elderly, our social system, with relatively high retirement benefits, is in the long run unsustainable with a graying population. Therefore the procreative aspect of human sexuality cannot be neglected. The acting out of human sexuality is not just a private matter, but involves a certain degree of social responsibility.

Since human sexual activity is not just a bodily function, it must be seen in the context of the mutual benefits of those who exercise it and those who are directly or indirectly affected by it. These benefits have ramifications for the wider human community so they are not just for the present moment, but must include consideration of the future. Here the issue of

103. See Wolfhart Pannenberg, *Anthropology in Theological Perspective,* trans. Matthew J. O'Connell (Philadelphia: Westminster, 1985), 428f., where he emphasizes this cultural formation.

sexual activity of the young and unmarried cannot be left out since eventually they will also impact the future.

As pornography blatantly shows, sexuality can degenerate into nothing more than a biological function satisfying sexual curiosity and desires. Since pornography is readily available on the internet, adolescents are prone to consume it. As recent studies have shown, however, they use it mainly for information and not for imitation. "Most adolescents do not believe exposure to sexually explicit websites has an influence on them."[104] But the out-of-control consumption of pornography can also become an addiction that may lead to a warped perception of reality and intimacy. This does not fulfill the reason for which sexuality was created, that is, the strengthening and deepening of the bond between the sexual partners. While young people are interested in the biological functions of sex, the decisive point for them is usually love, meaning longing and caring for the other.

But then there is the issue of sexual activity. It is interesting that the date of the first sexual activity for teenagers is later than it was just a few years ago. This again seems to confirm that the important point for adolescents is not biology but true affection. But next to this trend "toward a *new virginity*" there is also an immense drive in society for "sexual liberation."[105] The culture that forms and informs attitudes about sex is by no means homogeneous. If it is true, however, that sexual activity forms and strengthens the bond of communion with the other, this activity should ultimately lead to marriage. If it does not, it may hurt the other in the long run by eventually abandoning him or her in search of another sex partner or it may lead to promiscuous relativity that hinders the establishment of a lasting bond of mutual fidelity.

The Homosexual Controversy

Homosexuality has been practiced throughout the ages in a variety of forms, from the platonic ideal of young boys who accompanied older established men, to the sexual encounter in predominantly male environments, such as in the army or even occasionally in monasteries. Plato (428/427-348/347 B.C.) reported that Greek states each had different laws regarding homosexuality. He says that in Athens, for instance, having a young male as

---

104. So Judith K. Balswick and Jack O. Balswick, *Authentic Human Sexuality: An Integrated Christian Approach* (Downers Grove, IL: IVP Academic, 2008), 282.

105. Balswick and Balswick, *Authentic Human Sexuality*, 24.

a sexual lover "is held to be a very honorable thing."[106] But then he cautions: "The love of young boys should be forbidden by law, because their future is uncertain; they may turn out good or bad, either in body or soul, and much noble enthusiasm may be thrown away upon them."[107] Young boys who are still in their formative years emotionally and sexually can easily be harmed by such affairs. This has been widely recognized today and therefore there are usually laws prohibiting sexual activity with minors. But in his *Laws* Plato goes a step further, saying, "The intercourse of men with men, or of women with women, is contrary to nature, and that bold attempt was originally due to unbridled lust."[108] According to Plato, then, homosexuality in general is against nature and the result of unrestrained lust, something that he holds in contempt.

Nevertheless, homosexuality is a fact of life and even famous persons such as Erasmus of Rotterdam and Leonardo da Vinci (1452-1519) had "homosexual leanings."[109] Today, homosexuality is often considered a natural constellation caused by biological factors. Others argue that psychosocial factors, such as social learning, can contribute to homosexual orientation. But "there is no reliable evidence that sexual orientation is genetically inherited, neither is there evidence for the conclusion that it is the result of social learning."[110] As feminist biologist Lynda Birke (b. 1948) shows, "the relationship between human sexuality, sexual orientation and gender is immensely complex, involving multiple cultural responses to particular situations."[111] This is the reason why it is next to impossible to decide whether homosexuality is the result of biological determinism or whether it is the result of social constructivism. Perhaps it is some of both.

When we consult the Bible, Paul's perspective on homosexuality is quite prominent. American biblical scholar E. P. Sanders (b. 1937) points out that the choice of words in 1 Corinthians 6:9 "shows relatively unambiguously that Paul disapproves of homosexual activity of any kind" and in

---

106. Plato, *Symposium* (183), in *The Dialogues of Plato,* trans. B. Jowett, intro. Raphael Demos (New York: Random House, 1936), 1:311.

107. Plato, *Symposium* (181), in *The Dialogues of Plato,* 1:310.

108. Plato, *Laws* (I.636), in *The Dialogues of Plato,* 2:418.

109. So Balswick and Balswick, *Authentic Human Sexuality,* 95.

110. James D. Haynes, "A Critique of the Possibility of Genetic Inheritance of Homosexual Orientation," *Journal for Homosexuality* 28, nos. 1 and 2 (1995): 108.

111. Lynda Birke in her discerning study "Unusual Fingers: Scientific Studies of Sexual Orientation," in *Handbook of Lesbian and Gay Studies,* ed. Diane Richardson and Steven Seidman (London: Sage, 2002), 61, where she discusses recent studies in homosexuality.

Romans 1:26f. Paul condemns "male and female homosexuality flatly and indiscriminately."[112] New Testament scholar Mark Powell (b. 1953) makes an even more sweeping statement: "Every reference in the Bible to sexual relations between same-sex partners is negative."[113] And then he continues by saying that from a biblical perspective heterosexuality is identified "as demonstrative of the original intent of God." This means that the Bible presents a vision of what constitutes God's original design for humanity. But this design is tarnished through the fall. We have seen this already with sexuality in general. In this sinful world Jesus announced the twofold commandment of love: love for God and love for the neighbor (Mark 12:29-34). We are expected to extend our love to all people, irrespective of what or who they are, and we should "want them to have meaningful and satisfying lives."[114] Those who advocate homosexuality can hardly go to the Bible for approval. The biblical command is to love everyone and wish the best for them, but to approve of what they are goes beyond the biblical mandate (see John 8:1-11, where Jesus shows love but not approval).

Human sexuality occurs in the encounter between a man and a woman as a means of expressing mutuality in deepening in fidelity the bond between two persons. They open themselves to each other in their utter defenselessness, implying mutual trust and joy, in and with each other. Their encounter is neither casual nor fleeting, but lasting. Therefore it is appropriate to channel it into the sexual relationship in marriage.

4. Marriage

In talking about marriage we will notice a phenomenon like that of human sexuality. The official statements with regard to marriage have come primarily from the male perspective. Only recently has the female perspective also been considered. But in neither of the creation accounts in Genesis 1 and Genesis 2 is there a preference given for one sex or the other. In Genesis 1 we hear that humanity was created male and female, while in Genesis 2 though the male was created first, humanity did not come into its own until the creation of the female as the appropriate partner for the male.

112. E. P. Sanders, *Paul* (Oxford: Oxford University Press, 1991), 147.

113. Mark Allan Powell, "The Bible and Homosexuality," in *Faithful Conversation: Christian Perspectives on Homosexuality*, ed. James M. Childs Jr. (Minneapolis: Fortress, 2003), 19 and 21.

114. Powell, "The Bible and Homosexuality," 39.

Perhaps the sociocultural environment of biblical history as well as the history of Christianity helped to emphasize the male perspective. One might call this a patriarchal perspective, but it is more a family or clan perspective. There has always been a public interest in marriage because the survival of the clan or the family depended on the progeny that came from the woman. If the woman was received into the family (clan) of her husband and his immediate relatives, this was a gain for that family and a loss for the family from which the woman came. It was customary to compensate the family that lost the woman with some kind of bride price. This is still done today in many cultures, such as in Africa, whereas in others, such as in India, there is a dowry that the bride brings with her. To consider this as purchasing a woman would certainly be wrong, though occasionally it may be implied. It is much more a compensation for losing a family member and potential family members, namely, the woman and her potential children.

A marriage bond builds bridges as we can see from the famous Latin saying *"Tu felix Austria nube"* (You happy Austria marry). Among the European nobility, predominantly from the Austrian house of Habsburg, marriages were arranged in a strategic way. Through the newly won relations of sons and daughters by marriage, influence could be gained and new transnational family bonds could be established with the countries from which the new spouses hailed. This means a marriage exclusively based on love and resulting from the decision of two individuals was virtually unknown, contrary to what is now not just the custom but the rule in Europe and North America. This was also the case in Old Testament times.

a. Marriage in the Old Testament

Israelite society was organized according to kinship groups with the family as the smallest unit. The latter included "father and wives, their sons and their sons' wives, the unmarried daughters and the sons' offspring."[115] The family was multigenerational with a senior couple and their children plus their wives and the grandchildren. There was a profound interdependence in these self-sufficient agrarian families that "created an atmosphere of corporate family identity, in which one could not conceive of personal goals

115. S. Bendor, *The Social Structure of Ancient Israel* (Jerusalem: Simor, 1996), 48.

and ventures but only of familial ones."[116] Since marriage was not a private affair but one negotiated usually within the clan — marriage with a wife from the outside was generally frowned on — there are no biblical laws that deal directly with marriage or its dissolution.[117]

When a son wanted to marry, he or his father asked the father of the bride for permission to marry her. Then a bride price was paid to the father of the bride (Gen. 34:12). The bride could even be asked whether she wanted to marry the groom (Gen. 24:57). The bride also received some means from her family for the future household, such as maidservants (Gen. 24:59), land (Josh. 15:18f.), or other items. The engagement was not a trial period for marriage, but the betrothed was obligated to marital fidelity. Infidelity or being raped without crying for help was punished with death by stoning (Deut. 22:23f.). Though the rapist was also stoned there still was a double standard. Punishment of a married man was meted out for sexual relations with another married or betrothed woman, while for a married woman any sexual relations with a man, whether married or unmarried, was to be punished by death. Although this punishment by stoning is still executed in some Islamic countries today, such as Iran and Saudi Arabia, in the Old Testament we find only the written law but not one instance of its actual execution.

In the Old Testament marriage can be dissolved through the death of a spouse or through infidelity, or by the husband giving the woman "a certificate of divorce" (Deut. 24:1). Then the woman is free again to marry another man, but she cannot return to her first husband even if he would so desire. While we read at the beginning of Genesis that marriage is an intimate communion of love, including mutual support and respect (Gen. 2:21-24), the ruling of the husband over the wife (Gen. 3:16) and the man having more than one wife (Gen. 4:19) were seen as a result of the fall and a falling away from God's order. We read, for instance, that the Old Testament patriarchs and kings had more than one wife. Yet in Exodus 21:10 we read: if a man "takes another wife to himself, he shall not diminish the food, clothing, or marital rights of the first wife." This means that in polygamous arrangements women must be treated equally. Yet "it is noteworthy that the books of Samuel and Kings, which cover the entire period of the monarchy,

---

116. Carol Meyers, "Families in Early Israel," in *Families in Ancient Israel,* ed. Leo G. Perdue et al. (Louisville: Westminster John Knox, 1997), 21.

117. See Joseph Blenkinsopp, "The Family in the First Temple Israel," in *Families in Ancient Israel,* ed. Perdue et al., 58.

do not record a single case of bigamy among commoners (except that of Samuel's father, at the very beginning of the period). The Wisdom books, too, which provide a picture of society in their age, never mention polygamy."[118] This means that the most common form of marriage in Israel was monogamy. Virtually all passages in the Old Testament that extol the virtues of a wife presuppose a monogamous arrangement. When the prophets liken the relationship between Israel and God to that of wife and husband, they, too, presuppose a monogamous marriage (Isaiah 51). And Israel is called an adulterous woman in Hosea 1–3 because she has forsaken the Lord.

In the last commandment of the Decalogue ("You shall not covet your neighbor's house; you shall not covet your neighbor's wife, or male or female slave, or ox, or donkey, or anything that belongs to your neighbor"; Exod. 20:17), one gets the impression that the wife is subsumed under a man's possessions.[119] Yet she is not his property that he bought because the husband is also summoned to marital fidelity (Prov. 5:20). In Malachi 2:14-16 marriage is even portrayed as a covenant before God that should not be broken "for I hate divorce, says the Lord, the God of Israel, and covering one's garment with violence, says the Lord of hosts. So take heed to yourselves and do not be faithless" (Mal. 2:16). Breaking the bond of marriage is likened to violence and to faithlessness. This goes along with what Hosea shows in his parable of the covenant between God and Israel. Love and faithfulness were the foundation for a marriage in Israel. In early Judaism, then, the ideal marriage was considered to be an exclusive and lifelong arrangement. But reality did not always coincide with the ideal.

At that time the issue was even discussed whether the certificate of divorce could also be issued by the wife. But the Jewish patriarchal attitude and the lax Roman morals mitigated against such a change. It is perhaps for us today surprising to hear what reasons could be brought forth by a husband to present to his wife a certificate of divorce.[120] According to the view

118. Roland de Vaux, *Ancient Israel,* vol. 1, *Social Institutions* (New York: McGraw-Hill, 1965), 25.

119. J. Harold Ellens, *Sex in the Bible: A New Consideration,* foreword Donald Capps, preface Wayne G. Rollins (Westport, CT: Praeger, 2006), 69, states that in the earlier texts women were viewed as property of their fathers and then of their husbands, while in post-exilic times they were usually seen "as agents of their own destiny." This reflects a change in society from an agrarian to a more urban society where the wife in the latter was not so much needed for communal survival but could pursue her own tasks.

120. The quotations for the following are taken from the end of the Mishnah tractate

of Rabbi Hillel (ca. 30 B.C.–A.D. 9) and his school, a husband could reject his wife for almost any reason, for example, when she "spoiled his dish" (burning the noon meal). Rabbi Akiba (ca. 50/55-135) allowed divorce even if the husband "found someone else prettier than she" because it was his wife's fault that she was not more attractive. This shows that sometimes the flimsiest excuses could be adduced by the husband to divorce his wife. The school, or "house," of Shammai (50 B.C.–A.D. 30), however, differed fundamentally from the school of Hillel and admitted as a reason for divorce "only adultery committed by the wife and perhaps also suspicious adulterous behavior on her side."[121] This reflected the main tenor that the husband had a moral responsibility over against the woman and therefore divorce was not to be done cavalierly. It was especially forbidden to divorce a woman if as a divorcee she would be left without protection. Therefore the mental disability of a woman or her having become captive in war excluded a divorce by the husband. Eventually, the woman, too, could ask for a divorce and demand such a decree from her husband if he limited her personal freedom, for instance, if he no longer cohabitated with her or if his behavior was unbearable. The underlying maxim was that a wife is given to a man for life and not for suffering. Yet the wife always had to prove her case if she wanted a divorce.

b. A New View of Marriage: The New Testament

In the Old Testament and in early Judaism it was undisputed that one needed to marry and have offspring. Otherwise the early Israelites could not survive. They needed their children as helpers with their daily chores and also to ensure their protection in old age. But this expectation of marriage had changed with Jesus and the subsequent New Testament community. Since the kingdom of God was at hand, there was neither need for marriage nor for producing offspring. Marriage and children were an option, yet almost a secondary option. "Woe to those who are pregnant and to those who are nursing infants in those days" (Matt. 24:19), we hear Jesus say according to Matthew. And according to Luke, Jesus said, "Those who belong to this age marry and are given in marriage; but those who are consid-

---

Gittin, as quoted in James C. Crossley, *The New Testament and Jewish Law: A Guide to the Perplexed* (London: T&T Clark, 2010), 69.

121. Zeev W. Falk III, "Ehe/Eherecht/Ehescheidung," in *TRE,* 9:315 (*mGit* 9, 10).

ered worthy of a place in that age and in the resurrection from the dead neither marry nor are given in marriage" (Luke 20:34f.). Marriage is no longer a necessity for the new world to come; it can even be a hindrance. According to Jesus, discipleship is more important than one's family bonds (see Matt. 10:37).

Paul, too, must be seen with this perspective when he advised the virgins in Corinth: "I think that, in view of the impending crisis, it is well for you to remain as you are." Then he continued: "Are you bound to a wife? Do not seek to be free. Are you free from a wife? Do not seek a wife. But if you marry, you do not sin, and if a virgin marries, she does not sin. Yet those who marry will experience distress in this life, and I would spare you that" (1 Cor. 7:26-28). Paul emphasized that this was his own opinion. Since the time is short until the coming of the kingdom, one should simply remain as one is, but, as he said in conclusion, it will be easier for those who are unmarried. One has to be careful here not to interpret Paul's view as being in line with that of late Hellenism. In the Greco-Roman tradition some held marriage to be convenient for the man and others regarded marriage as a civic duty. But often marriage was held in contempt as inconvenient because one would be tied down with one particular person. Therefore divorce was exceedingly frequent.[122]

We see this new (Christian) approach to marriage especially well in Jesus' words in the Sermon on the Mount. It was clear that for Jesus marriage implied a lifelong commitment, not just verbally or technically, but in terms of exclusive fidelity. He also dismissed the idea of issuing a certificate of divorce. "Anyone who divorces his wife, except on the ground of unchastity, causes her to commit adultery; and whoever marries a divorced woman commits adultery" (Matt. 5:32). From Jesus' injunction, "Therefore what God has joined together, let no one separate" (Mark 10:9), comes now the conclusion: "Whoever divorces his wife and marries another, commits adultery against her" (Mark 10:11). In the following sentence the same is also said for the woman. The only exception for divorce is adultery. For Jesus, marriage is God's good order — one could say an order of creation — which should not be violated (see Matt. 19:8). Jesus maintains that marriage is for life.

But Jesus also concedes that people "were so hard-hearted that Moses allowed you to divorce your wives" (Matt. 19:8). As God's created order

122. For details about marriage in the Greco-Roman tradition, see O. Larry Yarbrough, *Not Like the Gentiles: Marriage Rules in the Letters of Paul* (Atlanta: Scholars, 1985), 31-63.

marriage cannot be dissolved because this would mean breaking God's own order. Yet there is human sinfulness and for that, as Jesus admitted, the Mosaic law allowed for divorce. In his stance against divorce Paul explicitly refers to the Lord, to Jesus (1 Cor. 7:10f.). The only exception Paul makes is if the marriage partner is not a Christian. Yet even then divorce, though possible, is not desirable, and, according to Paul, there is also no possibility of entering into a new marriage.

The New Testament also contains the story of the woman caught in adultery who is brought to Jesus by the scribes and the Pharisees who would like to apply the Mosaic command to stone her to death. Jesus confronts them with the admonition "Let anyone among you who is without sin be the first to throw a stone at her" (John 8:7). As one after the other went away, the story ends: "Jesus was left alone with the woman standing before him. Jesus straightened up and said to her, 'Woman, where are they? Has no one condemned you?' She said, 'No one, sir.' And Jesus said, 'Neither do I condemn you. Go your way, and from now on do not sin again'" (John 8:9-11). While some exegetes maintain that this story "was not originally part of the Gospel of John," they concede that "it may, however, be based on early oral traditions about Jesus."[123] Jesus does not approve of what the woman has done, but he will not condemn her, meaning that he will give her a chance to lead a decent life. We may conclude, then, that marriage must be held in sanctity. But if a marriage disintegrates, a new beginning is possible even if the dissolution of the marriage cannot be approved.

While marriage is part of the created order and divorce is a disturbance of that order, marriage is an interim institution. Though Jesus compared the kingdom of heaven to a wedding banquet (Matt. 22:2), he also suggested that marital bonds have no lasting significance in the resurrected state (Matt. 22:30). Marriage is lived on earth and is exclusively for the present age. Therefore it points to something new since the orders of this world will pass away. Marriage is then no longer obligatory and, as we have seen with Paul, forfeiting marriage can even be useful and so can abstinence within the marriage. When Paul expressed his own conviction he showed that marriage can also be an instrument to sanctify the non-Christian marriage partner through the behavior of the Christian spouse (1 Cor. 7:12-16).[124] In 1 Pe-

---

123. So *The Harper Collins Study Bible, New Revised Standard Version*, 2028, in a footnote. See also Ulrich Wilckens, *Das Evangelium nach Johannes* (Göttingen: Vandenhoeck & Ruprecht, 1998), 138, in his commentary to this passage, who claims that "it was not received in the common ecclesial canon until the 5th century."

124. Though this "sanctification" is difficult to interpret, it could very well mean that

ter 3:7 the significance of joined prayers is emphasized and husbands are enjoined to honor their wives since both are heirs "of the gracious gift of life."

In the Table of Duties (especially in Col. 3:18f. and more extensively in Eph. 5:21-33) we encounter a very elaborate and theological interpretation of marriage. The Table of Duties in Ephesians starts with a summons to mutual obedience: "Be subject to one another out of reverence for Christ" (Eph. 5:21). This is not a summons for obedience for the weaker members, women, children, and slaves under the stronger ones, but the encouragement of mutual service and love (see Gal 5:13). The mutual subjection to one another is anchored in Christ, reminding the Christian of his obedience in his salvation ministry. With such an introduction, marriage is not seen as a worldly affair but is anchored in Christ. The exhortation, which calls for obedience and subjection of wives to their husbands, may strike us as strange today. Most important and most significant, however, is the analogy drawn between the relationship of Christ and the church on the one hand, and that of husband and wife on the other. Yet through that analogy the relationship between husband and wife, including their sexual relationship, is sanctified. We could even say that marriage now becomes "a Christian institution."[125]

When admonishing women to be subject to their husbands the author of this letter stays within the customs of his time because this kind of obedience was deemed common in antiquity.[126] Yet the writer of this letter does not substantiate his argument with reference to the cultural environment, but by pointing to Christ. Since Christ is the head of the church, the church is subject to Christ. Analogously the wife should be subject to her husband. This reference should not cement a patriarchal arrangement. The church as the body of Christ comprises both men and women and their savior is Christ. Therefore husbands are commanded to "love your wives, just as Christ loves the church and gave himself up for her" (Eph. 5:25).[127] This

through the Christian wife her non-Christian spouse would bring "his behavior in line with both the Creator's intention in marriage (Gen. 2:24) and the Lord's directive prohibiting divorce." So Fitzmyer, *First Corinthians,* 300, on this passage.

125. So Ulrich Luz in his comments on Ephesians 5:22-33 in Jürgen Becker and Ulrich Luz, *Die Briefe an die Galater, Epheser und Kolosser* (Göttingen: Vandenhoeck & Ruprecht, 1998), 171.

126. So Ernest Best, *A Critical and Exegetical Commentary on Ephesians* (Edinburgh: T&T Clark, 1998), 532, who writes that a "husband would have had the right to enforce submission if it was not voluntarily offered."

127. Best, *A Critical and Exegetical Commentary of Ephesians,* 531, rightly comments

agape love that denotes love to God and to Christ and to the neighbor also includes sexual love. "That the love of husbands to their wives comes in the context of the comprehensive and holistic Christian love of the neighbor is for the future an important potential meaning of our text that can help to open up patriarchal structures."[128] When the writer continues, "he who loves his wife loves himself" (Eph. 5:28), then this is not self-centered love because he argues from the love of Christ for the church as his body. Since husband and wife are part of this body, then loving the wife means loving oneself. Therefore the union of husband and wife is maintained by their oneness in the one body, the body of Christ, which is identified here with the church.

This is very different from the argument we heard in 1 Corinthians 7, where Paul sees marriage as a means to prevent unchastity. In Ephesians marriage is an institution that receives its special dignity from Christ and through him it is related to God. This kind of argument allows a sacramental understanding of marriage and makes it impossible to dissolve marriage since such an act would compromise one's faithfulness to Christ. On the other hand, we see here the headship of the husband over the wife stemming from the same Christological reflection. This means there is a tension between the oneness of husband and wife and their mutuality as equal members of the body of Christ on the one hand, and the parallelism of Christ and church and husband and wife on the other. While the one would emphasize equality, the other emphasizes the opposite. This was the tension in which the early church found itself with regard to marriage, not to mention that the Pauline notion of marriage takes second place to virginity.

c. Against a Prevailing Culture: Early Christianity

"In their sexual code, Christians were conscious of standing apart from the pagan world. To find a virtuous people on earth, they remarked, a man had to look far away to the Seres, the people of China, who lived justly and in sexual modesty."[129] In the first centuries Christianity was a countercultural

---

that the analogy of human marriage and the Christ-church relationship is not perfect and should not be overstretched.

128. Ulrich Luz in his exegesis of Ephesians 5:25-28 in Becker and Luz, *Die Briefe an die Galater, Epheser und Kolosser,* 172.

129. Robin Lane Fox, *Pagans and Christians* (New York: Alfred A. Knopf, 1987), 341.

movement that was especially noticeable in its approach to sexuality and marriage.

For instance, in Egypt and much of the Near East, brothers married their sisters, a custom that helped to hold the family property together. In many cultural regions, bisexuality was taken for granted. Before marriage, a young man could turn to slaves or prostitutes, and abortion was freely practiced. "Marriage, finally, was only one social form of cohabitation and it was valued because it legitimized children and eased the transmission of property."[130] Many men lived with a partner as concubine, especially if she came from a different social class as was the case with young Augustine. Against this cultural stream Christian writers, such as Clement of Alexandria, pointed out: "Since pleasure and love seem to fall under marriage, it must also be treated of. Marriage is the first conjunction of man and woman for the procreation of legitimate children. . . . Nature has adapted us for marriage, as is evident from the structure of our bodies, which are male and female."[131] This simple quote makes three points. First of all, it is a natural order that human beings are male and female and are therefore made for marriage. Second, sensual pleasure and lust are channeled into marriage. They should not take place outside marriage. Third, marriage is for the procreation of children. Marriage is also lifelong as Clement points out when he says: "The Scripture counsels marriage, and allows no release from the union."[132] He also realizes that there is no necessity to get married. One can lead a celibate life. Since marriage is for life, widowhood was the preferred option when the husband died. The motivation for this was not the love of one's former husband, "but dependence on God."[133] But a widow could also remarry. This was also allowed for a husband whose wife had committed adultery. Yet with reference to 1 Corinthians 7:39, "A wife is bound as long as her husband lives. But if the husband dies, she is free to marry anyone she wishes," most early church fathers did not allow remarriage for a wife whose husband had committed adultery.

Chrysostom (ca. 349-407) in his *Homily* on Ephesians 5:22-24 strongly emphasizes conjugal love, saying, "For there is nothing which so welds our life together as the love of man and wife."[134] He sees in the harmony of hus-

130. Fox, *Pagans and Christians,* 344.

131. Clement of Alexandria, *The Stromata* (2.23), in *ANF,* 2:377.

132. Clement of Alexandria, *The Stromata* (2.23), in *ANF,* 2:379.

133. Fox, *Pagans and Christians,* 354.

134. See John Chrysostom, *Homilies on Ephesians* (20), in *NPNF,* first series, 13:143, for this and the following quote.

band and wife not only a good environment in which children are brought up, but also an influence on neighbors, friends, and relations. With reference to Genesis 1:27 he states that "there is no relationship between man and man so close as that between man and wife, if they be joined together as they should be." This means that the communion between husband and wife is a special one to which no other communion comes close, neither with parents nor with children or siblings, and not even with a friend. Yet at the same time in referring to the analogy of Christ and the church, Chrysostom says that Paul assigns each the proper place, the man that of authority and thought, and the woman that of submission. Both husband and wife, however, are subject to Christ, who is the ground and provision of their love.

Though Christians tried to maintain a lifestyle different from that of other people, they also had their problems, as Chrysostom shows when he writes in his picturesque style:

> It were meet indeed that ye had within you the wall to part you from women; but since you are not so minded, our fathers thought it necessary by these boards to wall you off; since I hear from the elder ones, that of old there were not so much as these partitions; "For in Christ, there was neither male nor female." And in the apostle's time also both men and women were together. Because the men were men, and the women women, but now altogether the contrary; the women have urged themselves in the manners of courtesans, but the men are in no better state than frantic horses.[135]

There was so much distraction between the women sitting on one side of the sanctuary and the men on the other that it was necessary to put up a dividing wall between them. Every theologian throughout the history of the church has dealt with marital issues. The reason was not that this was their favorite pastime, but that Christians were not immune to the temptations of the flesh. There have been marital problems as long as there has been marriage, and there have been sexual problems as long as human beings have been sexual beings.

While it was clear for the early church that marriage was a supernatural bond and God's good order, virginity was regarded to be superior to marriage. But neither virginity nor marriage merited salvation and therefore

---

135. John Chrysostom, *Homilies on the Gospel of Matthew* (73.3), in *NPNF*, first series, 13:443, in his homily on Matthew 23:14.

marriage should not be despised though it clearly held second place. Jerome, for instance, did not see marriage and virginity on the same level. "I grant," he says, "that even marriage is a gift of God, but between gift and gift there is great diversity."[136] In picking up on Paul's statement that he preferred that people remain celibate as he was, marriage is only a second option, and it is simply for sexuality's sake. Even there it takes one away from prayer and therefore the sexual act is only conceded to prevent more evil. Jerome writes: "I suspect the goodness of that thing which is forced into the position of being only the lesser of two evils. What I want is not a smaller evil, but a thing absolutely good."[137] The Pauline saying "it is good to marry" is for Jerome only something to avoid a greater evil. This means that the sexual act though sinful can be tolerated on account of a greater evil that could happen if it were not tolerated. This position says very little positive about the actual value of marriage constituted by mutual love and lifelong commitment. Jerome himself had in Paula, a wealthy Roman widow, a constant female companion for nearly twenty years. While their union may have been totally spiritual, it shows that even someone like him, who had little positive to say about marriage, still needed a female partner.[138]

The big question for the church, however, was whether the clergy could be married. The Council of Elvira (ca. 306/309), in present-day Spain, stated in canon 33 that all bishops, priests, and deacons who had been married at the time of their ordination should live in marital celibacy.[139] A similar action at the Council of Nicaea did not gain approval. Since there was no unanimity two different traditions developed. In the East, clergy, except

136. Jerome, *Against Jovinianus* (1.8), in *NPNF,* second series, 6:352.

137. Jerome, *Against Jovinianus* (1.9), in *NPNF,* second series, 6:352.

138. How emotionally attached he was to Paula can be seen in his reaction to her death. See J. N. D. Kelly, *Jerome: His Life, Writings, and Controversies* (New York: Harper & Row, 1975), 278, who cites Jerome's reaction: "All of a sudden I have lost her who was my consolation."

139. See Henri Crouzel, "Ehe/Eherecht/Ehescheidung V Alte Kirche," in *TRE,* 9:328. Here the account in "Proposed Action on Clerical Celibacy" at the First Council of Nicaea in 325 (in *NPNF,* second series, 14:51) states that the Synod of Nicaea as well as that of Elvira tried to pass such a law "that was to forbid all bishops, priests and deacons [Sozomen adds subdeacons] who were married at the time of their ordination, to continue to live with their wives." Yet the Egyptian bishop Paphnutius stood up at Nicaea against this injunction and thwarted the passing of this law. See also Sozomen, *The Ecclesiastical History* (1.23), in *NPNF,* second series, 2:256, regarding the action in Nicaea. It is still debated whether the Council of Elvira passed canon 33 or whether this and other canons were added later from other Iberian (Spanish) councils.

bishops, could marry before they were ordained and could continue to live a marital life. Since the drive for celibacy came mainly from the West (Spain), marriage was not really accepted there for ordained clergy. Yet strict celibacy was only enforced with the Counter-Reformation and the Council of Trent. Hippolytus of Rome (ca. 170–ca. 236) even tells us that during the papacy of Callistus (217-22) "bishops, priests, and deacons, who had been twice married, and thrice married, began *to be allowed* to retain their place among the clergy."[140] Yet this pope also allowed for abortion, which otherwise was considered murder. This means that in the early church the high standards that were espoused were often compromised.

For a long time the act of marriage was considered a worldly affair. Especially in Germanic culture fathers had the say over bride and bridegroom, and both were given in marriage either in the home or later at the church door. At the latter place it was more likely that a priest would perform the ceremony of joining the couple together. Yet when the Council of Lyon defined under Pope Gregory X in 1274 the seven sacraments this also included the sacrament of matrimony. Now marriage was an actual sacrament. It was constituted through the consensus of the marriage partners and could only be dissolved through ecclesial jurisdiction in case the conjugal union had not yet taken place.

d. Marriage Is No Second Choice: The Reformation

Erasmus of Rotterdam wrote in 1518 *Encomium Matrimonii* (Praise of Marriage) in which he highly praised marriage without discrediting the legitimate value of celibacy. Erasmus, the son of a priest, never broke with the Roman Catholic Church and never entered into marriage. It was different for the Reformers who all, sooner or later, got married. John Calvin emphasized especially the spiritual equality of husband and wife. He went beyond Augustine in calling marriage "the most holy of all ties."[141] As we noted previously, he does not call it a sacrament, but notes that "God instituted marriage for the common welfare of the human race."[142] With reference to

---

140. Hippolytus, *The Refutation of All Heresies* (9.7), in *ANF,* 5:131.

141. John Calvin, *The Epistles of Paul the Apostle to the Galatians, Ephesians, Philippians and Colossians,* trans. T. H. L. Parker, ed. David W. Torrance and Thomas F. Torrance (Grand Rapids: Eerdmans, 1965), 209, in his comments on Ephesians 5.

142. John Calvin, *A Harmony of the Gospels Matthew, Mark and Luke,* vol. 2, trans.

Ephesians 5:28-32, Calvin emphasizes that Paul shows men the unique love with which they should encounter their wives.

For all the Reformers it was clear that each husband should have only one wife, and vice versa. In some of the Anabaptist groups, however, polygamy was practiced. Already Martin Luther and Philipp Melanchthon (1497-1560), after much hesitation, had allowed the landgrave Philip of Hesse (1504-67) a second bigamous marriage since he had never really liked his first wife and always had attempted to escape from her.[143] Luther and Melanchthon referred to the Old Testament, where the patriarchs also had occasionally more than one wife and excused the landgrave's intention to marry a second wife by suggesting that by doing so he was avoiding a greater evil. Luther never publicly admitted that he gave this advice since it was given only in the confessional. While this advice caused great problems for the Protestants, another much greater scandal emerged.

An Anabaptist group attempted to erect the kingdom of God in the city of Münster in Westphalia, Germany, in 1534. These apocalyptically minded Anabaptists established a communism of production, meaning that all production was communally organized. A polygamous arrangement was also allowed in which one man could have several wives and all women without husbands were commanded to marry to fulfill God's command to humanity to "be fruitful and multiply" (Gen. 1:28). It was also said that the numerous progeny would qualify one for a place among the elect in the Holy City (Rev. 7:4).[144] While this utopian endeavor lasted for only a year until the city was taken over by the troops of the Roman Catholic bishop, another tendency had longer duration. In turning around Paul's comment in 1 Corinthians 7:15, "But if the unbelieving partner separates, let it be so," various Baptist groups and leaders allowed for the Anabaptist partner to separate from his or her non-Baptist spouse.[145] Both spouses should not only be in union in life, but also in faith. This means that marriage was a spiritual union and not a worldly thing as most Reformers had emphasized.

We have seen that **Martin Luther** in his view of marriage still followed

---

T. H. L. Parker, ed. David W. Torrance and Thomas F. Torrance (Grand Rapids: Eerdmans, 1972), 248, in his comments on Matthew 19:10-12.

143. For details, see Martin Brecht, *Martin Luther: The Preservation of the Church, 1532-1546*, trans. James L. Schaaf (Minneapolis: Fortress, 1993), 205-15.

144. For details, see George Huston Williams, *The Radical Reformation*, 3rd ed. (Kirksville, MO: Sixteenth Century Journal Publishers Inc., 1992), 782.

145. See Williams, *The Radical Reformation*, 778-81.

the Augustinian tradition, while also decisively moving beyond it. Expounding the sixth commandment in his *Large Catechism* Luther writes with regard to the state of marriage:

> He [God] also wishes us to honor, maintain, and cherish it as a divine and blessed walk of life. He has established it before all others as the first of all institutions, and he created man and woman differently (as is evident), not for indecency but to be true to each other, to be fruitful, to beget children, and to nurture and bring them up to the glory of God. God has therefore blessed this walk of life most richly above all others, and, in addition, has supplied and endowed it with everything in the world in order that this walk of life might be richly provided for. Married life is not a matter of jest or idle curiosity, but it is a glorious institution and an object of God's serious concern. For it is of utmost importance to him that persons be brought up to serve the world, promote knowledge of God, godly living, and all virtues, and to fight against wickedness and the devil.[146]

As this quote shows, for Luther marriage is one of the original orders of creation and not the result of the fall. Husband and wife are only outwardly (for the eyes to see) different. They are created for each other. Procreation is an important goal in marriage and so is the education of the children to the glory of God. In marriage, people are educated to serve the world. In this respect it is a worldly vocation. Marriage was not an emergency measure that God invented to limit human sinfulness. In a nutshell this is Luther's view on marriage.

Marriage, Sensuality, and Celibacy

"The origin of marriage is the will of God and not humanity."[147] Therefore God does not judge those who stand in faith and wish to do God's will on account of the sensual desires that take place in marriage. Despite the sin associated with it, marriage, if not by its nature then by the grace of God, receives God's gracious word of forgiveness and justification. Also, in spite of

146. Martin Luther, *Large Catechism* (sixth commandment), in *The Book of Concord*, ed. Kolb and Wengert, 414.

147. So Michael Parsons, *Reformation and Marriage: The Husband and Wife Relationship in the Theology of Luther and Calvin* (Edinburgh: Rutherford House, 2005), 142, in his excellent study. Parsons explicates Luther's understanding correctly in the kingdom to the left as a worldly vocation. Parsons also states that "both Luther and Calvin teach that marriage is a divinely given vocation" (103).

sin marriage remains a godly and holy estate. Luther sees sexual love, therefore, from a twofold perspective: from the perspective of God's good creation, and from the perspective of its distortion through sin.

Marriage, according to Luther, is the fundamental order of God from which all other orders and states are derived. It is commanded through God's creative will, for humans are driven to it by their very nature. Marriage cannot, therefore, simply be understood as God's command, but rather, by design of the creator, it is a necessary part of being human. Whoever does not enter into the estate of matrimony at some point, Luther surmised, inevitably falls prey to a loss of sexual discipline, prostitution, or self-abuse. These opinions are colored by Luther's own experiences with and observations of celibacy and contain a great deal of criticism specific to his time. Therefore Luther can also contend that the one who withholds himself from the estate of matrimony tempts God and does the will of Satan. Only within marriage is sexuality not a destructive force. Hence everyone should enter into the estate of marriage, if for no other reason than out of necessity and because of the sin inherent in our sexuality.

Yet Luther is aware of exceptions to marriage that are conceded by God. In the first place, there are some people who by their very nature are simply not suited for marriage. Likewise, there are others to whom God gives the exalted and supernatural gift of abstinence so that they are able to live a chaste life without being married. Such persons, however, are very rare, Luther observed. According to Luther, we would not find one among a thousand, for such persons are a "special miracle of God."[148] The Roman Church lost sight of this fact when they decreed priestly celibacy as law. If some genuinely have this gift from God, they should be thankful. No one, however, should put their trust in such abstinence and attempt a celibate life unless God has called them specially to be single, or unless they feel God's gracious gift of abstinence very strongly in themselves.

Luther, therefore, conceded the possibility of a celibate state and emphasized its special value and dignity. While it was a sin in the Old Testament to be without wife and child, this no longer applies in the New Testament. In agreement with Paul, Luther is even able to admit that the single state is better inasmuch as one without the responsibilities of marriage

> may better be able to preach and care for God's word. . . . It is God's word and the preaching which make celibacy — such as that of Christ and Paul

---

148. Martin Luther, *The Estate of Marriage* (1522), in *LW,* 45:21.

— better than the estate of marriage. In itself, however, the celibate life is far inferior.[149]

While a celibate life may provide more freedom to do one's professional tasks, from a moral perspective there is no higher estate than that of matrimony. Luther rejected, therefore, the qualitative superiority of the priestly estate. The marital estate, according to Luther, through the burdens that God lays on those who are married, contributes toward putting to death the old nature and is the advanced school of patient humility within God's will. Marriage provides innumerable opportunities to express patience and love that a single person does not have. Hence marriage is the rule and the celibate life the exception.

According to Luther, one should enter happily into marriage and should remain happy in marriage because God is well-pleased with marriage and with those who are married. The marital estate is adorned and made holy with the word of God. Hence marriage is a powerful source of joy in the midst of all burdens, crises, and disappointments. In marriage one finds peace in suffering, desire in apathy, and happiness in sorrow. "It is an art to see this estate according to the Word of God that alone makes both the estate of matrimony and those who enter into it lovely."[150] Luther therefore rejects the secular view of marriage that sees it only as a human and worldly institution that has nothing to do with God. Marriage is sanctified through God's will and word.

Seen from the perspective of human beings, however, marriage can only be holy when it is lived in the knowledge of God's involvement, that is, in faith. This does not contradict the characterization of marriage as an external, physical, or worldly thing, for even Luther is able to refer to his marriage as a "worldly business."[151] Marriage belongs to God's natural created order and not to Christ's redemptive order. Though it is a worldly walk of life, it is instituted by God and stands under God's blessing. Marriage is a holy estate even for those who are not Christians. Because it falls under the natural order, however, the church is not responsible for marriage as a legal institution. Marriage should not be subject to ecclesiastical laws and judgments but rather to those of the secular order. In those states that adopted

---

149. Luther, *The Estate of Marriage* (1522), in *LW,* 45:47.

150. Martin Luther, in a wedding sermon on Hebrews 13:4 from January 8, 1531, *Predigten des Jahres 1531,* in *WA,* 31/1:67.5ff.

151. Martin Luther, *Ein Traubüchlein für die einfältigen Pfarrherrn* (1529), in *WA,* 30/3:74.3.

the Lutheran Reformation, then, the legal aspects of marriage were soon administered by secular authorities. The church cannot establish laws in regard to this natural order of God any more than did Christ or the apostles, explained Luther. The only exception is to found in those matters when the issue at hand is one of conscience. Here there is also a place for the pastor to counsel and if necessary comfort people when they are uncertain about something in their own conscience and are confused, or when they have violated the true estate of marriage.

One sees the consequences of the doctrine of the two kingdoms in Luther's understanding of marriage. Marriage is part of the created order and belongs to the kingdom of the left. It is not a part of God's redemptive order for one can also be sanctified without marriage. Hence the question of what form marriage should take, patriarchal, partnership based, or egalitarian, is a question that must be solved in the secular realm and one to which the church is not able to contribute any special knowledge. The form of marriage is determined by the social conditions of different ages. Hence Katharina Luther "drove the wagon, cultivated the fields, fed the animals, did the shopping, and brewed beer."[152] She also was the "chief cook" and as "Lord Katie" she participated in the selection process of the boarders in their house.[153] In other words, she ran the whole household "and became a 'business woman' in her own right."[154] The independence of his wife allowed Luther to pursue his theological responsibilities. Both parents were responsible for the upbringing of the children, Katharina mostly during the day and when her husband was away on business and Luther mostly after he came home from work and when his wife was sick. But the children were also allowed to play around his desk while he was working. There was no clear separation of household duties for during his long years before marriage he had learned, for instance, to mend his own clothing, a practice he happily continued after his marriage despite the protests of his wife. It was clear, however, according to the custom of the time, that he would represent the family in important external matters, as, for instance, when a salary increase needed to be sought from the elector. His wife, on the other hand, was mostly responsible for internal matters, which included supervision of those employed within the household and on the little farm that she had purchased. With the cultural tradition of his times Luther was convinced of

152. According to Brecht, *Martin Luther*, 19.
153. Martin Luther, "Letter to Caspar Müller" (January 19, 1536), in *LW*, 50:126.
154. So Parsons, *Reformation and Marriage*, 204.

the husband's superiority over the wife. Yet when his former co-worker Veit Dietrich (1506-49) married in 1536, "Luther reminded him, undoubtedly referring to events in Luther's house, that a man must also yield to his wife, but without letting her dominate him."[155]

Although addressing marital problems was not a part of Luther's official pastoral duties since this was the responsibility of the secular authorities, he nevertheless gave advice on specific questions when asked in order to give counsel to the conscience. He frequently dealt with marital problems in a pastoral manner in his letters. According to Luther, the real responsibility of the pastoral office in regard to marriage was to proclaim to those who had entered into this estate not only the gospel but also God's will for marriage. Pastors should, therefore, inform those who are married about the power of faith and of love, without which one cannot have a good marriage.

The Practice of Marriage

In the practice of the wedding ceremony, Luther continued the traditional division. The actual wedding, that is, the pronouncement of the couple as husband and wife, took place before the church door. Inside the church, at the altar, the spiritual ceremony took place in which God's word concerning marriage was proclaimed, God's blessing announced, and the prayers of the congregation for the young couple sought. "The pastor in this way blesses the bride and groom, confirms their marriage, and testifies that they have accepted and publicly acknowledged each other."[156] The so-called church wedding is therefore only a confirmation of the marriage that has already taken place and is a belated act of ecclesiastical blessing.[157]

The public nature of marriage belongs to its very essence. Luther was careful to ensure that marriage as a public estate was always celebrated with a wedding before witnesses and the local congregation. A secret engagement and marriage, according to Luther, provides no certainty, and the testimony of both the parties is not sufficient to recognize their marriage. A

---

155. According to Brecht, *Martin Luther,* 21. Veit Dietrich had left Wittenberg since he did not get along with Katie.

156. Martin Luther, "Exempel, einen rechten christlichen Bischof zu weihen" (1542), in *WA,* 53:257.8ff.

157. In Germany today all marriages must officially take place at a government registrar's office before couples are allowed to proceed with a church wedding. The church wedding, then, usually follows the secular wedding by one or two days.

marriage should also not take place without the knowledge and consent of the parents, for this would violate the fourth commandment. On the other hand, parents should not force their children into a marriage against their will, nor should they forbid them to marry when they fall in love with someone.

Marriage has a twofold meaning in the relationship of the couple to each other and in their responsibility to procreate and rear children.[158] Husband and wife are there first of all for one another. The happiness of a marriage is secured when "husband and wife cherish one another, become one, [and] serve one another."[159] Sensual love alone is not enough because it can quickly cool. Marriage is much more a covenant of faithfulness.

> That is the ground and the entire essence of marriage, that a person gives him or herself to another and promises to remain faithful to them and not to turn to another. Meanwhile the one, therefore, is bound to the other and gives him or herself over as captive to the other.[160]

Within this covenant of faithfulness sexuality has a different context than it does outside of marriage, for it is no longer driven by self-seeking lust but by the desire to serve the other.

The physical relationship of a couple need not be limited only to that which is necessary to produce children. God allows couples sexual intercourse beyond what is necessary for procreation as an expression and consummation of marital love. Here Luther provides a corrective to Paul by contending:

> Although Christian married folk should not permit themselves to be governed by their bodies in the passion of lust, as Paul writes to the Thessalonians [1 Thess. 4:5], nevertheless each one must examine himself so that by his abstention he does not expose himself to the danger of fornication and other sins.[161]

Marital love and faithfulness proves itself above all in cases of disappointment in one's spouse, in times of conflict, and in the event that one's spouse is unbearable and mean-spirited.

Luther viewed marriage very soberly and recognized that it is always en-

---

158. For the following, see Althaus, *The Ethics of Martin Luther*, 92-97.
159. Martin Luther, *The Estate of Marriage* (1522), in *LW*, 45:43.
160. Martin Luther, *Ein Sermon von ehelichen Stand* (1519), in *WA*, 2:168.38–169.2.
161. Luther, *The Estate of Marriage* (1522), in *LW*, 45:36.

dangered when it is lived only on its own power. A Christian, however, does not draw superficially on happiness, but on the will of God. Luther argues similarly when he speaks of the illness of a spouse that prevents the fulfilling of the conjugal duty. In this situation one should not separate from the spouse but should serve God by serving the one who is sick. "Blessed and twice blessed are you when you recognize such a gift of grace and therefore serve your invalid . . . [spouse] for God's sake."[162] According to Luther, we can trust God that we will not be given more than we are able to bear. Everything depends on whether one enters and continues in a marriage with God, or self-confidently, that is, without God.

A first love or an initial falling in love is not, according to Luther, sufficient foundation for marriage. "It's easy enough to get a wife, but to love her with constancy is difficult."[163] It is an act of the devil that one becomes weary of one's spouse and casts his or her eye on others. One should arm oneself against this danger by beginning and leading a marriage under the eyes of God and praying for God's help. If another woman seems to me more beautiful and desirable than my own wife, wrote Luther, then I should say to myself: "I have at home a much more beautiful ornament in the person of my own wife whom God has given me and made beautiful above all others, whether she is physically attractive by nature or not or otherwise frail."[164]

The other aspect of marriage, according to the word and will of God, is its fruitfulness. Here the mother serves the loving will of God for his creature. She is made worthy with her whole being to be the tool and hand of God. This is true in pregnancy as well as with birth, seen in light of the crisis and danger of death associated with child-bearing that Luther poignantly witnessed as a result of the state of medicine and hygiene in his time. What the natural person sees as pure burden, limitation, and hard work, the eye of faith sees as a unique calling to serve God's gracious will and to foster new life. God therefore calls parents as apostles, bishops, and pastors of their children.

---

162. Martin Luther, *The Estate of Marriage* (1522), in *LW*, 45:35. Luther's original German here reads *Gemahl*, that is, "spouse," or even "husband," but not "wife" as the English version has it.

163. Martin Luther, "Table Talk" no. 524 (1542/1543), in *LW*, 54:444.

164. Martin Luther, in a sermon on Matthew 5:27-29, *Wochenpredigten über Matthew 5–7* (first printed 1532), in *WA*, 32:372.18-21.

Parenthood and Family

Parents, according to Luther, represent God and deserve to be seen by their children as the highest authority on earth, including both spiritual and secular dimensions.[165] Parents are the rulers of their children in the secular realm, providing rules to live by and nurture for their bodies. By virtue of the priesthood of all believers, however, they are also the spiritual authority for their children and are responsible to raise them in the Christian faith. Hence parents should not only love their children and prepare them for success in secular society, but they should also provide for them spiritually as they are able. Parents can earn blessedness for their children through a good upbringing, or damnation through neglect.

Luther did not agree with the opinion that one should not seek to influence children, that is, that they should be able to decide for themselves what they wish to believe. Although he constantly stressed that one cannot and dare not force someone to believe, he was well aware of the significance of parents as role models in worldly and spiritual matters, and of the truth of the proverb "The apple does not fall far from the tree." If parents do not have a positive relationship to faith then most likely their children will be brought up with an attitude of religious indifference. God, however, has established parents as his representatives. For this reason children should see their parents as representing God. Hence Luther wrote in his *Small Catechism* that we should "Honor, serve, obey, love, and respect" our parents. These five verbs belong together since to honor someone cannot be without love and respect. All this is not natural but requires a certain degree of obedience. Parents are the highest unified authority that their children initially know. This authority, however, is not grounded in any parental claim to power but finds its limits in the divine commission of parents for the children God has entrusted to them.

Luther attributes broad powers to the father as head of the household. A family of the late Middle Ages was composed of the parents and children and also frequently of servants, journeymen and apprentices of craftsmen, or boarders, all under one roof. In light of their physical and spiritual situations, Luther deduces that in the relationship between husband and wife, the husband is the head. Yet none of the normal tasks of wives are below the dignity of a husband to perform when necessary. Hence Luther can describe how the husband at night rocks the children, washes diapers, and cares for and works for his wife.[166]

---

165. For the following, see Althaus, *The Ethics of Martin Luther*, 99f.
166. Martin Luther, *The Estate of Marriage* (1522), in *LW*, 45:40.

The wife is the companion of her husband. She carried out the normal, lower-middle-class functions of her day — as Luther knew them — at home and on their property, and did this independently, and not under the supervision of her husband. The routine of the father of the house was coordinated with that of the wife and in regard to other household duties was not limited. Although the external function of a household is under the supervision of the government, its internal structure and the functions of the members in the household follow an order that is unique to each household and is appropriate to the order of creation. The father of the house, therefore, does not derive his authority from the government nor does he exercise this authority on behalf of it, but it is entrusted to him by God.

The primary concern of the wife is economic. The father, on the other hand, is primarily responsible for the religious aspect of family life. According to the preface of Luther's *Large Catechism,* "it is the duty of every head of a household at least once a week to examine the children and servants one after the other and ascertain what they know or have from it [i.e., the catechism]."[167] The father takes on the same function within the household as a pastor does in the parish. He is led by his spiritual care for his family appropriate to a catechetical instructor and receives this not by delegation from the church but through the position given him by God within the family as a baptized Christian.

The special function of the father is to be seen in that he cares for his children together with the mother, for these, at least until a certain age, are dependent on parental care. Children, therefore, stand in a similar relationship to their parents as do all persons to God who created them. The natural love for one's children, which arises from the biological connection to them, corresponds to the will of the creator. Yet this love dare not lead to a physical love for parents who rear their children for God and in God's stead. Hence parents should be just as concerned about the well-being of their children's souls as they are about the well-being of their bodies.

To bring up children for God does not mean that they should be sent to a monastery. Rather, they should be brought up to learn to serve and care for others, in fulfillment of their vocation, in availability for their congregation, and under the authority of God. The stubbornness of children who resist the authority of their parents is, according to Luther, the preliminary stage of the antisocial behavior of an adult and must be prevented through

---

167. Martin Luther, *Large Catechism* (preface), in *The Book of Concord,* ed. Kolb and Wengert, 383.

wise and if necessary strict discipline. "One should bring up children with great enthusiasm to have a healthy fear so that they fear those things for which one should have respect, but not so as to make them fearful, as many parents do, which hurts them throughout their life."[168] Unnecessary severity toward children is therefore foolish because it very easily has the opposite effect of what was intended. It is also a sin against the nature of children who, in their simplicity, are nearer to the original condition of our first parents than are adults. Luther therefore reprimands parents who do not compensate for the natural childishness of their children or who are unwilling to recognize their individuality.

One sees in Luther's view of the relationship between parents and children a fundamental ethical relationship built on mutual interaction. Also, one cannot accuse Luther of a patriarchal conception of the family in which the father is the unrestricted lord and master. This is true even though, as we have seen, Luther assumes the priority of the husband over the wife in the family. This was the naturally accepted family order for him and for his time. He based this view not only on tradition but also on natural law. Luther's analogy between parents and secular authority is certainly no longer applicable due to our democratically constituted government, even when we occasionally speak of a "father of the nation." Although our historical distance from Luther becomes very clear, we should not overlook the seemingly modern features of his understanding of marriage and family. The rights of parents, for example, find their limits in the first commandment. Luther himself went against the express will of his parents and entered the monastery. Also, as can be seen in Luther's own marriage, a wife had a certain amount of freedom that was not subject to the rule of her husband. One could even speak here of a partnership marriage in the sense of an "intellectual and spiritual partnership of the wife,"[169] whereby husband and wife are interdependent with each being concerned for the well-being of the other.

While we still could learn much from the Reformers, especially from Luther and his emphasis that marriage is the best educational institution in which we learn how to care for each other and to curb our egotistical inclinations, marriage has changed drastically since then. Although Luther mar-

---

168. Martin Luther, *Decem praecepta Wittenbergensi praedicata populo* (1518), in *WA*, 1:449.35-39.

169. Ingetraut Ludolphy, "Frau VI. Reformationszeit," in *TRE*, 11:443, in reference to Luther.

ried his wife without asking his parents for advice and against what most of his friends and especially his enemies considered appropriate, Luther and Katharina's marriage was no two-people-affair. They were embedded in a large, extended family that included boarders in their house, menservants and maidservants, and close friends. Today, however, much of this has changed.

In conclusion we want to summarize the most important points in Luther's view of marriage:

1. Marriage is a divinely instituted walk of life that is inferior to none.
2. Luther has a positive view of sexual activity within marriage, but due to his Augustinian thought formation sex is still tinged by human sinfulness.
3. Luther has a genuine appreciation of bodily/sexual intimacy.
4. Luther affirms an interdependence of husband and wife in their respective work, but as a child of his time is convinced of the superiority of the husband over his wife. The latter was compromised in his own home by the assertiveness of Katharina.
5. The upbringing of children is the responsibility of both parents. The father is more responsible for the spiritual side, the mother more for nurturing the physical side.

The Challenge of Today

German theologian Helmut Thielicke (1908-86) wrote: "Prior to romanticism people married, or were married, with a view toward individual love within the union thus effected, whereas since romanticism they marry on the basis of love they already experience."[170] This means that in Europe before nineteenth-century romanticism two people married, or they were married by arrangement, and then one expected or hoped that love would be kindled between husband and wife. But beginning in modern times one married only after such love was already kindled. In some regions of the world, however, marriages are still arranged by the respective parents or they exercise at least considerable influence on whom their children should marry.[171] We remember that Martin Luther confessed that he was not really

---

170. Helmut Thielicke, *Being Human . . . Becoming Human: An Essay in Christian Anthropology*, trans. Geoffrey Bromiley (Garden City, NY: Doubleday, 1984), 190.
171. See Joseph A. Fonseca, *Marriage in India: A Historical Social Theological Investiga-*

enthused about his future wife. He decided to marry Katharina since there was no one else around to marry her and because he had heard that she was attracted to him, not to mention the fact that he had become increasingly dissatisfied with the lonely life he was leading as the sole occupant of a big monastery. In the long run he really appreciated his wife and a deep bond of love developed between the two. In the modern world of Europe and North America, however, the gradual growth of love is more the exception than the rule.

In this day and age, the fire of love must first be kindled between two people, and only then is marriage discussed. Moreover, the couple often lives together for a number of years before they decide to marry. The reason for this is usually not because love is missing in the relationship, but because of secondary considerations such as graduation from school, employment opportunities, and the like. Marriage is no longer an arrangement made between two clans or two extended families, but the decision of two individuals. Since the larger support system of the families is often missing, marriage is more endangered now than in the past. This does not mean that there is less fidelity, but there is less comprehensive cohesion.

In our specialized and complex world our life is divided into different segments that have little or nothing to do with each other. We go to our workplace and are immersed in the work world. Once we are finished there we hurry home, perhaps doing a few errands on the way. The work world and time off from work usually have very little to do with each other. While Katharina knew exactly what her husband was doing, whether at home or away from home, marriage partners today have no idea what one another's workplace is like and often they are too tired when they return home to talk much about what happened at work. If both spouses are "gainfully employed," which today is more the rule than the exception, both have little idea what the other does when away from home. There is usually little or no time for sharing what was experienced during the day and work is often so specialized that the other partner would not understand it much anyway.

It is also significant that for us real work is only that for which we get paid while all the other duties in everyday life seem to be taken for granted. This was different during Luther's time, because his wife contributed substantially to the budget even if she did not earn any money by overseeing the farm work, brewing beer, employing the servants, and caring for the

---

tion (Bangalore: Redemptorist Publications India, 1988), 274, where he talks about the dowry system and the marital contract.

boarders in their home. The modern reduction of work to financially remunerated matters usually makes it necessary for both marriage partners to work outside of and away from their home and property.

This split between the work world and the world of non-work often results in marriage partners spending more actual awake time with their fellow-workers than with each other. A secretary/assistant often knows more about his or her boss than does the boss's wife or husband. This, of course, can become an emotional strain on the God-intended relationship between husband and wife, and is also a relatively new experience. Living in totally different worlds of experience and spending most of the time apart from each other in distant locations can create many problems. The marriage partners can become so immersed in their own respective worlds that the bond between the two is so attenuated that conversation between them stops. Moreover, since neither one knows the work of the other from firsthand experience, or understands the work world of the other, there is little common ground left between the two. When they finally get home to their joint living space, they are often too tired or simply too negligent to share with their marriage partner what they have experienced during the day. Since marriage, however, is a relationship that includes not only a segment of a person, but a person's whole being, we cannot exclude the partner from important segments of our life without estranging him or her from us. Once a third party enters the marriage scene, this signals that the marriage covenant is severely endangered. The relationship of mutuality that perhaps was already on shaky ground has now been destroyed.

At the beginning of a marriage there is always mutuality and sharing. As witnessed on the first pages of the Bible, and as Jesus affirms in many places, love is a natural power that draws one person to another and allows both to become one with the other. But marriage is not something that grows naturally. To the contrary, it requires commitment, discipline, and the courage to grow and change. In other words, nurturing a marriage is hard but rewarding work. Yet our competitive world militates against this. It often breeds egotism in which the self-assertion of the ego seems to be the most important factor for our advancement and well-being. Though there is much talk about love, this love is often reduced to biological love or sex. But what really draws us to the other person? Is it the feeling of (splendid) isolation and therefore a confirmation of the biblical insight that humans were created for each other? If this is true we cannot confine this relatedness to a few (convenient) moments or to the biological dimension without in the long run harming ourselves. This mutual relationship should encompass our whole lives. This means first of all that we do not sell ourselves in the marketplace for short-lived gains but create space and time for each other for mutual sharing and enjoyment.[172] Since sinfulness is self-centeredness, this means that our love for the other must fight daily against self-love. We must recognize that the other person is as much created and loved by God as we are. Once we are mindful of this we will affirm our partner in his or her personhood and not degrade the partner as an object. The more we overcome our egotism the more we will grow into the dynamics of this love relationship.

A mutual life relationship does not mean that we should become a duplicate of our partner. It is often the illusion of love that leads us to want to model ourselves exactly in the way the other wants us to be. Yet in a mutual relationship we should respect the desires and wishes of the other, without becoming their alter ego or renouncing our own ego and our own life. If we yield too much we have abandoned our common life and only the life of the other remains. Love, however, does not mean that each goes one's separate way, or that we only follow the way of the other. Both partners may and can be different and must have time and space for growth and development. Many marriages break apart or become boring because both partners continuously nag each other. Neither one wants to accept the other as he or she is, but wants to make the other a copy of oneself. Love does not mean that I own the other, but that together in our individual way we jointly encounter the future. As Jesus showed in his commentary on the sixth commandment in the Sermon of the Mount, the greatest enemy of marriage is a person's own ego, which would rather look in a mirror than turn to the other and say, "I love you."

The mutual life relationship that we affirm in marriage does not result from a contract between two people, though this may be involved. Marriage has a much larger dimension. As a basic form of human existence it is offered to us by God in creation. Since it is also a natural order, the government has a rightful interest in marriage and its success and therefore demands an official marriage ceremony. While a sizeable number of children are born out of wedlock, most future citizens are still born and raised within marriage. But there is also an ecclesial part to a Christian marriage. While the church building often serves as an ideal location for a beautiful wedding ceremony, there is much more to this ceremony than meets the

---

172. If I may append a personal note: when our son was asked on his internship in Singapore to work as a private investor for up to ten rich clients, his response was: "I will not sell my soul."

eye. We ask for God's blessing on the new marriage and take Jesus' promise seriously that marriage is under God's special protection.

God does not want a marriage to break apart, but to be transformed into a durable mutual life relationship. It is especially important that the marriage partners realize that there is indeed a third party involved in marriage, God, and that they daily include God in their marriage covenant. Once the married couple prays together in the Lord's Prayer, "Forgive us our trespasses as we forgive those who trespass against us," it will be difficult and even contradictory to be unforgiving toward one's own spouse. Therefore the saying "the family that prays together stays together" is not insurance against a broken marriage, but it can help to prevent breakage. A joined life under God's guidance helps to master problems in marriage and helps couples to remain in marital fidelity. If we allow God to rule in our lives, we may not be able to exclude our egotism completely, but it can at least be tamed enough that we do not endanger our relationship with our partner. The more we realize that God has accepted us the more we are also able to accept our spouse and to recognize and honor him or her as our partner. Marriage is not a state of being that one may simply enter into and stay in forever, but as is the case with Christian life in general, marriage, too, calls for daily renewal.

The biggest danger for a marriage is the illusion that everything runs by itself and things will be all right. Such self-satisfaction can lead to a deadening of the marriage or to the misunderstanding that one can become more daring outside of marriage. Yet the marriage is neither a place where we can come to rest nor is it an institution that we can intentionally burden. Though we watch this dangerous attitude quite often in movies or on TV, read about it in almost any magazine, or even hear it from friends, this is still the wrong attitude. As Jesus emphasized in the Sermon on the Mount, being frivolous with one's own marriage or with that of other persons is tantamount to breaking a marriage (Matt. 5:28). Love is not possible without renouncing one's own desires of egotism and escapism.

In Western societies today one usually only enters marriage out of love and affection. At the same time, couples can be more relaxed in engaging in sexual intimacy prior to marriage because of the availability of "the pill" and other methods of contraception to avoid pregnancy. The decision to abandon a marriage is also made much more quickly today than it was just a generation ago. But with all these "advantages" more readily available people have still not become happier. To the contrary, marital counselors and life counselors see more married couples than ever. In the pursuit of happiness and self-fulfillment we often consider the other only as a means through which we can satisfy our own ego. In so doing, we forget that we are intrinsically dialogical beings who cannot find our happiness in egotistic isolation, but only in opening ourselves to other people, and especially to our marriage partners. It is the tragedy of many so-called successful people that through their very success they become impoverished and isolated. In climbing the ladder to success they virtually stepped on so many people and their destinies that they forgot how to cultivate true friendship and intimacy. Fulfillment through the other person, however, consists not in using the person as an expendable object, but in cherishing him or her as a unique person loved by God. In marriage, self-fulfillment can only be attained in a continuous giving of the self and receiving from the other in return. It involves encouragement, not discouragement of the partner, and helping him or her, not triumphing over the partner.

If we live together in marriage and together approach the future that has been given to us, then we see marriage not as a straightjacket, but as an opportunity for joint planning, shaping, and working. Marriage will always lead us to new discoveries. Marriage is not a limitation imposed on us, but an opportunity to step out of isolation and into a joint union.

Since a marriage is lived on this earth and not in heaven, it is not without tension. Jesus plainly announced in the Sermon on the Mount that God does not want a marriage to be broken and will not approve of such. But marriages nevertheless can and do break. The same Jesus who categorically denounces the breaking up of a marriage with one's eyes and in one's heart, also says about the sinner who has broken her marriage: "I tell you, her sins, which were many, have been forgiven; hence she has shown great love" (Luke 7:47). Jesus even says to bystanders who quickly want to condemn a woman who has broken her marriage: "Let anyone among you who is without sin be the first to throw a stone at her" (John 8:7). Without attempting to justify the breaking of a marriage, those who come out of a broken marriage may live by Jesus' own words: "Neither do I condemn you. Go your way, and from now on do not sin again" (John 8:11). Those human catastrophes — and the breaking up of a marriage is a personal catastrophe — stand under God's forgiveness and God offers encouragement to do better in a new beginning. This shows us that marriage ultimately can only be lived through God's forgiving grace.

If marriage really means giving total attention to one's spouse, as Jesus proclaimed in the Sermon of the Mount, then every marriage must stand under the word of forgiveness and must be a continuous new beginning.

Christians are not just saints, but over and over again also sinners. They live in a world marked by human failure and guilt. With this realization they should be ready to forgive each other anew and be able to receive forgiveness and attempt a new beginning. Even if one thinks that a love has grown cold, one can learn to rekindle the fire of love, to approach the partner anew, to encourage him or her, and to venture a new beginning. We can learn from the Sermon on the Mount which view of marriage must be avoided (see Matt. 5:27-32). As Christians we will attempt to go into marriage in a different way than those who intentionally do not allow God to be a partner in their marriage covenant. If we realize that God is our creator who loves us and who is faithful to us, then this kind of love and faithfulness will also shine through us to our marriage partner.

Marriage contains a great promise because the more love we radiate, the more we will also receive, and the more faithful we are, the more faithfulness will we ourselves receive. Even today marriage is still a great opportunity for everyone. Yet those who, because of their personal history, are unable to find a marriage partner may be comforted to know that not everyone has to marry. It is an offer, not an obligation. Especially in our modern world, in which there are many more opportunities not only for work, but for leisure and meaningful societal engagement, those who remain single will also find many opportunities for sharing, for community, and for communion with others.

Children and Working Spouses

Since the divine intention for marriage is also to provide a context in which children are born and raised, we briefly want to address this complex but important dimension. With a child another human being enters the husband-wife relationship and thereby complicates it. Therefore having a child is no remedy for an already strained partnership. Yet it does not strain a stable partnership but asks for additional consideration. Though children are costly, financially and time-wise, they offer many rewards: affection, companionship, and the joy of seeing them grow, develop, and achieve. Like our spouses, each child is different and if we want to make our children into copies of ourselves, or what we wanted ourselves to be, we end up using them instead of nurturing and caring for them. The result will be problems and disappointment. The purpose of raising children is not to increase our own honor and prestige, but to "bring them up in the discipline and instruction of the Lord" (Eph. 6:4).

Raising children takes time, not just "quality time" but "quantity time." While children would prefer to have their parents by their side full-time, this is neither necessary nor possible. Parents also need free time even if it is just during the children's nap. But as we noticed above a "time deficit" in caring for the children can lead to developmental problems. Since most spouses are gainfully employed outside the home today, this may call for a reconsideration of that work. The traditional solution in industrial society was that mothers stayed at home with the children and fathers were the breadwinners. Yet this stereotype did not hold true for the financially less fortunate because for them child labor and women working in factories were often necessary means of survival. Sunday schools were initially offered so that children could at least attend school on Sunday since they worked during the week. Moreover, as studies have shown, the conventional division of work — women at home with the children and men outside the home and in the workplace — leads to little satisfaction with the spouses themselves, their relationship, and their role as parents.[173] More satisfaction was reported by those who had flexibility in their work schedule to be free to handle emergencies, stay at home with sick kids, and generally devote more time to family life.

There is no biblical mandate saying that the mother must stay at home with the children and the husband must work outside the home. The decisive question is not who does what, the question is one of priorities. The secular world tells us that we must achieve and this means climbing up the ladder and reaping the (financial) rewards. Yet this notion is basically self-centered and therefore intrinsically sinful. The best job and the best home are two items that are virtually impossible to bring together. Therefore compromises are needed but in such a way that the material concerns and the perceived financial needs do not win out over the actual overall needs of the family. Of course, any scaling back in gainful employment involves a reduction of one's finances. As Jesus reminded us, however, life is not just eating and drinking, but also has a spiritual and, we might add, a rewarding interpersonal dimension that is worth cultivating.

Some companies have noticed that satisfaction at home also results in better performance at work. They are helpful in many ways, assisting with housing concerns, providing child care so parents can remain active with their children, finding suitable employment for the other spouse, allowing

173. See the survey cited by Carrie A. Miles, *The Redemption of Love: Rescuing Marriage and Sexuality from the Economics of a Fallen World* (Grand Rapids: Brazos, 2006), 174f.

families of their employees to make use of company fitness facilities, and having family weekends when the family is able to go and see where the spouse actually works. In Germany, for instance, a new government rule has been in effect since 2007. It allows a new mother to stay at home from work and the government will pay her 67 percent of her last net income up to a certain maximum amount for one year. If the husband decides to stay at home, he will receive an extra two months of pay. This rule also encourages fathers to play an active role in raising the children and has been quite effective. For unemployed and single mothers the rules are adjusted accordingly. It came as a surprise that more and more husbands stay home to benefit from this rule. A genuine interdependence of husband and wife seems to develop in the upbringing of children.

From our review of the distinction and unity of man and woman the following points emerge:

1. The arrangement of power and influence between men and women was never fixed but has changed over the centuries. While in the Old Testament the status of the woman was considerably restricted, Jesus approached women in an egalitarian way. The New Testament trend of asserting equality between the sexes was continued in the early church. Women were very much involved in spreading the gospel. Yet, as we saw, Paul did not discard the cultural and societal traditions in which women found themselves even while he affirmed the mutuality between men and women sanctioned through Christ.

2. The Bible leaves no doubt that the proper place for sexuality is within the marriage of husband and wife. Yet the New Testament writers' expectation that the kingdom was coming soon meant that both marriage and sexuality lost importance. The nascent church then steered a clear course against both sexual promiscuity and Gnostic contempt for the body. But gradually virginity became the ideal while marriage was perceived as a second best. It was only in the period of the Reformation that sexuality was rediscovered as part of God's created order.

3. Until modernity, marriage was not a private affair but was part of a larger family or clan which provided support and stability for the married couple and the children. Especially in the early church, Christian marriage was a countercultural arrangement against the widespread contempt of marriage. This seems to be the case today, too, when many other forms of living together and sharing sexual intimacy are practiced.

4. Marriage is not divinely mandated. But it is an order of creation both for the benefit of husband and wife and for the upbringing of children. While gainful employment is important for the survival of a family, it is equally important that the respective members share their gifts and time with each other.

8. Human Destiny

There are two basic aspects to human destiny: we are put on this earth, and we look forward to a new earth. Concerning this world Paul sets the tone with his injunction "Anyone unwilling to work should not eat" (2 Thess. 3:10). For human beings work is a natural. Indeed, a human being has always been considered a *homo faber*, a craftsperson. For a long time it was thought that the invention and use of tools was peculiar to humans, but that opinion has changed. Animals, too, within certain limits, have the ability to invent and use tools. Yet when we fly in an airplane and look down on our planet, we see how humans have virtually changed the face of the earth. From the very beginning humans were asked to till and to keep the Garden of Eden (Gen. 2:15). In Genesis 1 we hear that humans should have "dominion over the fish of the sea, and over the birds of the air, and over the cattle, and over all the wild animals of the earth, and over every creeping thing that creeps upon the earth" (Gen. 1:26). This dominion would imply work. Work is not the result of the fall or the consequence of human sinfulness but it is natural for humans. The curse after the fall was not that humans now must work, but that there is drudgery connected with it (Gen. 3:17ff.). Though a man will toil from morning to night, often the ground will only yield thorns and thistles and therefore by the sweat of his brow a man will eat his bread.

As we have seen, humans are not created to be the servants or slaves of God. They are God's partners and even God's administrators on earth. The presupposition for success in human work is God's blessing, as we can gather from Genesis 8:22: "As long as the earth endures, seed time and harvest, cold and heat, summer and winter, day and night, shall not cease." In contrast to animals, human beings have the explicit commission, responsibility, and God's affirmation to be productively active. While the Sabbath is a day of rest, it is not a day of simply doing nothing, but another opportunity to remember that humans are ultimately related to God. The Sabbath as the end of the work week was to remind the Israelites both of the eternal Sabbath when all work will cease and that God is the end of all human efforts.

In contrast to Hellenistic ideas, work was the normal lot of every person and not reserved for slaves. As we hear in the context of the Ten Commandments: "Six days you shall labor and do all your work" (Exod. 20:9).[1] On the seventh day, however, the human being ought to rest. This joining together of work and rest and devotion to God was picked up in the monastic tradition of *ora et labora,* pray and work. Work therefore was not considered service to God, but it was a means of survival. As the psalmist says: "You shall eat the fruit of the labor of your hands" (Ps. 128:2). Yet the Israelites knew that without God's blessing no fruit of their labor would endure ("Unless the Lord builds the house, those who build it labor in vain," Ps. 127:1). There was no devaluation of bodily work over against mental work, especially since artistic faculties and craftsmanship were highly esteemed and considered as God's special gift (Exod. 31:2-6). Often, however, this led to the idea that if God blesses people their efforts will prosper and when God withholds his blessing their efforts come to naught. This then was connected with the idea that God's blessing was dependent on one's own merits; therefore the Israelites believed that for good behavior they were richly rewarded and for sinful acts they were punished. As the book of Job, however, shows, this belief was too simplistic. The story of Job conveys the message that the cause-and-effect sequence between our actions and God's reactions does not always hold true. Therefore Jesus reminds his audience: God "makes his sun rise on the evil and on the good, and he sends rain on the righteous and on the unrighteous" (Matt. 5:45).

1. Work and Vocation

In antiquity work with the hands was often thought to be the task of slaves and of servants; by contrast, free citizens should deal with the higher skills, such as poetry, science, and politics. Therefore both Plato and Aristotle

---

1. See Horst Dietrich Preuss, *Old Testament Theology,* 2 vols. (Louisville: Westminster John Knox, 1995-96), 2:199, for the Old Testament view on "work."

criticized working with one's hands.[2] Yet when we come to the New Testament, we notice that Jesus was a "carpenter's son" and was even called a "carpenter" himself (Matt. 13:55, Mark 6:3). At the same time, Jesus was also called "rabbi" (Mark 9:5). This means that Jesus may have had a dual profession: as a craftsperson he was a carpenter, and as an interpreter of the law he was a rabbi. Paul followed in that same tradition and also had a dual profession as "tentmaker" (Acts 18:3) and as missionary and apostle. It comes as no surprise that Jesus takes many of his illustrations and examples from the daily work of the people, whether shepherd, fisherman, laborer in the vineyard, or tax collector.

As the parable of the talents shows, using one's talents is expected by God and will have its reward (Matt. 25:14-30). Yet the parable of the rich farmer also shows that one cannot secure one's life through work alone (Luke 12:13-21), "for life is more than food, and the body more than clothing" (Luke 12:23). While Paul even encourages slaves to obey their worldly masters with fear and trembling, he tells some that they should actually do "the will of God from the heart" (Eph. 6:6). This means work is not an end in itself; ultimately, it is God's will that we not be lazy and idle, but we are to use to the fullest the various skills that God has given us.

Over against the Hellenistic disdain for bodily work, this holistic approach to this life and the life beyond seen in the New Testament prevailed in Christendom. For instance, Augustine asserts that God will feed and clothe us if by reason of either infirmity or occupation we cannot work. "But when we are able, we ought not tempt our God; because this very ability of powers we have by His gift, and in living by it, we live by His bounty Who has bounteously bestowed upon us that we should have this ability."[3] This means that God will take care of us if we are not able to take care of ourselves. Yet if we have the ability to work, then we should also use this as God's gift and dare not neglect it. When in medieval Europe cities developed and the mendicant orders, such as the Franciscans and the Dominicans settled there in the thirteenth century, a similar bifurcation of work developed as we saw in Hellenistic times. While common labor, especially that of the peasants, was frowned on, craftsmanship was held in high esteem, and from the donation of craftsmen these mendicant orders could

2. Plato, *Laws* (741e), in *The Dialogues of Plato*, trans. B. Jowett, intro. Raphael Demos (New York: Random House, 1936), 2:508; Aristotle, *Politeia* (1.5: 1254a.b and 3.5: 1278), in *The Basic Works of Aristotle,* ed. with an intro. Richard McKeon (New York: Random House, 1941), 1132 and 1182f.

3. Augustine, *On the Works of Monks* (35), in *NPNF,* 3:521.

survive and thrive. Often work with one's hands was even seen as penitence and there developed a stratification of society with three stations. On top were the nobility and the clergy, followed by those concerned with intellectual pursuits, including merchants and administrators, and on the lowest level were those who worked with their hands. The nobility, for example, was not allowed to engage in a profession or to be active in commerce but had to ensure peace and order in their respective territories.[4]

When we come to the Reformation period, we discern a positive evaluation of work. **John Calvin**, for instance, emphasizes that "the Lord bids each one of us in all life's actions to look to his calling."[5] He suggests that in order to realize our particular place in life God has named the various kinds of living "callings." In this regard we should be frugal and realize that we hold all earthly possessions in trust. Therefore Calvin admonishes the people: "Let each one see to what extent he is in duty bound to others and let him pay his debt faithfully."[6] This is true for the people, for the sovereign ruler, for the servants in the church, for the parents, and in whatever state one finds oneself. "In this manner let each man consider what, in his rank and station, he owes to his neighbors, and pay what he owes. Moreover, our mind must always have regard for the Lawgiver, that we may know that this rule was established for our hearts as well as for our hands, in order that men may strive to protect and promote the well-being and interest of others."[7] This means that work and its benefits are not to be enjoyed for oneself, but work is always for the benefit of other people.

Calvin maintains that the calling by the Lord is the starting point and the foundation for all proper actions. When you obey your calling, "no task will be so sordid and base, provided you obey your calling in it, that it will not shine and be reckoned very precious in God's sight."[8] All of us have a special calling and therefore it does not matter what kind of work we do. This shows in a nutshell that Calvin no longer distinguishes between menial and intellectual works or between secular and spiritual works. In his eyes all are of equal importance. The same can be said for Martin Luther.

Initially, **Martin Luther** followed the monastic idea that work is more

---

4. See Chuck Legoff, "Arbeit V: Mittelalter," in *TRE,* 3:634.

5. John Calvin, *Institutes of the Christian Religion* (III.10.6), ed. John T. McNeill, trans. Ford Lewis Battles, The Library of Christian Classics, vols. 20 and 21 (Philadelphia: Westminster, 1960), 1:724.

6. Calvin, *Institutes* (II.8.46), 1:410.

7. Calvin, *Institutes* (II.8.46), 1:411.

8. Calvin, *Institutes* (III.10.6), 1:725.

a curse than a blessing "for in Adam we are all condemned to work."[9] Work in this way is part of penitential activity because working and fasting crucify our flesh and therefore "fasting includes all kinds of work of crucifying one's flesh and staying awake, working, and so on."[10] Through his Reformation insight that we are justified through faith alone Luther then arrived at a new understanding of work. We cannot obtain merits through our work, but work is a fruit of faith and thereby a God-pleasing good deed. Because we have already received everything from God our creator, we cannot expect to be rewarded by God for what we do. Good works, therefore, have nothing to do with our justification. "Those things we do for God are not called good works, but what we should do for our neighbor, these are good works."[11] The fact that we perform good works here on earth is motivated solely by God's preceding grace toward us and the fact that our fellow human beings need our help. Whoever performs worldly tasks does so to the glory of God and as a service to the neighbor.

With this concept of worldly work as an expression of our gratitude toward God, and simultaneously as a help for our neighbor, Luther dispelled the widespread idea that only works that we do for God are pleasing to God, while the work we do in this world is basically drudgery and the result of our fallen state. This misconception led to the idea that only the clergy and members of monastic orders could devote themselves to doing good works. They had a real vocation by being called out of the mire of this world. For Luther, however, anything is a true vocation that we do out of gratitude to God and toward alleviating the plight of our neighbor. Through this new perception there occurred a great leveling of the hierarchic structure of work and a new appreciation of manual, intellectual, and artistic labor. We are not called out of this world to a better and higher vocational state, but we are called into this world by responding to the gifts God has given us in furthering the good of this world.

In our industrialized, urbanized society, however, this conception of vocation has largely disappeared. The modern understanding of one's "job" is characterized by cost control — minimizing investment and maximizing profits. But employers and employees today are increasingly taking notice of the fact that without personal engagement a "job," over the long run, simply amplifies the meaninglessness of life. Health problems,

---

9. Martin Luther, *Treatise on Good Works* (1520), in *LW,* 44:108.

10. Martin Luther, *Ein Sermon von Ablass und Gnade* (1517), in *WA,* 1:244.4.

11. Martin Luther in a sermon on John 20:21ff. (April 27, 1522), in *WA,* 10/3:98.26f.

lack of motivation, and a down-turn in the quality of work are only some of the results.

The meaninglessness of our work world is largely the result of our own doing. The manufacturing process, for instance, has in many places been broken down into such small entities that we no longer know how the item we manufacture or shape contributes to the final product.[12] Hence for more and more people the level of remuneration and the length of the workweek are no longer decisive. Most people desire that their work be interesting, challenging, and personally engaging. If one has no feeling for what one is doing, the work itself becomes more and more boring. Therefore Luther's emphasis on vocation as a service to one's neighbor needs to be rediscovered and brought back into the work process.

A new work ethic seems to have evolved that is characterized by the following "virtues":[13]

1. Sacrifice: we invest to meet the needs of others.
2. Service: when we say "May I help you?" we mean it.
3. Teamwork: the success of each depends on all working together.
4. Discipline: good intentions need to be carried through.
5. Honesty: trust builds relationships.
6. Creativity: we can try it a different way.

While these are indeed valuable virtues for both individuals and businesses, they focus on the work world. Yet for Luther vocation is more than just doing the kind of work for which we usually get paid. It includes all the stations of life, whether in the family or at the workplace, in private or in public. Therefore these virtues should also be considered for adoption in all avenues of life, in all of our vocations.

---

12. See Christofer Frey, "Die Reformation Luthers in ihrer Bedeutung für die moderne Arbeits- und Berufswelt," in *Luther und die Folgen,* ed. Hartmut Löwe and Claus-Jürgen Roepke (Munich: Christian Kaiser, 1983), 126.

13. Adapted from Michael C. Maibach, "The Virtues of a Commercial Republic," in *Business and Religion: A Clash of Civilizations?* ed. Nicholas Capaldi (Salem, MA: Scrivener, 2005), 28.

a. The Respective Station (Stand)
as Location for Mutual Responsibility

In his review of Luther's position Ernst Troeltsch claims: "Obedient service in the callings . . . comes to be considered the first duty of the Christian and the true and proper sphere for exercising the love of one's neighbor."[14] Yet it would be wrong to assume that with this emphasis on obedient service Luther was advocating a societal structure characterized by different classes. This can be shown by his notion of station *(Stand)*. A station is a place in society in which we find ourselves, depending on age, marital status, occupation, and so on. As we get older, these stations can change. Yet they are the respective places where our life is acted out. In 1630 hymn writer Johann Heermann expressed Luther's thoughts succinctly when he wrote: "Give me the strength to do with ready heart and willing whatever you command, my calling [*Stand*] here fulfilling."[15] These various stations are starting points for our actions. They are beyond our arbitrary decisions, for the creator has established them and placed us within a particular station. These stations are places to which God calls us so that we can carry out a specific and unique vocation. As God puts us in a certain situation we find ourselves in a web of human interdependence, for instance, as someone's customer, father, husband, employee, church member, and so on. We participate in most of these relationships simultaneously. And it is in these various stations that we are "actively engaged in shaping the lives of others as they are affecting ours."[16] They have a stabilizing function but unlike castes they are not closed in on themselves so that we are permanently assigned to them.

There is a certain mobility from one station to another. This becomes clear when Luther uses a traditional threefold division of estates, the economic, the political, and the ecclesial, and shows that a person does not belong exclusively to one station (estate) or the other. Luther comments: "This life is profitably divided into three orders: (1) life in the home; (2) life in the state; (3) life in the church. To whatever order you belong — whether you are a husband, an officer of the state, or a teacher of the church — look

---

14. Ernst Troeltsch, *The Social Teaching of the Christian Churches*, 2 vols., intro. H. Richard Niebuhr, trans. Olive Wyon (Chicago: University of Chicago Press, 1981), 2:557.

15. *Evangelical Lutheran Worship*, hymn no. 806, stanza 2.

16. So William H. Lazareth, *Luther on the Christian Home: An Application of the Social Ethics of the Reformation* (Philadelphia: Muhlenberg, 1960), 132, in his still very relevant application of Luther's thoughts.

about you, and see whether you have done full justice to your calling."[17] The stations describe the multidimensionality of human life and the different interpersonal relations that make up the structure of human existence. For Luther these are not secular relations, but they have a deep religious significance since we carry out our divine calling in the way we relate to each other and to the tasks involved in daily life.

In the category of the economic station Luther first of all subsumed marriage and household, meaning parents and children, menservants and maidservants, as well as widows and young girls. The political station comprises not only princes and lords, judges and officials, but also menservants and maidservants and all those who are in a subservient office. The ecclesial station not only includes those who preach and administer the sacraments, but also the custodians, the congregational treasurers, and those who serve these people. Indeed, all Christians can be included in the ecclesial station. This means that we find ourselves in several different stations, relations, and structures, depending on which aspect of our life we are considering.

"God has instituted many estates in life in which men are to learn to exercise themselves and suffer. To some he has commanded the estate of matrimony, to others the estate of the clergy, to others the estate of temporal rule, and to all he has commanded that they shall toil and labor."[18] Yet none of these stations is of higher value than the others and all have as their goal to serve the other stations. To be sure, each person is placed within a specific station, but one can also change from one station to another, for instance, from the spiritual station to the political or the economic. Yet every station has its own difficulties, so that none is better or easier than the others. There is also no station in which there is no sin for there is no station in which the command of God is fully carried out.

Why did God establish these stations in the first place? According to Luther's explanation the stations embody the will of God so that God might provide for order and serve the needs of human beings through these external forms. "Without these masks [i.e., stations] peace and discipline could not be preserved."[19] It is particularly important for us to remember that none of these stations is placed above or below the others. Luther strictly re-

17. Martin Luther, *Lectures on Genesis* (1535-45), in *LW*, 3:217, in his comments on Genesis 18:15. We should note that he says there that "life is divided into three orders" and not that society is divided into three orders.

18. Martin Luther, *The Holy and Blessed Sacrament of Baptism* (1519), in *LW*, 35:39.

19. Martin Luther, *Lectures on Genesis* (1535-45), in *LW*, 7:184, in his comments on Genesis 41:40.

jected a higher status for the spiritual station, for there must not exist any hierarchy of stations. Each of the stations is equally necessary for human life in its secular and spiritual dimension. A station, then, describes the place where I find myself at a certain time to execute the duties connected with this particular position within society. This means we wear different hats, depending on the place and situation in which we find ourselves.

b. Vocation and Calling

The term "station" is not synonymous with "vocation" or "calling," but only describes the situation or place where I fulfill my calling and exercise my vocation. For instance, every Christian belongs to the ecclesial station. In this station, or place, the housefather instructs his children in the Christian faith or the pastor preaches God's word and administers the sacraments. But the pastor is specifically called into this station to the pastoral office through human beings who represent God and exercise the church's right to call an individual person. Similarly, people are called to marriage because they are created as male or female to rear children and to establish a household. We notice with the latter example that the biological perspective of the station of the family and the individual's personal decision to marry a certain person become intertwined. Likewise, the station of a prince or that of a subject becomes a vocation once a specific directive is given to a person to take up the implementation of the tasks bound to this directive. A peculiar vocation, then, results from God's singling out an individual for a specific task.

Vocation as Divine Service

As everyone knows, being at a particular place in life does not automatically guarantee that we properly carry out the functions connected with that station. Therefore Luther never ceases to remind us that all vocations are for service to other people. Government, for instance, is intended for the benefit of the governed, not for those who govern; and the pastor works in the parish for the benefit of the faithful. This means we do not pick a vocation to see how much we can get out of the job by how little we invest. A vocation is not for us but for others. Luther suggests that if people properly attend to their vocation they are cooperators with God whether they are Christians or not. They are agents of God's unceasing preserving activity and through them God brings his love into the world. A Christian and a non-Christian can do things equally well. The difference is that what a Christian does is done through faith active in love.[20]

A station becomes a vocation if it is properly executed and thereby serves other people. In so doing one can exercise several vocations, not just the one which today is usually synonymous with a certain profession, but also a vocation within the biological orders, such as being a father, a mother, a son, or a daughter. As Swedish systematician Gustav Wingren (1910-2000) shows, according to Luther one cannot distinguish between a vocation or a profession that is exercised according to certain rules and regulations and the more intimate sphere of interpersonal relationships where we conduct ourselves in Christian love.[21] Wherever we encounter certain tasks and needs God summons us to master them properly in Christian love and to the best of our ability.

Luther reminds us:

> Every person surely has a calling. While attending to it he serves God. A king serves God when he is at pains to look after and govern his people. So does the mother of a household when she tends her baby, the father of a household when he gains a livelihood by working, and a pupil when he applies himself diligently to his studies. . . . Therefore it is a great wisdom when a human being does what God commands and earnestly devotes himself to his vocation without taking into consideration what others are doing. But surely there are few who do this.[22]

Luther is no utopian or romantic. He knows humanity and its proclivity to compare itself with others. Therefore he admits: "There are very few who live satisfied with their lot. The layman longs for the life of a cleric, the pupil wishes to be a teacher, the citizen wants to be a councilor, and each of us loathes his own calling, although there is no other way of serving God than to walk in simple faith and then to stick diligently to one's calling and to keep a good conscience." Yet Luther cautions that God "does not want people to change or abandon their vocations, as under the papacy it was consid-

20. See Martin Luther, "The Gospel for the Early Christmas Service, Luke 2[:15-20]" (1521/1522), in *LW,* 52:37, in the eighth point of his sermon.

21. See Gustav Wingren, *Luther on Vocation,* trans. Carl C. Rasmussen (Philadelphia: Muhlenberg, 1957), 29f.

22. See Martin Luther, *Lectures on Genesis,* in *LW,* 3:128, in his comments on Genesis 17:9, for this and the following quote.

ered piety to have given up one's customary way of life and to have with-drawn into a monastery."[23]

Since God hardly ever interferes directly with this world, God wishes to instill his gifts through our work and we become "the masks of God, be-hind which He wants to remain concealed and do all things."[24] This also means that all useful occupations are divinely ordained and without them no human community can exist. If we were to abandon them, we would ac-tually abandon God's calling and avoid what we are called to do. According to Luther, a vocation is God's calling for us to recognize in a given situation what God expects us to do. Whether we get paid for it or not, a vocation is much more than a means to "put bread on the table." It is one way in which God preserves and improves other individuals and the common good through us. Regardless of how different vocations may look to the outside world, they are ordained by God to sustain and further the created order. But Luther is realistic enough to recognize that we often do not keep our priorities in order. As he points out: "There are many people who are busy doing everything but that which is commanded of them."[25] Therefore it is important that we stop occasionally and ask ourselves what we are actually doing, and for whom we are doing it.

Helping our neighbor, being a parent, and rearing children demon-strate a commonality in our calling whereby the differences between rich and poor and between those in authority and those under authority disap-pear. "We should accustom ourselves to follow the order which He [God] has prescribed for us. Whatever you may be, son, servant, or maid in the meanest circumstances, stay where you are, because you are in a station where God has put you."[26]

It is an important element of Luther's concept of vocation that every genuine vocation, being derived from divine calling, demands the engage-ment of the whole person. Luther continually warned that the pre-eminence of one station over another is reprehensible because it implies contempt for the creator. "We should remain there [in our vocation] with a

---

23. Luther, *Lectures on Genesis* (1535-45), in *LW,* 3:62, in his comments on Genesis 16:7ff.

24. Martin Luther, *Commentary on Psalm 147* (1532), in *LW,* 14:114, in his explanation of Psalm 147:3.

25. Martin Luther, *Kirchenpostille* (1522), in *WA,* 10.1/1:307.13f., in a sermon on John 21:19-24.

26. Martin Luther, *Lectures on Isaiah* (1527-30), in *LW,* 17:384, commenting on Isaiah 65:12.

happy conscience and know that through such work more is accomplished than if one had made donations to every monastery and received every medal; even if it is the most menial housework."[27] Thereby we are reminded of Luther's comment: "If everyone served their neighbor then the whole world would be filled with divine service."[28]

Since a vocation should always be understood as God's calling and command, we can be sure that our activities in that vocation are pleasing to God. Being put in a certain place gives us certain challenges and we never have to be afraid that there is nothing for us to do. Since every vocation is ultimately for the benefit of others, choosing the right vocation loses significance. Luther presupposes that in some way there is a vocation already waiting for us, so we need not search for it through many trials and errors.

Vocational Mobility

While Luther did not insist that we are locked into a particular vocation for life, he held firmly to the idea of unchangeable givens that place us within particular vocations. Hence he argued, for instance, that "a woman must be a woman and cannot be a man," and that "we cannot all be princes, counts, preachers, noblemen, citizens, men, women, and servants."[29] Biological and educational differences allocate us to specific vocations. We are not only placed in a particular station but also in a particular vocation. Luther's view of stations and vocations remained, therefore, within the framework of the societal structure of his time. He had to allow that people were called into particular stations through their birth.

On the other hand, Luther in many ways broke through the idea that society is structured according to the stations into which people are born. He fought, for example, against the practice of barring those born out of wedlock from holding honorable vocations within the crafts and trades professions. He also demanded the possibility for the advancement of children of common parents, but he did not thereby sanction the motive of in-

---

27. Martin Luther, *Predigten des Jahres 1529,* in *WA,* 29:566.39–567.20f., in a sermon on Matthew 9:1ff.

28. Martin Luther, *Predigten des Jahres 1532,* in *WA,* 36:340.12f., in a sermon on Matthew 22:34ff.

29. See Martin Luther, *Sermon at the Dedication of the Castle Church, Torgau, 1544,* in *LW,* 51:348-53, in a sermon on Luke 14:1ff., where he emphasizes with many examples how one should not arrogantly seek to remove oneself from the station in which one has been placed. Quotations, 352 and 348.

creasing one's salary as justification for such advancement. Since every vocation is divine service, one cannot argue for a change in vocation on the basis of financial profit. Luther made parents vividly aware that through sufficient education their children could occupy all government, educational, and ecclesiastical offices. "It is not God's will that only those who are born kings, princes, lords, and nobles should exercise rule and lordship. He wills to have his beggars among them also, lest they think it is nobility of birth rather than God alone who makes lords and rulers."[30] "That is the way it will always be: your son and my son, that is, the children of the common people, will necessarily rule the world, both in the spiritual and the worldly estates."[31]

Advancement is open to all persons who have the prerequisite educational qualifications. Hence Luther impressed on the territorial lords the great importance of universities. He likewise wrote in 1524 an open letter, *To the Councilmen of All Cities in Germany That They Establish and Maintain Christian Schools.* He demanded that basic educational opportunities be available to all persons. Hence the children of poor parents were to be supported through governmental and ecclesiastical scholarships. Yet all these different possibilities are of no use if parents do not allow their children to take advantage of available educational opportunities. Parents, however, also have the responsibility of examining their children to determine whether they really have the necessary ability and interest to pursue higher education.

The fact that children have had a good education, however, does not automatically mean that they should demand to take up a more highly qualified vocation than what they would have had without this education. "Even though a boy who has studied Latin should afterwards learn a trade and become a craftsman, he still stands as a ready reserve in case he should be needed as a pastor or in some other service of the word. Neither will such knowledge hurt his capacity to earn a living."[32] For Luther there are no ethical distinctions of value between the different vocations, and a fulfilling life is possible within each of them. If we are unable to achieve a so-called career advancement, we should not consider ourselves deprived.

As we are often painfully aware, we can only choose our own vocation within certain limits, for the calling to a vocation always takes place through

---

30. Martin Luther, *A Sermon on Keeping Children in School* (1530), in *LW,* 46:250.
31. Luther, *A Sermon on Keeping Children in School* (1530), in *LW,* 46:251.
32. Luther, *A Sermon on Keeping Children in School* (1530), in *LW,* 46:231.

other people. Activity or training within a certain vocation precedes the actual reception of a call into this vocation. Therefore neither the choice of a vocation nor the carrying out of its duties is a purely private matter. Luther frequently cautioned parents and teachers to keep in mind the well-being of the whole community in influencing a child regarding vocation. Important in regard to Luther's thoughts on vocation is a person's readiness to serve and to love.

> See to it first of all that you believe in Christ and are baptized. Afterward concern yourself with your vocation. I am called to be a pastor. Now when I preach I perform a holy work that is pleasing to God. If you are a father or mother, believe in Jesus Christ and so you will be a holy father and a holy mother. Take watch over the early years of your children, let them pray, and discipline and spank them. Oversee the running of the household and the preparation of meals. Such things are nothing other than holy works for you have been called to do them. That means they are your holy life and are a part of God's Word and your calling.[33]

This mutual serving that we encounter in the family and in marriage as well as in the larger community has already been shown to us in the service of Christ. Humans are called to serve one another just as Christ served us.

Luther knew of no vocation that one could carry out without regard to the needs of the larger community. One is called when the community needs someone for a specific service and when one is qualified to meet the demands of this service. Hence one cannot derive from this either an inappropriate pride in one's vocation or the absolute right of an individual to perform a particular vocation. A vocation is a service and can only be required when both those who would serve in this vocation possess the necessary qualifications and the need for this service is present in the community. Under these conditions it is our duty not to forsake our vocation even if it becomes quite toilsome. If we have a genuine calling, we dare not forsake our tasks but should stand courageously before them and accomplish them.

Some may wonder why we have dwelt so long on Luther's understanding of vocation. We have done so for the following reasons:

1. Luther brought the concept of vocation down to earth. It is no longer just reserved for the clerics, but now all have a vocation. By bringing it

---

33. Martin Luther, *Predigten des Jahres 1534,* in *WA,* 37:480.2-8, in a sermon on Luke 5:1ff.

down to earth, he did not divorce it from God. Since God usually works indirectly in this world, we, in our respective vocations, are the "hands and means" by which God preserves and furthers the common good and his creation in general — though this latter point had not yet occurred to Luther. Therefore our vocation is a God-given duty by which we serve others.

2. Luther's view of vocation has had an impact far beyond his time. In the late eighteenth century and early nineteenth century vocation became a fundamental concept in the ethical teaching about duty. Immanuel Kant saw the universal law fulfilled in one's vocation. And through the influence of Luther, Frederick the Great, who ruled Prussia from 1740 to 1786, proclaimed: "The prince is the first servant of the state." The understanding of vocation as a duty was impressed on the Prussian officials and government workers who were known for the conscientious fulfillment of duty. Prussia's dominance in Germany led to the development of an efficient and incorruptible administration that in many ways is still exemplary today.

3. Luther's teaching on vocation could help us to counter an individualistic and self-centered striving for one's own advantage and allow us to rediscover the fact that our work is meant to serve the common good. Rediscovering Luther's teaching on vocation also helps us to understand that "Christian faith is not simply intellectual assent, but an active response to God in service to our neighbor's need."[34]

2. The Final Destiny of Humanity

Only utopian and chiliastic segments of Christian society have attempted to create the kingdom of God here on this earth by their own efforts. Yet such endeavors have always ended in disillusionment. For instance, the founding of the New World (North America) over against the Old World (Europe) carried with it decidedly messianic aspirations. Yet after little more than 200 years, this New World does not look much more promising than the Old World from which many Christian groups emigrated to build an earthly kingdom as "one nation under God." Even the secular millennium ideas of the "new man" that Mao Zedong (1893-1976) envisioned or

---

34. Louis T. Almen, "Vocation in a Post-Vocational Age," *Word & World* 4 (Spring 1984): 139.

the egalitarian society that Karl Marx espoused ended in a nightmare of apocalyptic proportions. Its inaugurators, Joseph Stalin and Mao, turned out to be the greatest mass murderers of all time. Adolf Hitler, too, who in chiliastic terminology inaugurated a *Third Reich*, theologically speaking the *Reich* (i.e., kingdom) of freedom and of the spirit, a *Reich* that according to his claims should have lasted a thousand years, fortunately only lasted twelve years. He put into concentration and extermination camps those who did not fit his image of the superior Aryan race, such as homosexuals, socialists, Marxists, Jews, and whoever else dared to doubt that Hitler and his scheme would bring about salvation.

There is no indication that our world is moving in the direction of the kingdom. To the contrary, natural resources are dwindling, human-made pollution is on the increase, and virtually everyone warns that a drastic climate change is in the offing, the full consequences of which no one can actually foresee. Even without any human interference, scientists tell us that our solar system and even the universe itself do not have a built-in sustainability. They will inevitably run their course and at the end there will be either empty space staring at us or all energy levels will have equalized and the sun and the moon and the stars in the present configuration will be no more.

Nevertheless, from its very inception humanity was not only a living species that made an imprint on the earth with its presence through artifacts, but through these artifacts also expressed the notion that death is not the ultimate end. The *homo religiosus,* the religious being, which a human being ineradicably is, is the only living species that has an acute death-awareness, knowing about its own finitude. At the same time human beings have never accepted death as finality but have interpreted it as a transition. Even Swiss-born American psychiatrist Elisabeth Kübler-Ross (1926-2004), who worked all her life with the terminally ill, stated: "Before I started working with dying patients, I did not believe in a life after death. I now do believe in a life after death, beyond a shadow of a doubt."[35] Since all of her patients died, it would have been natural for her also to conclude that death was the end. Yet she inferred from her work the opposite. Moreover, Kübler-Ross pointed out: "We have seen very few people who do not believe in some form of immortality."[36] Indeed, human beings are not content with their existence in the here and

35. Elisabeth Kübler-Ross, *Questions and Answers on Death and Dying* (New York: Macmillan, 1974), 167.

36. Kübler-Ross, *Questions and Answers on Death and Dying,* 159.

now. In some way or other they are looking forward to and hoping for their fulfillment of their lives in a final destiny.

a. The Discovery of Life beyond Death

When we ask to what extent humans have always reached toward the ultimate future, beyond their own death, we are confronted with the problem of reliable documentation. From archaeological finds we can gather that humanity has lived for approximately 2 million years, sustaining itself chiefly by hunting, fishing, and food gathering. But in terms of what earliest humanity thought and believed, we cannot go back any farther than the archaeological findings connected with Paleolithic hunters who entrusted their thoughts to rock art approximately 30,000 years ago. We also have excavations of human burials that date back 17,000 to 50,000 years. German paleontologist Karl J. Narr (1921-2009) writes:

> It is only from the Middle Paleolithic period onward that we know about funerals which, in their way, partly testify to the protection of the dead and, most likely, also to the provisions of food and tools offered for the dead and partly also for binding the deceased. Regardless of what the case may have been, loving care for the deceased or fear of the dead, it witnesses to the faith in a continuance of life after death in some form or other. . . . But even in earlier times (e.g. the Peking Man) there are indications that skulls or parts of skulls are separately preserved which we may explain by the idea of a further connection and a continuation of action after (for our conceptuality, physical) death in some form or other.[37]

Narr says the human beings he is talking about are *"in principle fully developed human beings,"* which means the transition must have been made from animal to humanity. In a similar way paleo-historian Jakob Ozols (b. 1922) states: "Though it may sound surprising, the oldest religious expression of early humanity accessible to us is the faith in a non-material form of soul indwelling in him."[38]

37. Karl J. Narr, "Beiträge der Urgeschichte zur Kenntnis der Menschennatur," in *Neue Anthropologie,* ed. Hans-Georg Gadamer and Paul Vogler (Stuttgart: DTV, 1973), 4:31-32 and 37. See also John Hick, *Death and Eternal Life* (New York: Harper & Row, 1976), 55-56, in his section on "primitive man." Hick states that humanity is unique in knowing that it is going to die but at the same time denies it and hopes for a life beyond (55).

38. Jakob Ozols, "Über die Jenseitsvorstellungen des vorgeschichtlichen Menschen," in

Historian of religion Mircea Eliade also states: "Belief in a survival after death seems to be demonstrated, from the earliest times, by the use of red ocher as a ritual substitute for blood, hence a symbol of life. The custom of dusting corpses with ocher is universally disseminated in both space and time, from Choukoutien to the Western shores of Europe, in Africa as far as the Cape of Good Hope, in Australia, in Tasmania, in America as far as Tierra del Fuego."[39] Eliade concedes that the religious meaning of these burials is anything but clear. As we know from the Parsees, even leaving a corpse in the open to be devoured by birds of prey does not signify the absence of the idea of survival beyond death. At least with some burials survival seems to be implied without a doubt. An example is when the corpses are bent and perhaps tied. This may express the fear of a possible return of the deceased to haunt the living. Yet burial in a bent fetal position may also signify the hope for rebirth.

During the Upper Paleolithic period (50,000-10,000 years ago) corpses sprinkled with red ocher were buried in graves together with a certain number of objects intended for personal use or adornment. As Eliade explains: "The presence of such objects implies not only belief in a personal survival, but also the certainty that the deceased will continue his particular activity in the other world. Similar ideas are abundantly documented, and on various levels of culture."[40] These burials confirm the belief in survival after death, not only by the use of red ocher, but also if the deceased are oriented toward the east. This shows a connection with the course of the sun, meaning the hope of a rebirth in the same way as the sun is born each morning in the east. In Palestine hundreds of Natufian Late Mesolithic burials (12,500-10,000 B.C.) have been found with either burials of the whole body or just the skull. Often grave goods were added for the dead.[41] The objects of personal adornment and even of food and tools seem to indicate belief in the continuation of specific activities and of some kind of life like the present life.

Archaic religious ideas have survived into later periods. For instance, a number of archaic civilizations, based on hunting, fishing, and gathering,

Tod und Jenseits im Glauben der Völker, ed. Hans-Joachim Klimkeit (Wiesbaden: Otto Harrassowitz, 1978), 14.

39. Mircea Eliade, *A History of Religious Ideas,* vol. 1, *From the Stone Age to the Eloysinian Mysteries,* trans. Willard R. Trask (Chicago: University of Chicago Press, 1978), 9.

40. Eliade, *A History of Religious Ideas,* 1:10f.

41. See Jon Davies, *Death, Burial and Rebirth in the Religions of Antiquity* (London: Routledge, 1999), 73.

survived until the end of the nineteenth century in races remote from a more global civilization. They are still present in the great tropical forests of Central Africa, in the Australian outback, and in the Arctic region. Despite influences from neighboring agricultural societies, the original structures of these civilizations have been left intact up until modern times. They have remained arrested at a stage like that of the Upper Paleolithic period of thousands of years ago, and thus are, in a sense, "living fossils." They still live largely by hunting and gathering and use no metal tools. It would be tempting to transpose the religious practices and mythologies of these still living civilizations back into the Upper Paleolithic period. With some degree of caution one can do this and thereby gain valuable insight into the distant past. Moreover, a Shamanic type of ecstasy still present among these "living fossils" is implied from archaeological studies of very early remains, especially from the Paleolithic cave paintings. This Shamanic ecstasy implies, "on the one hand, belief in a 'soul,' able to leave the body and travel freely through the world, and, on the other hand, the conviction that, during such a journey, the soul can meet certain superhuman beings and ask them for help or a blessing."[42] Once we have the idea of a soul as distinct from the body, death is no longer the absolute end of a human person.

The souls of the dead have their own realm of life in the beyond, a shadowy world that was a matter of fact for people living in the ice age. Since the skull is so important, we need not be surprised that we have burials of skulls only, and since animals were not thought to be that different from people, even the skulls of some animals were similarly buried. For prehistoric persons, the concept of life after death was determined primarily by the conviction of an immortal figure of the soul. "This conviction has remained a most important part of religions until most recent times. It is evidently shaped by the concept of events and dreams, but also by other events. The state without protection and participation during sleep has led to the assumption that this figure of the soul is the actual life and the protective power of the person."[43]

The recognition of an *anima* (spirit) residing in the human person that can move to different places, especially during sleep, as we may naively assume when we dream about things that are far away, was expanded to the conclusion that this *anima* leaves the body forever at death and continues

42. Eliade, *A History of Religious Ideas*, 1:24.

43. Jakob Ozols, "Über die Jenseitsvorstellungen des vorgeschichtlichen Menschen," in *Tod und Jenseits im Glauben der Völker*, ed. Hans-Joachim Klimkeit, 35.

to exist somewhere else. This primal human concept of a soul or spirit led to elaborate perspectives of an afterlife. This can be seen especially in Egypt, which developed a basically "death-driven culture." For the Egyptian, death "was an ever-present menace throughout his life and impinged to a greater or lesser extent upon his earthly existence. Its presence . . . was driven home upon him by the surrounding landscape. This oasis of culture was embedded in a lifeless waste, and his tombs were located on the edge of the hostile desert."[44] The narrow fertile strip of land along the Nile River was surrounded by the immense, life-threatening desert. The intense preoccupation with death is documented by elaborate funeral customs for the elite. First, the dead person was embalmed, so that the person could continue to exist in a life-like state after death. Second, the tombs were, to a large extent, patterned according to housing conditions in this life. Provisions for the deceased were enclosed in the tombs, and the walls and ceilings were elaborately decorated. Even the great pyramids show this obsession with death. As funerary monuments they were built to withstand the tides of time and they are a witness to the belief in immortality of their builders.

This cult of the dead in which the corpses were prepared for eternity by mummification and by the regular supply of provisions and gifts by which they could continue to participate in this earthly life in perpetuity should have precluded any thought of life in some other realm, for instance, in heaven or in the realm of dead. Yet the opposite is true. Because of the king's god-like status, heaven was at first accessible "only to the deceased king, but then became 'democratized,' as it were, and opened up to the commoners."[45] Initially only the king was thought to have a soul *(ba)* as distinct from the vital life force *(ka)*. But the Coffin Texts, which date from the First Intermediate period (ca. 2134-2040 B.C.) and the Middle Kingdom (ca. 2040-1780 B.C.), show that private individuals also acquired what had previously been reserved for the king; now they also were believed to have a soul. Two possibilities were open to them: either the soul was separated from the body and went to heaven while the dead body went to the netherworld, or both of them stayed together for the ascent to heaven. "In this way the preservation of the body in the tomb became the prerequisite for ascent to heaven."[46] To arrive in heaven one first had to pass through judgment.

44. Siegfried Morenz, *Egyptian Religion,* trans. Ann E. Keep (Ithaca, NY: Cornell University Press, 1973), 192.

45. Morenz, *Egyptian Religion,* 204.

46. Morenz, *Egyptian Religion,* 206.

This was again a frightening experience since the verdict did not depend on one's moral rectitude. One sought to avoid a negative decision by magical means as is seen from the Coffin Texts and the various Books of the Dead. According to Egyptologist Siegfried Morenz (1914-70) the reasons for reliance on magic in order to avoid the judgment of the dead "was the belief in equation with Osiris, the king of the gods and god of vegetation, the first to rise from the dead, who encompassed within himself every person buried with the proper ritual."[47] This means that the goal was to become like Osiris, who was brought back to life with the help of his consort Isis.

How tenuous, however, such hope for something positive beyond death was is shown by the Greek historian Herodotus, who relates an incident in Egypt that he himself observed. "At rich men's banquets, after dinner a man carries round a wooden image of a corpse in a coffin, painted and carved in exact imitations, a cubit or two long. This they show each other of the company, saying 'Drink and make merry, but look on this; for such shalt thou be when thou art dead.' Such is the custom at their drinking-bouts."[48] Life was not just focused on this world and the present existence, but on living well and enjoying whatever one could because one never knew when life would be over.

b. The Old Testament Account

The Israelites, in close proximity to Egypt and according to their own story, once enslaved in that country, did not develop a culture focused on death or afterlife. In Mesopotamia there is the story of Gilgamesh, who attempted to find eternal life for his dear friend Enkidu, but in the end realized that eternal life is not for humans. Then there is the rhythm between life and death, for instance, in the Canaanite religion with Baal, the god of life who dominated, and who through the winter rain caused the earth to turn green again and promised a good crop. The death god Mot, however, was thought to rule once summer set in when the merciless rays of the sun and the wind from the desert turned nature into a lifeless brown.

As Psalm 90 tellingly reminds us, the Hebrew people knew about the

47. Morenz, *Egyptian Religion,* 210. It is interesting that Jon Davies in his chapter on Egypt (27-39) does not even mention Morenz.

48. *Herodotus* (2.78), Engl. trans. by A. D. Godley in four volumes (Cambridge, MA: Harvard University Press, 1966 [1920]), 1:365.

power of death that nothing and no one can escape. But behind death there was God, who gave life and who also took it away.[49] Therefore death was seen as a normal end of life from which no one could escape. Death was also seen as evidence of God's wrath and therefore as a blessing when one died "old and full of days" (Gen. 35:29) and was gathered to one's people. There were stone-hewn family tombs where the dead were laid to rest on simple benches. Once the corpses had decayed, the bones were gathered into a lower pit so other family members could have their last rest on the same "beds." Of course, Israel was not completely immune to influences from its neighbors. We hear, for instance, that Saul consulted a medium at Endor to get in touch with the long-deceased Samuel. Though she complied with the wishes of the king, she knew that the king had outlawed such customs (1 Sam. 28:9). Also, when one touched a corpse, one had to purify oneself (Num. 19:13). There may well have been manipulations of the dead; otherwise injunctions against them made no sense. Indeed, "intolerance for any cult of the dead is the dominant position."[50]

Though a translation, or transference from this life to another life, is very rarely mentioned in the Old Testament (see Gen. 5:24), it was clear for the Israelites that death was not the end of a person's existence altogether. In their thinking there is a netherworld, Sheol, a place to which one "goes down" (Num. 16:30). Since Sheol is intimately connected with the grave, it is understandable that no one wanted to go there voluntarily. Hezekiah pleaded to be saved from the pit, the place in the tomb where the remains of the decayed corpse are preserved: "For Sheol cannot thank you, death cannot praise you; those who go down to the Pit cannot hope for your faithfulness" (Isa. 38:18). Since Hezekiah was only sick, we notice that death and Sheol can also be used in a metaphoric sense denoting the hostile and threatening powers and the anxiety they produce. Sheol can also be personified:

> Sheol beneath is stirred up to meet you when you come; it rouses the shades to greet you, all who were leaders of the earth; it raises from their thrones all who were kings of the nations. And all of them will speak and say to you: "You too have become as weak as we! You have become like us!" Your pomp is brought down to Sheol, and the sounds of your harps; maggots are the bed beneath you, and worms are your covering. (Isa. 14:9-11)

49. For the Old Testament understanding of death, see Preuss, *Old Testament Theology*, 2:106f. and 2:147-50.

50. Norman R. Gulley, "Death," in *The Anchor Bible Dictionary*, ed. David Noel Freedman, 6 vols. (New York: Doubleday, 1992), 2:109.

Besides the personification of Sheol we notice that it is a shadowy abode that every person must enter, even kings and rulers of the nations. Once they are there, they have no actual life, but are weak and are surrounded by worms and maggots. Sheol is nothing to aspire to. Therefore the hope of the Israelites initially was focused on this life and on Yahweh, who proved his power and faithfulness to the Israelites again and again. Individual "survival," so important for individualized Westerners, was relatively unimportant for the Israelites, who had put their faith in Yahweh who would sustain their corporate existence beyond the destiny of the individual. One continued to live on in one's sons and through them in the community. It was one of the most devastating fates to die without a male heir, for then there was no hope beyond one's own death. The end that the Israelites desired was to die in old age, with their sons assembled around them (Gen. 49:33). Of course, this was all viewed from a male perspective. The woman was guaranteed life and protection through sons she bore into this world. Death at a ripe old age was understood as a blessing, as we hear from Proverbs 10:27: "The fear of the Lord prolongs life, but the years of the wicked will be short." Early death was understood as a punishment for godlessness (1 Sam. 2:32).

Then came the devastating experience of the destruction of Israel, first the northern kingdom and then the southern kingdom of Judah, and with it the Babylonian exile. There the corporate existence of Israel was severely threatened. The prophet Isaiah already expects complete destruction and, afterward, universal salvation that is no longer confined to Israel, but is open to the whole world. In Isaiah 2:2-4 we read that all the nations will stream to the mountain of the Lord and he will teach them his ways. He will also judge between the nations, so they can "beat their swords into plowshares, and their spears into pruning hooks." The picturesque language there employs mythical imagery indicating that the new order of salvation reaches out beyond present historical reality. Not only will all nations listen to God and follow God's ways, but there will be eternal peace and wars will be something of the past. Everyone will have enough food and will enjoy a long life. The emphasis here is still not on the individual person, but on corporate existence, an existence, however, that includes the whole inhabited world. Even nature will be transformed since salvation is truly universal. Lions will no longer devour other living species, and serpents will not seek to endanger humans.

This universal view of human history is intensified in the period of the apocalyptic writers. While the prophets in their message of salvation had emphasized that the enemies of Israel were also God's enemies and therefore would either be converted or destroyed in the last days, in the apocalyptic period all anti-Godly powers were included. The apocalyptists viewed history as a unity and therefore believed that God was not only the God of all nations, but of the whole world. They felt that they were so near to the edge of history that they could see all history unfolding even to its conclusion, just as someone sitting on a high mountain can see a vast expanse of territory before her or his very eyes. While this present eon was still under the spell of wars and unrest, and while there were great disturbances in nature, the apocalyptists said that these travails already indicated the birth of the new eon when there would be the unlimited dominion of God. As Jürgen Moltmann emphasizes: "This historifying of the world in the category of the universal eschatological future is of tremendous importance for theology, for indeed it makes eschatology the universal horizon of all theology as such. Without apocalyptic theological eschatology remains bogged down in the ethnic history of men or the existential history of the individual."[51]

Indeed, there was a major emphasis on the universal scope of history. The fulfillment of history as the establishment of God's rule coincided, however, with the aspirations of Israel and also with the existential hopes of the individual. In Isaiah 26:14 we read: "The dead do not live; shades do not rise." But then we encounter in the same chapter the reversal of this statement when we read, "your dead shall live, their corpses shall rise. O dwellers in the dust, awake and sing for joy!" (v. 19). Similarly, we read in Psalm 49:15: "But God will ransom my soul from the power of Sheol, for he will receive me." In one of the earlier parts of the Old Testament we even read about a resurrection with a twofold outcome: "Many of those who sleep in the dust of the earth shall awake, some to everlasting life, and some to shame and everlasting contempt" (Dan. 12:2). Once Israel's corporate existence had collapsed, and the elite were led into the Babylonian exile, the once almost exclusive focus on corporate fulfillment no longer sufficed.

When the Israelites were allowed to return to their homeland after 539 B.C., as a result of the edict of Cyrus, the high hopes of Haggai and Zechariah were clearly mistaken since both saw Zerubbabel as the Messiah who was to come. Zerubbabel was never enthroned, so the hope for the fulfillment of the Davidic promise of the end-time kingdom had to be revised again. One generation before Zechariah, Deutero-Isaiah judged the situa-

---

51. Jürgen Moltmann, *Theology of Hope: On the Ground and the Implications of a Christian Eschatology,* trans. J. W. Leitch (New York: Harper & Row, 1967), 137-38.

tion much more realistically when he stated that true deliverance and fulfillment of salvation could only be brought about through the vicarious suffering of the true Servant of Yahweh. "We have all turned to our own way, and
the Lord has laid on him the iniquity of us all" (Isa. 53:6). Though the messianic element of the victorious king is not lacking in Deutero-Isaiah's description of the suffering servant, he ultimately did not dare to identify him
with a historic figure.[52] Fulfillment is not brought about in a new creation,
the realization of which could be traced in history, nor was it brought about
by the hope in an individualistic resurrection. Yet both hopes were still
present when the period of the New Testament began.

c. The New Testament Perspective

While the Old Testament is a portrayal of God acting in the history of Israel spanning more than a thousand years, the New Testament is primarily
focused on the life of only one person, Jesus of Nazareth, and the results
that came from that life. The Gospel of John summarized what all the New
Testament writings want to convey: these things "are written so that you
may come to believe that Jesus is the Messiah, the Son of God, and that
through believing you may have life in his name" (20:31). As Wolfhart
Pannenberg stated in his widely discussed "Dogmatic Thesis on the Doctrine of Revelation" (1961):

> The universal revelation of the deity of God is not yet realized in the his-
> tory of Israel, but first in the destiny of Jesus of Nazareth in so far as the
> end of all events is anticipated in his history. . . . According to the witness
> of the New Testament in the destiny of Jesus Christ, the end is not only
> proleptically viewed, but it has proleptically occurred. Because in him has
> already occurred with the resurrection from the dead, that which awaits all
> other people.[53]

The destiny of Jesus does not have a universal character just because the
end of all history was *envisioned* in that destiny. Pannenberg goes a decisive

---

52. See Walther Zimmerli, *Old Testament Theology in Outline,* trans. David E. Green
(Edinburgh: T&T Clark, 1984 [1978]), 221-23, on the Servant of Yahweh, where Zimmerli
concludes that ultimately Deutero-Isaiah is speaking "of a figure larger than life" (222).

53. Wolfhart Pannenberg, *Revelation as History,* ed. Wolfhart Pannenberg, trans.
D. Granskou (New York: Macmillan, 1968), 139 (thesis 4; my own translation).

step further, claiming that in Jesus the end of all history and therefore the end of the world has indeed occurred in proleptic anticipation. What has been anticipated as the end and fulfillment of history, the resurrection of the dead and a new world, in fact *happened* in a proleptic way, in and with Jesus. History has come to its conclusion in the destiny of Jesus and therefore this destiny is the key to understanding our own history and that of the whole world. At the end of the world there will occur on a cosmic scale only that which happened in and with Jesus on an individual scale.

The New Testament writers correctly called Jesus "the Christ," meaning in Greek "the anointed one," the same as was expressed in Hebrew with the title "Messiah." Through Jesus and his destiny we have the assurance and the intimation of what is going to happen at the end to the world and to us as individuals. Jesus and his destiny are, symbolically speaking, the lens through which, since the beginning of creation, the rays of all history are focused and projected into the future. This future has become predictable because it receives its future-directedness from Jesus the Christ who in his destiny has determined that future.

Those who had hoped for an ethnic or nationalistic salvation were disappointed when Jesus told Pilate "My kingdom is not of this world" (John 18:36). Indeed, there is no continuation of this world in whatever new form. As science has told us, at least since the twentieth century and as the Bible reiterates, this world has no ultimate future. Therefore the premier theologian and missionary of New Testament times, Paul, distinctively talks about a new creation when he writes about Christ: "And he died for all, so that those who live might live no longer for themselves, but for him who died and was raised for them. . . . So if anyone is in Christ, there is a new creation: everything old has passed away; see, everything has become new!" (2 Cor. 5:15, 17). Paul picks up here the Old Testament and Jewish image of the sacrificial lamb that was slaughtered to expiate for the sins of the people so that they might live. At the same time he connects this with the reality of Christ's resurrection, suggesting that the reconciliation, made possible through Christ's sacrificial death, leads to a new and everlasting life through his resurrection.

Especially instructive here is chapter 15 of Paul's first Letter to the Corinthians. Once he has narrated the tradition of Christ's resurrection, he concludes on the basis of this resurrection that there is also a resurrection for others. Paul does not conclude from the resurrection of one person that then others can be resurrected too. His decisive point is that since the resurrection of Jesus as the Christ has occurred, others will also be resurrected.

The resurrection hope is not a continuation of the hope that was already present at that time in Israel in the teaching of the Pharisees. Rather, the resurrection hope is based solely on the fact of Christ's own resurrection. Therefore Paul argues: "If Christ has not been raised, your faith is futile and you are still in your sins" (v. 17). If Christ has not been resurrected, then there is no forgiveness of sin and therefore no possibility of new life. So everything hinges on Christ's resurrection.

Yet again this is not an individualistic hope. As Paul explains: "For as all die in Adam, so all will be made alive in Christ. But each in his own order: Christ the first fruits, then at his coming those who belong to Christ. Then comes the end, when he hands over the kingdom to God the Father, after he has destroyed every ruler and every authority and power" (1 Cor. 15:22-24). While sinful humanity has no chance of life beyond death, Christ has reversed that death-bound course and enabled people to have hope beyond death. Yet there is a certain order of events: Christ has been raised first. When he returns at the end of time, all Christians will also be resurrected. Then all anti-Godly powers and authorities will be destroyed, so that there will be a universal rule of God throughout the world. Only then will God's creation find its fulfillment. This is the hope that the New Testament proclaims and with which the Christians confronted the world. Yet such hope, even at its inception, was not uncontested. There were at least two big rival options, reincarnation and immortality, which had been quite appealing in antiquity.

d. Rival Options: Reincarnation and Immortality

Reincarnation seems to be especially fascinating to the Western mind today, as we saw with the New Age movement. But it is not as clear-cut an option as the resurrection. With the resurrection notion, especially in connection with the last judgment, one is believed to either be received into eternal bliss or confronted with eternal damnation. With the notion of reincarnation, so the general feeling goes, one can be more relaxed. If one does not make it into a better life the first time around, one always has a second chance. Furthermore, one's resurrection is totally dependent on God's grace. Only God can resurrect us to new life. Resurrection, as we learn from the New Testament, is always undeserved. But with reincarnation human beings have a say. The individual person can more or less determine his or her own destiny. If a person accumulates more good karma, he or she can expect a higher form of reincarnation and at the end will enter fulfillment or Nirvana, but if a person puts forth less effort he or she must settle for a lower form of life. We should not forget, however, that in Eastern religions reincarnation is seen as a curse and not as a blessing. One hopes and strives for the day when the cycles of death and rebirth finally cease and the end goal will be reached.

There are also Western Christian theologians who approvingly look at the notion of reincarnation. John B. Cobb (b. 1925), for instance, writes: "The encounter with Buddhism may prove as an essential step for the West to free itself from its attachment to individualized personal existence as a final goal."[54] Cobb sees all our images of hope converging toward "a transcendence of separating individuality in a fuller community with other people and with all things. In this community the tensions between self and Christ decline, and in a final consummation they would disappear."[55] Yet the importance of individuality notwithstanding, it also holds true for the Christian faith that the communal aspect of the people of God rules supreme. Individuality is not finally extinguished as we have it in the concept of Nirvana. Being members of the body of Christ, we act in concert with each other, but not in uniformity.

Before we speak too loudly of an Eastern and a Western way of thinking concerning human destiny, we should note that the idea of further lifecycles after death has never been restricted to one geographical area. Especially during the formative years of the Christian faith, whether in Egypt, Rome, or Greece, ideas of reincarnation were widespread. Several of the church fathers took issue with this kind of thinking. Tertullian, in his eloquent manner, refuted the allegation that Jesus condoned reincarnation when he once mentioned the coming of Elijah (Mark 9:11-13). Tertullian's argument, though nearly 1,800 years old, is still persuasive today. He wrote:

> Heretics . . . seize with especial avidity the example of Elias, whom they assume to have been so reproduced in John (the Baptist) as to make our Lord's statement sponsor for their theory of transmigration, when He said, "Elias is come already, and they knew him not"; and again, in another passage, "And if ye will receive it, this is Elias, which was for to come." Well, then, was it really in a Pythagorean sense that the Jews approached John with the inquiry, "Art thou Elias?" and not rather in the sense of the divine prediction, "Behold, I will send you Elijah" the Tishbite? The fact, how-

54. John B. Cobb Jr., *Christ in a Pluralistic Age* (Philadelphia: Westminster, 1975), 220.
55. Cobb, *Christ in a Pluralistic Age,* 258.

ever, is, that their metempsychosis, or transmigration theory, signifies the recall of the soul which had died long before, and its return to some other body. But Elias is to come again, not after quitting life (in the way of dying), but after his translation (or removal without dying); not for the purpose of being restored to the body, from which he had not departed, but for the purpose of revisiting the world from which he was translated; not by way of resuming a life which he had laid aside, but of fulfilling prophecy, — really and truly the same man, both in respect of his name and designation, as well as of his unchanged humanity.[56]

Tertullian rejects the idea that Elijah has returned in the person of John the Baptist, but affirms that John the Baptist continued Elijah's work acting in his spirit and power. Since Elijah, however, did not die, but was simply translated into another sphere, he will come again as the same person in fulfilling the prophecy that Jesus espoused. Tertullian clearly rejected any notion of reincarnation. The same is true for most Christian theologians from the earliest time onward. They were acquainted with the idea of reincarnation, but refuted it in favor of the belief in resurrection.

Both reincarnation and resurrection emphasize that death is not the end of human life. Yet according to the Judeo-Christian tradition, God's animating Spirit is active in every living being. God's Spirit makes the difference between life and death and does not simply disappear at death, but causes new life to emerge and to exist. This life-giving power is strictly dependent on God, while a soul that migrates from one life to another is believed to function much more independently and needs no externally active power to survive and to strive.

Canadian-born psychiatrist Ian Stevenson (1918-2007) extensively researched a phenomenon by which, through age-regression, a person can recall an earlier life and relate provable knowledge of details from this life of the distant past. In many cases, it could be shown that these recollections of persons, items, or even of a foreign language of this earlier life, could not have been learned or later on acquired in some way or other. While these phenomena could give more credence to the notion of reincarnation, they could also be interpreted as "super-extrasensory perception," phenomena that also occur with extra-sensitive persons. These persons might have an extraordinary endowment for paranormal cognition and could get in touch with details about persons who lived long ago. Stevenson is also hesitant to

---

56. Tertullian, *Treatise on the Soul* (35), in *ANF,* 3:216-17.

consider these phenomena as a proof for reincarnation but rather "suggestive of reincarnation."[57] He sees them more as providing "important evidence for the survival of human personality after physical death."[58] Such a
survival of human personality after physical death is also expressed with the
notion of an immortal soul.

The *Catechism of the Catholic Church* teaches "that every spiritual soul
is created immediately by God — it is not 'produced' by the parents — and
also that it is immortal: it does not perish when it separates from the body at
death, and it will be reunited with the body at the final Resurrection."[59]
Many Protestant hymns, too, express the hope that once life on earth has
ended, the immortal soul will be united with God. Many leading Protestant
theologians of the past, such as Zwingli, Calvin, and to some extent Luther,
advocated the immortality of the soul. This is not surprising because it was
a common teaching of the church at the time. At the Fifth Lateran Council
in 1513, the Catholic Church condemned the "pernicious errors . . . concerning the nature of the rational soul, namely, that it is mortal, or one in all
men."[60] With this condemnation the Catholic Church took exception to
Ibn Rusd (Lat. Averroes, 1126-98), an Arabian philosopher who had taught
in commentaries on Aristotle that an individual human being has no substantial soul and therefore no personal immortality. There is only this one
life-force working in each human being that has immortality. With this he
thought he was following Aristotle, who taught about a spiritual soul that is
not created, but which pre-exists and therefore does not cease with human
death when the sensual soul of the body dies.[61] It is a non-sensual ideal entity connected with the eternal truth and the spirit that comes from the
gods and through which we return again to the gods. Plato was much

---

57. See Ian Stevenson, *Children Who Remember Previous Lives: A Question of Reincarnation,* rev. ed. (Jefferson, NC: McFarland, 2001), 3, where he also states that, in some cases
he investigated, the children may indeed have been reincarnated (254). But he more clearly
affirms "that mind and body are separate entities, joined during life, but not afterwards"
(254). Therefore he is skeptical "that the reductionist approach of nearly all neuroscientists
will contribute to understanding the mind-brain problem" (2).

58. Ian Stevenson, *Unlearned Language: New Studies in Xenoglossy* (Charlottesville:
University of Virginia Press, 1984), 158.

59. *Catechism of the Catholic Church* (366), rev. ed. (London: Geoffrey Chapman,
1999), 83.

60. "The Human Soul (Against the Neo-Aristotelians)," 738, in Heinrich Denzinger,
The Sources of Catholic Dogma (St. Louis: B. Herder, 1957), 237.

61. See Aristotle, *Generation of Animals* (2.3; 736f.), in *A New Aristotle Reader,* ed. J. L.
Ackrill (Princeton, NJ: Princeton University Press, 1987), 247f.

clearer on this point when he asserted that a demiurge, a creator-god, created both the soul of the universe and each individual human soul. The soul is something invisible, immaterial, spiritual, and trans-earthly. Each of these (human) souls would first reside in a star and then be "implanted in bodies. . . . He who lived well during his appointed time was to return and dwell in his native star, and there he would have a blessed and congenial existence."[62] The gods then gave each person a mortal body as the vehicle for the soul.[63] Once the person dies, then there is some kind of judgment, according to Plato, and after 1,000 years of migration there is a reincarnation.[64] After several of these rebirths, lasting altogether as long as 10,000 or as short as only 3,000 years, the soul can return to its point of origin, but then the migration cycle starts all over again. The human souls after death "go from hence into the other world, and returning hither, are born again from the dead."[65] Over against the soul, which was considered the principle of life, the body as its vehicle was regarded as inferior and its prison. At death, Plato claimed, the soul was "released from the chains of the body."[66]

Since the Christian message, including the New Testament, was communicated in *koine* Greek, the lingua franca for the eastern Mediterranean and Near East throughout the Roman period, Christians took over the cultural background that went with this language and naturally talked about the human person as consisting of body and soul, or body, soul, and spirit. In line with the Old Testament and also with late Judaism, one was also convinced that death was not the end of human life. Therefore the immortality of the soul was deemed by many Christians to be an appropriate conceptuality when they talked about the destiny of human life.[67] Yet such an idea could easily clash with the Christian belief in the resurrection of the dead.

When Paul preached for the first time in Athens, people listened intently, but laughter erupted when he spoke of the resurrection (Acts 17:32).

---

62. Plato, *Timaeus* (41f.), in *The Dialogues of Plato,* 2:23.

63. Plato, *Timaeus* (69), in *The Dialogues of Plato,* 2:48.

64. See Plato, *Republic* (10.615-21), in *The Dialogues of Plato,* 1:874-79.

65. Plato, *Phaedo* (70), in *The Dialogues of Plato,* 1:453.

66. Plato, *Phaedo* (67), in *The Dialogues of Plato,* 1:451.

67. See Catharine Cavanagh, "The Nature of the Soul according to Eriugena," in *The Afterlife of the Platonic Soul: Reflections of Platonic Psychology in Monotheistic Religions,* ed. Maha Elkaisy-Friemuth and John M. Dillon (Leiden: Brill, 2009), 79, who demonstrates the influence of Platonic thought on Christian theologians but also mentions that the Christians introduced many modifications of the Platonic scheme due to "the pressure of the Biblical text."

Such thought was deemed incredible to the Greek-speaking world since resurrection implied not only the continuation of an invisible and immaterial soul, but also the resurrection of the body. Of course, when Paul talked about the resurrection of the body, he did not mean a re-vivification of *that* body or a reassembling and rejuvenation of the decayed parts of that body. He knew that the perishable cannot inherit the imperishable, and therefore his antinomy of perishable-imperishable and mortal-immortal (1 Cor. 15:50-54) indicates a totally different existence of the resurrected person than she or he had before. Yet it is interesting that in his first letter to the Christians in Corinth he devoted a whole chapter (1 Corinthians 15) to explaining to them the Christian belief in the resurrection. As Paul mentions, "some" Christians there claimed that "there is no resurrection of the dead" (1 Cor 15:12).[68] Such a statement is not surprising since around A.D. 160 Justin Martyr also mentions people, evidently Christians, "who say that there is no resurrection of the dead, and that their souls, when they die, are taken to heaven."[69] Indeed, if the soul is by itself immortal, why would one need a resurrection?

When the *Catholic Catechism* emphasizes the immortality of the soul, the Roman Catholic Church does not disclaim hope in the resurrection. To that effect it also emphasizes in the same *Catechism* that the spiritual soul and the material body are united in forming "a single nature."[70] Nevertheless, the *Catechism* also states: "In death, the separation of the soul from the body, the human body decays and the soul goes to meet God, while awaiting its reunion with its glorified body."[71] If we read this statement, we could easily conclude that the human soul is immortal and therefore ascends to God on its own power. Only the rejoining of the soul with the glorified body is actually God's redemptive work. Here Karl Rahner (1904-84), the premier theologian of the Roman Catholic Church in the twentieth century, was much clearer. He asserted that things do not continue on "after death as though, as Feuerbach put it, we only change horses and then ride on — that is, as though the dispersion and the empty, undetermined and ever determinable openness characteristic of temporal existence continued on. No, in

---

68. Joseph A. Fitzmyer, *First Corinthians* (New Haven, CT: Yale University Press, 2008), 539f., writes: "In a sense, this is the most important problem that he addresses in this letter, and the instruction that he will give about this eschatological hope is the most important in the whole letter."

69. Justin Martyr, *Dialogue with Trypho* (80), in *ANF*, 1:239.

70. *Catechism of the Catholic Church* (365), 83.

71. *Catechism of the Catholic Church* (997), 227.

this respect, death marks an end for the whole person."[72] There is no recti-linear continuation possible from our empirical reality to an existence beyond death. Even a soul does not survive. But then Rahner cautions:

> But if a person thinks conversely that with death everything is over because human time does not really continue on, and because time which had a beginning also has to have an end, and finally because a time which spins on into infinity in its empty course toward something ever new which constantly annuls what went before is really unintelligible, and indeed would be more terrible than hell, this person is caught in the conceptual model of our empirical temporality just as much as is the person who has the soul continues on.[73]

Rahner asserts with the same vehemence as he did when he first affirmed that death is the end of the whole person, that with death not everything is over. Death is the demarcation between this life and the hereafter, a demarcation so radical that there is no continuation unless we talk about a "shadowy existence" like the existence in Sheol. But the Old Testament writers realized that this shadowy existence was no life in the real sense. A new creation and a resurrection, central convictions of the New Testament, are not derived from the concept of Sheol, but from the fact of Christ's resurrection. There is no suggestion in the New Testament of a continuity through and beyond death, nor of a reuniting of body and soul. It is only God's graciousness that allows for new life through resurrection, assuring that at death we do not fall into nothingness, but metaphorically speaking, into the all-embracing hands of God.

Since immortality as a gift of God is easily confused with an innate immortality of the soul, and thereby with a non-biblical soul-body dichotomy, we ought to be very careful in using the notion of the immortality of the soul at all. Karl Barth, for instance, mentioned the idea of the immortality of the soul only once in the more than 6,000 pages of his *Church Dogmatics* and called it "a typical thought inspired by fear."[74] The notion of the immortality of the soul, however, has little to do with fear, but is derived from the Hellenistic background of early Christianity. In Catholicism it often serves as an antidote to the frequent Protestant notion that at death we

---

72. Karl Rahner, *Foundations of Christian Faith: An Introduction to the Idea of Christianity,* trans. William V. Dych (New York: Seabury, 1978), 436-37.

73. Rahner, *Foundations of Christian Faith,* 437.

74. Karl Barth, *CD,* III/4:590.

completely die and perish. Then at some later date God reproduces us in the resurrection to new life just as a magician astoundingly pulls a rabbit out of a hat. As Martin Luther emphasized, however, time is a this-worldly entity and before God the concept of time must be done away with since for God there is no earlier or later. Therefore the assertion of a time (interval) after death, which this whole-death theory implies, has as little validity as the assertion of an immortal soul that separates from the body at the point of death.

Though there are many misunderstandings caused by the term "immortality," we should not discard its valid theological significance. Death is not the dissolution of the person. If that were so, death would provide an escape from this life and its consequences, and one could simply commit suicide to escape them. As the Old Testament emphasizes, God is a God of life. But God is not confined to this world. God is on this side of death and also on the other side. "God's relationship to people is a dimension of their existence which they do not lose even in death," as Jürgen Moltmann emphasizes.[75] God's relationship with us in this life is sustained and finalized in and through death. Thus death can result in eternal death as being eternally removed from God or it can result in eternal life as being joyfully brought into God's immediate presence. That the human soul or the human psyche can extend itself far beyond the human body is both attested to by extrasensory perception, such as precognition or telepathy, as well as by some near-death experiences.[76] Yet such phenomena are always associated with a still living person and not with a dead corpse and therefore they do not imply a self-existent soul beyond bodily death.

e. The Materialistic Attack

During the nineteenth century scientific materialism ruled supreme and people such as Ludwig Feuerbach and Karl Marx vehemently attacked religion and with it any human fulfillment provided by God. In 1830 Feuerbach published a little book entitled *Thoughts on Death and Immortality* in which he collapsed the Hegelian dialectic and claimed in pantheis-

75. Jürgen Moltmann, *The Coming of God: Christian Eschatology*, trans. Margaret Kohl (Minneapolis: Fortress, 1996), 76.

76. For more information on near-death experiences, see Hans Schwarz, *Beyond the Gates of Death: A Biblical Examination of Evidence for Life after Death* (Minneapolis: Augsburg, 1981).

tic fashion: "You exist in God, and therefore with immortality."[77] Therewith he rejected any personal immortality. The reason he was so negative on immortality was based on his understanding that any existence needs a material base. There is no disembodied existence possible. In his *Essence of Christianity* of 1841 he espoused for the first time his theory of projection in which he claimed that a person projects his or her life experience and its negativity into something positive, that is, a better life after death. "Faith in the future life is therefore faith in the freedom of subjectivity from limits of Nature; it is faith in the eternity and infinitude of personality."[78] Feuerbach was an important influence on Karl Marx and Friedrich Engels, as the latter admitted when he wrote: "Enthusiasm was universal, we were all for the moment followers of Feuerbach."[79] Today we have moved beyond this naïve materialism of the nineteenth century since even in the sciences, in terms of energy, existence is thought of as apart from its material base.

Feuerbach exhibited not only nineteenth-century materialistic ideas, but also the concomitant notion that things on this earth will get better and better. As a consequence, there was no need of a fulfillment in a hereafter because it was thought that there was already eternal progress here on earth. Charles Darwin's evolutionary theory provided the scientific undergirding for the hope in unlimited progress. World War I (1914-18) and the Great Depression (1929-33) made people wonder whether the world and history really are on a never ending upward spiral toward the better. But a very rude awakening came with the Nazi and the Marxist movements. One had promised a messianic Thousand Years' Reich, and the other had promised equality among all people and a universal brotherhood of all nations. But both ended as merciless tyrannies of unforeseen proportions. Both movements collapsed, Nazism in 1945 and Marxism in 1991.

It became clear that humans are not only inherently sinful, but that they also live with limited resources since they live on an earth whose natural resources are rapidly dwindling. Moreover, there seems to be a climate change with ever increasing calamities, induced by human carelessness over

77. Ludwig Feuerbach, *Thoughts on Death and Immortality: From the Papers of a Thinker,* along with an appendix of theological-satirical epigrams, edited by one of his friends, trans. with intro. and notes James A. Massey (Berkeley: University of California Press, 1980), 173.

78. Ludwig Feuerbach, *The Essence of Christianity,* trans. George Eliot (Buffalo, NY: Prometheus, 1989), 184.

79. Friedrich Engels, *Feuerbach: The Roots of the Socialist Philosophy,* trans. with intro. Austin Lewis (Chicago: Charles H. Kerr, 1903), 53.

against the environment. Humanity seems to resemble a species belea-
guered by enemies from within and without. If we are to overcome all these
obstacles to the future, from a scientific perspective our prospect still looks
quite bleak: sooner or later life as we know it will cease to exist.

It was in light of this precarious situation that Frank J. Tipler wrote
*The Physics of Immortality: Modern Cosmology, God, and the Resurrection of
the Dead.* We have mentioned this book before in which he deals extensively with the future of humanity. Tipler continues the materialistic bend
of the nineteenth century with a curious updating. He assumes that all
forms of life, including human life, are subject to the same physical laws as
electrons and atoms. A human being is nothing "but a particular type of
machine," the human brain only "an information processing device," and
the human soul "a program run on a computer called the brain."[80] Tipler asserts that in this book he wants to describe the Omega Point Theory, which
he calls a testable physical theory stating that one day in the distant future
an all-present, all-knowing, and all-powerful God will resurrect each of us
to an eternal life that in all its essential features will correspond to the
Judeo-Christian heaven. This God will exist primarily at the end of time.

Tipler knows that the future course of the universe is such that life as
an information process cannot continue forever in its present form, that is,
as a carbon-based organism. If life as an information process that can sustain communication is to continue at all, it must continue to exist on some
other basis. Tipler is convinced that in the not too distant future computers
will possess the capability for autonomous information processing and
communication and finally will even be able to reproduce themselves. Since
Tipler understands a person as an entity capable of autonomous information processing and communication, and since computers will be able to assume these functions, he sees the only possibility of future "life" on the basis
of computers.

On this premise the physical mechanism of the individual resurrection
is the emulation of all persons who have long since died, including their
worlds, in computers of the distant future. These computer emulations are
identical with the persons who have actually lived.[81] Tipler is convinced
that within thirty years we will be capable of building a machine that is at
least as intelligent as we are. The reason for developing intelligent machines

80. Frank J. Tipler, *The Physics of Immortality: Modern Cosmology, God, and the Resurrection of the Dead* (New York: Doubleday, 1994), xi.
81. See Tipler, *The Physics of Immortality,* 14.

lies in the fact that without them we are prone to end in extinction. In the long run life has no other choice but to move beyond this earth in order to survive. Tipler asserts that life can continue only by reproducing itself through artificial intelligence mechanisms.

Tipler tells us that the extinction of humanity is the logically necessary consequence of eternal progress. Since we are finite beings, we have definite limits. Our brains can contain only a limited amount of information. Since the advance of life to the Omega Point is a fact, the furthest developed consciousness must one day be a nonhuman one. But everything that we as individual beings contribute to culture will survive our individual death. The next step of intelligent life will be information-processing machines. The closer we move to the Omega Point the more computer capacity is available to store our present world and to simulate it exactly. Finally, there will also be the possibility of simulating all possible visible universes, or simulating virtual universes. At the end "not only are the dead being resurrected but so are people who have never lived."[82] All people and all histories that could have existed will then indeed exist. In a more recent book Tipler claims that "human history will end in about fifty years: computer experts predict that computers will exceed human intelligence within fifty years, and the dematerialization mechanism can be used to make weapons that are to the atomic bombs as atomic bombs are to spitballs. Such weapons and superhuman computers would make human survival unlikely."[83]

The dead will be resurrected as soon as all the computers in the universe have reached such an enormous capacity that all possible human simulations can be stored in only an insignificant fraction of the total capacity. According to Tipler, the "resurrection will occur between $10^{-10^{10}}$ seconds and $10^{-10^{123}}$ seconds before the Omega Point is reached."[84] He claims: "The Omega Point Theory is the first physical resurrection theory to be fully consistent which totally agrees with the Christian resurrection theory. It is also the first redemption theory justified by reason, not by faith."[85]

Even Tipler is aware that the world he portrays must finally turn in on itself, that it must collapse through its gravitational pull. One wonders whether the facts that Tipler extrapolates are more credible than the trust

82. Tipler, *The Physics of Immortality*, 223.

83. Frank J. Tipler, *The Physics of Christianity* (New York: Doubleday, 2007), 4. In this book Tipler also "proves" with the laws of physics God as "the Cosmological Singularity," the Trinity, the miracles including the virgin birth, and Christ's resurrection.

84. Tipler, *The Physics of Immortality*, 225.

85. Tipler, *The Physics of Immortality*, 247.

that Jesus evokes through his message and destiny. If theology is subsumed under physics and eschatology under cosmology, what avenues are there to counterbalance that which German philosopher Karl Jaspers called "scientific superstition, our modern overestimation of the capabilities of science"?[86] Once the scientific theories of the future are no longer mindful of the finitude of space, time, and matter, they are prone to replace Christian eschatology in the same manner as the latter will lead to religious superstition if it is oblivious to the earthly conditions to which it adds its ultimate evaluations.

The project of Frank Tipler shows that even after Christian premises are discarded, modern humanity has still a deep-seated urge to ascertain that there is a future in store for us. If it is not here or in the hereafter, maybe on other planets or in other life forms. Since its very beginning humanity has always had the feeling that life on earth is not all that is. There is something beyond this life. It is interesting that even in scientific garb this urge of humanity is now continued. The same observation can also be made with the intelligent design movement. It is not just the dethronement of Darwinism that is most important there, but the assertion that there is indeed a teleology discernible in this world. Charles Darwin, who introduced only natural causes in his evolutionary concept, was convinced of such teleology while conceding at the same time: "I cannot look at the universe as the result of blind chance."[87] Even such an astute scientist as Darwin could not rid himself of the existential question whether there was a teleology and therefore an eternal significance to our lives. Here Augustine's insights in his *Confessions* hold true: "You have made us for yourself, and our heart is restless until it rests in you."[88] Therefore a fulfillment of human destiny seems inevitable.

f. Ultimate Fulfillment

But what will this fulfillment be like? When we talk about the ultimate fulfillment for the human being, we have to heed the accusation of Ludwig

86. Karl Jaspers, *Philosophy and the World: Selected Essays and Lectures,* trans. E. B. Ashton (Washington, DC: Regnery Gateway, 1963), 12, in his essay on "The Present Task of Philosophy."

87. See page 33, note 8, above.

88. Augustine, *Confessions* (1.1), trans. with intro. and notes Henry Chadwick (Oxford: Oxford University Press, 1992), 3.

Feuerbach that this fulfillment results from the negation of our insufficiencies here on earth. The seer of the book of Revelation narrates:

> Then I saw a new heaven and a new earth; for the first heaven and the first earth had passed away, and the sea was no more. And I saw the holy city, the new Jerusalem, coming down out of heaven from God, prepared as a bride adorned for her husband. And I heard a loud voice from the throne saying, "See, the home of God is among mortals. He will dwell with them as their God; they will be his peoples, and God himself will be with them; he will wipe every tear from their eyes. Death will be no more; mourning and crying and pain will be no more, for the first things have passed away. (Rev. 21:1-4)

What is depicted here as the final fulfillment are allusions to Old Testament expectations in Isaiah 65:17; 66:22; Ezekiel 37:26; and Isaiah 25:8. These could be easily made into projections that on the last pages of the Bible are claimed to be fulfilled in the future. Yet the second to the last verse of the Bible concludes: "Amen. Come, Lord Jesus!" (Rev. 22:20). The coming of a new heaven and a new earth is intimately tied to the coming of the Lord Jesus. As the exclamation mark indicates, this expresses not just a desire, but is also an affirmation.

What has occurred already in Christ's own destiny, in his resurrection, urges for and necessitates a completion. Envisioned is not an individualized destiny, either of Jesus or of individual human beings. Rather there are two things that are intimately related to each other: (1) The first resurrection that occurred on Easter was not an individualized event, but the proleptic anticipation of that which is to be fulfilled on a universal scale. There will be new life for all of humanity. (2) This second point is as important as the first, namely, God's own homecoming. The ugly, broad ditch between humanity and God is finally overcome, not by human striving, but by God's own doing. The last and the first pages of the Bible belong together; that which God has created God will also redeem.

Does this mean that there is a universal homecoming and that everyone and everything will be redeemed? Two cautions are in order here. The Israelite community was very practical and not theoretical in its reflections about God. Their primary question was: Does anyone care? The answer they received through God's acts in history was that God indeed was with them and had not abandoned them. Only gradually was their view widened when they realized that God is indeed the Lord of all people and of the whole universe. The same caution is in order for the New Testament. The

Christian message is not a theory about everyone and everything, but an existential address first proclaimed by Jesus himself: "the kingdom has come near; repent, and believe in the good news" (Mark 1:15).

Those who respond to that call, as far as they are able, are certainly included in the new world. All others are not the object of theoretical speculations. But they are the concern of the church when it prays for the redemption of all people. How that redemption is accomplished, and whether it is a universal redemption, is God's business alone. The same holds true with myriads of people who might live on other earth-like planets. To speculate about them was still a favorite subject of Immanuel Kant at the conclusion of the eighteenth century. If there are indeed such human-like beings on other planets, their destiny is not for us to decide, but it lies in the mercy of God.

As the church confesses in the Apostles' Creed with the phrase that "Christ descended to the dead," and as we read in such verses of the New Testament as 1 Peter 4:6 where it states that "the Gospel was proclaimed even to the dead," the God whom we know is indeed a gracious God. On the other hand, we also notice in the New Testament that only through Christ are people able to come to God. How this is accomplished is God's own prerogative and not for us to decide. Therefore we should proclaim with Christ the joyful victory over all negativity, and rest assured that human beings are not lonesome wanderers at the fringe of the universe staring into eternal nothingness, but children of the heavenly Father who has provided for them an eternal destiny of joy and fulfillment.

In Conclusion

We have traversed the huge field of anthropology, asking ourselves first who we are, then whether or to what extent we are free in our own actions, and finally focusing on humans as a community of men and women. We listened to the biblical account, followed historical transformations, took the insights of the life sciences into account, and finally formulated our own conclusions. Many more aspects of anthropology could have been covered. We hardly touched on culture as a typical human way of self-expression, we left unmentioned the mentally and physically challenged though they are part of the human family too, and we said hardly anything about the pressing ecological problems that confront us. That these points and others were hardly mentioned does not mean that they are unimportant but that space did not permit a more extensive treatment.

Four points, however, have become evident.

1. Humans are something special. Though we share much with other living species we have made this world our own in an unprecedented way. In the last three centuries we have increased our population tenfold and have shaped the face of the earth so drastically that Dutch chemist and Nobel Prize winner Paul Crutzen (b. 1933) claimed that since the eighteenth century a new geological epoch has arisen, the Anthropocene period. Crutzen's claim received a very positive response. He wrote: "Unless there is a global catastrophe — a meteorite impact, a world war or a pandemic — mankind will remain a major environmental force for many millennia. A daunting task lies ahead for scientists and engineers to guide society towards environmentally sustainable management during the era of the Anthropocene. This will require appropriate human behaviour at all

scales."[1] Since we are charged with representing God in caring for God's creation, an immense task lies ahead. That task includes sensitizing ourselves and others, and forming communities of care. The question is whether we are able and willing to assume this obligation.

2. In this context the issue of human freedom becomes decisive. Paradise is irrevocably lost. Any attempt to attain heavenly bliss by our own efforts is doomed to failure. In this respect we can only appeal to God's mercy. Though we are not as free as we would want to be in our earthly pursuits, the life sciences attribute to us a certain degree of freedom. Though there is an inherent tendency of seeking our own advantage at the expense of others, once we become cognizant of it, much is gained. Liberation theologies have especially shown us how humanity has constructed structures of injustice and how they can be dismantled. This should also give us new insights into eco-justice, liberating the earth from the debilitating impact of humanity which in the long run will endanger our own lives. Here it is especially important that we work together as a human community.

3. Though humans have an inherent tendency to be self-centered since they live under the spell of the fall, no human being can live by himself or herself. Our modern industrial society shows how interdependent we are. We need the assistance of others, be it the doctor, the airline pilot, the garbage collector, or the security guard. While their remuneration varies, the right performance of their tasks is of equal value. This leads us to the necessity of rediscovering the value of a vocation, a calling to serve others. We are not simply doing a job, but we have a God-given duty to serve others, if for no other reason than to expect that we will be served too. But this interdependence goes beyond those whom we serve though we may not even know them. The very fact that we are here on earth depended on two persons who are our biological parents. This nucleus of society, broken as it may be, is a stabilizing factor in any society. The proclamation of free love in Marxist socialism soon gave way to rather restrictive divorce laws, and for Marx especially his own family was very important to him. This suggests that we need this kind of intimacy and support that we cannot get anywhere else. Moreover, for raising children no other institution is equal to the family. Yet how a family works internally and how the respective tasks are distributed varies greatly, depending on the respective time and circumstances.

4. Finally, humans are acutely aware of their own finitude. But humans not only recognize their finitude, they also yearn to overcome it and as a re-

---

1. Paul J. Crutzen, "Geology of Mankind," *Nature* 415 (January 3, 2002): 23.

sult they invent all kinds of schemes and ideas to try to do so. The idea of immortality, the notion of self-transcendence, or the final anthropic principle witness to the longing for overcoming finitude. Through the resurrection of Jesus the Christ the Christian faith has provided a foundation of hope that has inspired believers over the centuries. Yet it is not an escape valve by which we can overcome the strictures of our earthly existence. As Paul pointed out, since we are new creatures, participating already to some extent in the hoped-for new existence, we are obligated to evidence this in some way in our present life. Stated another way, Christians are Easter people living from and toward that Easter experience of a new creation. This "daunting task" which Paul Crutzen laid before us, need not paralyze us. Rather, it could be taken as an opportunity to show that we take seriously our task to be God's administrators to take care of God's creation, instead of spoiling it for God and ultimately for ourselves.

Index of Names

Index of Subjects

Index of Biblical References
and Other Ancient Texts